Palgrave Studies in Prisons

Series Editors
Ben Crewe
Institute of Criminology
University of Cambridge
Cambridge, UK

Yvonne Jewkes
Social & Policy Sciences
University of Bath
Bath, UK

Thomas Ugelvik
Faculty of Law
University of Oslo
Oslo, Norway

This is a unique and innovative series, the first of its kind dedicated entirely to prison scholarship. At a historical point in which the prison population has reached an all-time high, the series seeks to analyse the form, nature and consequences of incarceration and related forms of punishment. Palgrave Studies in Prisons and Penology provides an important forum for burgeoning prison research across the world.

Series Advisory Board
Anna Eriksson (Monash University)
Andrew M. Jefferson (DIGNITY - Danish Institute Against Torture)
Shadd Maruna (Rutgers University)
Jonathon Simon (Berkeley Law, University of California)
Michael Welch (Rutgers University)

More information about this series at
http://www.palgrave.com/gp/series/14596

Ben Crewe · Susie Hulley ·
Serena Wright

Life Imprisonment
from Young
Adulthood

Adaptation, Identity and Time

palgrave
macmillan

Ben Crewe
Institute of Criminology
University of Cambridge
Cambridge, UK

Susie Hulley
Institute of Criminology
University of Cambridge
Cambridge, UK

Serena Wright
Department of Law and Criminology
Royal Holloway, University of London
Egham, Surrey, UK

Palgrave Studies in Prisons and Penology
ISBN 978-1-349-84993-2   ISBN 978-1-137-56601-0   (eBook)
https://doi.org/10.1057/978-1-137-56601-0

This Palgrave Macmillan imprint is published by the registered company Springer Nature Limited
The registered company address is: The Campus, 4 Crinan Street, London, N1 9XW, United Kingdom

Foreword

The impact of long-term imprisonment is hard to imagine for those who have never experienced it first-hand. Most who haven't don't particularly care what it's like. Unless connected in some way to someone serving a long sentence why should anyone care? When we think about prisoners, generally all we see in our mind's eye are faceless, nameless, voiceless criminals safely locked way from the rest of us. How they feel, about their crimes, their victims and their incarceration—what they think as they serve their time inside, their hopes and their fears—is of little concern to the rest of us.

A popular misconception on the outside is that prisoners are having an easy life with their three-square meals a day and a warm bed at night—with no regrets for their criminal actions. Taxpayers are regularly regaled by the press with tales of prisoners lording it up with televisions, phones and pool tables. The public's ignorance of prison life has allowed the popular press a free reign to report prison stories however it pleases. Prisoners are 'lags', jails are 'cushy'—every Christmas at least one tabloid newspaper will publish a prison's Christmas day menu and contrast it with the deprivations of pensioners. Media portrayals of prison life usually contain at least a kernel of truth. But even then it is mostly served up as entertainment or titillation. We may be fascinated, intrigued and horrified by what we see on TV or films, or by what we read in the tabloid press—but mostly we're just glad it's them doing time and not us.

It might not always seem apparent to the observer, given the amount of violence in our jails today—but the fact is our prisons are brimming with self-loathing, remorse and contrition. Vulnerability, psychological dysfunction, poor mental health and intellectual impairment abounds. As a long-term prisoner, I remember the mental and emotional exhaustion of living day after day, year after year trying to adjust to living in chaotic captivity. It's hard to imagine an environment more inappropriate than our prisons to address problematic human behaviour. In his most recent annual report, Chief Inspector of Prisons Peter Clarke described the levels of suicide and self-harm in our prisons as 'a scandal' and suggested an independent public inquiry into the issue. People in the so-called care of the state, he said, 'are dying unnecessarily.' One reason is surely that we imprison more people in the UK than anywhere else in Europe. We have more life-sentenced prisoners than Russia or Turkey—more in fact than France, Germany and Italy combined. But the chasm between the public's perception of prison and the reality has never been greater.

'Murderers, rapists and paedophiles deserve all they get, and more,' say the politicians, and the proverbial man in the street, outraged by such crimes, is hardly going to disagree. Violence against the person of any kind causes so much pain and distress, and victims of crime quite rightly want their perpetrators to be punished; in many cases, the more severe the punishment the better. So many times after a high-profile conviction, we hear cries that the sentence was 'not long enough.' But how long is long enough for any crime, and what is it we expect years of incarceration to achieve?

Sensational reporting of violent or sexual crime in particular has no doubt helped prison sentences to creep ever longer over the past forty years. In 1979, the average time a life-sentence prisoner spent in custody before release was around nine years. In 2001, it was thirteen years; today it is seventeen years. The average minimum term judges imposed for murder rose from twelve and a half years in 2003 to twenty one years in 2016. In the 1980s, there were two globally reported UK serial killer trials, at the end of which each perpetrator was convicted of having killed over a dozen people. Each was given a minimum tariff to be served in custody of 25 years. Such terms then were considered unusually lengthy.

Today, however, we think nothing of it when young men in their early twenties, or late teens even, caught up in youth gang culture who end up with murder convictions receive tariffs of 25, 30 or 35 years. Our society has become inured to the idea of sentencing people we consider to be violent and dangerous to longer and longer periods of imprisonment. In 2006,

Lord Phillips, the former Lord Chief Justice said, 'Some murderers are being sentenced to a minimum of 30 years, or even full-life terms. But I sometimes wonder whether, in 100 years' time, people will be as shocked by the length of sentences we are imposing as we are by some of the punishments of the 18th century.'

Always missing from the debate on prisoners and prisons however are the voices of those serving the longest sentences. They are voices that need to be heard, and finally, this book allows them to speak. Poignant and powerful, it should be the required reading for ministers, judges and especially the Sentencing Council. A common theme among the subjects is their endeavours to survive—I've often described my own twenty years of imprisonment as a long-term exercise in survival—some will make it, but the sad truth is that many of them will never get the chance to breathe free air again. Too often a long prison sentence turns into a death sentence. I hope this book brings the much-needed reasoning and rationality back to our thinking about prison sentence length.

North Wales, UK   Erwin James
July 2019

Acknowledgements

We wish to acknowledge a number of people collectively. Funding for the project was provided by the Economic and Social Research Council (grant ES/J007935/1) and subsequently by the University of Cambridge's Newton Trust. We are extremely grateful for their support.

We are also thankful to all those people who enabled and championed the research from its early days onwards, including a range of practitioners without whose assistance the study would not have been possible. Those deserving of special mention include Steve Wagstaffe, Richard Vince, Phil Wheatley, Michael Spurr, Gordon Davison and all of the governors who granted us permission to undertake fieldwork in their establishments as well as the staff who facilitated us during our time administering interviews and organising interviews. Many front-line practitioners made us feel welcome and assisted us enormously, and we particularly want to thank Dave, Scott and Simon at HMP Gartree, who helped us on our way during our prolonged fieldwork period there. We are also grateful to Adam Spriggs and Sam Cuthbertson who provided us with the information that enabled us to sample and locate our participants.

We received a huge amount of support from colleagues at the Institute of Criminology, many of whom we thank individually below. The Prisons Research Centre deserves special mention for providing such an exceptionally nurturing environment: a true intellectual home. Beyond the Institute of Criminology, we have been inspired and stimulated by a range of academics and practitioners and wish to express our gratitude to members of our advisory board, whose expertise we should have used much more: Jamie Bennett, Peter Bennett, Phil Boardman, Gwyneth Boswell, Rod Earle, Adrian Grounds, Yvonne Jewkes, Ruth Mann, Shadd Maruna and Tara Young. Thank you to Josie Taylor and Liam Inscoe-Jones at Palgrave, who remained very patient.

Throughout the study, we were always aware of the people whose murders were at the heart of our study, and the families and other loved ones left bereft at their deaths. As we try to highlight throughout the book, these victims were an absent-presence in the narratives of our participants, the majority of whom—particularly once they had been in prison for a few years—reflected with deep remorse about the people whose deaths they had been involved in. At times, we asked ourselves how the tone and content of our writing might feel to those people on the other side of the criminal act. In the end, we do not feel that there is any contradiction between providing a humanistic portrayal of long-term prisoners and their circumstances, and feeling deep sympathy for the direct and indirect victims of murder. We do, however, want to make explicit acknowledgement of the latter. The tragedy of murder is deep and enduring.

We are most grateful to the men and women who participated in our study, especially those whom we interviewed. Thank you sincerely. We hope we have done the job that we pledged to you we would try to do.

Ben Crewe Acknowledgements

This was a very challenging study, and it would have been far less successful without my co-researchers, their incredible commitment to the study and our shared orientation to our participants. Susie, I'm enduringly grateful for your good sense and wisdom, and for all of the conversations over the years, which have been more significant than you might realise. Serena, thank you for the endless enthusiasm and for pushing me into places of discomfort. Working with both of you, and seeing you develop, was an absolute pleasure, and I'm sorry for the bad decisions along the way. I make no apologies, though, for overruling those various PowerPoint designs.

Within the Institute, I am particularly grateful to Alison Liebling, for the ongoing intellectual and personal friendship. It makes a huge difference. Sincere thanks too to very many staff and Ph.D. students, in the PRC and beyond, but especially Ruth Armstrong, Tony Bottoms, Loraine Gelsthorpe, Adrian Grounds, Ben Jarman, Borah Kant, Caroline Lanskey, Ben Laws, Amy Ludlow,

Nicky Padfield, Bethany Schmidt and Jason Warr. Members of the COMPEN research team—Claire Bonner, Alice Ievins, Julie Laursen, Kristian Mjåland and Anna Schliehe—also merit a special mention, for the number of conversations they've endured that have begun 'When we did the long-term prisoners' study', and for their friendship, understanding and collegiality in recent years. I also want to thank a number of people beyond the Institute of Criminology who have shaped and sustained me and this study, even if it might not be apparent to them: Catherine Appleton, Jamie Bennett, Peter Dawson, Tomer Einat, Kate Gooch, Yvonne Jewkes, Shadd Maruna, Fergus McNeill, Ian O'Donnell, Thomas Ugelvik and Dirk van Zyl Smit. I feel very fortunate to have so many sources of support, challenge and good company.

My parents, plus Deborah, John and Daniel continue to form a bedrock that underlies so much of what I do. Most of all, thank you to Nicole, for everything, and to Eva and Joseph, who give my life so much meaning.

Susie Hulley Acknowledgements

Thank you to all my colleagues at the Institute of Criminology for ongoing support and inspiration, particularly: Alison Liebling for her loyalty to me, in finding me projects in the early years and for being an inspiring scholar; Caroline Lanksey for listening when things got tough and for the moral support; Julie Laursen and Alice Ievins for being all-round lovely people and supportive colleagues; to Eliza Preece for the short-term but high impact camaraderie (and long-term friendship) and to Ruth Armstrong and Amy Ludlow for their ongoing advice and support. To my current co-investigator Tara Young, at the University of Kent, for always providing a confidence boost and some light relief on the tricky days!

Thank you to Ben, for being a great mentor, an inspiring colleague and a good friend. You made my first ride out as co-investigator on this study straightforward and enjoyable. I have learnt so much over the last decade from you, not only from our discussions but also from observing and reading your work.

I am grateful to you, Serena, for throwing yourself into this study with full force. Your infectious cheerfulness brightened our stays in grim hotels during fieldwork and charmed prisoners and prison staff within minutes of arrival. You were my support when interviews were emotionally gruelling, and with your warmth and kind nature, you are a valued friend.

Finally, thank you to my amazing family. To Ruth and Steve Howell, for being unbelievably kind people, for taking me in and being stuck with me 23 years later. To Lynn and Ian McHugh, and Annie and Ollie Browning, for sharing your families with me—the wonderful Anneliese, Sophia, Florence, Matilda and Kitty. To June and Ken Rutherford, without whom it would literally be impossible for me to work, for being so supportive and generous. To Graeme, Sarah, Frankie and Millie, for your support (often in times of need!). To Matthew Hulley and Eve Rowland for being so supportive and Matt for being a brilliant brother—our daily chats make me happy and politically more informed! To my husband Paolo, for being brilliant, funny, kind and (inconspicuously) unbelievably supportive. I couldn't have done this without you. To my favourites—Isla Mae and Rory Matthew. A prisoner in this study asked me what I wanted my legacy to be, and at that moment, it was clear: you are all that matters. As long as you are happy, kind and brave, my life project is complete.

To my Mum and Dad—in the short time, you were both here with me and Matt, whatever you did, you did an amazing job. We are happy and strong and surrounded by love. I am Dr. Hulley because of you. We are so lucky to have ever had you.

For Isla and Rory and for Mum and Dad.

Serena Wright Acknowledgements

My first and biggest thanks go to my co-authors, Ben and Susie. You both nurtured, supported and guided me through my first research post, and helped me to grow from a nervous doctoral student to an assertive early career scholar, with a raft of publications and a wealth of empirical experience and knowledge that I will continue to draw upon for the rest of my academic life. More than just co-authors though, I think of you both now as life-long friends and look forward with enthusiasm to our wild nights out (i.e. discussing books over beer—and *most* of a burger—or tea, cake, and those awful weak, half-shot decaf lattes). Susie, you have always been the most amazingly wonderful and compassionate person and never too busy to lend an ear to me when I was struggling. I could not have wished for a better fieldwork comrade; thank you. And Ben—thank you for your wisdom, kindness and awful sense of humour (FYI, your taste in PowerPoints, however, remains your least endearing attribute).

A massive thanks also to my friends and colleagues, past and present, at the Institute of Criminology, Cambridge, who made my four years there such an inspiring, challenging and fondly remembered venture. Thanks to Alison Liebling, who provided academic guidance and cultivated my desire to excel in the field of prisons sociology and to Loraine Gelsthorpe, who gave me much-welcome opportunities to co-author with someone whose work on women and justice I had long respected. Thanks also to Caroline Lanskey, Ruth Armstrong and Amy Ludlow for their warmth and tea-fuelled chats, and to Giulia Conto, Zetta Kougiali, Jules Laursen, Tomer Einat, Matt Skipper, Ben Laws and Alice Ievins for all their support over the years.

A host of other long-term academic friends were also instrumental in supporting me during both the duration of the long-term prisoner project and the write-up period, particularly Isla Masson, Fi Wadie and Yvonne Jewkes, all of whom provided wise words, tea and cake. I have also begun to collect new friends at Royal Holloway, whose support has also been incredibly important in trying to balance book writing with full-time lecturing. A huge thank you to my friend and Learning Together partner in crime Morwenna Bennallick and particularly to my long-suffering office-mate Michelle 'Stealth' Webster; DW, the academic sparring, Thorpe dates and laughter you bring to my life saw me over the final hurdle, so thank you.

Thank you also to my lifelong friends back in Portsmouth, particularly Jo, Laura, Lau, Hannah and Faye, for always being so proud of me and keeping me grounded. For those I have parted ways with, thanks to Nina and Jess, and particularly to Jasmin, for the years of support. To Jacko, no longer with us, thank you for your care and compassion, for teaching me how to be a better person and for always believing in me, even when I didn't believe in myself. I miss you every day.

And lastly, thank you to my wonderful parents, Rita and Graham Wright—I am so incredibly proud to be your daughter—and to the world's best siblings, Mark and Zoe Wright, whose unique humour always provides welcome light relief from the constant academic hellfire that is term-time.

For Mum and Dad, Mark and Zoe, and—as always—for Jacko.

Praise for *Life Imprisonment from Young Adulthood*

"In all the attention to mass imprisonment in recent years, criminologists have only turned recently to what is clearly one of the most significant and problematic features of it: life sentences with no possibility of release for decades, especially when imposed on the very young. In *Life Imprisonment from Young Adulthood*, Crewe, Hulley, and Wright go beyond the legal transformations that have accompanied this revolution in punishment in England and Wales, to give us the deepest empirical look at adaptation and survival in long-term imprisonment for over forty years; a generation that has seen the life imprisonment sanction explode across the common law world."

—Professor Jonathan Simon,
University of California, Berkeley, USA

"Changing trends in sentencing and the use of imprisonment have resulted in the imposition of prison tariffs so lengthy that they were only recently regarded as highly unusual and barely survivable. In *Life Imprisonment from Young Adulthood*, Crewe, Hulley and Wright explore this peculiar manifestation of our deep cultural attachment to incarceration and describe the ways in which very long sentences are experienced by the men and women serving them. At the core of this book is violence—the violence of the offences that result in lengthy sentences, the violence that has saturated the lives of those serving them, and the violence of a system that fractures lives and consigns the people it punishes to squander decades behind bars. It is meticulously researched, imaginatively constructed, elegantly written and quietly passionate about the injustices and cruelties surrounding its subject matter. *Life Imprisonment from Young Adulthood* will undoubtedly quickly become a classic in the canon of sociological studies of the prison."

—Professor Yvonne Jewkes, *University of Bath, UK*

"*Life Imprisonment from Young Adulthood* is a masterwork of social science. The book is original, comprehensive, balanced, and insightful. The authors draw on a rich body of scholarship spanning a wide range of disciplines to bring moral, existential, and psychological insights to bear on a complex subject that is assessed with a thorough set of mixed research methods, the rich findings of which are all reported with clear, concise, and often compelling prose.

This study of life-sentence prisoners embodies social science at its best. The authors provide a ground-breaking analysis of life sentence prisoners—their crimes and their punishments; their trials and tribulations in relation to their crimes and their imprisonment as they grapple with what they have done, what they are now, and what they might yet become; and ultimately their remarkable human resilience in the face of profound and life-changing adversity that is analyzed with great empathy and insight. For life sentence prisoners there is persisting damage and loss, but also enduring growth and hope for lives worth living. Reformers can take a cautious hope from this seminal study, which offers fruitful guidance to students of correctional policy and practice.

Everything one would want to know about the nature of the crimes and punishments of life-sentence prisoners as full-blooded human beings working out their lives in harsh and often unforgiving circumstances is concisely and often eloquently presented inside the covers of this marvellous text. I am confident this book will mark a turning point in the study of prison life and adjustment that will move the field to greater and more nuanced understandings of crime and punishment in general as well as in the context of life-sentence prisoners. By probing the outer edges of crime (homicide) and punishment (life terms), Crewe, Hulley and Wright shed a bright light on timeless questions about human nature that are at the heart of our understanding of crime and punishment."

—Professor Robert Johnson, *American University, USA*

Contents

About the Authors

Ben Crewe is Deputy Director of the Prisons Research Centre and Professor of Penology and Criminal Justice at the Institute of Criminology, University of Cambridge. He is interested in all aspects of prison life, including prison management, staff-prisoner relationships, public and private sector imprisonment, penal power, and prisoner social life. He is the author of *The Prisoner Society: Power, Adaptation and Social Life in an English Prison*, as well as a number of edited collections.

Susie Hulley is a Senior Research Associate at the Institute of Criminology, University of Cambridge. She is interested in how young people are affected by the criminal justice system, particularly their experiences of criminalisation and imprisonment. Her recent work focuses on the application of 'joint enterprise' by criminal justice practitioners (police and lawyers) and the impact of this legal doctrine on young people.

Serena Wright is a Lecturer in Criminology and Researcher in the Department of Law and Criminology at Royal Holloway, University of London. Prior to this, she worked for four years as a Research Associate at the Institute of Criminology, University of Cambridge. Her research on prisons and penology has focused chiefly on long-term, life imprisonment, but also extends to short-term sentences and 'frustrated desistance', particularly among women. She is particularly interested in the intersection between trauma, addiction and criminalisation, and between health, gender and criminal justice.

List of Tables

1

Introduction

All of one's plans and life-goals are very much put on hold until one's re-emergence
into the light of day. Perhaps the better analogy is of a cocoon. We are trapped in
a chrysalis while the outside world rushes on without us, yet within the chrysalis
a metamorphosis is taking place. We change as people, we achieve certain things,
removed from the real world. And so what emerges is a transformed individual, for
better or worse [...] One can never truly be the same or simply take off from where
we left off. [...] Whatever happens in here, I will be catching up on all those lost
years of my youth. [...] Think of all the things I should be doing now: establishing
my career, getting married, having a family, settling down, and amassing all the
various accoutrements of living – a home, a car, etc. (Dan, 20s, early)[1]

In the absence of capital punishment, depriving people of their liberty for extremely
long periods is the most extreme sanction of the state. Dan's description in the
quotation above illustrates the elemental profundity of this sanction. When men
and women are confined for very significant terms, they encounter the normal
pains and burdens of imprisonment, but also confront a range of more acute

---

[1] As we explain in Chapter 2, throughout the book, when quoting prisoners, we specify their pseudonym, their
age by decade, and their sentence stage at the time of the interview.

© The Author(s) 2020
B. Crewe et al., *Life Imprisonment from Young Adulthood*,
Palgrave Studies in Prisons and Penology,
https://doi.org/10.1057/978-1-137-56601-0_1

anxieties about who they are, their place in the world, the kind of life they are able to construct inside prison and what they have lost as a result of their sentence. The aim of this book is to describe and make sense of such experiences. Focusing on the prison system in England and Wales, it seeks to address the questions of how men and women who are given long life sentences at an early age experience sustained imprisonment, how they cope with its burdens, how they deal with issues of selfhood and meaning, and how they establish a social lifeworld within a carceral environment.

The Abolition of Capital Punishment and the Growth of the Long Life Sentence

When the Advisory Committee on the Penal System reported in 1968 on the prison regime for long-term prisoners in conditions of maximum security, 168 individuals were serving custodial terms of longer than 10 years and 489 serving life sentences or their equivalent (Radzinowicz 1968). At the time, only two 'lifers' had served more than 15 years of continuous custody, while only six had served over 12 years. Of the individuals released from prison between 1959 and 1963 who had committed murder, the period spent in prison ranged from four to 14 years (House of Commons 1964, c. 612).

Today, however, very long sentences are comparatively commonplace. In 2003, the *average* minimum period (or 'tariff'—see below for further explanation) to be served for mandatory life sentences (excluding whole-life tariffs) was 12.5 years; by 2013, this had reached 21.1 years (see Table 1.1). Indeed, over recent years, there has been a significant increase in the number of people serving long sentences, in average tariff lengths and in the overall amount of time spent in custody by prisoners serving life sentences.

It was the abolition of capital punishment as the mandatory punishment for murder—a result of changing penal sensibilities alongside a series of high-profile miscarriages of justice—that effectively created the long life sentence as a widespread penal phenomenon. The *Homicide Act 1957* had already introduced partial defences to murder (provocation and diminished responsibility), reducing such offences to 'manslaughter', and had abolished the use of capital punishment for murder except in certain circumstances, for example: any murder by shooting; any murder of a police officer acting in the execution of his duty; or any murder

Table 1.1 Average tariff length for murder in England and Wales (2003–2013)

Year of sentence	Average tariff (years)
2003	12.5
2004	14.5
2005	15.9
2006	17.1
2007	15.6
2008	17.8
2009	17.5
2010	18.9
2011	18.8
2012	20.4
2013	21.1

Source Ministry of Justice (JSAS/FOI 89346) (Thanks to Jonathan Bild for granting us permission to cite the data from his Freedom of Information request. A more recent Freedom of Information request (170904015) produced different figures, based on the same question, suggesting that the average tariff for prisoners serving mandatory life sentences went from 15.3 years in 2003 to 21.3 years in 2016, an increase of almost 40%)

committed in the course or furtherance of theft. The abolitionist goal of eliminating the mandatory death penalty for the remaining 'capital murder' offences in England and Wales was advanced in 1965, when Royal Assent was granted to the *Murder (Abolition of Death Penalty) Act*, suspending—though not abolishing entirely—capital punishment for all forms of murder.[2]

In the eight years between the enactment of the *Homicide Act* and the *Murder (Abolition of the Death Penalty) Act*, the question of what imprisonment for 'life' meant was, in political circles, a cause of 'grave disquiet' (House of Commons 1964, c.612). Following the 1965 Act, all individuals convicted of murder were to be given sentences of mandatory life imprisonment. However, as the number of life-sentenced prisoners rose rapidly, the unintended consequence was to place a significant burden on the prison system. In a House of Lords debate in 1980, the Earl of Longford brought to the House's attention the 'dramatic increase' in 'long-sentence prisoners'. In 1957, he noted, there had been 133 prisoners serving life imprisonment. By the late 1960s, the number had risen to almost 600 (House of Lords 1971, c.623) and, by 1979 to 1322, representing a tenfold increase in 22 years (House of Lords 1982, c.870). As the Earl went on to argue, the 'miserable conditions' created by overcrowding in English prisons compounded the 'mental

---

[2]Wholesale removal of the death penalty as a legally defined, if unused, punishment from the statute books in England and Wales did not occur until 1998.

torture which we inflict on long-term prisoners, to whom we hold out no prospect of human happiness as one dreary year passes slowly into another' (House of Lords 1982, c.870). Moving forward, he suggested, penal policy should be focused on one matter alone: to achieve a 'substantial reduction in the prison population', an act which would require both limiting the number of 'long-term' prisoners and reducing the length of such terms.

This reduction has not materialised; indeed, the 'rapid' rise of indeterminate sentences in the first decade of the twenty-first century has seen a 75% increase in mandatory life sentences handed down per year—the 'largest proportionate increase' in the prison population of England and Wales (Ministry of Justice 2009: 2). The number of individuals within the prison system serving life sentences increased from 1322 in 1979 to almost 2000 by the end of the 1980s, a decade after the Earl of Longford's plea. By the end of 2019, this figure stood at 7046 (Ministry of Justice 2019a).

Within these general increases, there has been a rise in the number of prisoners with lengthy tariffs. As Table 1.2 shows, the number of people aged 18 or over given minimum sentences of 15 years or more increased from fewer than 100 individuals per year between 2000 and 2003 to as high as 249 in 2008 (Freedom of Information, ref: 68520). At the end of 2010, out of 8309 prisoners in custody serving a life sentence, 2309 had minimum terms of 15 years or more (Freedom of Information, ref: 68152); of these, 319 had been sentenced when aged between 18 and 20 inclusive (Freedom of Information, ref: 68520).

By the end of September 2019, there were 3555 individuals in custody serving life sentences with tariffs of between 10 and 20 years and 1827 with tariffs of greater than 20 years (Ministry of Justice 2019a). 880 individuals had a tariff of more than 25 years, 291 of more than 30 years and 264 of more than 32 years (Freedom of Information, ref: 191009017). These numbers were substantially higher than at the start of 2014, when 543 individuals were serving life sentence with a tariff of more than 25 years, 179 of more than 30 years and 137 of more than 32 years (Freedom of Information, ref: 89346). Thus, while the overall number of individuals serving life sentences fell slightly between 2011 and 2019, a higher proportion have tariffs of greater than 20 years (Ministry of Justice 2019a). Meanwhile, the average length of time that life-sentenced prisoners spend in custody (i.e. including the period beyond their tariff point) has also increased, from 9.1 years in 1979 to just over 14 years in 1997 (Cullen and Newell 1999) and—for those serving mandatory life

Table 1.2 Number of individuals receiving life sentences, 2000–2010

	Less than 18 (Current age)		18 or over (Current age)	
	Tariff less than 15 years	Tariff 15 years or more	Tariff less than 15 years	Tariff 15 years or more
2000			413	70
2001			410	88
2002			479	72
2003			422	96
2004			460	136
2005			444	178
2006			370	215
2007	1		310	191
2008	10	3	269	249
2009	7	2	208	238
2010[a]	8	1	91	196

[a]Information available as of 18 November 2010

sentences specifically—from 14 to 17 years between 2002 and 2017 (Ministry of Justice, 2019b).

This upward trend has continued. By the beginning of 2014, when we began the fieldwork for this study, 44 prisoners in England and Wales were serving a whole-life tariff (without any possibility of release); 543 were serving life sentences with a minimum term of more than 25 years; 179 with a minimum term of more than 30 years; and 32 with a minimum term of more than 32 years (Freedom of Information request ref: 89346).[3]

Such dramatic rises in the number of people sentenced to long—and lengthening—prison sentences primarily reflect changes in 'the political dynamics of crime and punishment' (Travis 2002: 29). Writing about the United States, Mauer et al. (2004: 5, 9) commented that:

> The number of persons serving life sentences has grown along with the increase in the overall prison population of recent decades. [This] is not primarily a by-product of increasing crime rates [...] clearly factors other than crime rates have contributed to those trends.

Likewise, with regard to England and Wales, the Prison Reform Trust (2012: 3) noted that:

---

[3]These figures exclude whole-life tariffs.

In twenty years the prison population has all but doubled. This is largely due, not to any crime wave, but to increased sentence lengths, the introduction of mandatory penalties and an earlier recourse to custody for those who, in the past, would have been required to pay a fine or do community service.

These trends reflect a set of changing sensibilities and practices that have been well documented elsewhere (Bottoms 1977; Garland 2000; Travis 2002; Simon 2007). In practice, they involve the increased use of forms of expressive punishment designed to communicate moral outrage (Feeley and Simon 1992; Garland 2000) and a political culture that is less resistant to punitive demands, cultivated by the popular press.

At the level of policy and legislation, in England and Wales, the introduction of longer minimum sentences for serious offences was the outcome of three main phenomena, which we detail below: first, the creation of the 'tariff' system for life-sentenced prisoners; second, the specific measures of the 2003 *Criminal Justice Act;* and third, the up-tariffing of certain forms of homicide, alongside the rise in the use of 'joint enterprise' in prosecutions for murder and other serious offences. The common thread between these measures is the exercise of increased legislative control over minimum sentencing (leading to average 'increased length of stay' in prison) (cf. Ministry of Justice 2013), the need to satisfy public concern regarding 'dangerous criminals' or serious offenders, and the reduction of judicial discretion.

The 'Tariff' System for Life-Sentenced Prisoners

Now a standard feature of 'life' and other indeterminate sentences, the 'tariff' represents the minimum period of time that a prisoner must serve before being considered for release (i.e. 'parole', under licence conditions). The tariff system was created in 1983 by then Home Secretary, Leon Brittan, as a political response to growing public fear regarding perceived increases in violent crime, as well as wider concerns relating to the perceived disjuncture between the ostensible length of sentence being given to prisoners and the amount of time they actually served (House of Commons 1983, c.506). The creation of the tariff signalled the commitment of the government and the criminal justice system to the retributive aims of sentencing, in the sense that its purpose was evidently punitive: to communicate the severity of the act committed and punish the offender for a related period. The remaining time to be served, known as the 'risk' or 'preventative' element, was based on sentencing aims related to the protection of the public (House of Commons 1983, c.506) and remains so today. That is, the expiration of the tariff does not represent the release date, but rather the point from which the prisoner *might* be released, subject to approval by the Parole Board. There are no set limits to the length of this second preventative period; indeed, the explicit order regarding life-sentenced prisoners is that they are to be detained for 'as long as [is] necessary' (i.e. until they are no longer a risk or threat to the public) (Ministry of Justice 2010, para. 3.1).

Initially, it was made clear that life-sentenced prisoners were to be kept under tri-annual review and that, after a period of ten years' incarceration, ministers were obligated to review the individual case (House of Commons 1983, c.507). Over the intervening years, however, the ministerial power to set punitive periods in England and Wales has passed to the courts, and trial judges have become responsible for setting the tariff period for adult mandatory life sentences. Further, the discretion available to judges to apply themselves in such cases has since been greatly restricted by the Legislature, primarily as a result of two developments. The first is the introduction of further mandatory life sentences, for example under the *Crime (Sentences) Act 1997*, i.e. the 'two-strike' life sentence for adults convicted of a second serious violent or sexual offence, and the introduction of 'whole life tariffs' under the *Criminal Justice Act 2003*. The second involves changes in the minimum tariffs that judges are obliged to consider as the 'starting point' in deciding on the sentence length that they impose.

The Criminal Justice Act 2003 (Schedule 21)

In *The Story of the Prison Population: 1993–2012*, the Ministry of Justice (2013) outline a series of legislative changes that impacted on the increasing number of receptions into prison as well as the average length of custodial stay, including the *Criminal Justice Act 1993*, the *Crime (Sentences) Act 1997*, the *Tackling Knives Action Plan (2008)* and the *Legal Aid Sentencing & Punishment of Offenders Act (2012)*. However, the piece of legislation enacted in this period that effectuated these shifts most significantly was the *Criminal Justice Act 2003*. The Act introduced a series of mandatory tariff 'starting points' for murder, which resulted in a broad 'up-tariffing' of certain types of homicide, particularly those carried out with a bladed weapon or firearm. Schedule 21 of the Act dictated the point, in years, at which a judge was required to begin when deciding on the length of a custodial term for those found guilty of a listed offence. Judicial discretion could then act only to shape the direction in which the tariff decreased or increased from this starting point, depending on the mitigating or aggravating factors in a given case. For example, Section 5 ([1] and [2]) of Schedule 21 stated that a tariff starting point of 30 years had to be adopted where an individual was aged 18 or over and was convicted of an offence involving 'a degree of seriousness that is particularly high', listing such offences as: murder involving a firearm or explosive; murder of a police/prison officer in the course of their duty; murder done for gain; or a murder that is racially or religiously aggravated, or aggravated by sexual orientation. The equivalent minimum starting point for defendants aged under 18 when the offence was committed became 12 years' imprisonment.

The Up-Tariffing of 'Knife Homicides' and the Rise of 'Joint Enterprise'

Controversially, Schedule 21 of the 2003 Act also stipulated that, where a defendant was aged 18 years or over and was convicted of a murder of a type that did not fall within Section 4 (whole life orders) or Section 5, the minimum starting point was 15 years. At this time, this included murder committed with a knife. In 2009, a Home Affairs Select Committee was convened to discuss whether existing sentencing frameworks for murder committed with such weapons required revision. In the months following the Committee meeting, the Justice Minister, Jack Straw, announced that the minimum starting point for sentencing those convicted of 'knife murder' would be increased from 15 to 25 years, in situations 'where the weapon is taken to the scene with the intention of committing an offence or having it available for use as a weapon, and is then used to kill' (Ministry of Justice 2010, para. 2.1).

The Sentencing Guidelines Council had, in fact, been consulting on increasing sentences for all offences involving bladed weapons since 2006. But the eventual up-tariffing for 'knife murder' in 2010 is more often attributed to two phenomena. The first is the apparent and consistent rise in violent homicide involving bladed weapons. Between 2005/2006 and 2006/2007, the number of such offences rose by 26.9%, and the year that followed saw the highest recorded total of 'knife homicides' since the introduction of the Homicide Index in 1977: 270 in total, representing 35% of all recorded murders that year (Home Affairs Select Committee 2009). In attempting to explain this, the 2009 Home Affairs Select Committee on the matter noted that 'as with overall violence, the majority of knife victims and perpetrators are young men in their late teens and early twenties', linking the rise in such incidences to 'an increase in street violence between groups of young people who are sometimes referred to as "gangs"' in urban areas (para. 40). The second determinant, according to the Committee, was the occurrence of a series of high-profile fatal stabbings which 'dominated the headlines' in 2008 and 2009 (2009: 1.1). Chief among these was the murder in North London in 2008 of the teenager Ben Kinsella, acknowledged at the time by Justice Secretary Jack Straw as the event underpinning the 'understandable concern' regarding sentences for murders involving knives (Press Association 2009). In explaining the rationale behind the tariff increase, the 2010 Statutory Instrument that introduced the new 25-year minimum sentence also cited 'considerable [public] concern that the starting point for this type of murder should be higher than the current 15 years, particularly as the starting point for murder using a firearm is 30 years' (Ministry of Justice 2010, para. 7.2).

Public and political concerns about knife murder and gang violence have also featured prominently in justifications for the growing use of the doctrine of joint enterprise. 'Joint enterprise' represents a complex set of legal principles, which have existed for hundreds of years and allow for more than one person to be convicted of a single offence (Hulley et al. 2019). It has been estimated that, over an eight-year period (2005–2013), up to 4590 prosecutions for homicide involved the use of joint enterprise (Bureau of Investigative Journalism (2014: 7). In practice then, joint enterprise has multiplied the number of people convicted of murder and sentenced to long-life tariffs. As Crewe et al. (2015: 252) note, the 'blunderbuss' approach of joint enterprise (hereafter JE) to prosecute murder cases means that, regardless of whether the defendant was a 'principal or an accessory' to the death, he or she is equally liable to mandatory life imprisonment. While Parasitic Accessorial Liability (PAL)—the most controversial aspect of joint enterprise, since it enabled secondary parties to be convicted based on a lower burden of proof (foresight) than the principal party (intent) (Green and McGourlay 2015; Bennathan and Taylor 2016)—was abolished in 2016 (see CPS 2018), in practice, multiple individuals continue to be convicted for single homicide offences. For example, in 2017, thirteen individuals were charged with a single murder, with seven receiving murder convictions and life sentences with tariffs ranging from 16 to 25 years (see *R v Wright and others [2017]* and *R v Walters and others [2017]*).

The result of such developments is that a growing number of men and women are serving the kinds of sentences that, until recently, were not only highly unusual but were also considered to be barely survivable. The consequences are manifold. Although, in recent years, the problems facing men and women serving short sentences have generated most interest from penal policymakers and commentators (e.g. Howard League for Penal Reform 2011; Player 2005; Killias et al. 2010), the management of the long-term prisoner population has been long considered 'one of the most difficult challenges facing correctional administrations' (Flanagan 1995a: xi). As Flanagan (1995a: xi) notes, one issue is that long-term prisoners have generally been managed within prison regimes not originally designed to cater to them:

> [W]hen an inmate reaches the sally port with a sentence of 36 months, we prescribe a set of experiences with discrete learning objectives directed towards measurable improvement in skills and knowledge by the time of release. When an inmate arrives who is facing 36 *years*, however, our muddled response reveals that, except for selected work assignments and a few educational programs, we have little insight into planning institutional careers for long-term prisoners.

Flanagan's comments about the US prison system resonate with an intermittent discourse in England and Wales, in which resource constraints have at times produced a language of 'parking' long-term prisoners—that is, leaving them relatively unaided, and instead steering attention and interventions towards prisoners approaching release—until the point in their sentence when they themselves are on the cusp of freedom. More recently, however, high-security prisons in England and Wales have placed considerable emphasis on building 'rehabilitative cultures', while coming to recognise the risks of neglecting men and women in the early stages of very long prison terms (Justice Select Committee 2019). These risks have coalesced around three linked anxieties: a concern about how to make life meaningful for men facing decades of confinement; the fear that disillusionment and alienation might push this population towards extremist ideologies; and considerable unease about issues of order and control in prisons holding large proportions of very long-term prisoners. In her valedictory lecture, the former Chief Inspector of Prisons warned that high-security prisons and young offender institutions were becoming 'less stable, more difficult to run and potentially more unsafe' as a result of holding 'a growing proportion of men, often young men, serving very long sentences, who may feel they have little to lose' (Owers 2010). The following year, Michael Spurr, the Chief Executive of the National Offender Management Service (NOMS), made similar observations[4]:

> In high security prisons the population is younger than it was before and serving sentences that are longer. [...] There are similar issues in the young offender institutions where we have gangs and longer sentences and we have got to work through how best we manage those challenges. [...] It is one of the biggest operational challenges we have at the moment. How we can best deliver to a longer sentenced population, and many more younger prisoners, who don't buy into the system, with the risk that that can lead to concerted disorder? (Spurr, interviewed by Lloyd 2011: 28)

Part of the concern expressed by senior practitioners at this time was that the profile of the long-term prisoner population was changing, from an older, largely white cohort of professional criminals to a more volatile population comprising young, ethnic-minority men, involved in forms of serious and violent crime that were largely disorganised. Such men, observed the Director of High Security Prisons (personal communication), seemed to be entering the prison system with a much greater degree of shock and disaffection than traditional 'gangsters', while their relationships both with staff and with other prisoner subgroups, including men convicted of terrorist offences, were somewhat more opaque. In this context, a study of long-term prisoners—their adaptations, social relations and sense of penal legitimacy—had practical as well as scholarly value.

---

[4]NOMS was the name of the organisation that oversaw prison and probation services in England and Wales from June 2004 until April 2017, at which point it was renamed Her Majesty's Prison and Probation Service (HMPPS).

Defining 'Long-Term' Imprisonment[5]

As Flanagan (1995b: 4) notes, '[t]here is no uniform definition of long-term incarceration'. Attempts to quantify its meaning have ranged considerably, both in policy and in scholarly domains, and some studies make no clear attempt to define the parameters of this population (e.g. Porporino 1991; Short 1979; Brown 1998). As long sentences have become more common, what is considered a 'long' period of imprisonment has quietly inflated. As former Director-General of NOMS, Phil Wheatley noted, sentence lengths once considered exceptional have been normalised:

> It's almost like a currency. So if [previously] you read in the newspaper that somebody had got a 20-year sentence, you all thought that was a *very* long time. [...] And everybody looked at it and thought 'How can you do that?'. [...] And we've somehow managed to devalue that currency [...] We've got a different view about what is a 'long' time. (Phil Wheatley, interview, August 2014)

The normalisation of such sentences is reflected in policy and academic writing from the closing decades of the twentieth century. Forty years ago, scholars and political institutions (e.g. Council of Europe 1977) were 'confident' (Flanagan 1995b: 4) in adopting five years of continuous confinement as an appropriate definition of a 'long-term' sentence. Similar definitions were being adopted in England and Wales during this period. Towards the end of the 1960s, the Home Office (Radzinowicz 1968) defined sentences of four or more years as 'long', while a UK study of 'long-term prisoners' (Gunn et al. 1973) used the five-year mark as the threshold between 'short' and 'long' sentences. By the mid-1980s, definitions of 'long-term' incarceration had stretched, to around six to eight years (MacKenzie and Goodstein 1985; Mackenzie et al. 1989). Designations of 'long-term' imprisonment as confinement of no less than a decade were a feature of a number of studies in the 1970s and 1980s (e.g. Richards 1978; Banister et al. 1973; Zamble and Porporino 1988), and continued to be used in the 1990s (e.g. Weekes 1995) and beyond. By the mid-1990s, Flanagan (1995b) suggested that

---

[5]'Long-term' sentences can be split into two clear categories—determinate and indeterminate sentences. Life sentences and indeterminate sentences for public protection (or 'IPPs') fall within the latter, and some of the studies cited here are referring to all of these groups when discussing the nature and impact of 'long' sentences.

only a sentence of eight to ten years would 'qualify a US prisoner as a long-term inmate' (p. 4).

Understanding Long-Term Imprisonment

Considering such definitional boundaries through an optic of harm, the Council of Europe (1977) suggested that a period of incarceration should be regarded as 'long term' at the point after which 'there could be no doubt that the specific problems of long-term imprisonment became noticeable' (Council of Europe 1977: 7). Considering 'long term' in relation to damage caused, rather than years served, points to the importance of the subjective experience both of time and imprisonment itself—matters that we focus on throughout this book. Yet our understanding of what these experiences entail is highly limited. Since their heyday in the latter half of the twentieth century (e.g. Radzinowicz 1968; Cohen and Taylor 1972; Banister et al. 1973; Gunn et al. 1973; Council of Europe 1977; Heather 1977; Richards 1978; Sapsford 1978; Short 1979; Porporino 1991; Flanagan 1982, 1995b, 1995c; Weekes 1995; Brown 1998), academic studies into the nature and consequences of long-term imprisonment have become much less common. Although there has been a considerable amount of research into the development of 'life without parole' in the United States (see, for example, Rhodes 2004; Johnson and McGunigall-Smith 2008; Ogletree and Sarat 2012), the absence, in such situations, of the possibility of release makes the sentence rather different from in European contexts, where only a very small minority of prisoners are serving equivalent terms. Meanwhile, the body of literature in England and Wales specifically—widely considered to have originated in earnest with Cohen and Taylor's (1972) seminal study—is now, in many respects, outmoded. The studies that comprise it tell us relatively little about the distinct subset of the long-term prisoner population serving '*very* long sentences' who were identified some fifty years ago as presenting 'special problems' (Radzinowicz 1968: 57), but who are confined in a very different kind of prison system from at that time: one that is often considered more decent and humane, yet is more preoccupied with risk, more secure and more restricted by notions of 'public acceptability'. These shifts bring their own unique challenges.

Nonetheless, the research literature on long-term imprisonment points to a number of key themes (for a very comprehensive recent overview, see Van Zyl Smit and Appleton 2019). The first of these is time. As many scholars note (Cohen and Taylor 1972; Sapsford 1983; Cope 2000; O'Donnell 2014), time is the essence of any term of coercive confinement, since it is the unit by which the deprivation of liberty is inflicted. Meanwhile, to quote Flanagan (1981: 212), 'the element of *time* exacerbates all of the deprivations [of prison life] and transforms them […] into major problems of survival'. Long sentences also have a particularly distortive effect on the way that time is experienced (O'Donnell 2014). While time in prison feels endless, empty and unreal (a 'misty abyss', to quote Cohen and Taylor 1972: 95; see also Jewkes 2005; O'Donnell 2014)—something to try to deplete—the long-term prisoner remains aware that time outside the prison is all too precious (Jamieson and Grounds 2005). Time is too abundant in the world that the prisoner inhabits, and too scarce in the world from which he or she has been removed. One of the greatest struggles for prisoners serving long, indeterminate sentences is dealing with the overwhelming nature of the time ahead, which may feel impossible to contemplate (Cohen and Taylor 1972; Flanagan 1981; Liebling et al. 2011), particularly because of its indeterminate nature (Sapsford 1983; Van Zyl Smit and Appleton 2019). O'Donnell (2014: 178) argues that since 'the currency of the past is soon spent', and thoughts of the future generate anxiety, prisoners instead focus on and live within an 'extended present'.

A second theme in studies of long-term prisoners is the struggle to find meaning and purpose, and to cushion the self against the assault of institutional life. Sapsford (1983: 77) notes that 'The prisoner has to live with potentially no sense of direction, movement or purpose, which is a constraint beyond the scope of our culture's repertoire of normal-life adaptations'. Receiving a life sentence may generate deep existential crisis, with prisoners overwhelmed by a sense of hopelessness and despair about their predicament, or in a 'state of almost psychological "paralysis"' (Liebling et al. 2011: 271). In particular, Cohen and Taylor's (1972) *Psychological Survival* documents a range of anxieties among long-term prisoners about 'mundane and untested matters as the passage of time, the making and breaking of friends, the fear of deterioration, the role of self-consciousness and the loss of identity' (p. 39). The search for existential meaning—which Viktor Frankl (1959/1985) regarded as a primary motivational driver—is often fulfilled through religion (Irwin 2009; Liebling et al. 2011) or education (James 2003; Warr 2008), both of which enable narrative reconstruction while offering a broader re-evaluation of selfhood and society.

A third theme is shame, remorse and redemption. Toch (2010) speculates that many serious and long-term offenders come to feel themselves to be substantially different from the person they were at the point that they committed their index offence. Some undergo 'crucial regenerative change pretty much on their own' (p. 8), and many narrate sincere scripts of redemption, which come to dominate their orientation to both life in prison and post-release (see also Schinkel 2014; Munn and Bruckert 2013). As Irwin (2009: 66) explains:

> Awakening begins when lifers fully appreciate that there has been something fundamentally wrong with their former behaviour. […] they come to sincerely regret that they have taken a life of another human being. They further realize that there may be something fundamentally deranged in their personality or character. […] They take inventory and ask themselves who they are and what they should do to reform themselves.

A final theme is coping, adaptation and change. Sustained imprisonment may only be survivable with the support of some kind of protective ideology (Cohen and Taylor 1972) or—conversely—through acquiescence to the terms and parameters of the sentence (Schinkel 2014). Jewkes (2005) draws on the idea of liminality to describe the state of social limbo that long-term prisoners occupy, when detached from both their past and from a predictable future. As Jewkes goes on to argue, though, this sense of ambiguity is eventually supplanted, as prisoners 'construct new narratives of self' (p. 376). For those who are sentenced late in life, narrative retention may be more significant than narrative redefinition in protecting against the symbolic degradations of imprisonment. That is, older prisoners may defend their sense of self by clinging to markers of decency and achievement from the life they had established prior to their imprisonment (Crawley and Sparks 2005).

Whichever the case, the literature suggests that most prisoners serving very long sentences do not succumb to the forms of 'prisonisation' (Clemmer 1940) and 'learned helplessness' (Seligman 1975) that might be expected, in which sustained exposure to institutional conditions makes them dependent or apathetic. As Sapsford (1983: 63) summarises: 'prisoners did not deteriorate, because they found ways of coming to terms with the prison environment and using it for their own purposes'.

The Impact of Long-Term Imprisonment

Sapsford's statement is consistent with a number of quantitative studies that have concluded that extended periods of incarceration do not have a debilitating impact on such matters as cognitive functioning or self-esteem (*inter alia*, Banister et al 1973; MacKenzie and Goodstein 1985; Rasch 1981; and see Van Zyl Smit and Appleton 2019 for a very clear digest). Such studies suggest that, if anything, the problems of imprisonment seem to be less rather than more severe among prisoners who are further into their sentences (Richards 1978; Flanagan 1980; Leigey and Ryder 2015; and see Hulley et al. 2016). Indeed, there is evidence that some long-term prisoners attribute positive meaning of some kind to their experience (Schinkel 2014), and that some men and women held in the most extreme conditions of long-term isolation not only survive the experience, but may feel themselves to have improved as a result of it (see O'Donnell 2014). But such conclusions are contested, particularly by scholars whose orientations are more qualitative. Liebling and Maruna (2005) argue that the implication that prisoners are impervious to the impact of incarceration, or that its effects are impermanent, is to some degree based on measurements of harm that are highly partial (see also Cohen and Taylor 1972, for a more acerbic critique). That is, most quantitative studies do not take into account the 'affective dimension' (p. 3) of imprisonment, such as feelings of loneliness and injustice, whose effects might surface indirectly or at points in time well after release from prison (cf. Grounds 2005; Liem and Kunst 2013).

Despite these differences, qualitative and quantitative studies are consistent in suggesting that long-term prisoners find strategies for alleviating the difficulties that they encounter, which make the problems of imprisonment more manageable over time. A number of scholars have highlighted the way in which long-termers exhibit a distinctive attitude of 'maturity', in which they seek to avoid trouble, 'consider alternatives prior to action' (Flanagan 1980: 216), adjust to the imposition of authority and use their time constructively. To quote Johnson and Dobrzanska (2005: 8), 'lifers come grudgingly to accept the prison as their involuntary home for life', accommodating to their situation through personal routines and behaviours that provide a localised sense of autonomy and a sense of wider purpose. In one of the few longitudinal explorations of adaptive behaviour among long-term male prisoners—and it should be noted that the literature on long-term female prisoners is even sparser (although see Walker and Worrall 2000; Lempert

2016; Crewe et al. 2017)—Zamble (2016: 421) reports that, over time, such men deliberately withdraw 'from the diffuse social networks that are typical of inmate interactions', maintain their emotional ties with people in the community, become more positive in their attitudes towards the criminal justice system and become progressively more preoccupied with the future. 'In effect, they sometimes seemed to be living within a world of their own, inside the prison but separate and apart from its ordinary discourse […] if their bodies were in prison, their cognitive focus was elsewhere' (p. 421).

Long-Term Imprisonment from Young Adulthood

This book engages with all of the issues listed above, while drawing heavily on two further implications of the literature. First, long-term imprisonment represents a profound rupture in the prisoner's existence, selfhood and life course, and a deep shock to his or her sense of what was previously taken for granted (Cohen and Taylor 1972; Jewkes 2005; Aresti et al. 2010; Liebling et al. 2011). Like all prisoners, those given a life sentence are extracted from a set of social relations and familiar routines, and 'cast into a completely unfamiliar and seemingly chaotic one where the ordering of events is completely out of [their] control' (Irwin 1970: 39). On entry into prison, the long-term prisoner 'has to come to terms with the fact that he is starting a new life, one in which the routines which previously obtained in every area will be transformed' (Cohen and Taylor 1972: 43). To quote Sapsford (1983: 61), for life-sentenced prisoners first entering custody, 'the shock is very great. Suddenly they have lost the whole pattern of their lives and the whole of the reinforcement to which they are accustomed'. Writing on the 'turbulent transition' of acclimating to life without parole, Leigey (2015: 35) likewise cites one prisoner's reflection that: 'In a blink of an eye, your whole life has changed right in front of you', and quotes another who describes the disorientation of imprisonment as 'like going to another country' (p. 36).

Jewkes (2005) relates long-term imprisonment to chronic or terminal illness, characterising both as states that are imposed upon (rather than directly chosen by) the individual, are inconsistent with his or her existing sense of self and entail a 'sudden interruption of the lifecourse'. This comparison is redolent of Cohen and Taylor's (1972) argument that long-term imprisonment is analogous to experiences such as being in a car accident, suffering a chronic illness or being evacuated to an unfamiliar area. Such experiences 'are literally and metaphorically shattering' (Cohen and Taylor 1972: 43): so extreme and disruptive that they disturb a set of foundational and normally tacit assumptions about selfhood and society: who one is, how the world functions and a range of 'everyday matters as time, friendship, privacy, identity, self-consciousness, ageing and physical deterioration' (p. 41). For Jewkes, this interruption to the lifecourse, alongside the realisation of what the prisoner has lost, 'may be regarded as the ultimate sanction of life imprisonment' (2005: 370), producing a sense 'of bereavement for oneself; the loss involving lost worlds, lost futures and lost identities' (p. 370).

The second key point is that prisoners do not remain perpetually in this state of shock, grief and disorientation, but instead find ways of coming to terms with their actions and circumstances. As John Irwin (2009: 2) asserts:

> … whoever they were and whatever crime they committed, the vast majority of lifers become completely different people after serving years in prison. Two things unavoidably happen to them. First they are removed from the social contexts that in many complicated ways influenced their orientation, values, and viewpoints and contributed to their crimes. Second, they mature. Beyond these two inevitable changes, most of them consciously undertake a transformation of their thinking, orientation, and personality. This leads to their actively taking advantage of every resource available to prepare themselves for a different life when they are released.

Irwin's notion of 'awakening' has found considerable support in other studies (e.g. Leigey 2015; Liem 2016; Herbert 2018), and Liebling et al. (2011: 37) report a similar process: 'One of the gradual reactions to the crisis of a long sentence was the eventual realisation that there was an urgent need to change, if prisoners wanted to progress, be released, and lead a life without crime'. The suggestion in both analyses is that, after some time, long-term prisoners actively reflect upon themselves in relation to their circumstances, engaging as conscious agents in a process of existential contemplation and self-reconstitution not just within a context of severe constraint but because of it. A second key feature of this book, then, is its attempt to bring into relief this dynamic, in which individuals come to terms with, and reflexively negotiate, being in what Cohen and Taylor (1972: 58) summarise as an 'extreme and immutable environment, imposed upon them as a punishment'.

Here, Margaret Archer's work on reflexivity and late modernity is particularly instructive. In a series of publications, Archer (2003, 2007, 2012) has set out a framework for understanding the role of 'reflexivity' in the social world. Reflexivity is defined as: 'our power to deliberate internally upon what to do in situations that [are] not of our making' (2003: 342), or as 'the regular exercise of the mental ability, shared by all normal people, to consider themselves in relation to their (social) contexts and vice versa' (2007: 4). Archer argues that it is through reflexivity that individuals (or 'agents') engage with the structural circumstances that they confront: 'Situations do not directly impact upon us; they are reflexively mediated via our own concerns' (2003: 139). That is, agents encounter objective circumstances, which constrain and enable their range of actions, but the particular constraints or enablements that become activated are determined according to priorities that are subjectively defined by each individual ('the causal power of social forms is mediated through social agency' [Archer 2003: 2]). As she summarises,

> ... agents *subjectively* deliberate upon their courses of action in relation to their *objective* circumstances. Reflexively they must seek to establish a *modus vivendi* at the nexus between their voluntarily defined priorities and the social determined characteristics of the contexts that they now confront (2003: 244; italics in original).

Archer generally refers to these voluntarily defined priorities as 'ultimate concerns'. It is these concerns—this sense of 'what matters to me'—that provide the compass or sounding board for practical action, allowing agents to navigate unpredictable situations and work out 'what to do, what to think and what to say' (Archer 2003: 26). They do so, in practice, through what Archer calls 'internal conversations'. These introspective, inner dialogues are used by agents both to work out their ultimate values and desires—'who they are and how they see their lives progressing' (Akram and Hogan 2015: 3)—and, when confronted with circumstances and opportunities, to help plan actions and practices accordingly. As Farrugia (2013: 287) summarises, 'In this sense, human reflexivity is the engine of social life'.

Central to Archer's argument is her characterisation of late modernity as an era that produces a 'reflexive imperative'. Whereas, in previous eras, there was relative *continuity* between the social conditions in which people were socialised and those they subsequently encountered as they moved through life, there is now considerably more *incongruity* between these contextual domains. Rapid social transformations mean that individuals are thrust into an array of novel situations:

new kinds of contexts, organisations and social relations. As a result, they are unable or unwise to rely on 'habit', tacit knowledge or previous experiences to steer their course of behaviour:

> Whereas the 'past', in the form of one's background, used to be a help in the present towards the future, it increasingly has nothing to give and, at worst, represents a hindrance. [...] Swift change renders habitual guidelines to action of decreasing relevance or positively misleading. (Archer 2012: 41, 64)

Without authoritative or established guidelines for what to do or how to act, reflexive deliberation becomes all the more important in determining behaviour.

While Archer makes no direct comment on prisons and imprisonment, her framework is apposite for an understanding of the condition of long-term prisoners. As noted above, having been given long sentences following convictions for murder, such prisoners face a form of extreme incongruity, a radical rupture between past, present and future. This rupture has three primary components, whose terms provide the structure for this book. First, it dislocates long-term prisoners from the social worlds and relationships in which they were previously embedded. Second, it produces a major existential breach, in which the murder offence itself forces such prisoners to reassess whether they are the person they thought themselves to be. Third, it requires a radical revision of the assumptions that they held about their futures. This triple rupture—relationships, self and future—represents an acute breach in almost everything that the prisoner could previously assume, requiring them to adjust from life in the community to protracted confinement, and to rethink who they are and what they might become. In such respects, the murder conviction is a 'fateful moment' *par excellence* (Giddens 1991), a point at which life is forever changed in a manner that reshapes 'the reflexive project of identity' (Giddens 1991: 143) precisely because the episode decouples the individual from the moorings of their past.

Archer emphasises that there are different modes of reflexivity, congruent with specific eras or, for our purposes, social circumstances. Of particular relevance to our analysis are Archer's ideas of 'fractured reflexivity' and 'meta-reflexivity'. Fractured reflexives are people who, as a result of profound social discontinuity or personal change (such as serious illness or marital breakdown), exist in a state of disorientation about what their priorities are and how to realise them. Such individuals hold almost no internal dialogue at all, or the forms of self-talk in which they engage give them 'no instrumental guidance about what to do in practice' (p. 299). Their internal conversations are inhibited or expressive: rather than acting purposefully in pursuit of a goal, they dwell emotionally on their condition, in ways that, if anything, exacerbate their distress and confusion. While some reflect nostalgically on a past that no longer provides a guide to action, others 'grasp in desperation at unrealistic projects' (p. 303), or rely on 'gut feelings' to guide their actions. Whichever the case, lacking the kind of 'strict personal identity' which enables the formation of personal projects, they are 'passive agents', lacking in purpose or direction, whose subjectivity makes no difference to the play of objective circumstances upon them' (p. 299).

Meta-reflexives are disengaged from their family backgrounds, divorced from the behavioural repertoires set out by their past and keen to forge lives that differ from those they experienced in childhood. Rather than consulting with or prioritising family and friends (like 'communicative reflexives') or making decisions pragmatically and strategically (like 'autonomous reflexives'), they pursue a *modus vivendi* and judge their courses of action according to ideals, values and relatively abstract life projects. In contrast to fractured reflexives, they are engaged in a constant and transformative process of self-examination. Specifically, they are reflexively preoccupied with themselves and their personal projects, rather than with tasks and external actions. Archer considers this form of reflexivity to be emblematic of late modernity, where there is significant incongruity between how things are and how they used to be. Clearly, though, fractured reflexivity and meta-reflexivity might be regarded as alternative reflexive responses to situations in which individuals are radically and suddenly dislocated.

It is significant that the environment into which long-term prisoners are thrust is particularly constraining. By definition, and over a sustained period of time, as well as removing prisoners from their former lives, imprisonment imposes a vast range of everyday restrictions on their actions and severely curtails their potential to autonomously construct their futures. In this respect, while Archer's account of contextual incongruity provides a useful framework for thinking about social and biographical dislocation, its fit is imperfect. Among the central criticisms of Archer's work are that it implies that, within late modernity's 'situational logic of opportunity', people are 'free to self-actualize' (Farrugia and Woodman 2015: 627), constructing their ultimate concerns as sovereign individuals. In this respect, Archer has been criticised for understating the impact of family background on life outcomes, for under-estimating the strength of habitual action (Akram and Hogan

2015) and for being unable to account for why people adopt particular ultimate concerns over others (Farrugia 2013; Farrugia and Woodman 2015). That is, her emphasis on the novelty of the situations produced by social transformation leads her to suggest that, as meta-reflexives, people act in ways that are more or less unhindered by embodied dispositions or structural determinants.

Clearly, this formulation of 'opportunity' and relatively unconstrained agency makes little sense within the context of the prison. Accordingly, Chapter 4 emphasises the overwhelming nature of the pains and problems that prisoners experienced during the early phase of the sentence, and the reactive adaptive responses that resulted. Nonetheless, as Chapter 5 goes on to describe, even within conditions that restrict choices and actions to an almost unparalleled degree, individuals interpret and reflexively engage with the world in ways that give them some sense of control, meaning, purpose and hope. That is, prisoners who were beyond the initial phase of the sentence were not so much in a mode of 'coping-survival' as 'coping-adaptation'. The chapters that follow correspond with the ruptures and dislocations that we have noted above, and the adaptive imperatives that they generate: first, the need to reformulate personal relationships and ensure the maintenance of relational goods in radically altered social circumstances (Chapter 6); second the impulsion to reconsider matters of personal selfhood and identity in the context of long-term confinement and in relation to the offence of murder (Chapter 7); third, the challenge of dealing with the everyday and long-term burdens of time, and of coming to terms with the relocation of life to the domain of the prison (Chapter 8). Throughout, we suggest that the experiences and adaptations of long-term prisoners, sentenced at an early age, can only be understood with reference to what we call the 'offence-time nexus': the nature of the offence of murder, and the sheer amount of time that they have to serve (as well as, for the female participants in particular, biographical experiences of abuse). In the concluding chapter of the book, we outline the implications of our findings and reflect on their implications: in doing so, we return to the essential issue with which the study originated: what we are we doing to people when we deprive them of their liberty for such life-changing periods.

References

Akram, S., & Hogan, A. (2015). On reflexivity and the conduct of the self in everyday life: Reflections on Bourdieu and Archer. *British Journal of Sociology, 66*(4), 605–625.

Archer, M. (2003). *Structure, agency and the internal conversation.* Cambridge: Cambridge University Press.

Archer, M. (2007). *Making our way through the world: Human reflexivity and social mobility.* Cambridge: Cambridge University Press.

Archer, M. (2012). *The reflexive imperative.* Cambridge: Cambridge University Press.

Aresti, A., Eatough, V., & Brooks-Gordon, B. (2010). Doing time after time: An interpretative phenomenological analysis of reformed ex-prisoners' experiences of self-change, identity and career opportunities. *Psychology, Crime & Law, 16*(3), 169–190.

Banister, P. A., Smith, F. V., Heskin, K. J., & Bolton, N. (1973). Psychological correlates of long-term imprisonment. *British Journal of Criminology, 13*(4), 312–330.

Bennathan, J., & Taylor, P. (2016). *Jogee and joint enterprise—Where to from here? Historic convictions, appeals, and the Criminal Cases Review Commission.* London: Doughty Street Chambers. Accessed 30 May 2018 from https://www.doughtystreet.co.uk/documents/uploaded-documents/2016_02_-_Bennathan_and_Taylor_on_Jogee.pdf.

Blom-Cooper, L. (1987). The penalty of imprisonment. The Tanner lectures on human values. *Lecture, Delivered at Clare Hall.* University of Cambridge.

Bottoms, A. E. (1977). Reflections on the renaissance of dangerousness. *The Howard Journal of Criminal Justice, 12*(2), 70–96.

Brown, A. (1998). Doing time: The extended present of the long-term prisoner. *Time & Society, 7*(1), 93–103.

Bureau of Investigative Journalism. (2014). *Joint enterprise: An investigation into the legal doctrine of joint enterprise in criminal convictions.* London: The Bureau of Investigative Journalism.

Clemmer, D. (1940). *The prison community.* New Braunfels: Christopher Publishing House.

Cohen, S., & Taylor, L. (1972). *Psychological survival: The experience of long-term imprisonment.* Middlesex: Penguin.

Cope, N. (2000). Drug use in prison: The experience of young offenders. *Drugs: Education, Prevention and Policy, 7*(4), 355–366.

Council of Europe. (1977). *Committee on crime problems: Treatment of long-term prisoners.* Strasbourg: Council of Europe.

Crawley, E., & Sparks, R. (2005). Hidden injuries? Researching the experiences of older men in English prisons. *Howard Journal of Criminal Justice, 44*(4), 345–356.

Crewe, B., Hulley, S., & Wright, S. (2017). The gendered pains of life imprisonment. *British Journal of Criminology, 57*(6), 1359–1378.

Crewe, B., Liebling, A., Padfield, N., & Virgo, G. (2015). Joint enterprise: The implications of an unfair and unclear law. *Criminal Law Review, 4,* 249–266.

Crown Prosecution Service. (2018). *Secondary liability; charging decisions on principals and accessories.* Accessed 23 May 2018 from https://www.cps.gov.uk/legal-guidance/secondary-liability-charging-decisions-principals-and-accessories.

Cullen, E., & Newell, T. (1999). *Murderers and life imprisonment: Containment, treatment, safety and risk.* Winchester: Waterside Press.

Farrugia, D. (2013). The reflexive subject: Towards a theory of reflexivity as practical intelligibility. *Current Sociology, 6*(3), 283–300.

Farrugia, D., & Woodman, D. (2015). Ultimate concerns in late modernity: Archer, Bourdieu and reflexivity. *British Journal of Sociology, 66*(4), 626–644.

Feeley, M. M., & Simon, J. (1992). The new penology: Notes on the emerging strategy of corrections and its implications. *Criminology, 30*(4), 449–474.

Flanagan, T. J. (1980). The pains of long-term imprisonment: A comparison of British and American perspectives. *The British Journal of Criminology, 20*(2), 148–156.

Flanagan, T. J. (1982). Correctional policy and the long-term prisoner. *Crime & Delinquency, 28*(1), 82–95.

Flanagan, T. (1995a). Preface. In T. Flanagan (Ed.), *Long-term imprisonment: Policy, science and correctional practice* (pp. xi–xiv). Thousand Oaks: Sage.

Flanagan, T. (1995b). Long-term incarceration: Issues of science, policy and correctional practice. In T. Flanagan (Ed.), *Long-term imprisonment: Policy, science and correctional practice* (pp. 3–9). Thousand Oaks: Sage.

Flanagan, T. (Ed.). (1995c). *Long-term imprisonment: Policy, science and correctional practice.* Thousand Oaks: Sage.

Flanagan, T. J. (2016). Dealing with long-term confinement. *Criminal Justice and Behavior, 8*(2), 201–222.

Garland, D. (2000). The culture of high crime societies. *British Journal of Criminology, 40*(3), 347–375.

Giddens, A. (1991). *Modernity and self identity: Self and society in the late modern age.* Cambridge: Polity Press.

Green, A., & McGourlay, C. (2015). The wolf packs in our midst and other products of criminal joint enterprise prosecutions. *The Journal of Criminal Law, 74*(4), 280–297.

Grounds, A. T. (2005). Understanding the effects of wrongful imprisonment. *Crime and Justice, 32,* 1–58.

Gunn, J., Nicol, R., Gristwood, J., & Foggitt, R. (1973). Long-term prisoners. *British Journal of Criminology, 13*(4), 331–340.

Heather, N. (1977). Personal illness in "lifers" and the effects of long-term indeterminate sentences. *British Journal of Criminology, 17*(4), 378–386.

Herbert, S. (2018). Inside or outside? Expanding the narratives about life-sentenced prisoners. *Punishment & Society, 20*(5), 628–645.

Home Affairs Select Committee. (2009). *Knife Crime,* HC (2008–9) 7. Retrieved from https://bit.ly/2l6JH95.

House of Commons. (1964). *November 19 Debate* (vol 702, col 612–3). Retrieved from http://bit.ly/2kQtQf1.

House of Commons. (1983). *November 30 1983* (vol 49, cc 506–507). Retrieved from http://bit.ly/2l6H86Z.

House of Lords. (1971). *February 17 Debate* (vol 315, col 623). Retrieved from http://bit.ly/2mugkxT.

House of Lords. (1982). *April 28 Debate* (vol 429, col 870). Retrieved from http://bit.ly/2m9EDAW.

Hulley, S., Crewe, B., & Wright, S. (2016). Re-examining the problems of long-term imprisonment. *British Journal of Criminology, 56*(4), 769–792.

Hulley, S., Crewe, B., & Wright, S. (2019). Making sense of 'joint enterprise' for murder: Legal legitimacy or instrumental acquiescence? *British Journal of Criminology, 59*(6), 1328–1346.

Irwin, J. (1970). *The felon.* Englewood Cliffs, NJ: Prentice-Hall.

Irwin, J. (2009). *Lifers: Seeking redemption in prison.* New York: Routledge.

James, E. (2003). *A life inside.* London: Atlantic Books.

Jamieson, R., & Grounds, A. (2005). Release and adjustment: Perspectives from studies of wrongly convicted and politically motivated prisoners. In A. Liebling & S. Maruna (Eds.), *The effects of imprisonment* (pp. 33–65). Cullompton: Willan Publishing.

Jewkes, Y. (2005). Loss, liminality and the life sentence: Managing identity through a disrupted lifecourse. In A. Liebling & S. Maruna (Eds.), *The effects of imprisonment* (pp. 366–388). Cullompton: Willan Publishing.

Johnson, R., & Dobrzanska, A. (2005). Mature coping among life-sentenced inmates: An exploratory study of adjustment dynamics. *Corrections Compendium, 30*(8–9), 36–38.

Johnson, R., & McGunigall-Smith, S. (2008). Life without parole, America's other death penalty: Notes on life under sentence of death by incarceration. *The Prison Journal, 88*(2), 328–346.

Justice Select Committee. (2019). *Prison population 2022: Planning for the future,* HC (2017–19) 16. Retrieved from https://bit.ly/2YLf1JF.

Killias, M., Gilliéron, G., Villard, F., & Poglia, C. (2010). How damaging is imprisonment in the long- term? A controlled experiment comparing long-term effects of community service and short custodial sentences on re-offending and social integration. *Journal of Experimental Criminology, 6*(2), 115–130.

Leigey, M. E. (2015). *The forgotten men: Serving a life without parole sentence.* New Brunswick: Rutgers University Press.

Leigey, M. E., & Ryder, M. A. (2015). The pains of permanent imprisonment: Examining perceptions of confinement among older life without parole inmates. *International Journal of Offender Therapy and Comparative Criminology, 59*(7), 726–742.

Lempert, L. B. (2016). *Women doing life: Gender, punishment and the struggle for identity.* New York: NYU Press.

Liebling, A. (2014). Moral and philosophical problems of long-term imprisonment. *Studies in Christian Ethics, 27*(3), 258–269.

Liebling, A., & Maruna, S. (2005). Introduction: The effects of imprisonment revisited. In A. Liebling & S. Maruna (Eds.), *The effects of imprisonment* (pp. 10–32). Cullompton: Willan Publishing.

Liebling, A., Arnold, H., & Straub, C. (2011). *An exploration of staff-prisoner relationships at HMP Whitemoor: 12 years on.* London: Ministry of Justice.

Liem, M. (2016). *After life imprisonment: Reentry in the era of mass incarceration.* New York: NYU Press.

Liem, M., & Kunst, M. (2013). Is there a recognizable post-incarceration syndrome among released "lifers"? *International Journal of Law and Psychiatry, 36*(3–4), 333–337.

Lloyd, M. (2011). Interview: Michael Spurr. *Prison Service Journal, 193,* 23–28.

MacKenzie, D. L., & Goodstein, L. (1985). Long-term incarceration impacts and characteristics of long-term offenders: An empirical analysis. *Criminal Justice and Behavior, 12*(4), 395–414.

MacKenzie, D. L., Robinson, J. W., & Campbell, C. S. (1989). Long-term incarceration of female offenders prison adjustment and coping. *Criminal Justice and Behavior, 16*(2), 223–238.

Mauer, M., King, R. S., & Young, M. C. (2004). *The meaning of "life": Long prison sentences in context.* Washington, DC: The Sentencing Project.

Ministry of Justice. (2009). *Population in custody monthly tables—February 2009: England and Wales (Ministry of Justice Statistics bulletin).* London: Ministry of Justice.

Ministry of Justice. (2010). *Explanatory memorandum to the Criminal Justice Act 2003 (Mandatory life sentence: Determination of minimum term) Order 2010 (No. 197).* London: Ministry of Justice.

Ministry of Justice. (2013). *Story of the prison population: 1993–2012: England and Wales.* London: Ministry of Justice.

Ministry of Justice. (2019a). *Offender management statistics quarterly April–June 2019.* London: Ministry of Justice.

Ministry of Justice. (2019b). *Offender management statistics quarterly: October to December 2018—'Prison releases 2018'.* London: Ministry of Justice.

Munn, M., & Bruckert, C. (2013). *On the outside: From lengthy imprisonment to lasting freedom.* Vancouver and Toronto: UBC Press.

O'Donnell, I. (2014). *Prisoners, solitude, and time.* Oxford: Oxford University Press.

Ogletree, C. J., & Sarat, A. (Eds.). (2012). *Life without parole: America's new death penalty.* New York and London: New York University Press.

Owers, A. (2010, July 13). *Valedictory lecture.* Westminster Central Hall. Retrieved from https://bit.ly/2mbeIZN.

Player, E. (2005). The reduction of women's imprisonment in England and Wales: Will the reform of short prison sentences help? *Punishment & Society, 7*(4), 419–439.

Porporino, F. J. (1991). *Differences in response to long-term imprisonment: Implications for the management of long-term offenders.* Ottawa, Canada: Correctional Service Canada.

Press Association. (2009, November). Knife killers will serve minimum 25 year jail term, Jack Straw says. *The Guardian.*

Prison Reform Trust. (2012). *Prison: The facts (Bromley Briefings Summer 2012).* London: Prison Reform Trust.

Radzinowicz, L. (1968). *Report of the Advisory Committee on Penal System on the regime for long-term prisoners in conditions of maximum security* (The Radzinowicz Report). London: HMSO.

Rasch, W. (1981). The effects of indeterminate detention. *International Journal of Law and Psychiatry, 4*(3–4), 417–431.

Rhodes, L. A. (2004). *Total confinement: Madness and reason in the maximum security prison* (Vol. 7). Berkeley, Los Angeles, and London: University of California Press.

Richards, B. (1978). The experience of long-term imprisonment: An exploratory investigation. *British Journal of Criminology, 18*(2), 162–169.

Sapsford, R. J. (1978). Life-sentence prisoners: Psychological changes during sentence. *British Journal of Criminology, 18*(2), 128–145.

Sapsford, R. (1983). *Life sentence prisoners: Reaction, response and change.* London: Open University Press.

Schinkel, M. (2014). Punishment as moral communication: The experiences of long-term prisoners. *Punishment & Society, 16*(5), 578–597.

Seligman, M. E. (1975). *Helplessness: On depression, development, and death.* New York: W.H. Freeman.

Short, R. (1979). *The care of long-term prisoners.* London: Macmillan Press.

Simon, J. (2007). *Governing through crime: How the war on crime transformed American democracy and created a culture of fear.* New York: Oxford University Press.

Toch, H. (2010). "I am not now who I used to be then": Risk assessment and the maturation of long-term prison inmates. *The Prison Journal, 90*(1), 4–11.

Travis, J. (2002). Invisible punishment: An instrument of social exclusion. In M. Mauer & M. Chesney-Lind (Eds.), *Invisible punishment: The collateral consequences of mass imprisonment* (pp. 15–36). New York: The New Press.

Trebilcock, J. (2011). *No winners: The reality of short term prison sentences.* London: Howard League for Penal Reform.

Van Zyl Smit, D., & Appleton, C. (2019). *Life imprisonment: A global human rights analysis.* Cambridge, MA: Harvard University Press.

Walker, S., & Worrall, A. (2000). Life as a woman: The gendered pains of indeterminate imprisonment. *Prison Service Journal, 132,* 27–37.

Warr, J. (2008). Personal reflections on prison staff. In J. Bennett, B. Crewe & A. Wahadin (Eds.), *Understanding prison staff* (pp. 17–29). Cullompton: Willan.

Weekes, J. R. (1995). Long-term offenders in Canada. In T. Flanagan (Ed.), *Long-term imprisonment: Policy, science and correctional practice* (pp. 22–28). Thousand Oaks: Sage.

Zamble, E. (2016). Behavior and adaptation in long-term prison inmates. *Criminal Justice and Behavior, 19*(4), 409–425.

Zamble, E., & Porporino, F. J. (1988). *Coping, behaviour and adaptation in prison inmates.* New York: Springer Verlag.

2

Methods

The study originated in a previous research project, in which two of the authors (BC and SH) had interviewed men who were at the beginning of very long sentences and wondered at the difficulties of coping with such an extreme sanction. Both had been struck by the fact that their interviewees were serving sentences that were longer than the number of years they had been alive, and yet who seemed coolly resigned to their circumstances. Initial discussions with senior figures within what was then the National Offender Management Service (NOMS) suggested a dovetailing of interest in the long-term prisoner population.

The Director of High Security Prisons expressed a keen interest in understanding more about the changing nature of the long-term prison population, having observed that such men seemed different from the traditional lifer: younger, less criminally 'professional', more likely to be from minority-ethnic backgrounds, more shocked and alienated on entering custody and with fewer stable ties to networks in the community. At the time of such discussions, practitioners were also concerned about the growth of 'Muslim gangs' within high-security prisons and a set of opaque connections between prisoners convicted of terrorist offences and traditional, organised 'gangsters'. In the event, our study focused more on long-term prisoners located throughout the prison system than on the emerging social dynamics of the high-security prison estate, but research on such matters by

© The Author(s) 2020
B. Crewe et al., *Life Imprisonment from Young Adulthood,*
Palgrave Studies in Prisons and Penology,
https://doi.org/10.1057/978-1-137-56601-0_2

Liebling et al. (2011) and Liebling, Armstrong, Bramwell, and Williams provided findings that were highly complementary to our own (see Liebling et al. 2015, and see Liebling and Arnold 2012; Williams 2017).[1]

Research Design

The study employed a mixed-method approach, involving surveys and in-depth interviews. The population of interest was established at the outset of the study with assistance from the NOMS Offender Management and Public Protection Group, which provided data on all current prisoners who had been given a life sentence with a tariff of 15 years or more when they were aged 25 years or less. At that time (February 2013), there were 808 people who met these criteria, composed of 789 men, spread across 73 prison establishments and 27 women, in nine separate establishments. In total, 309 men and 21 women participated in the study, over a fieldwork period of 22 months (from February 2013 to December 2014). This represented 39% of the men within the population and 72% of the women. Participants were drawn from 25 prisons, all located in England, 16 of which held men and nine of which held women.[2]

Initially, the men's prisons were selected based on the concentration of male prisoners who fitted our criteria in each. Thus, to access as many eligible participants as possible within each fieldwork visit, we initially chose a selection of establishments that held at least one per cent of our target population, although we did not seek to conduct research in each of the 21 prisons that did so. Only three prisons that held fewer than one per cent were included in the sample, in order to access prisoners who were serving time in Category D 'open' prisons, approaching

---

[1] In England and Wales, male prisoners are classified according to four security categories. Category A prisoners are those that would pose the most threat to the public, the police or national security should they escape. Category B prisoners do not need to be held in the highest-security conditions but are kept in conditions that make the potential for escape very difficult. Category C prisoners are those deemed not to be trusted in open conditions but unlikely to make a determined escape attempt. Category D prisoners can be trusted in open conditions. Adult prisons for men are high-security (holding prisoners who are Category A or B), Category B, C or D (also known as 'open prisons'). Female prisoners are categorised differently, being deemed Category A or 'Restricted status' (if their escape would present a serious risk to the public) or as being suitable either for closed or open conditions.

[2] None of our participants self-identified as gender non-binary.

release. Few prisoners who met our criteria were at this sentence stage, because the increase in the length of life sentence tariffs is a relatively recent phenomenon.

The selection of individual prisons was also influenced by the granting of access by individual governors and by the practical realities of undertaking a large-scale empirical study. In some cases, where more than one establishment met the general research criteria, our decisions about inclusion and exclusion were determined by the relative convenience of reaching them and the minimum period they would require us to stay away from home (up to three days per week). We have no reason to believe that these sampling decisions impacted our findings. Male prisoners were generally not contacted prior to our arrival in the prison, because time was built into the fieldwork to allow for some personal interaction prior to interviews. In such establishments, once on-site, we asked each prison to provide an up-to-date list of prisoners who fulfilled our criteria, for the purpose of further sampling.

The female prisons were selected based only on the location of the population. We visited all nine prisons holding women who matched our research criteria, spending brief periods in each. Unlike our approach to the men's prisons, a letter was therefore sent to every woman prior to our arrival in each establishment, to ensure that each was informed about out study in advance of our arrival. The letter provided details of our study and our plans to visit the establishment, with an invitation to potential participants to meet us during our time there and decide at that point whether they would like to take part.

The design of the study was not consistent with the form of 'slow research' that we would normally advocate. Whereas, in previous studies, we have tended to make *the institution* the primary object of enquiry (see, e.g. Crewe 2009; Hulley et al. 2012; Crewe et al. 2014), in this project, the primary focus was individual prisoners, located across the prison system. This meant that the time we spent in each research site ranged from a single day (most often, in the female estate and in Category D prisons, which held only one or two people who met our criteria) to up to seven weeks in the Category B prisons, where almost two-fifths of the sample were located. In the former cases, we often felt uncomfortable that we were 'parachuting' into the prison and into the lives of our participants, without sufficient opportunity to develop the level of trust and rapport that characterises ethnographic immersion, and with the associated risk that we were unable to follow up on the well-being of prisoners following our interactions with them. Even in the establishments where we were based for longer periods, we spent less time than we would have liked engaging in the kind of 'deep hanging out' that strengthens research relationships outside the formal moments of fieldwork. Spreading ourselves thinly contributed to a different form of research depth, based on our sample size, but this trade-off sometimes left us feeling slightly anxious that our research engagement was shallower and more fleeting than was ideal.

Access

The study was logistically highly complex, not least because of the various layers of access that we had to negotiate in order to undertake the fieldwork. When first applying for funding, we sought, and were granted, a letter of support by the Chief Executive of NOMS. Once funding had been secured, the research was approved by the NOMS National Research Committee, through the standardised application process. However, permission then had to be obtained from the governing governor of each of the many research sites. In practice, due mainly to the relations of trust that had been established by members of the research team over the course of their careers, we were granted access to every prison that we approached, sometimes at very short notice. At different stages of the study, though, we had to negotiate other forms of access. Prior to Christmas each year subsequent to the fieldwork, we sought permission to send each of our interviewees a 'Season's Greetings' card, with an update on our progress and dissemination activities. Since our participants had often moved establishments, this required us to trace their locations—again, with the assistance of the NOMS Offender Management and Public Protection Group—and approach an even larger number of governors to obtain approval to make contact. Our requests were always granted, but the process was time-consuming and unwieldy.

For the initial fieldwork, once permission had been granted by the governor of each prison, we faced differing institutional demands, generally determined by the security team of the particular prison, and not always with an intensity that corresponded to the establishment's security level. These included: the need for proof of a valid Criminal Records Check; the requirement to participate in 'security talks' (which ranged from a five-minute test of our existing knowledge of security issues to much longer, more formalised security inductions); the demand—in a high-security prison holding sex offenders—for a member of discipline staff to be present during some of our interviews[3]; and in one women's prison, the requirement to carry out interviews in the legal visits area.[4] Security teams also dictated the extent of access in each prison. In almost all prisons, we were permitted to carry keys, which enabled us to move freely within the establishment. In some cases, however, organising keys was too burdensome for the prison, given the brief nature of our presence (or, in the case of open establishments, was not necessary).

Access was also required when, having undertaken an initial analysis of our data, we undertook targeted feedback sessions with prisoners in six establishments. These sites comprised four men's prisons (one high-security and three Category B training prisons) and two women's prisons. Typically, we spent around 30 minutes providing a short summary of our findings and then invited the prisoners in attendance to ask questions and reflect on our data and interpretations. Around 80 prisoners attended these sessions overall, often validating our thinking, sometimes pushing us to think further, and generally thanking us for taking the time to revisit them. One feedback session with female prisoners enabled us to interrogate the significance of the fact that the most severe problem reported by the female sample was 'Having to follow other people's rules and orders'—a finding that surprised all of the women in one feedback group. While we were not able to work out exactly what this statement 'meant', we were reassured that our uncertainty was not the result of having missed an obvious explanation. A discussion group with male prisoners confirmed to us that the concept of 'contextual maturity' (see Chapter 8) had intuitive validity, while another, with female participants, supported our thinking about the undertow of mistrust among female prisoners ('That doesn't surprise me

---

[3]This situation was unsatisfactory, but was non-negotiable. In four interviews, therefore, a prison officer sat in the corner of the large interview room, intervening only when interviewees turned to him for confirmation or reassurance. Clearly, this arrangement compromised normal promises of anonymity and confidentiality, but did so without interviewees being in any way misled about these terms.

[4]Interviewing in such circumstances was problematic. It was difficult to build rapport, not least because legal visits areas—where prisoners meet their solicitors to discuss their cases—carry such different meanings from the kinds of non-descript office spaces on wings in which we normally conducted interviews. One prisoner made explicit that her reason for declining to be interviewed was her emotional association with this particular space. Furthermore, because legal visits are located 'outside' the main prison building, we were unable to contact prisoners following interviews to check properly on their well-being. In one instance, an interviewee did not return for the second part of her interview, following the lunch break. The interviewer (SH) asked an officer to convey to the prisoner her regret and to check that she was not unduly upset by the research encounter, but this kind of arms-length communication felt extremely inadequate. As a result, to establish whether the interview had caused her any distress, SH sent a letter to the prisoner—the most efficient means by which to contact her. The interviewee responded, explaining that she had found the interview 'difficult'. This experience generated a great deal of worry on our part, and we agreed, as a team, that we would decline any subsequent request to conduct interviews in such spaces even if this meant foregoing interviews entirely.

at all – I do not trust anyone. At all'). Beyond the benefits of obtaining feedback of this kind, one of our aims in organising these sessions was to ensure some degree of reciprocity in the research process. If nothing else, we felt, our findings might give our participants a way of making sense of what they were going through and a sense that they were not alone in their emotional responses, adaptive trajectories and preoccupations. In our subsequent dissemination activities—for example, in *Learning Together* initiatives in HMP Grendon, HMP Full Sutton and HMP Bronzefield—our feeling that prisoners can find it empowering to be exposed to scholarship that captures and conceptualises their experiences has been corroborated. Given that part of our argument is that long-term prisoners cope with their sentences through forms of reflexive deliberation and planning, this seems especially apposite.

Ethics

Ethical approval for the study was granted by the Institute of Criminology ethics committee and, as part of its access process, by NOMS. Our processes followed standard practice for prison research, involving the distribution of a very detailed information sheet and a brief consent form, in which—among other, more prosaic details—we noted the normal limits of confidentiality: risk to self, risk to others and risk to the security of the establishment. At the request of NOMS, participants were also given the name of an individual working within their organisation whom they could contact should they wish to ask further questions about the research, make a complaint about it or communicate further with us. No-one made use of this contact point; however, a number of prisoners wrote to us directly in response to our festive cards, and we always sought to respond. Some correspondences remain on-going, with prisoners who have updated us on their psychological and institutional progress and congratulated us on developments resulting from the study and our own professional achievements.

We left participants with information sheets for twenty-four hours prior to asking them whether they were willing to be involved in the research. In prisons where we knew we would be on-site for less than a day, we contacted potential participants prior to our fieldwork visit, posting letters with information sheets attached, and following up with a face-to-face discussion once we had arrived. In all prisons, once consent was obtained, prisoners who agreed to fill in the survey were given a sealable envelope, which, along with the survey, contained the information sheet, a consent form and a 'support note' which signposted prisoners to available sources of support should they wish to talk to someone following survey completion. Practices varied a little in each prison, but, typically, surveys were given directly to participants by members of the research team rather than by prison staff.

While levels of literacy among prisoners are known to be lower than among their community counterparts (Prison Reform Trust 2018), almost all prisoners were able to complete the survey without assistance. Where literacy issues were highlighted, a member of the research team supported the prisoner by presenting the questions orally. On the whole, however, prisoners were left with their surveys for around half a day or over the lunchtime period of lock-up. Because of the content of the survey, one section of which asked prisoners about the main problems that they encountered, we ensured that prisoners were never left with surveys overnight, when they might be most vulnerable to distressing forms of rumination. On completion of the survey, a short debrief was held with each prisoner to ensure they were not emotionally troubled by the exercise: specifically, we committed ourselves to looking each respondent in the eyes when they handed back the survey and asking them if anything within it had upset them. In only two cases, prisoners requested more extensive discussions with one of the research team.

Prisoners who participated in interviews were debriefed in person at the end of each session (many interviews took place over two or three encounters): that is, asked whether had been upset by anything that they had discussed. As with the survey, we also provided each participant with a formal 'support sheet'. If anything, though, our very strong impression—based both on overt statements and less explicit forms of communication—was that most participants felt themselves to have had a valuable opportunity to talk about themselves and their predicament. Some seemed to use the interviews as an opportunity to practice a self-narrative, and others to off-load emotionally to someone who, within the environment, was unusually neutral. Our expressions of concern were sometimes met with confusion. On one occasion, a participant expressed unease that his interviewer was asking him so often whether he 'was okay', since such prompts for reassurance had begun to make him wonder whether he should be 'less okay'; on others, interviewees sought reassurance from us that we did not mind them telling us details that we might find traumatic or emotive.

In the field, ethical dilemmas rarely offered the kinds of straightforward solutions implied by formal ethics procedures. In one interview, a participant who was appealing his conviction hinted at his own guilt, though with sufficient vagueness for us to feel comfortable that we need not consider how to deal with this insinuation. Throughout the research, we were faced with the mundane ethical dilemmas of fieldwork in practice: how hard to try to persuade people to participate, whether to inform staff about prisoners who seemed highly vulnerable, but who had stated explicitly that they did not want us to mention this to staff, and other such issues.

Some ethical matters did not make themselves directly visible to us at the time. At a conference some months after the end of fieldwork, BC was approached by a former staff member of one of the fieldwork sites, who reported that the research had 'created some difficulties' within the prison. Some of the participants had been involved in forms of slow, therapeutic engagement, and our intervention—in the form of interviews that had encouraged them to open up rather rapidly about their offences and experiences—had disturbed a planned timetable of disclosure and induced some unhelpful emotional responses. The discussion was an important reminder of the potential for research to have unintended consequences, particularly when participants are vulnerable and researchers spend relatively short periods at each research site.

Interviews

Interviews were conducted in two parts, almost always one-to-one, in offices on prison wings. The first part was a detailed life history interview, which drew heavily on the literature on narrative inquiry and life stories (e.g. Hollway and Jefferson 2000; McAdams 1988) and focused on various aspects of life prior to this particular sentence, such as family circumstances, education, engagement in work, and previous contact with criminal justice and other state services. The second part of each interview focused on participants' lives inside prison during their current sentence. Our main interests were the particular problems of serving a very long-life sentence and prisoners' strategies for managing them; their social adaptations, specifically, the relationships they developed with other prisoners and staff; and their thoughts on the legitimacy of their situation. Interviewees were not asked directly to disclose the details of their index offence, as this was not the focus of the research. However, they were not discouraged from doing so, and often it was clear that the circumstances of their offence, or their feelings of shame or anger about their conviction, were relevant to various aspects of their prison experiences.

Interview Sample

In total, 126 men and 21 women participated in interviews. This represented 16% of the male population and 72% of the female population who fitted our criteria. We did not keep a formal count of the number of prisoners who declined to be involved, but these numbers were certainly low overall: we estimate them to be less than one in five men and women whom we approached. While we did not ask potential participants their reasons for declining, those who did so were very rarely hostile to the research so much as uninterested in it. Younger prisoners were the most likely to express some degree of suspicion about the research, particularly those who were involved in legal appeals and were wary about disclosing information to people other than their legal representatives. We suspect that others among our younger cohort had not come to terms with their situation and were still in such a state of shock and disorientation that they were almost incapable of participating in a reflective discussion.

Within the overall sampling frame, we purposefully sampled the male interviewees to reflect the proportion of prisoners within the overall population at different sentence stages and in each kind of prison (Young Offender Institution, High-Security Prison, Category B, Category C, and Category D 'open' establishments). Specifically, we sought out prisoners for interview who were in the *early stage* of their sentence (within the first four years), the *mid-stage* (calculated as half of the overall sentence tariff, plus or minus two years) and the *late stage* (two years prior to their tariff point, or beyond their tariff point). Early-stage prisoners were deliberately over-sampled, for three reasons: first, because they represented the fastest-growing cohort of prisoners serving such sentences; second, because they were the group generating most concern among practitioners; and third, to maximise this sub-sample for the follow-up study that we intend to conduct in due course.

Towards the beginning of our fieldwork period, there was natural congruence between sentence stage and prison security level: most high-security and Category B training prisons held a higher proportion of 'early-stage' prisoners. However, as the research continued, prisoners within particular establishments were purposefully approached to broadly satisfy the quota at each sentence stage in the overall population. Given the much smaller number of women within the population, we sought a total population sample, regardless of sentence stage.

Table 2.1 shows the proportion of male prisoners at each sentence stage who participated in interviews, in each category of prison, with the 'late-stage' prisoners split into those who were pre-tariff and post-tariff.

Interviews were long, generally lasting between one and four hours. Those undertaken with younger prisoners tended to be shorter, often because of these prisoners' relatively short-life histories but also because they generally had a more limited capacity to articulate their experiences—something that, in itself, alerted us to the difficulties that prisoners experienced in coming to terms with and reflecting upon such a dramatic turn in life. Notably too, prisoners in the mid- and late-stages of their sentences were noticeably more expressive and reflective than early-stage participants, often seeming to use the interview as an opportunity to externalise their internal conversations.

Our original intention was also to interview around 20 prison officers about the specific challenges of managing prisoners serving very long sentences from an early age. However, it was soon apparent that such interviews were unlikely to generate data of real value. Officers had relatively few views that were specific to our population, mainly because the number of prisoners serving long sentences was so large that they had little to say about the differences between such men and those with shorter prison terms or did not know who, on their wing, was serving the kind of sentence we were interested in. This was in itself telling. In the end, then, it proved more productive to engage with staff informally, during lunch breaks and through interactions on the wings.

Table 2.1 Interview sample breakdown by sentence stage and prison type

Sentence stage	Total number of male prisoners	Number (proportion) residing in each prison type				
		YOI	High security	Cat. B	Cat. C	Cat. D
Early	61	25 (41%)	16 (26%)	20 (33%)	0	0
Mid	37	1 (3%)	9 (24%)	23 (62%)	4 (11%)	0
Late	6	0	1 (17%)	1 (17%)	2 (33%)	2 (33%)
Post-tariff	22	0	1 (5%)	4 (18%)	5 (23%)	12 (55%)
Total (in sample)	126	26	27	48	11	14

Table 2.2 shows the demographic details of the male and female interview sample. As can be seen, these groups were broadly similar, although with a wider range among the male sample with regard to age, tariff length and time served in prison.

Surveys

Surveys were administered in 16 men's prisons and nine women's prisons, with all prisoners who met our criteria being considered eligible for participation. The survey instrument replicated that used by Richards (1978), Flanagan (1980), and Leigey and Ryder (2015) in their studies, with some adaptations and significant additions, outlined below. For that reason, Table 2.3 provides a summary of the methodological details of our research alongside studies that are broadly comparable. The table demonstrates the breadth of our research compared to previous studies, both in terms of the range of prisons and the number of prisoners within the sample. It also highlights differences between each study's definition of 'long-term imprisonment', which ranged from five years' of continuous confinement to life sentences with a minimum term of 15 years.

Development of the Survey Instrument

In adopting the survey instrument used in previous studies, our aim was to ensure some degree of cross-temporal and international comparability in our findings.[5] However, two of the 20 problems presented to prisoners by Richards (1978), and subsequently Flanagan (1980) and Leigey and Ryder (2015) were omitted and the wording of two others was changed. Specifically, 'Being worried about becoming a vegetable' was removed due to its form of language, which we felt was out-dated and potentially offensive, while 'Longing for a time in the past' was removed because it seemed vague and unclear (to the extent that we did not feel that we would know how to make sense of any arising data). 'Keeping out of trouble' was changed to 'Finding it hard to keep out of trouble', to make it consistent with

[5]This is despite some difficulties in claiming direct comparability, with regard to such matters as mean age at the time of being sentenced (ranging from 21 in our study to over 28 in Richards [1978]), and ethnic composition of the sample (over 50% White in our study, compared to 29% White in Flanagan [1980]).

Table 2.2 Demographics of male and female interview sample

		Male sample	Female sample
No. of participants		126	21
No. of prisons		15	9
Ethnicity	White	53.2%	85.7% (18)
	Black/Black British	30.2%	4.8% (1)
	Asian/Asian British	8.7%	0
	'Mixed race'	7.9%	9.5% (2)
	Other	0	0
Age range at time of research (mean)—in years		18–67 years old (30)	20–45 years old (28)
Age at time of research	18–21 years old	23.0%	4.8% (1)
	22–30 years old	38.9%	66.6% (14)
	31–40 years old	21.4%	19.0% (4)
	41–50 years old	8.0%	9.6% (2)
	51–60 years old	7.1%	0
	Over 60 years old	1.6%	0
Sentence stage[a]	Early	48.4%	52.4% (11)
	Mid	29.4%	19.0% (4)
	Late	4.8%	23.8% (5)
	Late (post-tariff)	17%	4.8% (1)
Age at sentence (mean)—in years		13–25 (20)	16–25 (20)
Age at sentence	13–15 years old	0.8%	0%
	16–18 years old	23.8%	19.0% (4)
	19–21 years old	40.5%	47.6% (10)
	22–25 years old	34.9%	33.3% (7)

	Male sample	Female sample
Tariff range (mean)—in years	15–35 (20)	15–25 (19)
Tariff length		
15–19 years	56.3%	57.1% (12)
20–24 years	23.9%	38.1% (8)
25–29 years	15.8%	4.8% (1)
30 years or more	4.0%	0
Time served range (mean)—in years	10 months—42 years (10)	10 months—22 years (8)

[a] *Note* for the men, sentence stage is defined as 'early'—up to four years of the sentence; 'mid'—the median of an individual's sentence, plus or minus two years; 'late'—two years prior to the end of the tariff; post tariff—beyond the tariff date. Sentence stage for the women is defined by 'thirds' of their sentence. In almost all places in the book where we use the term 'sentence', we are referring to the custodial element of the life sentence, i.e. the period spent in prison rather than on life licence in the community

Table 2.3 Comparison of current study with previous studies using problem statements

Author/s and period of study/year of publication	Geographic location	No. of prisons	Prison type/s	Sentence length	No. of participants
Crewe, Hulley & Wright (fieldwork undertaken between 2013–2014)	UK	25	Young Offenders Institutions High security Category B Category C Category D Female prisons	Life-sentence with tariff of 15 years or more	330
Richards (1978)	UK	1	Male high security	At least 10 years of life	22
Flanagan (1980)	United States	5	Male maximum security	Served at least 5 years of continuous confinement	49
Leigey and Ryder (2015)	United States	Unknown	Male prisons, type unknown	Served at least 15 years of a 'life without parole' (LWOP) sentence	18

the wording of other problem statements, and 'Being afraid of going mad' was changed to 'Worrying about your mental health', again due to concerns about appropriate terminology.

Towards the end of the seven-week fieldwork period in our first research site, prior to any surveys being administered, we developed some additional statements to represent the set of problems that prisoners were raising in our initial wave of interviews but which did not feature in Richards's original survey. For example, in order to address issues that were particularly pertinent to contemporary imprisonment, we devised a number of items relating to the 'tightness' of contemporary imprisonment (Crewe 2011)—the role of risk assessment practices, written documents and specialist staff in determining prisoner progression. These included problems such as: 'Worrying about how you are described on file' and 'Feeling you have to be careful about everything you say or do'. Other supplementary problem statements reflected concerns whose correspondence with the established literature on 'the pains of imprisonment' (Sykes 1958) means that they were almost certainly relevant in earlier periods. Among these problems were 'Feeling you have no control over your life', 'Having to follow other people's rules and orders' and 'Feeling worried about your personal safety'. Having devised a large number of potential additions, we eventually reduced these to 21 additional problem statements, in part because we (and representatives within NOMS, who had requested sight of the final survey) were concerned that a longer list might generate distress. Overall, then, participants were asked to consider 39 potential problems of long-term imprisonment overall, as shown in Table 2.4.

For the purpose of the current study, the problems were not—as in Richards (1978)—separated into 'outside' and 'inside' problems, since this was considered to offer limited analytic benefit. We agreed with Richards' (1978: 166) own critique, that the distinction made between these categories was 'crude', particularly in relation to some of the original problems such as 'feeling sorry for yourself' and 'wishing that time would go faster'. This was also the case for many of the supplementary problems such as 'feeling that you have no-one to talk to about the things that really matter to you' and 'feeling lonely', which might easily fall into either or both categories. Instead, we attempted to make more precise post hoc distinctions between problems, by grouping them thematically and statistically into a number of dimensions (see Table 2.8).

We also added two further parts to the survey, which were designed to explore how individuals felt they had changed (or not changed) during the sentence (part

Table 2.4 Richards' (1978) original problem statements (as revised) and additional problem statements included in the current study

Richards' (1978) problem statements (with revised wording shown in italics)	Additional problem statements included in the current study
Wishing that time would go faster	Feeling that you are losing the best years of your life
Wishing you had more privacy	Feeling that the system is ignoring you and your individual needs
Feeling that your life is being wasted	Thinking about the crime that you committed
Losing your self-confidence	Feeling that you are losing contact with family and friends
Feeling sorry for yourself	Prison officers making life harder
Missing little "luxuries", e.g. your favourite food, home comforts	Feeling that you have no control over your life
Finding it hard to keep out of trouble (replaced 'keeping out of trouble')	Not feeling able to completely trust anyone in prison
Feeling angry with yourself	Prison psychologists making life harder
Missing social life	Feeling that the length of your sentence is unfair
Feeling suicidal	Feeling lonely
Feeling angry with the world	Feeling worried about your personal safety
Missing somebody	Feeling frustrated that you are not progressing through the system
Getting annoyed or irritated with other *prisoners* (replaced 'inmates')	Worrying about people outside
Being afraid of dying before you get out	Feeling that you have no purpose or meaning in your life
Feeling sexually frustrated	Worrying about how you are described 'on file'
Being worried about your mental health (replaced 'being afraid of going mad')	Feeling anxious about the uncertainty of your release date

Richards' (1978) problem statements (with revised wording shown in italics)	Additional problem statements included in the current study
Worrying about how you will cope when you get out	Feeling that you have no-one to talk to about things that really matter to you
Being bored	Thinking about the amount of time you might have to serve
	Having to follow other people's rules and orders
	Feeling that you need to be careful about everything you say and do
	Being afraid that someone you love or care about will die before you are released

3 questions in Table 2.5) and attitudes to other parts of their sentence (part 4 questions in Table 2.6). In addition to this, prisoners were given space to write their 'three most positive' and 'three most negative' things about their 'life at the moment'.

Table 2.7 summarises the demographics of the male and female survey sample.

The datasets that we were given at the start of the study by NOMS supplied limited demographic data (age, but not ethnicity) and sentence information for the populations of interest. When the data were extracted, the 789 men in the population were on average 30 years old, the same mean age as our interview sample, and very close to that of our survey sample (29). Their mean age when sentenced—22 years old—was slightly higher than both the interview and survey samples (20). It is noteworthy that that one male reported being sentenced at 13 years old. The men in the NOMS data were serving sentences with tariffs of between 15 and 49 years, with a mean of 20 years.[6] While the male interview

Table 2.5 Part 3 of the survey: the extent to which prisoners felt they had changed since the start of their sentence

I am becoming/have become less tolerant of other people
I am learning/have learnt to deal with my emotions
I am learning/have learnt how to avoid the things that get me into trouble
I am learning/have learnt useful skills
I am gaining/have gained a good education
I am becoming/have become a less mature person
I am making/have made good friends in prison
My mental health is better than before I came to prison on this sentence
I am becoming/have become less respectful of other people
I am becoming/have become more distant from my family
My drug use is more serious than before I came to prison on this sentence
I am becoming/have become less positive about my future
I am becoming/have become more polite and considerate towards other people
My life feels more stable now than before I came to prison
I feel safer than before I came to prison
I feel less fit and healthy than before I came to prison on this sentence
I feel happier than before I came to prison
I am becoming/have become a better person overall

---

[6]The tariff was computed by calculating the difference between the sentence date and the tariff expiry date, so that the tariff data may show figures slightly lower than actual tariff lengths, due to remand time not being accounted for in the data.

Table 2.6 Part 4 of the survey: prisoners' attitudes about other aspects of their sentence

There is no point trying to beat the system
I have a lot of respect for prison officers
A prisoner should always be loyal to another prisoner rather than to staff
I rely on staff to help me get through my sentence
I am completely compliant with the system
I would be willing to 'get involved' on behalf of a friend, whatever the consequences
I rely on other prisoners to help me get through my sentence
I have no power in here
It is sometimes okay to tell staff about another prisoner's business
I am hopeful about my future

and survey sample range were 15–35 years, the mean was the same as the overall population.

Within the population, there were more male prisoners with tariffs of 15–19 years (63.1% compared to 48.3% in the interview sample and 56.3% in the survey sample). The proportion of men in the population serving tariffs of 20–24 years (21.5%) was slightly smaller than the survey sample (23.9%) and interview sample (27.7%). The study, then, slightly oversampled male prisoners with tariffs of 25 years or over—15.4% in the population, compared to 24% in the interview sample and 19.8% in the survey sample.

Women in the population data provided by NOMS were aged between 16 and 25 years at the time of their sentence, with a mean age of 21—one year higher than the mean of the women in both our interview and survey samples. The tariff range and mean among the population of women were the same as the female survey and interview participants, with one exception. The longest tariff for those in the population was 24 years, while for the interview and survey sample was 25 years. This was due to one woman identifying her tariff as 25 years, despite the NOMS data showing her tariff to be close to 24 years. The discrepancy may be accounted for by the period time that she might have served on remand, which is not included in the NOMS data. A breakdown of tariff length shows that the study oversampled women serving longer sentences, with 47.3% of the interview sample and 42.9% of the survey sample having tariffs of 20–25 years, compared to 29.6% of the population. The remaining were serving less than 20 years (70.4% in the population, 52.6% in the interview sample and 42.9% in the survey sample).

Table 2.7 Demographics of male and female survey sample

		Male sample	Female sample
No. of participants		294	19
No. of prisons		16	8
Ethnicity	White	50.2%	78.9% (15)
	Black/Black British	28.7%	5.3% (1)
	Asian/Asian British	6.1%	5.3% (1)
	'Mixed race'	5.8%	10.5% (2)
	Other	3.0%	0
Religion	No religion	25.3%	66.7% (13)
	Christian	28.1%	16.7% (3)
	Buddhist	3.2%	0
	Hindu	0.7%	0
	Jewish	1.1%	0
	Muslim	33.7%	5.6% (1)
	Other	8.1%	11.1% (2)
Age range at time of research (mean)—in years		18–67 years old (29)	20–45 years old (29)
Age at time of research	18–21 years old	10.5%	5.3% (1)
	22–30 years old	61.2%	63.2% (12)
	31–40 years old	21.8%	21.1% (4)
	41–50 years old	3.7%	10.5% (2)
	51–60 years old	2.4%	0
	Over 60 years old	0.3%	0
Sentence stage	Early	19.5%	52.6% (10)
	Mid	21.0%	15.8% (3)

		Male sample	Female sample
	Late	21.7%	31.6% (6)
	Late (post-tariff)	20.9%	
Age at sentence (mean)—in years		13–25	16–25
		(20)	(20)
Age at sentence	13–15 years old	0.7%	0
	16–18 years old	18.6%	21.1% (4)
	19–21 years old	43.0%	36.8% (7)
	22–25 years old	37.8%	42.1% (8)
Tariff range (mean)—in years		15–35	15–25
		(20)	(19)
Tariff length	15–19 years	48.3%	52.6% (10)
	20–24 years	27.7%	36.8% (7)
	25–29 years	16.8%	10.5% (2)
	30 years or more	7.2%	0
Time served range (mean)—in years		10 months—42 years	16 months—21 years
		(10)	(9)

Conducting Team Research

Working as a team was highly productive and generated very few serious disagreements or tensions. Most of the difficulties that we encountered were practical rather than relational: perhaps most notable was that our interview schedule grew more often than it shrank, because it was difficult for anyone to feel that they had sole authority to remove questions that others had suggested and because our sense of which questions 'worked' was not always shared. To give one example, while BC found the question 'how does time *feel*?' very illuminating, SH and SW found it difficult to ask in a manner that felt natural to them.

In general, we tried to work alongside each other when collecting data, although our differing contractual commitments to the project (SW: 100%; SH: 60%; BC: 40%) meant that our time in the field varied considerably. Often, it was difficult for us to retain as sharp a sense of each other's movements and findings as we would have liked, although the pen portraits that we produced following each interview assisted greatly in ensuring that we were mutually apprised. Wherever possible, we tried to debrief contemporaneously—in the evenings following days within the research sites. However, this was inhibited by some of the practical difficulties of combining fieldwork with family commitments. Both BC and SH had very young children during the main fieldwork period and were keen whenever possible to return to their homes in time to see them before their bedtimes. As noted above, such considerations shaped our sampling decisions to some extent (and we wondered why we had encountered so little discussion in any literature we had read about the impact of parental demands on research design and fieldwork decisions). They also meant that SW was often alone overnight in rather unglamorous hotels, a situation that felt unavoidable but was certainly unfortunate.

Once the process of data analysis began, our most productive occasions were always face-to-face meetings in which we talked through our current thinking, clarified our goals and plotted journal articles and other outputs. Typically, spending half a day in a meeting room or café clarified and accelerated our thinking very considerably, in part because it was so difficult through other means to maintain a collective sense of our thoughts and objectives. Disagreements about matters of analysis and interpretation were rare. Where there were tensions, these were relatively minor: disagreements about how to deal with fieldwork dilemmas or about the marginal benefit of adding in additional research sites, for example.

In writing this monograph, we divided up responsibilities, each taking the lead for different chapters, with BC taking overall responsibility for editing and seeking to ensure a consistent tone. As each chapter was completed, it was circulated, discussed and edited iteratively, each chapter going through a number of drafts as it changed hands. To write in a truly collaborative way requires considerable trust (and sometimes a relatively thick skin), and we were lucky to have this. As is customary, all the names that we have given to interviewees in the text are pseudonyms—any similarity to the real names of specific long-term prisoners is simply coincidental. Where possible, we have also included details of their sentence stage and age (by decade). One of the aims of doing so is to illustrate the relative youth of many of our early- and mid-stage interviewees, and the considerable age of some of those who were post-tariff. Our decision to make very liberal use of direct quotations—edited for the sake of clarity, but with care not to alter meaning—reflects our desire to provide a vivid and humanistic representation of our participants: to fully evoke their subjective experience.[7] It is also consistent with the book's aim of emphasising the role of agency and reflexivity in the process of adapting to serving a long prison sentence.

One of our primary findings is that there was a relatively common shape to the adaptive trajectories of long-term prisoners. Accordingly, we present our analysis in a manner that emphasises common rather than individuated experiences. In doing so, we do not wish to suggest that there were no variations between our participants, and within the text, we note these differences where relevant, particularly those between male and female interviewees, between participants in different parts of the prison system, and between prisoners convicted of 'mainstream' and sex offences. Meanwhile, although we recognise that it is generally preferable to quantify the number of prisoners who expressed a particular point or represented a particular orientation, to avoid giving a false sense of precision, we have tended towards the use of terms such as 'some', 'many', and 'most'. Our interviews were fluid and did not cover exactly the same ground, and since many participants expressed views of considerable complexity, their content was not easily amenable to simple categorisation. All of this means that providing more concrete quantification would be misleading, even if it were to be possible. Despite

---

[7]The symbol '[…]' indicates where we have removed text that was present in the transcript.

their ostensible vagueness, we believe that the terms that we have used more accurately communicate patterns of feeling and experience than specific numbers could do.

The Research Process

We spent a good deal of time discussing differences in our fieldwork and interview styles. Such differences became especially apparent to us as a result of a decision to analyse each other's interviews (rather than our own), to help familiarise ourselves with as much of the interview data as possible. This attempt at supportive evaluation proved hugely constructive, if somewhat challenging. Our differences were less to do with the variables typically assumed to shape research dynamics, such as class and gender, and more to do with our research 'temperaments', and the ways that we each managed our personal boundaries. Compared to BC and SH, SW's style was particularly open, and she was more inclined to draw on, or sometimes 'leak', her own life experiences and emotions within her interviews. This closer, looser style generated exceptional levels of rapport and greater disclosure about personal matters relating to sex and intimacy, for example (see Rubin and Rubin 2012). It appeared to lessen the potential social gulf between prisoners and an academic researcher from an established university, with all of the signals and assumptions that result from such distinctions (to quote one participant: 'I'm not stereotyping, but you look … I don't know. You don't come across like you've grown up on a council estate'). However, it occasionally risked being collusive and meant that interview content was sometimes less bound to the research questions.

BC and SH sought to show empathy without recourse to so much personal disclosure. Their questioning was slightly more focused and direct, producing less superfluous data and reducing the risk of leading participants' responses. Trust was established through the demonstration of 'professional' interest and from communicating that they were honest, open, respectful and non-judgmental (Rubin and Rubin 2012), rather than fellow emotional travellers. The risk of this approach was that it generated a shallower understanding of subjective detail and, because it was less fluid, produced fewer 'surprise findings'. Despite these differences in approach, each of us felt that we had an empathic, responsive interview style, and all of us were told by prisoners that—for example—they had 'never talked to anyone about this before'. We are sceptical that our idiosyncrasies led to significant differences in what we concluded, and our ongoing reflections helped us to hone our styles and deploy ourselves within the field according to our individual strengths.

The fieldwork was, in many respects, less challenging than we had anticipated. From the start of the project, we had discussed the possibility that we might feel moral ambivalence about some participants or that some might be hostile towards us. All of us were experienced prison researchers, who had very rarely met participants whom we disliked, and we were all committed to a form of person-centred, non-judgmental interviewing. But humanistic research leaves room for researchers to have aversive responses precisely because it seeks to engage honestly with people and to recognise their moral complexity rather than present a sanitised and sainted version of who they are and what they have done. Rather than mask any such responses in the interest of signalling our research skills and personal virtues, we were keen to be candid about them.

Typically, on the very rare occasions when we struggled to connect with participants, it was not due to what they had done, but because of personality traits. And in the great majority of cases, we did not find it at all difficult to establish points of personal connection. If anything, we more often reminded ourselves not to be naïvely credulous, to engage with something close to 'unconditional positive regard' (Rogers 1956) while avoiding sentimentality. However, the nature of our sample produced some distinctive dilemmas. Almost all of our participants' trials had generated media coverage, creating the possibility of 'knowing' them, via online searches, in advance of encountering them in person. While we agreed that we should not 'look people up' prior to interviewing them, our practices did not always correspond with our pledges. Sometimes, this was helpful, for example, in working out who might be best or least suited to undertaking particular interviews. On other occasions, being unaware of participants' index offences was beneficial, in the sense that we were able to approach and address them in ways that were not moulded by legal and media discourse. In one interview, for example, SH's question 'are you still in contact with your girlfriend?' produced the response: 'No, I killed her'. But, despite the brief awkwardness that ensued, the participant explained that it was refreshing for him to be interviewed about his experiences rather than his offence or his official diagnosis as a psychopath.

Each of us carried different sensitivities, linked to our life histories and circumstances, which shaped our responses to descriptions of bereavement, loneliness, mental health problems and other such matters. In one interview, for example, a participant's account of parental loss resonated with SH's own experiences, producing an unexpected emotional response and the kind of tacit recognition of commonality that can bridge otherwise divergent life circumstances. For SW, the grief of prisoners who had been recently bereaved was a particular challenge, as she herself was struggling with having lost her best friend to cancer in the previous year. BC's most challenging interview was with a man who had been convicted of torturing and murdering a child not that much older than his own daughter; in another interview, he found himself very affected by a participant's description of a recurring dream, in which he could hear his young child crying behind a wall that he was unable to scale. By the end of the fieldwork, however, we were also aware that we had become to some degree desensitised to sentence lengths that had initially bewildered us. In some of the establishments where we spent time, there were just so many men with tariffs of 20 years or more that it was not difficult to see why prison staff were rather blasé about such disposals.

It was difficult not to be drawn into our participants' claims of innocence and their related narratives of desperation. This was particularly the case when interviewing people who had been convicted as secondary offenders under the doctrine of joint enterprise, which we all felt to be unjust. We reminded ourselves that we could never know the facts of individual cases, that our instincts might be flawed, and that the specific details of individual cases were not directly relevant to our study. Yet certain prisoners remained imprinted in our memories well after we completed our fieldwork, and these were often people whose sentences seemed highly disproportionate to their acts or whose distress was especially acute: for BC, a meek prisoner, with chronic mental health problems, who proclaimed his innocence; for SH, a young women, highly distressed by her conviction as a secondary offender under joint enterprise, who had suffered multiple serious sexual assaults from her early childhood onwards, and many additional traumas, including the death of two children; for SW, an 18-year old with learning difficulties who was struggling to come to terms with his secondary role in a murder, as well as the recent attempted suicide of his girlfriend.

We experienced all of the normal, prosaic aspects of prison research: challenges, including suspicion of our motives, unwanted sexual attention, cynicism from some staff and fatigue; basic fieldwork mistakes, such as temporarily misplacing a voice recorder (BC), and getting into a 'borderline argument' with a prisoner who was critical of our survey (SW); and moments of humour, humanity and exhilaration, when we made real connections with our participants or felt that we had gained significant insight into a research issue. The fieldwork was bleak and uplifting at the same time, and as we left prisons at the end of the day, we often veered between contemplative silence and animated analysis.

Interviewing Women

It was striking, however, that some interviews were considerably more traumatic than others. While we heard much that moved us during our interviews with the men in our study, the women whom we interviewed communicated considerably more trauma and distress.[8] As we have noted elsewhere (Crewe et al. 2017), the acute and multiple experiences of abuse that the female prisoners narrated felt qualitatively different from the adverse and traumatic experiences described by the men. Almost all of the women had experienced physical and sexual abuse from an early age, often being victimised at every life stage, i.e. within the family home, in local authority care, and then within intimate partnerships. Many had experienced serial bereavement, including the deaths of their own children, as well as periods of homelessness from a young age, addiction to drugs and/or alcohol, and a multiplicity of abuse at the hands of men: exceptionally severe domestic violence ('he tried slashing my throat, and he tried to ram my head through [the window] and he wrote all over the walls in blood, "I'm going to kill you"'), coercive control ('I wasn't allowed to straighten my hair. I wasn't allowed to be on Facebook. I wasn't allowed to walk anywhere'), and victimisation at the hands of trusted partners ('I was with him for eight years and he beat me every day'). While such events had occurred in the lives of some of our male participants, their intensity and multiplicity—as described to us, at least—were lesser.

The result was that every interview with the female prisoners felt like an out-pouring of anguish. While we would not want to imply in any way that our own difficulties, in listening to such accounts, were in any way equivalent to those of our research participants, their impact on us was still significant. In engaging actively and emotionally with the recounting of traumatic events, in which participants 'externalised' and, in some senses, relived the events they were describing, we absorbed a considerable amount of their distress.

---

[8]Interviews with female prisoners were conducted only by SH and SW.

Operating without any clinical training or support, despite hearing 'narratives as miasmic as any that might surface in a therapist's office' (Klempner 2000: 71), meant that, at times, SH and SW—who conducted all of the interviews with the female participants—felt haunted by the content of what they had heard. Team debriefs were, in this respect, all the more important. For a short period, we considered investing in some professional therapeutic assistance, although this did not, in the end, feel necessary. We reflect on this not, we hope, as an exercise in 'navel-gazing' or self-pity, but to highlight the potential for some interviews, with some individuals, to generate particularly strong and difficult feelings.

Analysis

Interview Analysis

Interviews were recorded whenever possible, with the consent of participants, and all recordings were transcribed and then coded in full, using NVivo software. A small number of interviewees requested that only written notes were taken. Coding and analysis proceeded based on an iterative analytic approach, in which the material was addressed based both on pre-defined and emerging themes.

The first stage of interview analysis came in the form of 'pen portraits' (see Hollway and Jefferson 2000), which we compiled for each interviewee while we were in the field. These profiles, no more than two pages long, combined our observations and summaries of key details with snippets of our interviewees' own phrasing. The core idea of the 'pen portrait' is to 'capture the richness, complexity and dimensionality of human experience in social and cultural context' (Lawrence-Lightfoot and Davis 1997: 3), through maintaining a focus on the contextual realities within which participants' unique stories are located (cf. Hill 2005). That is, such portraits maintain the 'aesthetic whole' and integrity of the life story, and situate 'data' within the parameters of personal life narrative (Chapman 2016). This is in contrast with data coding, which crumbles individual narratives into thematic heaps, often rendering invisible participants' full and unique personhood.

Writing the pen portraits had a number of functions. First, it served as a means of producing an initial analysis of each interview; second, it was often cathartic, allowing us to put our thoughts about the person, the process and our reactions to both on paper soon after the interview encounter; third, it enabled us to communicate our findings to each other, at points when we were not conducting fieldwork together. We have included a range of pen portraits in the following chapter, primarily because they offer natural, vivid and humanising characterisations of individual research participants, an objective that felt particularly important given the topic in question.

Survey Analysis

As with the studies undertaken previously by Richards (1978), Flanagan (1980) and Leigey and Ryder (2015), participants in the current study were asked to score each problem on a 'Frequency' (F) scale (reporting how 'often' they experienced the problem, on a Likert scale from 1 to 5, where 1 was 'never' and 5 was 'very often') and on what the previous authors called an 'Intensity' (I) scale. As this asked prisoners to report how easy the problem was to deal with when it was experienced (on a Likert scale of 1–5, where 1 was 'very easy' and 5 was 'very difficult'), we replaced the term 'Intensity' with the more intuitively accurate idea of 'Solubility' (Sol): how soluble, or solvable, the problem was felt to be. As such, problem 'Severity' (Sev) was calculated by multiplying the Frequency score by the Solubility score ($F \times Sol = Sev$) (note that, as in the previous studies, where prisoners reported 'never' experiencing the problem, the Severity score was 0). As with the previous studies, overall mean Severity scores could range from 0 to 25, with 25 being the most severe rating possible.

Principal Components Analysis (PCA) was conducted on the problem severity data, in order to group the variables into meaningful subsets of 'problems'. Due to the distributions of the severity data being significantly non-normal for all problems (demonstrated by the Kolmogorov–Smirnov test, which was significant for all problems—$p < 0.001$), a 'normalizing (Blom) transformation' was conducted on the data. This adjusted the raw score values to allow for 'meaningful comparisons between tests' (Solomon and Sawilowsky 2009: 448) and to help with model selection (Hicks et al. 2004: 924). PCA was subsequently conducted on the rank scores output. From the first analysis, ten factors emerged and four were retained due to their substantive importance, confirmed using Kaiser's criterion. Some changes were made to the extracted factors based on conceptual thinking (items were removed where they did not fit conceptually and were placed back into the analysis). The process of PCA was repeated on the remaining items (including those removed from the extracted factors), from which four further factors emerged. A final round of analysis was undertaken with eight items that had not worked elsewhere conceptually. This produced two further factors. Thus, the final nine dimensions, and one standalone item, emerged through an iterative process, involving reflection on both the theoretical grounding of the problem statements and the empirical knowledge that we derived through our fieldwork. A list of the dimension names, their respective Cronbach's alpha (standardised) reliabilities and the survey items included in each dimension are shown in Table 2.8.

Methodological Issues

A methodological difficulty in relation to the analytical groupings, used for the survey analysis and interview sampling, is that, since the study is cross-sectional rather than longitudinal, we cannot draw strong conclusions about 'change' over the course of the sentence. Indeed, there is considerable potential for cohort effects, not least because it has become far more common in recent years for people receiving life sentences to be given very long tariffs than it was when our late-stage prisoners were sentenced. The result is that these groups might not be directly comparable. Among our survey respondents, for example, compared to the 'post-tariff' group, prisoners in the 'very early' stages of theirs sentences were: eight times more likely to be serving sentences of 20 years or more; 15.5 times more likely to be denying their guilt; and 2.8 times more likely to be Black or from a minority ethnic group (the difference between groups on each of these variables was significant).[9] Moreover, differences between prisoners in the post-tariff stage and those in the other groups may also reflect a methodological limitation related to the concept of 'selective release' (Zamble 1992); that is, prisoners who remain in prison beyond their tariff date may be different from those who are granted release. Period effects may also affect the experiences of the different groups of prisoners, in that changing penal sensibilities may impact differentially on prisoners according to the particular eras in which they have served their sentences. Establishing the

---

[9]There was a significant association between sentence stage and: tariff length (defined as under 20 years or 20 years and over—$\chi^2(4) = 53.29$, $p < 0.001$); guilt ($\chi^2(4) = 36.74$, $p < 0.001$); and ethnicity ($\chi^2(4) = 12.55$, $p < 0.05$).

Table 2.8 Dimensions generated from survey items

Factor 1—Deprivations (male survey $\alpha = 0.800$; female survey $\alpha = 0.795$)

Missing little luxuries

Missing somebody

Feeling sexually frustrated

Missing social life

Wishing you had more privacy

Being bored

Factor 2—Autonomy/Control (male survey $\alpha = 0.726$; female survey $\alpha = 0.621$)

Finding it hard to keep out of trouble

Getting annoyed or irritated with other prisoners

Prison officers making life harder

Feeling that you have no control over your life

Having to follow other people's rules and orders

Factor 3—Progression (male survey $\alpha = 0.753$; female survey $\alpha = 0.530$)

Feeling frustrated that you are not progressing through the system

Prison psychologists making life harder

Feeling that you need to be careful about everything you say and do

Worrying about how you are described on file

Factor 4—Anger/Frustration (male survey $\alpha = 0.731$; female survey $\alpha = 0.722$)

Feeling angry with yourself

Feeling that your life has been wasted

Wishing that time would go faster

Feeling angry with the world

Factor 5—Emotional and physical vulnerability (male survey $\alpha = 0.768$; female survey $\alpha = 0.892$)

(continued)

Table 2.8 (continued)

Feeling that you have no one to talk to about the things that really matter to you

Feeling that the system is ignoring your individual needs

Feeling worried about your personal safety

Not feeling able to completely trust anyone in prison

Factor 6—Mental well-being (male survey $\alpha = 0.769$; female survey $\alpha = 0.874$)

Being worried about your mental health

Feeling suicidal

Feeling sorry for yourself

Feeling that you have no purpose or meaning in your life

Feeling lonely

Factor 7—Time (years) (male survey $\alpha = 0.809$; female survey $\alpha = 0.808$)

Feeling that the length of your sentence is unfair

Thinking about the amount of time that you might have to serve

Feeling that you are losing the best years of your life

Factor 8—Outside relationships (male survey $\alpha = 0.659$; female survey $\alpha = 0.738$)

Worrying about people outside

Feeling that you are losing contact with family and friends

Being afraid that someone you love or care about will die before you are released

Factor 9—Release anxiety (male survey $\alpha = 0.670$; female survey $\alpha = 0.752$)

Losing your self-confidence

Being afraid of dying before you get out

Feeling anxious about the uncertainty of your release date

Worrying about how you will cope when you get out

Stand alone

Thinking about the crime that you committed

contribution of period and cohort effects is complicated, however, and the similar survey results across the various studies undertaken over 40 years suggest that the impact of such issues may, in certain respects, be relatively minor.

With regard to our qualitative data, we generally found very strong similarities between what early-stage prisoners reported to us in the present and what mid- and late-stage prisoners reported when recalling their earlier years of custody. While we have therefore been careful, in our analysis, not to adopt misleading language around matters of change or to assume that the prisoner experience is itself unchanging, we are quite confident that many of the adaptive changes described to us by prisoners who were many years into their sentences are likely to be reproduced by those who are at earlier sentence phases. A second major limitation of our study is that it did not include prisoners who had been transferred during their sentences to secure psychiatric hospitals, having been sectioned under the Mental Health Act. According to official data obtained at the end of 2013, this applied to 191 prisoners—a significant proportion of our population of interest. Unavoidably, then, given the scope of our fieldwork, our findings systematically exclude the experiences of a large proportion of men and women with the most acute psychological and psychiatric difficulties.[10]

References

Chapman, T. K. (2016). Expressions of "voice" in portraiture. *Qualitative Inquiry, 11*(1), 27–51.

Crewe, B. (2009). *The prisoner society: Power, adaptation and social life in an English prison.* Clarendon and Oxford: Oxford University Press.

Crewe, B. (2011). Depth, weight, tightness: Revisiting the pains of imprisonment. *Punishment and Society, 13*(5), 509–529.

Crewe, B., Hulley, S., & Wright, S. (2017). The gendered pains of life imprisonment. *British Journal of Criminology, 57*(6), 1359–1378.

Crewe, B., Liebling, A., & Hulley, S. (2014). Heavy-light, absent-present: Re-thinking the 'weight' of imprisonment. *British Journal of Sociology, 65*(3), 387–410.

---

[10] An application for funding to extend the study, in order to interview people who met our criteria but were within secure hospitals, as well as prisoners given very long life sentences when older, was unsuccessful.

Flanagan, T. (1980). The pains of long-term imprisonment: A comparison of British and American perspectives. *The British Journal of Criminology, 20*(2), 148–156.

Hicks, B. M., Markon, K. E., Patrick, C. J., Krueger, R. F., & Newman, J. P. (2004). Identifying psychopathy subtypes on the basis of personality structure. *Psychological Assessment, 16*(3), 276.

Hill, D. A. (2005). The poetry in portraiture: Seeing subjects, hearing voices, and feeling contexts. *Qualitative Inquiry, 11*(1), 95–105.

Hollway, W., & Jefferson, T. (2000). *Doing qualitative research differently: Free association, narrative and the interview method.* London: Sage.

Hulley, S., Liebling, A., & Crewe, B. (2012). Respect in prisons: Prisoners' experiences of respect in public and private sector prisons. *Criminology and Criminal Justice, 12*(1), 3–23.

Klempner, M. (2000). Navigating life review interviews with survivors of trauma. *Oral History Review, 27*(2), 67–83.

Lawrence-Lightfoot, S., & Davis, J. H. (1997). *The art and science of portraiture.* San Francisco: Jossey-Bass.

Leigey, M. E., & Ryder, M. A. (2015). The pains of permanent imprisonment: Examining perceptions of confinement among older life without parole inmates. *International Journal of Offender Therapy and Comparative Criminology, 59*(7), 726–742.

Liebling, A., & Arnold, H. (2012). Social relationships between prisoners in a maximum security prison: Violence, faith, and the declining nature of trust. *Journal of Criminal Justice, 40*(5), 413–424.

Liebling, A., Arnold, H., & Straub, C. (2011). *An exploration of staff-prisoner relationships at HMP Whitemoor: 12 years on.* London: Ministry of Justice, National Offender Management Service.

Liebling, A., Armstrong, R., Bramwell, R., & Williams, R. J. (2015). *Locating trust in a climate of fear: religion, moral status, prisoner leadership, and risk in maximum security prisons—Key findings from an innovative study.* Prisons Research Centre, Institute of Criminology: University of Cambridge.

McAdams, D. P. (1988). Biography, narrative, and lives: An introduction. *Journal of Personality, 56*(1), 1–18.

Prison Reform Trust. (2018). *Prison: The facts (Bromley Briefings Summer 2018).* London: Prison Reform Trust.

Richards, B. (1978). The experience of long-term imprisonment: An exploratory investigation. *British Journal of Criminology, 18*(2), 162–169.

Rogers, C. R. (1956). Clientcentered theory. *Journal of Counseling Psychology, 3*(2), 115.

Rubin, H. J., & Rubin, I. S. (2012). *Qualitative interviewing: The art of hearing data* (3rd ed.). Thousand Oaks, CA: Sage.

Soloman, S. R., & Sawilowsky, S. S. (2009). Impact of rank-based normalizing transformations on the accuracy of test scores. *Journal of Modern Applied Statistical Methods,* *8*(2), 9.

Sykes, G. (1958). The pains of imprisonment. In *The society of captives: A study of a maximum security prison* (pp. 63–78). Princeton: Princeton University Press.

Williams, R. J. (2017). Finding freedom and rethinking power: Islamic piety in English high security prisons. *British Journal of Criminology.* https://doi.org/10.1093/bjc/azx034.

Zamble, E. (1992). Behavior and adaptation in long-term prison inmates: Descriptive longitudinal results. *Criminal Justice and Behavior, 19*(4), 409–425.

3

Life Histories

This book details considerable consistency in the adaptive patterns of prisoners serving very long sentences for murder. In doing so, it emphasises the ways in which the nature of the offence and the severity of the sanction flattened out many aspects of the prisoner experience, overriding many characteristics that might otherwise be expected to shape it. We would not wish to imply that our sample was homogenous, however. Throughout the text, we detail some of the distinctive experiences of the women in our sample, since these were made especially apparent in our interviews. To more adequately convey some of the particularities of our participants' experiences, both prior to and during their imprisonment, below we provide six qualitative pen portraits. These portraits have been selected to represent the interview sample along certain dimensions (such as sentence stage, gender, ethnicity and attitude towards the conviction), to demonstrate its heterogeneity, and to flesh out our participants in ways that animate them as human beings and bring to life their biographical and emotional complexities.

© The Author(s) 2020
B. Crewe et al., *Life Imprisonment from Young Adulthood*,
Palgrave Studies in Prisons and Penology,
https://doi.org/10.1057/978-1-137-56601-0_3

Seb, 20s, Early Stage

Seb had grown up in a small northern English town: a place where 'there's not much prospects. [You] either get out - and that's a rare lot that do get out - or you come to jail. Or you end up on benefits. Or you end up on drugs'. Despite the conditions of his hometown, he described his childhood as 'good'. Problems started to arise at school in his early teens. This, Seb reflected, was linked to his discovery of alcohol and smoking weed [marijuana]. In his mid-teens, he was excluded from school and sent to a Pupil Referral Unit to continue his education. By his late teens, his relationship with his parents had fractured to the point that Seb had moved out of the family home. Yet 'life was good' for him: selling weed, 'partying' and 'doing what young lads do'. He was also playing sport at a high level and hoped to make a career of this.

Seb had been convicted of the murder of a young male who died during a fight outside a local pub. The conviction and sentence felt deeply illegitimate to him, and he was immersed in the appeal process in the hope of having his conviction overturned in favour of a verdict of manslaughter. He acknowledged that his blows had killed the victim, but argued that they were acts of self-defence. At trial, Seb explained, he accepted a plea bargain due to pressure placed on him by his own barrister ('they were basically telling me, "Oh, you're fucked, everything's on you. [...] the best thing for you to do is go guilty"') and by the prosecution, who argued: 'Go guilty, and we'll give you 25 years. [But] if you go not guilty, and get found guilty, you're getting 30 years *or more*'. Seb stated simply: 'All I thought of is my mum - I need to get a less sentence for my mum, really. So I've gone guilty'.

Like 56% of our male survey sample, and 89% of our female survey participants, this was Seb's first custodial sentence, and he described the initial period in prison as very difficult.[1] He responded by retreating into drug use, while his anger at his conviction and sentence manifested themselves in non-compliance with the prison regime. He refused to go to work, got into fights with other prisoners on a regular basis, and was 'running round like an idiot [...] not really caring about the rules'. While he had initially come into the prison system as a Category B prisoner, his attitude and behaviour, in addition to considerable security intelligence about his trade in drugs and mobile phones, saw him swiftly transferred to a high-security establishment.

---

[1] As such, this was not a sample characterised by serious prolific offending.

Since entering the high-security estate, however, Seb had changed: 'When I come to jail, I weren't grown up […] but when I come to Dispersal,[2] that's when I had to proper mature'. Seb's relationship with his mother had also influenced his decision to stop 'fighting the system', once he realised how much he was hurting her through his actions. He filled his days with reading and writing, going to the gym, playing computer games, cooking and spending time with a 'tight' group of trusted friends. He had converted from Christianity to Islam before coming to prison, in his mid-teens, and his faith and religion were central to his everyday life. It was important to Seb that his time inside was not 'wasted' and he took every opportunity to engage in 'learning, education [and] different trades'.

Seb found the relational losses associated with his sentence hard, particularly the absence of sex and intimacy, and the difficulties associated with trying to maintain familial relationships. He was also struggling to get back to a Category B prison, despite having completed all offending behaviour courses on his sentence plan. There was nothing left to do except 'keep my head down' and 'hope'. Asked where he thought he would be in five years' time, Seb replied: 'In a better state than I am now. […] Hopefully doing an Open University [degree] [and] in a Cat B'. When reminded about his appeal, he explained:

> I'm just not pinning my hopes on it. Because if they pull you off [the appeal is rejected], it's just going to kill you off […]. So I just think to myself, 'It's probably not going to happen'. Carry on doing my studying and that. And then if it does happen it's a bonus; if it doesn't happen, then I was prepared for it anyways.

Gail, 30s, Late-Stage

Gail described her childhood as having been marred by violence, and she would often arrive at school covered in bruises. She had a far more positive relationship with her father ('I was a real Daddy's girl') and so was 'devastated' when, in her early teens, her parents split and her mother remarried a man who perpetrated extreme acts of violence against Gail and her siblings; 'the second day I met him, he beat me up. And it wasn't a case of just hitting us - he had me down on the floor with

---

[2] 'Dispersal': a high-security prison, or the high-security prison system.

the hair and he was like kicking me in the head and punching and things'. Almost overnight, she said, she went from being a highly compliant, high-achieving child ('I was in the top sets for everything at school') to a 'rebellious teenager', and her desperation to escape her violent home life saw her turn to alcohol and drugs (initially 'weed, a bit of LSD, a bit of speed' [amphetamines] and glue-sniffing).[3] Having run away from home to escape the physical abuse, Gail described moving in with her then-partner, who himself 'started getting really violent'. Whenever she tried to leave him, he would threaten to kill himself or increase his level of violence.

Gail talked little of the events leading up to the murder she was convicted for, or of the killing itself. She disputed the legitimacy of her conviction under joint enterprise, because she had not 'physically killed someone' and felt that her tariff length was unduly long in part because she was a woman. Nevertheless, she acknowledged that she deserved to be punished for 'contributing to the murder'. Once sentenced, she found the length of her tariff particularly difficult to process and could not 'deal with it in one go'. Her coping strategy involved being occupied and goal-orientated:

> This is how to get through your time; to stay busy and to stay focused. [...] For me, coming into prison learned me that I need goals – need something to aim for, I need something to hope for. I need something that pulls me forward and drives me along.

Still, she struggled: 'I used to hit the "five-year wall", and... I suppose I'd crash for a bit. I'd give myself a couple of weeks and just crawl into bed'. Mostly these 'crashes' centred on affective issues, particularly around the anniversary of the murder, as she was consumed with feelings of guilt and shame: 'the guilt from [the victim], the guilt from the effect it had on [the victim's] family, the guilt for anybody who has to have anything to do with it'.

When turning to the future, Gail did so with trepidation and an impending sense of panic about the 'massive' task of having to build a life post-release:

> I can't even imagine what life is like out there. [...] The world has changed; it's not the world it was when I came to jail. The level of traffic on the road is phenomenal,

---

[3] 68% of female survey participants, and 43% of male survey participants, reported having had a problem with alcohol or drugs (or both) before they came into prison on their current sentence.

technology is phenomenal, the choices are phenomenal, and it's like a very, very different world. And I can't kind of - thinking about being in here until I'm in open [conditions] and I'm going out into it, and coping with it, I can't imagine. I can't imagine. I haven't got the ability to imagine that world and me in that world.

Beyond the fear, however, Gail expressed tentative hopes for life beyond prison. Primarily, such reflections centred on overcoming many of the material deprivations of the past two decades, interspersed with aspirations for autonomy, material comfort and what many might consider to be the more mundane aspects of life at liberty:

[I'd like] my own flat done exactly how I'd like it. A huge, big bed [...]. A quilt that actually weighs something. A mattress that's comfy. Doing something that I want to do, like doing something that I enjoy doing. [And] being able to take walks, and sit outside in the dark, and look at the stars.

Campbell, 30s, Mid-Stage

The youngest of seven children, Campbell had been raised by his mother on a council estate in a Midlands town. He described his father ('absent from my life from the age of two') as a well-known armed robber. Growing up was 'tough': money was tight, and many people in his extended family were involved in crime or in prison. At a young age, Campbell 'started hanging around with an older lot'— his 'notorious' older brothers, and other males who were much older than him. He started 'getting in trouble' with this group, and 'almost overnight' went from being 'a young kid at home; a mummy's boy' to 'being a man [...] And then the life of crime started'. His offending was initially 'petty [...] purely [for] my pleasure and enjoyment'. As he got older, he switched to stealing cars, motivated primarily by money because 'with money comes respect'. By his mid-teens, violence was also a central part of Campbell's offending, and from the age of 15, he received custodial terms for offences including 'kidnap and torture', robbery, intimidation of witnesses, grievous bodily harm and attempted murder. He explained: 'I thought I was the big man [...] making decisions that held people's life in the balance [...] I thought that was just normal life'.

In his 20s, Campbell was one of several men convicted of murder, under the principles of joint enterprise, for the death of a young male. Although he had been at the scene, he had not wielded the weapon, as such, and originally pleaded not guilty at trial 'because my solicitor told me [...] "You haven't actually committed murder"'. On being found guilty, he was sentenced to life imprisonment with a very significant tariff. He refused, however, to 'be bitter' or 'start appealing' against his sentence ('I didn't feel I had a right to do that'), accepting a portion of the responsibility for the young man's death. He was clear that, but for his actions, the victim would not have lost his life: 'I can't take away the fact that my actions led to it happening, in certain kinds of ways'.

While being in prison 'didn't frighten' him ('I've been doing it since I've been 15 [...] It's just this time it was for the long haul'), Campbell remembered being 'fucking shell-shocked' by the length of the tariff: 'I daren't [look] at the years or anything [...] I think that would have probably broke me'. Having initially been designated as a Category A prisoner, he had spent the first five years of his sentence in a high-security establishment. While life there was, in some respects, 'good'—'I had a laugh, played football, a lot of gym, eating proper food'—there was 'no progress [...] You ain't learning nothing, [or] thinking about what you've done. You're just living for the moment. [...] Basically getting older and fatter'.

Campbell felt able to cope with the experience of imprisonment, but the relational losses inherent in long-term confinement affected him significantly, for example: the 'daily loss' of 'time out there with your family'; his ex-partner leaving him; and the 'helpless[ness]' he felt when, several years into his sentence, his brother and mother both died. Describing the loss of his mother, he reflected, 'my fucking world collapsed. [And] there is absolutely nothing you can do, you know?' It was this event that made him realise 'something's gotta change', and so—after serving a third of his tariff—Campbell asked to be transferred to a (prison-based) therapeutic community. While initially sceptical, he described this as an 'eye-opening' experience, which had helped him to reinvent himself and move away from his previous life and worldview: 'I'm a changed man now'.

The realisation that his nieces—young children when he first came to prison—had now 'got kids, [and] drive cars' troubled him, because it brought to life his relative stagnation:

I feel the same [as I was]. I feel like I achieve nothing. I've grown up in my head as such, you know, but in terms of what I should have been doing out there, I just feel I've missed out.

However, he drew strength from his family and friends, and from the fact that he still 'had a life'. While being released was a 'frightening prospect' ('It will have been at *least* 20 years since I've been out there'), he was hopeful about his future, grounded in a set of relational ambitions:

[Firstly] I want to make my mum proud. [She] had to die knowing her son was locked up. I at least wanna make something out of my life, you know? [And secondly I want] kids. [...] A family. A loving family. [...] And it's about having the support around me and not surrounding myself with idiots. And also not thinking about my reputation anymore, you know? I wanna try and do things that are positive. And that's basically it.

Deena, 20s, Mid-Stage

Deena had been brought up by her mother (an 'emotionally weak woman [with] drug problems') and grandmother (who, conversely, was 'incredibly strong... a 'pick-yourself-up-and-get-on-with-it' kind of woman'). Her father, an alcoholic, had been absent throughout much of her early childhood; a period that passed with little comment during the interview. As Deena entered secondary school, her mother had met a new partner, who over the course of the next few years assaulted her physically. As a consequence—and like at least six of the other women in the interview sample—she was taken into the local authority care.[4] Within six months, she had been raped by one of the male care workers. By her mid-teens, Deena had already served a term in a secure children's unit, for a serious violent offence. Following her release from the unit, she had not returned to school and spent her days selling drugs with her first serious boyfriend. At this point, Deena

---

[4]This is higher than the proportion of female prisoners in other studies (e.g. one in five, in Caddle and Crisp 1997), and far higher than the general population, of whom two per cent have been in care at some point during their childhood (Dodd and Hunter 1992).

was also taking drugs herself, 'but only recreationally'—she had been 'too scared' by her parents' addictions 'to go too far down *that* road'.

With an ironic laugh, Deena said that, before coming to prison in her late teens, she had slowly begun to build herself a more positive life and was even undertaking a vocational college course which she had hoped would translate into a career—'things finally started to pick up for me'. By this time, she was also living with her partner, which she described as the first time that she had ever felt safe and had a 'stable' life. However, her partner had remained an active drug dealer, making it more difficult for Deena to leave behind that life entirely. These circumstances were relevant to the murder for which Deena was convicted. Prior to this, however, she had had no real sense that prison was a likely part of her future. She was excited at the prospect of living a 'normal life', with a partner, children, a job and a stable home—'all the things I never had'.[5]

Deena had not challenged or appealed any aspect of her sentence or conviction, despite it involving joint enterprise. When asked about this, she said that she often reflected on how she would feel in the shoes of the victim's children: 'I ask myself, "If that was my parent, would I think 16 years was long enough?" Probably not'. She felt deep remorse for what she had done. In the initial years of the sentence, these feelings, in addition to the sentence itself, left Deena overwhelmed: 'I was really numb [...] I couldn't see a way through it – I couldn't see the end; I thought "This is it now"'.

Deena identified the first four to five years as the most difficult part of her sentence, culminating in her 'lowest point', when the reality and permanence of her new life finally 'sank in'. She responded with what she described as a 'fuck it attitude [...] like what's the point? [...] I didn't feel that I had anything to work towards'. In addition to the emotional distress she was experiencing ('I tried to commit suicide and ended up in hospital'),[6] and because of this sense of having 'nothing to lose' and little purpose, Deena spent those initial years 'acting out':

---

[5] 12 of the 19 women who we interviewed identified themselves as having children, either in the survey or in interview. One woman noted having two children in the survey, despite them both having passed away prior to her sentence. The stark nature of collecting such data quantitatively was not lost on us. Very early on in the process, we recognised the complex and emotive nature of asking women about their children. Many had experienced miscarriages, abortions (often forced upon them by others), infant deaths, and children being taken into care.

[6] 67% of female survey participants had self-harmed or attempted suicide prior to their imprisonment, and 89% during their current sentence. For the male survey participants, these figures were 15% for both.

fighting other prisoners, assaulting offers, 'disobeying orders and just silly little things'.

Within prison, among Deena's chief concerns were: her diagnosis as 'schizoid' ('they told me I was going to get all this support, and all I got was a label'); the impact of 'doing all my growing up in a false environment'; and the long-lasting effects of too many years learning to 'detach [from] your feelings'. Since passing the five-year point, however, Deena had started to make more constructive use of her time, and she identified a number of deeply rewarding qualifications that she hoped to convert into employment on release. Moreover, she reflected that the here and now was 'the first - I think - *positive* experience of being somewhere and feeling safe and having an education and getting my needs met'. When asked where she saw herself in five years' time, she replied 'Hopefully, in an open prison [or] going out to work. Start[ing] to reconnect with the community'. Her long-term ambitions were clear and simple: 'Get to my family again. Be successful in whatever I do, and, yeah – just living my life and doing all the things I missed out on'.

Richard, 50s, Post-tariff

Since the age of 18, Richard had spent only a few months at liberty. In his childhood, he had regularly witnessed his father 'severely beating' his mother. His experience of school was almost wholly negative—he 'didn't mix well with other children', and at the age of seven found himself in 'child guidance' ('what would be psychiatric child support nowadays') for support with 'controlling [his] temper and tantrums'. Richard described himself as an 'uncontrollable kid', who would also turn his violence in on himself when he became angry or upset: 'as a youngster I used to claw my face to bits just out of pure frustration'.

At the age of twelve, Richard was sent to a 'special boarding school', where he was subjected to serious and repeated sexual violence. This only stopped when Richard became a senior, and 'ended up doing to the juniors what the seniors did to me'. This was behaviour he would come to repeat in the prison system: 'I'd manipulate [other prisoners] to give me what I wanted without [the victim] running to his mates looking for help, or going to the staff'. It was at the boarding school that Richard felt his 'criminal career began'. While he listed 'shoplifting, thieving, fraud, [and] arson' as some of his convictions, the majority at that time were for what he referred to as 'sexual offences'. As a consequence, he spent significant periods of time in youth detention centres.

Richard had been convicted and sentenced for the rape and murder of a young girl. While he had pleaded not guilty at his trial, his conception of his culpability for the victim's death was complex. He acknowledged that he had killed the victim ('I've never denied that I did what I did'), but strongly rejected the label of 'murderer': '[Psychology] are saying that's me being "in denial" of the premeditated thought of the murder, but [it happened] in a moment of panic. [...] I will never *ever* accept it was murder'.

The nature of his offence had caused Richard's family and friends to 'disown [him] straight away'. He therefore did not have the relational ties that bound the majority of our interviewees, at least to some degree, to the outside world. For Richard, this absence of external relationships underpinned his non-compliance in the first five years of his sentence:

> I knew I had 20 years ahead of me, and at the beginning of the sentence - because I had nothing to lose - I spent the first three-to-five years smashing up, giving [prison officers] hell, making their job as hard as possible.

This response was also directly linked to what Richard saw as the illegitimacy of his conviction: 'you want to treat me like a murderer, fine; treat me like a murderer. But you will reap what you sow'. For Richard, the entire prison system was devoid of legitimacy, especially prison psychologists, who held 'too much power' and whom he blamed for his lack of progression. While he understood that the need to protect the public underpinned the systemic reluctance to release him ('I think, "Wait a minute – I wouldn't want a child killer living next door to me!"'), this had caused Richard to develop 'twisted' thoughts. He now conjured up ways to justify the extra time he had served: '[I think] "Well fuck you—I've done the time, I could now go out and do the bloody crime. What can I do which is equivalent of what a judge might give me 16 years for?"'.

Richard hoped, in five years' time, to be in 'a low secure hospital' and on his way to 'getting NHS secure accommodation' in the community. His current focus was obtaining this transfer, because he 'need[ed] to know why I killed [the victim]'; insights he felt required 'more experts than prison psychologists to explain'. Although he could not think about the possibility of life beyond release ('I don't have dreams about the future anymore'), he recognised the importance of trying to maintain hope. Since becoming a born-again Christian some time ago, he had drawn his strength from religion: 'what keeps me going through all their negativity is my Christian faith'. He strongly believed that 'at the end of the day, Christ is going to get me through this - one way or another'.

Mahmood, 30s, Mid-Stage

Mahmood grew up in a large city in the Midlands. He had lived with his mother, father and siblings and described a 'really difficult' childhood marred by domestic violence: 'My dad was an alcoholic. So he used to beat my mum up, beat me and my siblings up'. Such beatings were routine, 'kind of like déjà vu - every day of my childhood was very similar'. Cultural constraints meant that Mahmood had felt unable to confide in others about the violence: 'coming from [my ethnic] background, anything that happened in the house stayed in the house. We weren't allowed to talk about it - not even to close family'. Years later, Mahmood would be diagnosed with post-traumatic stress disorder and severe depression as a result of these experiences. He explained how he 'hated' school—'I could never get into it'—something that was related to his domestic circumstances, since his father would begin drinking when he returned from work late at night:

> …and that's when he would beat [us] up. So basically all night we didn't sleep, and all night I'd be thinking 'I don't wanna go to school'. And then when I'd get home I'd be […] scared of what's going to happen at night. So it was kind of like that fear of every part of the day. [And] I struggled all the way through school.

In his younger years, Mahmood's coping strategy had been 'going out, and playing football with my mates'. At 16, when he started sixth-form college, he began to enjoy a sense of autonomy and freedom for the first time:

> Up until I was sixteen, I felt trapped. […] Because I couldn't get out of the house. But after that, I started going out with my cousin, and I'd get into fights, and I'd drink [and] I started college. […] I felt free.

However, Mahmood had been left with deep feelings of guilt about his own escape from violence: 'Basically I was a coward – I left my mum and siblings at home; I kind of ran away'. In addition, he had struggled with an intense anger towards his father, and his inability to express it. He also began to resent the disempowerment he felt as soon as he crossed the threshold at home: 'As loud as I'd been outside, and getting into fights, as soon as I got home it was like I felt like that little kid again'.

Between the age of 16 and the time of his index offence, Mahmood had been a 'hurricane of emotions. [...] I was a complete mess'. He had taken a series of low-paid retail jobs but had struggled with the relative inactivity: being 'kind of stood about; quiet, and stuff like that'; 'I wanted to be loud, and around a lot of noise and action, so I could forget what was going on at home'.

When he was in his early 20s, Mahmood killed a stranger. In the initial years of his sentence, he had felt hopeless and feared he was 'never going to see outside again'—'I come in and my head was all over the place. I can't even remember the first few weeks being inside. [...] I was a mess'. He reported that no psychological support was offered at any of the high-security prisons he was located in, despite the fact that he was 'breaking down'. He 'coped' by making the acquaintance of another prisoner who knew one of Mahmood's relatives ('I was lucky. [...] I kind of just played a bit of pool with him. [...] If I weren't doing that, I'd be in my cell, breaking down. That was kind of how I coped') and by denying the offence, to others and to himself ('I blocked it out'). After having admitted to the murder eight years into his sentence, Mahmood thought about it 'constantly'. He talked a little about the impact of his offence on himself, but the 'most difficult part' of his sentence was the pain and shame he had brought upon his family members: 'What I've kind of put my family through is [...] going to hurt me for the rest of my life'. Although he sometimes felt he was 'drifting away' from his family, he had retained strong bonds with his mother, siblings, other family members and friends from home and drew great strength from their support. It was only the thought of how it would 'crush' his family that had stopped him taking his life in the early years of the sentence: 'One hundred per cent I wouldn't be here today if I didn't have my family'.

After almost a decade in high-security prisons, Mahmood was 'angry, depressed, really insecure, really nervous, and I needed a change - I needed to sort my life out'. This arose both from a desire to come to terms with the offence and from a need to escape the pervasive racism he had experienced from staff ('Under the ties like they'd have National Front icons.[7] I got called 'Paki' – I'd hear that more than my name'). They would 'lose' his application forms, place him on report for things he had not done, and 'knock into me in the corridor': it was 'just little things, but it was continual'. The result was a 'breakdown' and led to Mahmood applying for a transfer to a therapeutic community.

Since being based at the therapeutic community, Mahmood felt that he was 'finally on the right path. [...] I can see where I want to get to'. His aspirations for life post-release centred on gaining employment with a 'generative' focus:

> I want to learn from my mistakes [and] help people - I'd love to like be in a position where I could help kids, and because of everything that I've gone through in my life, and things that I've done, I wouldn't want any kids following my path.

His future plans also reflected the importance for Mahmood of living life relationally:

> I've got a niece and nephew… I just want to get to a point where I can like take them to the park, or take them shopping, and take my little nephew to football… I want to be part of their lives in the future, and I want to be helping my family. So I've got to kind of use that as a kind of motivation really.

References

Caddle, D., & Crisp, D. (1997). *Imprisoned women and mothers*. London: Home Office.

Dodd, T., & Hunter, P. (1992). *The national prison survey 1991: A report to the Home Office of a study of prisoners in England and Wales carried out by the Social Survey Division of OPCS*. London: HMSO.

---

[7]National Front: an extreme far-right, white supremacist political party in the UK.

4

The Early Years

I spent the first month in complete shock and I thought I would wake up and go home. It wasn't real […] And it hurt - it felt like somebody was ripping my chest open. I saw no future, no point to tomorrow. (Maria, 20s, early)

This chapter seeks to convey the experiences of prisoners in the early period of life sentences for murder, as they confronted the deep existential fractures and 'contextual dislocations' (cf. Archer 2003) produced by such prison terms. Specifically, it brings into focus the combined effect on prisoners of being convicted of the particular offence of murder and of being given a very long sentence at a relatively early age: what we call the 'offence-time nexus'. Our analysis extends Bury's (1982) notion of 'biographical disruption' to one of existential dislocation and biographical *rupture*, in which individuals had to come to terms with an almost total breach of their sense of self, their relational ties and their expectations of how their lives would pan out. A key part of our overall argument is that the sheer length of the sentence and the enormity of the offence compounded and intensified the standard 'pains of imprisonment' (Sykes 1958), giving them an affective quality that resulted in some distinctive adaptive responses. The chapter

© The Author(s) 2020
B. Crewe et al., *Life Imprisonment from Young Adulthood*,
Palgrave Studies in Prisons and Penology,
https://doi.org/10.1057/978-1-137-56601-0_4

details these pains in a loosely chronological manner—from offence to trial, conviction and sentencing—before outlining the various adaptive reactions that they generated.

Being 'in Shock': Acute Stress Reactions to Conviction, Sentencing and Initial Incarceration

The initial pains of long-term incarceration began prior to conviction, at the point at which prisoners were first remanded in custody. Periods on remand were often long—sometimes many months—in overcrowded local prisons lacking in opportunities for purposeful activity. Many participants described heavy restrictions being placed on their daily activities, due to the severity of the charge against them ('they wouldn't let me go to education and they wouldn't let me go to gym' [Harris, 20s, early]) and extended periods of inactivity: 'sat in a cell, twenty-three hours, sometimes twenty-four hours a day [...] doing nothing' (Stephen, 20s, mid). The toll of the remand period was evident in the narratives of many early-stage prisoners, in terms of a lack of self-care ('I didn't eat [...] couldn't sleep. I sat there smoking myself [stupid]' [Tamara, 20s, early]), and many first-time prisoners described one of the most 'stressful' elements of the initial remand period as the absence of an effective schema for negotiating prison life: 'The worst bit [...] is being new to prison and you don't really know how to deal with it' (Darrin, late teens, early). For those prisoners who were serving a prison sentence for the first time—56% of the men and 90% of the women surveyed—the result was a brutal form of entry shock: being a prison novice, contemplating their offence and facing the possibility of a life-changing sentence.

Such experiences left an indelible mark. Recalling his experience almost two decades later, Bernard (40s, post-tariff) described the 'humiliating and degrading' process of reception into prison for the first time: being 'stripped off, room full of people, stark bollock naked', feeling 'helpless', and having 'no control, no power'. Aged eighteen at the time, 'surrounded by career criminals and gangsters' in a notoriously rough prison, and struggling to acknowledge what he had done, he had tried to take his own life: 'because I felt that it would prove that I'm not guilty, you know, and they would let me go home'.

However, such pains paled in comparison with the experience of the trial, and being convicted and sentenced. Indeed, it is difficult to overstate the extent of despair and disbelief associated with this period. Episodes of amnesia were common, as were feelings of paralysis, numbness, surrealism and a sense that the moment of conviction or sentencing was 'not real' ('I'm still expecting to wake up from this' [Maria, 20s, early]).[1] Campbell (30s, mid) recalled being 'fucking shell-shocked' when he was first sentenced; Maria's (20s, early) 'head was spinning for weeks'; while Kathryn (20s, early) explained that: 'I was very much in shock [...] I was just quite numb with it all, and I think that's why I couldn't cry when I got back to the prison'. Experiences of this kind bear strong similarities to the symptoms of acute stress responses (Bryant et al. 2015). Moreover, echoing Archer's (2003) description of 'fractured reflexives', the terms in which they were communicated were predominantly 'expressive' in nature, conveyed in almost exclusively emotive language, with scant reflective consideration of 'instrumental resolutions'.

These reactions were not merely affective in form. Many interviewees described a distinct physiological reaction to their conviction and sentencing. Accounts of collapsing upon conviction were not uncommon: Julius (30s, mid) recalled that his legs had 'buckled' when the verdict was delivered, while Fiona (20s, early) described 'falling to the floor' of the court and being carried out from the dock by prison officers. Others described aspects of the experience of conviction and sentencing that might be best understood in the clinical language of depersonalisation: the sense of 'watching oneself' or feeling 'disconnected' from one's behavior' (Moskowitz 2004: 26). Dan (20s, early), for example, explained that the early days following his guilty verdict 'felt like an out-of-body experience', where the steps he was taking did not feel like his own, while Ray, reflecting back on his early experience, said:

> I felt that the whole experience wasn't real - like it was still a dream. [...] I'm just sitting in this cell, and I'm looking at these walls, and it's just not registering. Shock. Meltdown. (Ray, 50s, post-tariff)

Karen (20s, mid) similarly described spending the early weeks post-conviction 'walking around in like a dream state - a sad dream state'. Some of these feelings

---

[1] Such experiences were compounded for a number of women by the fact that they were heavily medicalised during their trials. One recalled having fallen asleep while in the dock because of the strength of the tranquilisers she had been prescribed. Several reported being 'so smashed' that they could tell us nothing about their time in court and said that they had been returned to their prison cells without realising they had been found guilty, much less sentenced to life imprisonment.

were linked strongly to the dizzying experience of being handed down such a long sentence: a feeling of 'temporal vertigo' about the prospect of so many years in prison (see Chapter 8). In clinical terms, this was an acute stress reaction to the shock of conviction, the sheer length of the tariff and the sense that life, as one had known it up to that point, was 'over'. Commonly, individuals at this stage explained that they were simply incapable of processing the length of their sentence, consistently linking this to the young age at which they had received their sentence:

> To be honest, when I was convicted, I really did think it was over. I just thought, like, '18 years? At *that* age?' I thought to myself, 'I haven't even *lived* 18 years [..] This is madness, this'. I thought, 'I'm *never* getting out of jail'. (Kenny, 20s, mid)

Carl, convicted in his late teens, recalled his bodily reaction when the judge started his sentence consideration at 30 years—he had been briefed by his lawyer to expect 25—as he began to consider the implications for his future:

> My legs were shaking and I was scared, I was proper scared [...] Because there's a big difference between - I mean, if you look at it logically it's only five years, but there's a big difference between coming out of prison when you're 38/39 and coming out when you're like 45, do you know what I mean? (Carl, 20s, early)

The intensity of these reactions was all the more significant for individuals who had been anticipating acquittal or conviction of a lesser offence. Many participants said they had been reassured by their trial solicitor that they would be 'going home' after the trial ('I didn't expect to get sentenced - my solicitor bought me a coach ticket to go home and told my dad to expect me home' [Eileen, 30s, late]). Being found guilty under these circumstances made the reality of the outcome even harder to bear and exacerbated feelings of entry shock. As Maria (20s, early) explained, conviction represented the death knell of hope that life would ever return to 'normal': 'once you're convicted', she explained 'home seems further away from you than it's ever been in your life'.

This disjuncture between the expectation and reality of the trial result was particularly profound and painful for participants convicted in accordance with the principles of joint enterprise. Such individuals represented over half of our survey sample (52% of men and 56% of women), the majority of whom considered themselves to be 'not guilty' of the specific offence of murder. In this respect, their conviction typically felt both unexpected and illegitimate.[2] Many were convinced prior to trial that they did not meet either the *actus reus* and/or *mens rea* components of murder—that they had neither killed the victim nor intended to cause them serious harm or death—and were unaware of the existence of joint enterprise altogether (see Hulley et al. 2019). This rendered the shock of being officially identified as a 'murderer' and receiving a long custodial tariff all the greater. Jeremiah, charged alongside several peers, explained:

> In the trial I thought I was just going to get [convicted for] the violent disorder charge. When I took part, I never knew about the whole joint enterprise concept or anything. So when I got the murder conviction, I didn't know, and it just hit me - I didn't know whether to laugh, cry, I didn't know anything and I just got back to my cell and just sat down. I haven't cried and [pauses, reconsidering] I *have* cried, when I got convicted. It was just a big shock to me and I just didn't realise that this would be the outcome of it. [...] Even my lawyer never knew, and my lawyer was saying that the worst-case scenario would be manslaughter [...] My solicitors kept on saying 'There's *no way* that this jury would convict you of murder on the basis of that...' But it happened, man. (Jeremiah, 20s, early)

Even those individuals who acknowledged their guilt and accepted their conviction felt little protection against the shock and despair of receiving such a long sentence at such a young age. As Antone—handed a 17-year tariff at 22 years old—explained:

> When I was given my sentence [I was] devastated. I kind of knew it was coming - as I say, I never denied what I did. I've taken someone's life; I deserve to pay the price. But to hear that from the judge - that I received a 17-year sentence - it just knocked me off my feet. I was sitting in a box in a court and there was a mandatory translator with me, because English is my second language, and I hadn't asked her for anything in terms of translation, but when the sentence was rolled out I actually asked her 'Did he say *seventeen*? He said seventeen?' She said 'Yes', and I - I had to sit down and I was shaking. I didn't [pauses] I was devastated. I realised it would be

---

[2] Notably, however, there were few significant differences in the severity scores for those convicted in accordance with the principles of joint enterprise and those who were not, with only 'feeling that your length of sentence is unfair' felt by the former to be a more severe problem to a degree that was statistically significant.

long. [...] but when you actually *hear* the words coming out, you [pauses]. Your whole world just drops down. (Antone, 20s, early)

Antone's reflections underscore the fact that no amount of preparation or acknowledgement of guilt could serve as an emotional bulwark at the point of conviction and sentencing. It was at these moments that our participants had to confront a reality that was often beyond their comprehension.

Post-conviction: The Initial Pains of Long Indeterminate Sentences

Male prisoners in the early sentence stage, particularly those in the very early stage (i.e. the first sixth of their tariff), reported experiencing almost all of the problems of long-term imprisonment with a greater degree of 'severity' than those at later sentence stages. Table 4.1, illustrates this with reference to the ten survey dimensions described in Chapter 2.

Compared to their 'mid', 'late' or 'post-tariff' counterparts, male prisoners at the very early and early stage of their sentence reported significantly higher severity scores for three dimensions: *Deprivations, Autonomy/ control* and *Time*.

Similarly, as we see in Table 4.2, women in the early sentence stage reported significantly higher severity scores than those at the late stage for five dimensions: *Deprivations, Autonomy/Control, Time, Anger/Frustration* and *Mental Well-being*.

The overall data patterns are consistent with those of previous studies that have employed the survey that we adapted (e.g. Richards 1978; Flanagan 1980; Leigey and Ryder 2015), in that there is little ostensible indication that the problems of such sentences accumulate or worsen according to time served.[3] Indeed, as the wider literature on the effects of imprisonment anticipates (see, e.g., MacKenzie and Goodstein 1985; Liebling et al. 2005; Harvey 2012), for almost every item, the severity scores were highest in the earliest sentence stages and decreased at each

---

[3] It is striking in itself that there is such common ground between the findings of studies in different jurisdictions and during different decades, indicating that long-term imprisonment has some more or less essential qualities. In all such studies, the findings point to the primacy of 'missing somebody', the pains associated with basic deprivations (social life, luxuries and sexual relations) and the sense of life being lost or wasted. Meanwhile, among the least severe problems in all previous studies are such matters as feeling suicidal, being concerned about mental health issues, being afraid of dying before release and 'feeling sorry for yourself'. For further details, see Hulley et al. (2016).

Table 4.1 Mean dimension severity scores according to sentence stage—male prisoners[a]

Dimension	Mean severity score (no. of respondents in each group)				
	Very early (VE) (53–57)	Early (E) (96–99)	Mid (M) (81–83)	Late (L) (27–28)
Deprivations	14.17***PT, *M	12.72***PT	11.72*PT	11.05
Autonomy/control	11.17**PT	10.80**PT	9.29	9.82
Progression	9.49	9.87	9.59	9.80
Anger/frustration	10.08	8.72	8.14	8.17
Emotional and physical vulnerability	9.93	8.98	8.30	9.60
Mental well-being	6.16	5.75	5.68	6.76
Time	16.04***PT, *M,L	14.85***PT	12.28	11.39
Outside relationships	14.09	13.34	12.38	11.54
Release anxiety	7.18	7.65	8.12	9.13
(Single item) thinking about the crime you committed	8.53	13.76	12.78	13.31

[a] * $p < 0.5$, ** $p < 0.01$, *** $p < 0.001$. The letters indicate which group the figure is significantly higher than: PT—Post-tariff, L—late stage, M—mid-stage

Table 4.2 Mean dimension 'severity' scores according to sentence stage—female prisoners

Dimension	Early (10)	Mid (3)	Late (6)[a]
Deprivations	15.85[*L]	13.22	8.94
Autonomy/control	14.01[*L]	10.53	8.60
Progression	13.28	9.50	7.88
Anger/frustration	15.79[**L]	9.00	7.63
Emotional and physical vulnerability	15.95	8.17	8.33
Mental well-being	13.91[*L]	6.53	6.20
Time	19.33[**L]	12.67	8.06
Outside relationships	18.77	12.89	12.94
Release anxiety	15.65	7.42	9.17
(Single item) thinking about the crime that you committed[b]	25.00	16.33	13.20

[a]For the female participants, sentence stage is organised by thirds, that is 'early' means within the first third of the sentence, mid within the second third and late (including post-tariff) in the final third of their sentence or beyond the tariff point
[b]Significance tests could not be conducted on this item, as one group had only one respondent within it

stage thereafter. Significant differences were found for 14 out of 39 problems, in almost all cases, between prisoners who were at earlier phases of their sentences and those who were post-tariff. As we clarify in subsequent chapters, however, we would warn against taking such findings at face value.

For current purposes, some further examples provide illustration. In relation to 'deprivations', for example, men in the early stage—and in particular the *very* early stage—of their sentence reported 'missing little luxuries' with far greater severity than those in later stages (with severity scores ranging from 13.75 among very early-stage prisoners to 9.93 and 5.35 among late-stage and post-tariff prisoners, respectively). Those in the early sentence stage also ranked this problem much higher (10th out of 39 problems) than those in the late or post-tariff period (19th and 32nd, respectively). Similarly, women in the first third of their sentence reported experiencing 'Missing little luxuries' with greater severity than women who were in the final third of their tariff or were post-tariff (severity scores: 19.40 and 5.17, respectively, and rankings of 10 and 33, respectively).

Kathryn (20s, early), who was less than four years into a tariff of over two decades, identified such 'home comforts'—including flannels, hairclips and being allowed more than seven sets of underwear—as crucial in keeping her 'linked with the real world'. Other early-stage prisoners listed audio-visual equipment, such as television, radio, CD players and sometimes games consoles, as 'luxuries' that made prison 'liveable'. The inclusion of phone calls home within prisoners' accounts of such 'extras' signalled the difficulty that some participants experienced in being able to access and afford such communications. In this regard, as O'Donnell (2014) notes, the initial phase of imprisonment is 'especially painful' because of the contrast between the prisoner's recent life, as a free citizen, and his or her restricted present (p. 207; see also Liebling et al. 2005).

During this period, then, prisoners were particularly aware of the comforts that were no longer available to them or to which their access was limited. As Carl explained, the initial period of imprisonment entailed a sharp encounter with the elemental deprivations and lack of autonomy of prison life:

> It went from being able to go to the shops and order whatever you wanted, to having to order your items once a week. For someone who is just coming into prison and who has never been in it before, it's a wake-up call, it's a shock. [...] To have your meals given to you at a certain time, I mean, you can be hungry at ten o'clock at night, and if you've got nothing to eat then tough shit! (Carl, 20s, early)

With regard to autonomy and control—to which we return in Chapter 5—while the deprivation of liberty was felt acutely in the remand stage, especially by those with no prior custodial experience, the realisation after the point of conviction that this state of confinement and restriction was to be endured indefinitely generated an extreme level of emotional distress:

> I spend every day doing something and then thinking, 'I'll just help my mum', 'I'll just go and see my mum', 'I'll just'- but there is no 'just' about it, there is no - this is the reality. And at the moment, I struggle with the reality. And, like I said, sometimes I do silly things and I get up at 2am to go to the toilet and forget that I'm actually locked in a cell. And for at least the next 25 years I can't get up and decide 'I'm going for a walk today'. I can't decide when I will and won't eat my meals. I can't decide when I will or won't go to bed. I am told what to do from the minute I get up until the minute I go to sleep. I have got to live by somebody else's rules, and I have got to do things in just a certain way. (Maria, 20s, early)

In relation to time, compared to female prisoners in the late stage of their sentence, those in the early stage rated as significantly more severe all three items of relevance, i.e. 'Feeling that your life has been wasted', 'Feeling that you are losing the best years of life' and 'Feeling that you have no purpose or meaning in your life' (see

Table 4.3). Among the male participants, as shown in Table 4.4, such differences did not always reach statistical significance, but the pattern of higher severity at the very early and early sentence stage was again clear. As we discuss in greater detail in Chapter 5, individuals at this point of their sentence felt life to be 'almost pointless' (Carl, 20s, early). Billy (20s, early), for example, described himself as: 'rotting […] Just existing for pretty much no purpose at all really'.

Similar to Williams' (2000: 43) observations of the relational impact of chronic illness, the consequences of the sentence for family members were often uppermost in the minds of our participants:

[When I was sentenced], all I was thinking about was my family and friends, and what effect it was going to have on them and on my little sister. When they said 'guilty', I looked to the box where my sister was in, and I just saw her crying […] and I just burst into tears. I just couldn't help it. It's very difficult. (Paul, 20s, early)

Such concerns were reflected in the survey data that formed the *Outside Relationships* dimension, where male and female prisoners in the very early and early stages of their sentences were particularly worried about the people they had left behind

Table 4.3 Mean 'severity' scores according to sentence stage for the dimension 'Time'—female prisoners

	Early (1-10)	Mid (2-3)	Late (5-6)
Feeling that your life has been wasted	19.50*L	11.33	9.67
Feeling that you are losing the best years of your life	18.10*L	16.33	8.67
Feeling that you have no purpose or meaning in your life	18.10**L	7.67	5.50

Table 4.4 Mean 'severity' scores according to sentence stage for the dimension 'Time'—male prisoners

	Very early	Early	Mid	Late	Post-tariff
Feeling that your life has been wasted	15.75	14.52	13.29	13.57	14.65
Feeling that you are losing the best years of your life	17.09**PT	16.02*PT	13.79	12.68	10.35
Feeling that you have no purpose or meaning in your life	8.14	6.57	6.24	6.21	7.70

on the outside, while also reporting 'missing social life' as a more severe problem than those further into their prison terms (see Tables 4.5 and 4.6).

Similarly, 'missing somebody' represented one of the most painful aspects of our participants' experiences—ranked first overall by the men and second overall by the women—and was rated as a more severe problem by men in the very early stage (the first sixth of the sentence) than at any other stage (see Table 4.7).

Explaining these experiences, and their greater severity at the early sentence stage, requires a twofold process: first, an analytic explanation of the dislocations that produced them and, second, a detailed account of their substance. To this end, the section that follows focuses on the existential and biographical consequences of receiving a long life sentence for murder as a young adult. The chapter then moves on to consider the affective dimensions of these experiences, particularly the specific forms of anger and grief that were generated by being convicted and sentenced.

Table 4.5 Mean 'severity' scores according to sentence stage for survey items 'Worrying about people outside' and 'Missing social life'—male prisoners

	Men's sentence stage				
	Very early	Early	Mid	Late	Post-tariff
Worrying about people outside	17.13**PT	15.99*PT	15.13	14.00	10.05
Missing social life	15.24***PT	13.64**PT	11.95	10.93	7.70

Table 4.6 Mean 'severity' scores according to sentence stage for survey items 'Worrying about people outside' and 'Missing social life'—female prisoners

	Women's sentence stage		
	Early (10)	Mid (3)	Late (6)
Worrying about people outside	21.60	18.00	12.67
Missing social life	14.90*L	19.67	6.83

Table 4.7 Mean 'severity' scores according to sentence stage for survey item 'Missing somebody' ('Deprivations' dimension)—male prisoners

	Men's sentence stage				
	Very early	Early	Mid	Late	Post-tariff
Missing somebody	19.55***PT	17.19***PT	17.56***PT	17.14**PT	10.20

Existential Dislocation and Biographical Rupture

Once the trial had finished, individuals were left scrabbling to make sense of what had happened within the broader context of their personal biographies. In particular, early-stage prisoners struggled to absorb the fact that the futures that they had anticipated had, in effect, been cancelled. Indeed, the extreme biographical fractures that were rendered by the sentence were often most acute when interviewees engaged in optimistic, counterfactual explorations of their ideal or expected futures prior to conviction. Such 'upward counterfactuals' (i.e. where imagined futures are 'better than reality' as it currently stands) (Boninger et al. 1994: 298) often mirrored conventional life goals, including such aspirations as going on regular holidays, starting a family, going to university and having a meaningful job. Narratives of this kind were found predominantly (but not exclusively) among those who, like Bethany and Jim, had no prior criminal record:

> We were going to go on holiday with [my boyfriend's] family in the August [before the murder]. And I said to him, 'I'm due my [contraceptive] injection in a couple of weeks. [...] Shall I stop taking it?' [...] And he was like, 'Yeah'. We were ready to start our own family. (Bethany, 20s, early)

> I had high aspirations. I was very motivated. Confidence bordering on over-confidence, looking back now. [...] I'd just turned 21 [and] I had the consumerist, capitalist ideal of being highly successful, highly wealthy, and I equated happiness to a large degree to that: acquiring as many assets as possible, all of these things. Having a good-looking girlfriend, having a good quality life. Those were the things at that time that I valued. (Tim, 20s, early)

In contrast, other interviewees described having had little or no vision of their future before coming into prison. Such lives were characterised by living 'day-to-day', in the kind of 'extended present' (O'Donnell 2014) that is more often associated with the experience of 'time' *inside* prison (see Chapter 8). For many of the women, particularly those with substance addictions, the everyday battle to survive the present had left no space for fantasies about a rosier future:

> *Did you have a vision of your future at all?*
> No, I never - I wasn't even thinking about the future, I was just thinking about each day, and getting through each day. Because the months and weeks before my crime

happened, I was drinking every day, I was using cannabis, so it was just 'Where are we going to get money from for tomorrow?' I never imagined what my future would be like or anything like that - I was just living day-to-day, just surviving from one day to the next. (Eileen, 30s, late)

Oscar (late teens, early) likewise described 'living in the moment' prior to his imprisonment, explaining that his thoughts of the future extended only to spending time with friends and having enough money in his pockets to 'go out and have a good time'. Having been a prolific drug user from the age of thirteen, he had rarely considered the years ahead of him: 'I never thought about it, to be honest with you - [I was] off my face most of the time'. Having served several short custodial terms prior to his life sentence, the only certainty of his anticipated future was that he would be at some point reincarcerated: 'I knew I was coming back to jail at some point'.

Nonetheless, his current sentence represented a substantial shock because of his assumption that his criminal career would continue to involve relatively petty offending and short sentences: 'I never thought I'd be back in jail for this long'. Such comments were echoed across the accounts of those who had been incarcerated previously. That is, while they had regarded imprisonment as almost inevitable, they had not foreseen a conviction for murder and the resulting life sentence. Martin, for example—two years into a 25-year tariff—noted that he:

… expected to come back to prison someday. […] But not for what I am here for. […] Probably for a drugs offence, maybe a fight or something - I never ever thought that I would get more than four or five years. (Martin, 20s, early)

In this sense, then, however participants depicted their anticipated futures, being awarded a very long life sentence produced a significant existential and biographical rupture.

The relational consequences of this breach were varied and far-reaching, as we discuss in greater detail in Chapter 6. The burden carried by the families of serious offenders (see Condry 2007) was not lost on those serving such terms—for example, Maria (20s, early) noted the pain of realising that 'you're not the only one that's being punished - your whole family is being punished too'. As Zubair likewise explained, one of the most difficult aspects of the early stage of his sentence was seeing the deterioration in his parents' health and the burden of feeling responsible for their decline:

> My dad was a big man. And he comes to see me now and he's skinny, he's lost weight - I can see he's aged with all the stress he's under just thinking about me. Same with my mum [...] You start thinking 'It's them that are going through the hard time, not us'. (Zubair, 20s, early)

Often, the temporal dimension of the tariff was thrown into sharpest relief when prisoners considered its impact on family members. Prisoners who were parents described the pain of knowing they would miss the entirety of a son or daughter's childhood and adolescence. Christopher (20s, mid) explained that one of the hardest aspects of his 17-year tariff was 'thinking about [my] kids growing up without me' and the tendency, in the initial sentence phase, to ruminate on the 'stuff that you'll probably miss'. Terrance (20s, early) described a recurring nightmare in which he could hear his young child crying, beyond a wall too high for him to surmount. Those without children reported fears about whether their parents would live to see them released and whether they would ever again spend time with family members in conditions of freedom. Zubair recalled returning to his cell, after being sentenced to a 30-year tariff, and immediately working out the age his parents would be at his earliest possible release date: 'I was like, "Shit, dad's gonna be *this* old, my mum is gonna be *that* old"'. Accordingly, the severity scores for the problem 'Being afraid that someone you love or care about will die before you are released' was highest for men and women in the early sentence stage compared to other phases (for women: early 17.90, mid 8.33, late 12.17; for men: very early 14.30, early 13.44, mid 11.25, late 10.71, post-tariff 10.00).

In some cases, relational disconnection was instigated at the behest of the person serving the sentence, as Ashley explained:

> [When I first came in] I didn't give a fuck about the world anymore, I didn't care about outside. I was cutting myself off from out there, and I didn't want any connection with it. I hardly had visits when I first came in. My girlfriend, she would always come and see me [...] but I didn't want any connection with the outside and I tried telling her 'Just go away - just live your life and leave me alone', and she wouldn't. I didn't want any connection with anything. (Ashley, 30s, mid)

While Ashley's relationship had survived, other participants described terminating intimate relationships following their sentencing. While appearing to represent an act of altruism for the partner, such acts also served to safeguard prisoners from anxieties relating to infidelity or fading love:

> I just had to end it, cos it was not fair. I couldn't expect that to happen. And I'd just always have in the back of my head that something was happening outside. Like, I'd start getting paranoid and stuff and that's not- I used to see people and they were shouting down the phones and arguing with their girlfriend, and I thought 'that's not for me'. (Scott, 30s, mid)

In most instances, however, family members, intimate partners and the majority of friends drifted or moved purposefully away from those serving such sentences. As Earl (20s, early) noted: 'when you have a longer sentence, people *do* forget about you'. In some situations, these decisions were out of the hands of the prisoner—in some cases, for example, friends and relatives had broken off contact because of the nature of the offence. Bethany (20s, early), who had been convicted of the murder of a family member, reported being 'basically disowned' by her relatives, who said she 'deserved to rot' in prison. Harry (30s, mid) explained that he and his family were no longer in contact as a direct result of the terms of his index offence ('my mum [...] got involved in my case and she picked a side. [...] I've never heard from her since'), while Richard (50s, post-tariff) likewise had no contact whatsoever with the outside world, because of the moral repugnance felt by his family members in relation to his offence.

As well as dislocating prisoners from their anticipated future, and from their existing relational ties, the experience of being convicted of murder also forced many participants to confront a radical threat to their self-concept. As we discuss specifically in Chapter 7, in the wake of a murder conviction, prisoners had to come to terms with the shattering of their sense of self and social identity, and find some way of reconstituting biographical selfhood. The profundity of these ruptures produced a range of affective responses that we discuss in the section below.

The Affective Dimensions of Long Indeterminate Sentences

Anger

Terms such as frustration, aggression and anger are often used interchangeably outside clinical contexts, and sociological analyses of prison life are no exception (e.g. Toch and Adams 2002; Toch et al. 1989). However, decades of work on the psychology of emotions have sought to differentiate between such notions, conceptualising 'anger' as a toxic combination of negative emotional reactions including frustration, aggression, distress, reproach and shame, and a desire to identify 'blame-worthy agents', i.e. those assumed to be causally responsible for these negative affective outcomes (Clore and Centerbar 2004: 139). Indeed, Averill (1983 cit. in Quigley and Tedeschi 1996: 280) suggests that 'more than anything else [anger] is an attribution of blame'.

Indeed, over time (sometimes hours, sometimes years), prisoners found that their initial sense of shock, numbness and dissociation gave way to an avalanche of affective reactions, among which 'anger' was primary:

> First few hours [post-conviction] like… the first few minutes I was just shocked, obviously. But the first couple of hours after that? I was [emphasises] *Pissed. Off.* Man, like, I was mad - nothing but hate in me. (Errol, 20s, early)

> *How did you feel when you were given your sentence?*
> Obviously I was devastated, yeah. […] Then I was pissed […] I was angry, I was upset, you get me? (Kendrick, 20s, early)

Here, there are clear parallels with Kübler-Ross' (1969, 2014) work on the 'stages of grief' (see also Kübler-Ross and Kessler 2005).[4] While heavily contested, particularly in its most proscriptive forms (see, e.g., Fitchett 1980; Stroebe et al. 2017), this theoretical framework for making sense of loss shares common ground with the experiences of young life-sentenced prisoners. As with terminally ill individuals trying to come to terms with their own mortality (see Jewkes 2005), early-stage

---

[4]These are denial, anger, bargaining, depression and acceptance (Kübler-Ross 1969; Kübler-Ross and Kessler 2014).

lifers found that, as numbness and disbelief receded, the emotions that had previously been held at bay flooded in, with anger 'at the front of the line' (Kübler-Ross and Kessler 2005: 11). In some cases, such anger could best be understood as what Archer (2003: 299) has described as the 'exclusively affective' rage of the 'fractured reflexive', serving little purpose beyond the 'expressive'. For example, Bethany (20s, early), who was serving an 18-year tariff, described regularly screaming at short-term prisoners, who 'took the piss' by complaining to her about their sentences. In this sense, like the narratives of shock and dissociation described above, such descriptions were rarely connected to meaningful action or 'instrumental guidance' about the way to move on from such feelings. More commonly, however, and in line with Clore and Centerbar's (2004) reflections, when states of shock and numbness gave way to despair and frustration, expressions of 'anger' tended to involve disavowal of responsibility for the victim's death and the externalisation of blame.

In the early sentence stage, responsibility for the deeply negative affect experienced by our participants was frequently directed at 'the system'. That is, feelings of anger were linked to the perceived illegitimacy of the conviction and sentence. For example, Martin explained that his anger at being found guilty stemmed from a combination of despair at the outcome of the trial coupled with a sense of injustice about a process that he perceived to be faulty in convicting him:

> Of course I feel angry! I am here for something that I have never done. [...] I don't deserve to be here. [...] Even the judge said to the jury that there is no evidence against me - there is nothing that says that I was there [...] there's nothing that says I am even involved. [The judge said] it is 'highly likely' that I wasn't even a part of it. And I *still* get found 'guilty'. (Martin, 20s, early)

This tendency to implicate 'the system' as blame-worthy agent and object of anger was common among individuals like Martin who had been convicted under the principles of joint enterprise.

Typically, what mattered to such prisoners was not the procedural fairness of the trial, but rather the perceived injustice of the law itself—its 'legal illegitimacy' (Hulley et al. 2019)—and its extreme outcome.[5] In this regard, anger was almost

---

[5] In this sense, the experiences documented here diverge from findings within classic studies of 'procedural justice' (e.g. Tyler 1980, 2003) which suggest that the key factor shaping perceptions of the actions of the legal apparatus relates to the 'fairness of the processes used when dealing with them' (Tyler 2003: 283). Such

exclusively linked to the feeling that the conviction and sentence length were unfair because the law itself was unjust, driving forms of conduct that were emotionally highly charged (see Beijersbergen et al. 2015). For example, when asked if he had settled into his sentence, Andre—who had been given an 18-year tariff at the age of 15—responded that he went 'through stages' of acting 'mad' whenever he thought about the length of his prison term:

> For six months I'll be alright, and then I'll lose it and then I'll lose it for, like, six months, and then I get it back [...] Like, for instance, if I get up in the morning and say 'fuck it... fuck it, that's it'. That day I'm gonna cause havoc [...] Once I go to 'Basic' and I don't have no TV, I don't stop.[6]
>
> *Right, because?*
>
> I've nothing to lose at all. [...] [When I think about my sentence], that's when I just come up and do something mad. (Andre, late teens, early)

Having identified himself as being caught up in a murder case in which they 'don't know who done it', Andre did not consider himself to be legally guilty of the murder. As a result, he felt compelled to 'do something' to justify his imprisonment and redress the imbalance caused by the perceived unfairness of his conviction ('I'm saying to myself "I'm in jail for something I haven't done, so I might as well [do something]"') (see Adams 1965, cit. in Beijersbergen et al. 2015 on equity theory). Here, then, perceptions of injustice among early-stage prisoners generated considerable anger and non-compliance.[7]

Physical manifestations of anger and attempts to manage perceived injustices were not only evident in externalised aggression and rule-breaking, but also in violence acted out upon the self. Tamara (20s, early), who said that she 'didn't really self-harm too much outside [prison]', explained how her anger at 'society' was internalised in the form of self-injury. In other cases, early-stage prisoners' accusations of responsibility both for their anger and for their predicament were

---

theories indicate that people are 'not so much concerned with the outcomes they receive in encounters with authorities [...] [than with] the fairness of the procedures and the interpersonal treatment they receive in these encounters' at the system level (Beijersbergen et al. 2015: 198). However, when the stakes are as high as two or three decades of incarceration, the consideration of process seems likely to be trumped by assessments of the law itself and the outcomes it generates.

[6] 'Basic': the lowest level of the system's incentives and earned privileges scheme ('basic', 'standard' and 'enhanced').

[7] Our analysis helps account for why disciplinary infractions tend to be more common during prisoners' initial sentence stages (see, e.g., Toch and Adams 1989).

also directed at victims themselves. Stephen (20s, mid), who had served half of his 16-year tariff, explained that, at the start of his sentence, he was 'angry with the victim [...] I was looking to blame him'. In some respects, this mirrors the tendency of people who are bereaved to feel anger towards the deceased (e.g. see Maercker et al. 1998). Here, however, anger was directed towards the person for whose death its bearer was deemed at least partly responsible.

The complexity of such feelings was evident from Maria's reflections on the anger she felt towards her victim, whom she had killed following what she described as a serious sexual assault. Only ten months into a 25-year tariff, Maria (20s, mid) explained that her resentment towards her assailant was overshadowed by the anger she felt towards herself because her actions meant that he would never be 'brought to justice' for what he had done to her: taking his life meant that 'all the bad things he ever did [become] non-existent [...] I will live with those scars alone'. In the main though, the primary function of anger was to keep at bay other, potentially overwhelming, emotions—specifically shame and remorse. In this sense, the victim served as a scapegoat for feelings of guilt and responsibility that, as Asad notes, prisoners were unable or unwilling to acknowledge:

I was angry when I got my sentence, I was *really* angry.
Angry at the world, or angry at the judge, angry at the victim, or just generally angry?
Generally angry. I was angry [pauses] - I was angry with me, I was angry with how my life turned out. Deep down, I know I had a lot more potentially in my life, to do so much more, so much good with my life, that it was a sad sight. And because I had no one else to blame, I couldn't blame myself. Or I could, but I didn't want to, so I was just angry. Yes, I was angry with myself, but I didn't want to admit that to myself [...] Because at that time I can't see no light at the end of the tunnel, and I'm just thinking 'I guess jail is me for the rest of my life', innit? 'This is as good as it gets for me'. (Asad, 30s, mid)

Asad's reflections on the nebulous sense of despair and resentment that he had felt during the initial years of his sentence indicate how anger was often a displacement or deflection of acutely unpalatable truths about the self. As reported in other studies of convicted homicide perpetrators (e.g. Irwin 2009; Adshead et al. 2015), however, internal conversations acknowledging the root of such feelings were relatively rare during the initial years of incarceration. We return to such matters in Chapter 5.

Grief Reactions and Intrusive Recollections

A plethora of studies attest to the experience of post-traumatic stress reactions among individuals affected by homicide or attempted homicide, focusing in particular on the family members of homicide victims (e.g. Clements and Burgess 2002; Wickie and Marwit 2001; Kashka and Beard 1999). Much less work explores what Pollock (2000: 176) describes as the 'spectrum of reactions to involvement in the killing of another', including when the perpetrator reports being 'shocked, experiencing disbelief akin to being traumatized by involvement in the event itself' (p. 176). Yet it was clear from our interviews that the death that had given rise to the conviction often left deep psychological scars on the perpetrators of, or secondary parties to, the killing.

Participants commonly described symptoms consistent with the clinical criteria for acute stress disorder (see Bryant et al. 2015), which were both psychological and physiological, and were felt both in the immediate aftermath of the murder and during the years that followed:

> It's only, maybe, days later or whatever time later that these images come forward to the surface, and the emotion then comes up and then you vomit, you may shake, you may cry. (Ivan, 50s, post-tariff)

As Michenbaum (1996, cit. in Pollock 2000) notes, acts of homicide are often 'indelibly etched' on the minds of their perpetrators. In some cases, participants cried as they recalled the details of the offence, often many years after the event. Sylvester, who had served eight years of an 18-year tariff, broke down as he talked of his shock and grief in the aftermath of killing his own partner:

> I was just - in my mind, I was in shock. So I was standing there all stressed and I got my mate, and I was so nervous. And he said, 'What's going on?' and I said, 'Oh, I think I killed her. I think she's dead'. [...] I was so upset - and I get in the shower and there was blood on my face. I was so shocked. I was so nervous and just so upset. That time I was so upset, I was so angry, sad, scared. (Sylvester, 30s, mid)

Such observations are consistent with the literature on 'complicated grief'; a term which relates to the ways in which an individual's initial grief reactions following bereavement are not—in clinical terms—'integrated', resulting in a 'persistent disturbing sense of disbelief regarding the death' (Shear and Shair 2005: 253). This sense of disbelief was common among prisoners in the study, many of whom recognised the moral complexity of grieving for a death that they had caused.

Others described shock, dissociation and amnesia as dominating any attempt to recall the index offence. In a particularly graphic account, Jonathan recounted 'blanking out' during the attack and then being 'shocked' by what he had done once his 'rage' had subsided and he was 'back in control':

> I'm just a normal guy and [pauses] It was an accident. [...] It weren't a planned murder. [...] I know it was over the top.
> *And I would imagine that the drugs and the alcohol probably had quite a lot to do with that...?*
> Yeah. And the steroids and stuff. [...] I just went in some sort of rage I never felt before. And then when I realised what I'd done, and, like, obviously, I'd just...I'd blanked out, couldn't stop hitting him. I knew what I was doing but I couldn't control myself from doing it, and then when I got back in control I was shocked, like. I had blood all over my[self]. And I was, like, 'Fucking hell - what have I done here?' and run, you know? (Jonathan, 20s, early)

Jonathan's emphasis on being 'a normal guy', and the pains taken to distinguish his own actions from that of a 'planned murder', was indicative of a broader pattern. Although a small minority of young participants talked with some degree of indifference or bravado about their offence, none expressed pride or pleasure; few stated that they had intended to kill. Far more often, offence narratives were 'confrontation gone wrong' and conflict that 'went too far'. Both Maria and Ivan, for example, described altercations with people who had abused them which had gone irrevocably beyond what was intended:

> All I wanted to do [in attacking him] was get away - it never *once* entered my head that he was actually hurt [pauses] I did what I did with a reason, but I never intended for it to end the way it did. (Maria, 20s, early)

> My intention was to go back and confront [my abuser]. But it's almost like you're working on automatic. [Pauses] All the things that we had done together - all the nasty things, all the intimate things, whatever - came to the surface in multi-coloured of sounding, and it was just too much all at once, and my head just exploded, so I [pauses] unfortunately, I killed her. (Ivan, 50s, post-tariff)

The extent to which such claims were forms of neutralisation, or 'cover stories' that helped align events with narratives of self (Adshead 2011), is difficult to tell, although it was clear that many prisoners sought to ward off the implications of accepting full responsibility for the index offence as a means of demonstrating ethical selfhood. We return to these issues in Chapter 7. For current purposes, the aim is to highlight the complex cluster of emotions that related to matters of morality, culpability and grief, and the enduring, affective preoccupation with the experience of the index offence that many participants described.

Distressing dreams connected to the death of the victim were particularly common—and especially acute—in the initial years of the sentence. As Cary (20s, early) stated, 'Everyone has nightmares. Whoever tells you not, they'll be lying'. Ashley (30s, mid) described being haunted by 'terrible nightmares' about his mother being killed in front of him as revenge for the murder he had committed, while Sean—a year and a half into a 19-year tariff—explained that he dreamt about his victim repeatedly:

> I've been having fucking dreams, haven't I? *Every* night I have a dream. [In one dream] I've been running over a field that was wet and I fell. Like, I fell in a hole, yeah, and I was just drowning and drowning, yeah, and I've looked up and the police was there, and [the victim] was there and I begged him - *begged* him - for getting me out. And I woke up. [...] But they're so *real.* (Sean, 20s, early)

Such visions were not limited to the realm of sleep, sometimes taking the form of intrusive recollections: 'involuntary' and distressing memories experienced while awake.[8] Most commonly, these took the form of 'dissociative flashbacks', which Hackmann et al. (2004: 232) describe as not simply 'recall' of a traumatic event, but episodes where an individual 'loses all awareness of present surroundings, and literally appears to relive the experience'. Re-experiencing the events of the murder 'as if they were features of something happening right now, rather than being aspects of memories from the past' (p. 232) was relatively common, particularly among female participants:

> I was having these flashbacks [in my cell] and these horrible nightmares, and I didn't get it; I didn't understand why I was standing there with a knife, or why a knife,

---

[8] Such experiences fall within the *DSM-V* clinical diagnosis of both acute stress reaction (cf. Bryant et al. 2015) and post-traumatic stress disorder (cf. Pai et al. 2017).

why [the victim] was on top of me and it was all very, very confusing and I didn't understand. (Nadia, 20s, early)

I suffer with PTSD [post-traumatic stress-disorder], and I have done all through my sentence. [...] I just was living in fear of my next flashback and going back to that [room where the victim died]. [...] If I was locked in the cell at night, it was as if I was there and I could see it, and it was like my victim was there in front of me, and I could see it, and I just couldn't get it out of my head, it was just constant. (Jenny, 20s, mid)

Flashbacks often extended beyond the visual, into highly sensual auditory and olfactory experiences:

It was like it was happening again, I was there all over again; I could smell it, I could hear it, I could see it. Sometimes, I could feel the heat, I'd feel the heat [of the victim set on fire]. (Jenny, 20s, mid)

That was when I was struggling with hearing voices and ... well, hearing my victim. It wasn't hearing voices, it was hearing my victim. (Tori, 30s, mid)

For others, particularly those convicted under joint enterprise as secondary parties, it was the shock of witnessing, rather than being the primary perpetrator of, the index offence that haunted them. Jill (40s, post-tariff), for example, complained that she had never had counselling 'for the fact that I watched two brutal murders', involving someone being stabbed at least 'sixty, seventy times', while Zufar explained that, in addition to trying to come to terms with his 25-year tariff, he was struggling to process having watched someone be killed:

[The primary offender] stabbed the other victim 12 times, I believe. I was there when it all happened, which was the first time I ever seen such a thing. [...] I'm suffering flashbacks, get flashbacks from the event what happened. I pray to god every day that it goes away; I don't want it to be with me for the rest of my life. (Zufar, 20s, early)

Zufar was among the minority of early-stage prisoners who reflected at length about the murder and its 'ripple effects', the impact of which was evident in his emphasis in the final line of the following quotation:

I would often just be thinking about the event and [...] how someone my age didn't deserve to die - I think about that. And one thing that I *really* think about is his parents - I wonder how the family of the guy [trails off]. That's something that really, really, really, really affects me - it *really* affects me.

Taken together, these reflections on intrusive recollections and 'complicated grief' help to illustrate the psychic enormity of the offence of murder: that is, the psychological and physiological implications of being directly or indirectly involved in someone else's death. While felt most acutely during the early sentence stage, the ongoing impact of such experiences demonstrates the salience of the offence itself, as well as the sentence length that resulted from it, to the experiences of long-term lifers. Indeed, the ways in which such individuals made sense of, defended against, and—eventually—coped with their sentences can only be understood by first acknowledging the initial struggle to process the permanent and enduring nature of being responsible for someone's death and being imprisoned for such a long period.

Surviving the Early Stage

For the reasons outlined above, participants consistently described the initial years of their sentence as a period of time to be *survived*: a situation that was managed—with greater or lesser success—through a range of reactive defences. Among our participants, these practical and psychic mechanisms were complex and multifarious and alert us to the inadequacy, in this context, of the conventional literature on prisoners' adaptive responses to the pains of imprisonment, which have generally been conceptualised in terms of compensatory social dynamics such as solidarity and exploitation, or forms of individualised resistance (see, e.g., Sykes 1958; Crewe 2009; Ugelvik 2014). In the section that follows, we describe the range of reactive forms that prisoners adopted and enacted as a way of seeking to survive the chaos and 'tumult' (cf. O'Donnell 2014) of the early years of their sentences.

Suppression

Cramer (2000) identifies the act of suppression as an important and 'high adaptive' psychic defence mechanism. It is, Vaillant (1994: 45) argues, 'far more than a simple neglect or repression of reality'; rather, it is a form of mental cognizance which allows painful affective feeling and situations to be acknowledged at certain times and suppressed at others. This separates it from the less mature defence of 'repression', in which conscious awareness of raw emotions and realities is banished *in toto*. For many participants, then, being consciously able to dull or suppress their awareness of where they were and how much time they had to serve was critical to psychological and physical survival. For example:

> If it's too stressful to think about, I just don't think about it. (Liz, 20s, early)

> The less aware you are [in the first years] the easier it is to deal with, innit? [...] Blank nothingness—that's what gets you through. And if you can put yourself in that kind of state, that's how you survive. (Neil, 30s, mid)

As we discuss in more detail in Chapter 8, psychological retreat from the pains of the early years was often achieved through temporal suppression. In a similar vein, as described in the quotations below, the use of substances served to 'kill' or 'numb' the implications of being given a life sentence[9]:

> For the first few years of prison, I always had something in. I was on prescribed drugs anyway, but then if there was [illicit] drugs we'd have it; if there was heroin there, we'd smoke it.
> *And why were you taking the drugs then, do you think?*
> I suppose, like, to kill reality (Jill, 40s, post-tariff)

> I can remember I was smashed enough every day, off my face. [...] And I didn't care. [...] It was making me feel lovely.
> *And what does it make you feel like?*
> Numb. That numbing effect. [...] Like everything was gone. (Nadia, 20s, early)

---

[9] Notably too, some participants reported having been forcibly medicated in their early sentence phase, seemingly as a means of managing their behaviour rather than treating a specific diagnosis. Nathan (30s, mid) described being 'fed drugs' as a means of securing his compliance ('They just [...] medicate you, until you're not a problem anymore'), while Carly (30s, post-tariff) identified her experience of being medicated on Largactil—an anti-pscychotic drug—as a standard institutional response at that time to those with long-life sentences ('back then, if you've come in for a big sentence, [the response was] "Just drug 'em up", kind of thing. And that was just normal').

Substance use was effective not only for suppressing the reality of the sentence, but also for avoiding contemplation of the offence. Brian (40s, late) recalled that, during the initial months and years, he 'was probably stoned most of the time' to avoid thinking about 'what I'd done'. Similarly, when asked why he had taken drugs during the early stage of his sentence, Victor replied:

> I think it was just to get rid of all of my memories that I had, because on top of all my past and everything like that, I had on top of me murder as well. It's like the shame inside of me. (Victor, 30s, post-tariff)

Kendrick, who was four years into a 29-year tariff, believed that, without marijuana to calm him down and help 'block out' reality, he would have taken his own life during the first month of his sentence:

> That first night, like, I ended up I was feeling suicidal, you get me? I never did do anything, but those thoughts that ran through from my head – 'I ain't lived for that long, so how am I going to be in jail that long?' […] But around those times I had weed. So I suppose if I didn't have that then, I don't know [if I would still be alive], you get me? Obviously, I'd smoked it and it calmed me down - I'd say for the first month after I got sentenced, I was smoking that whole time. It was like blocking everything out. (Kendrick, 20s, early)

In this example, Kendrick identified drugs as his saviour, and certainly suppression was adaptive in the short term in ensuring physical and psychological survival. However, when reflecting on such methods of 'seeking refuge' or 'maintaining sanity', many individuals beyond the early stages regarded them as ultimately mal-adaptive (see Toch and Adams 1989), in that they represented a retreat from, rather than engagement with, meaningful and sustainable problem-solving behaviours. Jill (40s, post-tariff), for example, commented that: 'I couldn't say I was 'coping' back then. I suppose I was just hiding. Hiding behind the drugs, anti-depressants, whatever'.

A second means of suppression existed in the form of non-suicidal self-harm. This was a heavily gendered phenomenon. Female participants were much more likely than male participants to have self-harmed or attempted to take their own life before coming into prison (67% of women compared to 15% of men). Additionally, almost six times as many of the women compared to the men reported self-harming or making an attempt against their own life during their current sentence (89% compared to 15%, respectively). In some instances, self-harm within the initial years of the sentence was a means of suppressing intrusive and involuntary thoughts. This is consistent with Suyemoto's (1998) assertion that self-mutilation is a form of 'affect regulation' which 'stems from the need to express or control anger, anxiety, or pain that cannot be expressed verbally or through other means' (p. 537). Similarly, Haines and Williams (2003) regard self-mutilation as a behaviour used by individuals who have no other viable strategies of affect management. For our participants, deliberate, non-suicidal self-injury very often represented a means to convey or suppress extreme distress, very often linked to feelings of guilt, as Carly explained:

> When [the guilt] started to hit me, like kind of thing, I couldn't cope. [...] [In the first years] my head was just messed up. [...] I tried- oh my god, I tried, like, [pauses] Oh god, it just sounds really mad! I was looking in mirrors and hoping that I would see the victim, so I could talk to them. [...] It was just really messed up crap, and [pauses] that's when I started cutting myself. I started hurting myself in ways as well, you know, like stupid madness things? Like hitting myself with batteries on my knees and everything. (Carly, 30s, post-tariff)

Rather than being more actively directed to a set of goals, as in the forms of 'sublimation' that we discuss below, such acts were primarily motivated by avoidance.

Escape

While many individuals tried to suppress reality, others sought to escape it. One means of doing so was through self-isolation: withdrawing from the social milieu of the prison and retreating into a private world as a means of 'maintaining sanity' (cf. Toch and Adams 1989, 2002: 133). Eileen (30s, late), for example, described having become 'a bit of a recluse' in the first six months of her sentence, cutting off all family contact as a 'way of coping' with the feelings of shame at having let down her parents: 'It took me six months to actually phone my dad and say, "Hi, I'm still alive, I'm okay". [...] I couldn't cope. I couldn't cope with the fact that I'd let [them] down again'.

For others, retreat from family members and prison peers was linked to mental health problems precipitated by the sentence:

The first year was remand, so I was thinking I was going home. [...]. The second year just after I got my sentence, it was hard - that was a hard year. I was trying to shut people off or shut people out of my life.
And why were you doing that?
I was depressed, man. [...] I think I was going through a bad case of depression. (Julius, 30s, mid)

Can you remember the first few days after that, and how you felt?
I didn't come out of my room, I just stayed in bed; I just didn't want to do anything. [...] I was in healthcare for a couple of nights, because I literally just didn't eat, I couldn't speak. [...] I just kept myself in my room. (Tamara, 20s, early)

Other forms of 'escape' were intended to be more permanent, as Jared explained:

It was a couple of weeks after I got sentenced. [...] I remember sitting on the yard one morning with two fellas and I said to them like, 'How would you feel if you [had 25 years to serve at the age of 19]?' [...] They both said, 'Well, put it this way, I wouldn't be here right now'. [...] I went back to my cell and for about three weeks I planned on hanging myself, and I did end up hanging myself. [...] I did try and kill myself a few times. (Jared, 20s, early)

Similar to Jared, Darrin (late teens, early) explained that the prospect of spending his twenties and thirties in prison had led him to consider taking his own life because there seemed 'no point in living anymore', while Karen's despair at being 'asked to do a sentence longer than I'd actually lived' caused her to attempt suicide:

I was adamant that I was just going to kill myself, because [...] I was very depressed, very angry. [...] I remember drinking a whole 100 grams of Nescafe, with about *that* much water [indicates an inch against the side of a mug], because I read in the newspaper that a girl died of a heart attack after drinking fourteen espressos. [...]. Then I tried to slit my wrists a few times. (Karen, 20s, mid)

For others, such plans were related to feelings of guilt and shame, as well as despair at the prospect of long-term confinement:

My last two or three attempts [with ligatures] were suicidal - I tied a ligature quite bad. [...] My impulse then was on self-destruct. I wanted to hurt myself because I didn't wanna ever hurt anybody else again. I wanted to hurt myself.

And why did you want to hurt yourself so much?
Cause I'd murdered somebody. I had taken somebody's life who... who had a whole
life ahead of her. (Tori, 30s, mid)

I never had any intention of serving the sentence - I never had any inkling I was
going to do it. My plan was to commit suicide; that's what I'd planned, and I just
thought, 'as soon as I get an opportunity, I'm going to do it'. [...] And bearing in
mind that I'd killed somebody, I was full of guilt and remorse, and confusion and
[pauses]. You know, I'd just had a baby, and all my life I'd just [pauses]. My life had
finished, and also I'd finished someone else's life, you know? I'd ended two lives by
my actions, so I was in a bad place mentally, I really was. (Stuart, 40s, post-tariff)

Finally, the intention or consideration of self-inflicted death was identified as a
means of escape for both the prisoner and their loved ones: a way of relieving
families and friends of the burden of an individual's offence and subsequent incarceration. In this respect, and as a way of communicating the web of affective
reactions experienced by young lifers, Arshad is worth quoting at length:

The thought [of taking my life] came through my head- when I thought 'This is
it for me', you know. That was when the first visit came, and I saw my mum and
everyone. And dad, he was broken. I've never seen my dad cry, but he was broken.
I seen my missus crying her eyes out [...] I seen her stomach, you know, she was
giving birth soon. It was hard to bear, that first few days. And then as soon as the
conviction happened, I thought 'I'll never see my little girl... I'm never going to be
able to take you out, never going to be able to do all this stuff that a father wants
to', you know? [...] And I'm thinking 'Can I handle this, can I do this, can I put
on a brave face and phone home and say "oh, don't worry about it, everything's
cool?"' [...] I remember going back to my cell and sitting there thinking 'Would it
be easier [if I died]? Can I just put an end to all this - this headache, this heartache?'.
It nearly got to that stage where I really was considering it. [...] I was in a bad place.
(Arshad, 30s, late)

The virtual ubiquity of suicidal ideation among early-stage prisoners was startling:

I think everyone who gets a life sentence probably spends the first year or so secretly
debating whether they are going to actually do the sentence or not, [...] in terms
of suicide. (Rafe, 30s, mid).

This is quite a bleak question, but have you ever thought about hurting yourself or?
Yeah, everyone thinks about that, but I would never kill myself. I have thought about it, yeah I might as well just kill myself… there is no point. […] Just randomly you think like that, there's no point in living anymore. I might as well kill myself. (Darrin, 20s, early)

Meanwhile, a large number of participants reported periods of depression, the gravity of which they often identified only in retrospect: 'deep, deep depression' (Kenny, mid); 'I was a lot depressed, a lot' (Jared, early). Some who were still in the early years of the sentence expressed doubt that they would be able to cope with many more years in prison ('There's certain days or weeks where I would be, fucking, "How am I supposed to do this?" [Hugo, early]; others declared that they did not want to cope:

If I end up having to do this whole sentence I am not going to want to go on. […] I am 21 now, I have not even done 21 years outside, so I have got to do that and more inside, so there's no point. […] I would rather die in here than go out, if I have to do that length of time. It is pointless. (Martin, 20s, early)

As we discuss in the chapter that follows, the fact that, for our participants, such intentions were not executed demonstrates that such phases of deep depression were, mostly, overcome.

'Jailing'

The term 'jailing' has been used by a number of scholars to refer to an adaptive style of 'making a world out of prison' (Irwin 1970: 74) by seeking positions of influence, engaging in illicit activity (Toch and Adams 1989) and related activities such as fighting, trade and involvement in volatile relationships—what Owen (1998) refers to as being 'in the mix'. Along with suppression and escape, 'jailing'— particularly through committed involvement in the informal economy or activities such as stealing, accruing contraband and using drugs recreationally—represented the principal activity in the defensive repertoire of many early-stage prisoners.

Many participants—particularly male prisoners—reported (or intimated) that they had engaged actively and continually in the prison's informal economy in the initial period of their sentence, from sourcing extra canteen items and tobacco to the procurement of pornography, mobile phones and drugs[10] Such pursuits were generally motivated by a desire to regain some small sense of control and make prison life more comfortable and survivable. Willis (30s, mid), for example, described how he had traded in drugs at the start of his sentence because it was his only means of accessing the 'creature comforts' he was missing. For others, such as Christopher (20s, mid), trade was a way of maintaining self-respect, enabling him to purchase expensive clothes ('keep fresh') and helping him provide for his family and their material needs ('the kids are getting older. They need more stuff. Shit's expensive outside').

For such prisoners, the parole date was 'not really relevant … it's too far away' (Ignacio, 20s, early), and the benefits of involvement in trade outweighed any possible costs:

> *If they said to you 'you definitely will have to serve an extra three or four years for doing this', would you still be doing it?*
> Yeah. Cos then I'd get it and I'd live comfortably. […] Like, when I get out I would still live comfortably. […] I'd rather come out sitting on a load of money than come out and have to get a nine-to-five job. (Ignacio, 20s, early)

Others expressed an underlying attitude that there was 'nothing to lose' from such activities: that you would 'only gain from it' (Andre, late teens, early). Core to Andre's belief was both that the likelihood of being caught was low and that punishments were meaningless in the context of the length of the sentence, especially relative to the potential benefits:

> I got caught on visits getting [drugs] in. I got seven days block [segregation], four days losses [of privileges]. […] Cause I'm a lifer, the only thing I actually can get is block.
> *And does that not matter to you?*
> No. […] You're gonna make sixteen hundred pounds off one package. On the road,[11] you would have made five hundred pounds, so it's more than double the money. (Andre, late teens, early)

---

[10] A much wider group of participants 'dabbled' in such activities in minor ways, but here, our discussion is about more committed involvement in *sub rosa* activity.

[11] 'On road' or 'on the road': outside prison, often indicating a criminal lifestyle.

Comments of this kind were indicative of the general sense of nihilism among many early-stage prisoners, expressed in phrases such as 'not giving a shit' (Ignacio, 20s, early) or having 'nothing to live for at all' (Ashley, 30s, mid). Diego, who was two and a half years into his 28-year tariff, exemplified this attitude:

> When I first came in, I always had a phone, always had drugs and was always selling drugs so I was occupied. Didn't care about nothing, didn't give a shit about nothing. (Diego, 20s, early)

The tone of such claims represented a form of 'lucid indifference' (Camus 1954: 94): a tactical disregard designed to ward off or mitigate existential fears and uncertainties. Put another way, 'in an absurd world, one that is unpredictable and continually threatens the self' (Douglas 1984: 85), the individual seeks to detach from painful experiences by professing defiance and indifference. In refusing to 'invest his [or her] positive emotions in the world [...] vital emotions are saved from destruction' (Douglas 1984: 85), Ignacio, for example, claimed that, when sentenced, he 'just didn't give a shit at all, I really didn't' (Ignacio, 20s, early). Other prisoners, in recalling having been 'boisterous' during the early period of their sentence, used a related language of not caring about the consequences of assaulting staff or fighting with other prisoners.

> *So in the earlier days you said you got into a bit of trouble with assaults, and things like that. Did you ever have a sense of the impact that might have on when you might be released?*
> No, because I was in that stage where nothing mattered. I was going back to my little dark world. [...] I didn't care. I knew right from wrong, but being early in my sentence you're like 'what have I got?'
> *Does it feel like you've got nothing to lose?*
> Yeah. [...] I didn't care, I was always getting in trouble, always getting up to no good. (Victor, 30s, post-tariff)

Attitudes of this kind were frequently linked to the persistence of an 'on road' mindset, imported into the prison by those 'used to that [lifestyle]' (Christopher, 20s, mid). As Christopher added, those 'mixed up' in selling drugs and mobile phones inside prison were most often people who had been involved in such activities in the community: 'coming to jail is just the same'. For some prisoners, then, early-stage behaviour was continuous with the pre-prison self:

> When I first come to jail I didn't really think of the consequences, so I was just
> getting up to everything, arguing - I was still in the mentality of when I was outside,
> so if I got into an argument I used to see red, I couldn't control my anger, so I was
> always fighting, always arguing. I was just anti-everything. (Seb, 20s, early)

The extracts above help to highlight some key analytic points. First, prisoners who
were relatively newly imprisoned often retained a pre-prison orientation and were
still involved in networks that entangled them in conflicts or facilitated trade.
In this respect, many early-stage prisoners remained embroiled in external relationships, even when they were physically dislocated from them. Second, some
aspects of 'jailing'—in particular, forms of violence—were not so much instrumental acts as the uncontrolled outcome of the affective struggles described earlier
in the chapter:

> The way I was feeling, if anyone did try and rob me or anything like that, I would
> have hurt them, because I was so angry and the time, back in them times. I would
> have just kept punching him and punching him. (Jonathan, 20s, early)

> I was constantly angry, constantly angry big time. [...] Even if somebody looked at
> me the wrong way I'd probably have to go and fight with him.
> *And about what, do you know?*
> Just angry, not angry at anything, just at everything, yeah. (Ignacio, 20s, early)

Third, as Victor implies through the term 'I knew right from wrong, but...', some
accounts provided a sense of a temporary moral suspension, produced by the shock
of being imprisoned for such a long period: 'I was struggling to get my head around
it, [...] I'd just steal instead [...] it was my way of coping (Karen, 20s, mid); 'I had
nothing to live for anymore [...] I was stealing, I was smoking drugs [...] I think
I didn't give a fuck about the world anymore' (Ashley, 30s, mid). Finally, while
many studies have noted that it is a fallacy to believe that long-term prisoners and
those with no prospect of release might be more inclined towards misconduct as
a result of having 'nothing to lose' (see, e.g., Flanagan 1980; Sorensen and Reidy
2019), among our sample, this attitude was very characteristic of prisoners in the
early sentence stage. This was primarily due to unresolved emotional turmoil and
the feeling—at this point—that life was without purpose:

My attitude was, 'what's the point, I'm not getting out [...] What are you going to do, send me to prison for 20 more years?' (Tommy, 50s, post-tariff)

I got [a] 'fuck it' attitude, like what's the point, do you know? I didn't feel that I had anything to work towards. (Deena, 20s, mid)

We return to these kinds of sentiments in Chapter 5.

Sublimation

We have characterised the mechanisms outlined so far as ways of blocking out or numbing a range of painful realities, often through 'self-destructive or self-injurious' means (Toch and Adams 1989, 2002: 4), or activities that delayed the adaptive processes that we detail in Chapter 5. To quote John Irwin:

> Awakening begins when lifers fully appreciate that there has been something fundamentally wrong with their former behaviour. They realize that their actions have brought them to this disastrous end. [...] [This process, however, is delayed by] joining the prison 'convict' social worlds, [...] hostilities, drug use, gambling, fighting and assassinations. (Irwin 2009: 66–67)

However, a very small number of early-stage participants described strategies that already appeared to be productive rather than defensive in their adaptive direction. Such activities—forms of *sublimation*—involved the channelling of negative affect into 'self-satisfying and socially acceptable means' (Diehl et al. 2014: 636), including 'artistic and intellectual endeavors' (Baumeister et al. 1998: 1103), which allowed the initial pains of imprisonment to be 'acknowledged, modified, and directed toward a relatively significant [...] goal' rather than 'dammed or diverted' (Vaillant 1971: 118).

For some participants, sublimation involved the pursuit of higher education with the specific aim of gaining a degree (see Chapter 5).

> I want to be able to do a degree while I'm in here. [...] If I've got that potential, then I might as well see fit to put good use to it. (Carl, 20s, early)

My short-term goals are: stay healthy, stay fit [...] and [complete a] law degree. (Jim, 20s, early)

Jim's short-term goals also included more artistic pursuits, such as playing musical instruments, and featured as part of an overarching annual strategy: 'at the end of a year I will look back over the year that's gone and say "OK, have I achieved what I set out to achieve at the start of that year?" And then I'll set goals for the year ahead' (Jim, 20s, early). For others, appealing the sentence represented a means of sublimation in that it channelled energy into pseudo-legal activity: sifting through case papers, looking for 'loopholes' to challenge a conviction and launching formal appeals. We return to the particular activity of appeal in due course.

Denial

As Anna Freud (1937/1993) explained, *denial* represents an effective psychic tool for defending against painful existential realities, by ignoring or disavowing their very existence (Modell 1961: 533). This, Cramer (2000) suggests, is a less 'mature' defence than the conscious postponement of pain through suppression or the 'creative' pro-activity of sublimation. The distinctiveness of denial from these 'high adaptive' defences is that it 'disowns' or seeks not to acknowledge the problematic reality at hand, instead making a 'counterclaim' that involves the positing of an alternative version of the problematic elements of a given situation (cf. Modell 1961: 533). However, denial is rarely absolute (Cohen 2001/2013), in the sense that some aspect of the reality is always registered at some level. For our purposes, then, denial existed on a continuum and centred on three key domains: denial of the offence and denial of the sentence, which we explore below, and denial of time, which we discuss in Chapter 8.

Adshead (2011: 186) notes that individuals charged with serious violent offences 'often deny any responsibility' for these acts, for reasons that most commonly include 'being advised to do so by legal counsel, not yet being able to accept what they have done, and actual innocence'. Among prisoners convicted of serious and sexual offences in particular, denial is commonly regarded as a way of coping with stigma, shame and self-disgust (Blagden et al. 2014), and of suppressing anxiety (Johnson 2019). In relation to death row prisoners in the United States, for example, Johnson (2019: 81) describes denial as:

... an outgrowth of shocked disbelief, which is then converted into a thoughtful and rational set of assertions about one's immunity from the death penalty. [...] Others adopt a denial strategy that is premised on the deferral of anxiety. [...] The lengthy appeals process that must be completed for capital cases is taken as a grace period – a planned limbo during which the prisoner worries less about the prospect of execution and more about the technicalities of his case.

It is important at the outset to note that we are not suggesting that offence denial was always disingenuous or misleading. There is good reason to believe that some interviewees who contested the legitimacy of their conviction did so not because they were 'in denial', but because they were innocent. However, the reflections of participants at the mid-, late- and post-tariff stages revealed a strong narrative of *denial of the offence* as a means of maintaining sanity and support networks in the early years of the sentence. Indeed, among our participants, the majority (59% of both the men and the women) identified themselves as not guilty of the offence for which they had been convicted. Such claims were significantly more common among those in the early stage of their sentence, with only 13% of men in the very early stage—the first sixth—of their tariff considering themselves to be guilty of murder. This figure increased according to sentence stage, to 32% of those in the early stage, 56% of those in the mid-stage, 52% of those in the late stage and 70% of those beyond their tariff point.

For some prisoners—as participants who were further into their sentences articulated—denial was an attempt to manage external perceptions of the self and maintain familial support, which they feared would evaporate if they were to acknowledge guilt:

When I got arrested, I come up with a lie, basically—a bullshit story that I wasn't there. And I stuck with that story. I couldn't change it cos I knew that if I had changed it, it would look bad upon me. [...] I was scared of rejection from my family. (Curtis, 20s, mid)

My mother put me in a very awkward position. [...] She said 'You know, if I find out that you've done this, I will disown you.' And so I had to adopt a denial stance on it. (Ray, 50s, post-tariff)

More often, however, denial of the offence was about managing internal perceptions of the self. That is, it was a way of evading the painful reality of what it meant to accept that you were the kind of person who was 'capable of taking another person's life' (Mathiassen 2016: 3). As we discuss in greater detail in Chapter 7, taking a life represented a profound assault on prisoners' perceptions of themselves as moral beings (see Pollock 2000). Maintaining innocence allowed the deep 'guilt, remorse [and] shame' associated with 'being a murderer' (Ferrito et al. 2012: 329) to be circumvented or at least diminished:

> The reality of it all is you did [pauses, and then emphasises] *I* did kill someone. *I* did sexually assault them. [...] But I wasn't prepared to accept that was me. (Ivan, 50s, post-tariff)

Much like the terminally ill patient rejecting the reality of their diagnosis (see Kübler-Ross 1969), then, denial of the offence 'function[ed] as a buffer' between the individual and an 'uncomfortable and painful' reality (p. 51).

For many prisoners, in the despair and darkness of the early period of confinement, some hope was found through denial of the permanence of the reality of their sentence: 'I was in denial for a while. [...] I was just thinking "I'll get out soon possibly" [...] I was looking for the light at the end of the tunnel' (Dean, late teens, early). As Tamara indicated, denial of the sentence could also entail an attempt to act oneself into the belief that the sentence, and the pains that it generated, was somehow unreal:

> I don't feel like I've got 25 years. I feel like I'm going home tomorrow. But I'm not. I know I'm not, but I just don't think - in my head I don't think I want to come to terms with my sentence. Because I think I'd probably hit the floor and I probably would never get back up. And I think that's why I always put such a front on, like I'll walk out of my room and I've got a big smile on my face, and I'm like, 'Are you all right?' and everyone's just like, 'Really? We know you're depressed'. I don't act like it, I don't, and I'm all right.
> *But is it self-preservation?*
> Yeah, it's like...It's like I'm in a movie every day. Every day I come out and it's like I'm acting. (Tamara, 20s, early)

However, the primary means of denying the sentence was through the process of legal appeal, an act that was critical in generating hope and 'maintaining sanity' (cf. Toch and Adams 1989), particularly during the initial phase of the sentence.

Indeed, among our participants, attempting to overturn the sentence and/or conviction via the appeals process was exceptionally common: 81% of male respondents in the very early stage (first sixth of their tariff) and 48% in the early stage (second sixth of their tariff) were currently appealing their conviction for murder, their sentence, or both.[12]

Appeal, then, was a key mechanism of psychological survival. As Roger (40s, post-tariff) explained, 'every lifer up and down the country does the same thing. For the first 10 years [appealing] is another coping mechanism to get you through'. Many early-stage prisoners located hope in the imminent possibility of release, however fanciful ('People are getting royal pardons every day, year, for just silly things, so if they can give them royal pardons, they can give me a royal pardon') [Diego, 20s, early]). Most recognised that the appeal process was a long shot, some because they knew that their grounds were questionable, others because they were aware that successful outcomes were rare. Many acknowledged that appealing was an act of distraction or desperation:

> Most people in jail appeal, it's a way of distracting themselves. [...] it's just some other way of giving themselves hope, innit? As human beings we all need hope. The day that you take hope away from a man is the day you cripple a man, innit? [...] We can deal with a lot of extreme stuff, as long as we've got hope. (Asad, 30s, mid)

> *Do you think that the appeal process can be a coping mechanism?*
> Appeal? Yeah, it's hope, innit? It's hope. (Kendrick, 20s, early)

> I was very angry about [the sentence length]. I was affected by it, but I suppose it didn't affect me that much because I always had the mindset that 'This is not it', you know? It's not final, I've always got a chance of appeal', and I was always thinking, 'I'm going to get out, I'm going to get out, there's no *way* I'm going to stay 16 years'. And as time went by, I was just living with that hope. (Linwood, 30s, mid)

---

[12]This was comparatively high compared to those further on in their sentence, with only 24% of those in the second third of their sentence and 14% in the final third of their sentence currently appealing. At the post-tariff stage, only 5% were appealing at the time of the study. At least part of this disparity can be explained by the fact that many of those beyond the mid-point of their tariff had already exhausted the options for appeal at an earlier point in their sentence, or no longer saw the point in appealing once they had served a number of years.

As Linwood suggested, then, appeal was a means of alleviating anguish and persuading oneself that the sentence was non-definitive.

For Willis and Alan, who had reached the mid-point of their tariff period, and were no longer maintaining innocence, appealing against the sentence had been unrelated to matters of innocence and guilt. Rather, they acknowledged, it was a 'bid for freedom' in the absence of other possibilities of escape:

> I couldn't take responsibility, and I didn't want to live with a life sentence. I was saying I didn't do it, I was just in denial. [...] I think it's just a bid for freedom though, you know? Like in the olden days, people used to escape and nowadays there's none of that. [Appealing] is just a natural thing to do. (Willis, 30s, mid)

> I was thinking '18 years it's a long time' like, [and] I thought, 'Well, I can't escape', and I first was denying the offence, thinking about maybe I can get out on appeal, and it's like you're just grasping for hope. (Alan, 30s, mid)

Yet maintaining innocence was not always cynical. Some prisoners were no doubt innocent; others felt themselves, with very good grounds, to be guilty of much lesser offences than murder (see Crewe et al. 2014; Hulley et al. 2019); and others still reported that, for many years, the extent of their denial was so deep that they were genuinely convinced of their innocence. In this sense, appeal included elements of *suppression* and *escape*, as well as denial.

Concluding Comments: 'You just Cope; You've Got no Other Choice'

In their study of life without parole, Johnson and McGunigall-Smith (2008) note that long-term prisoners tend to 'adjust' with the passing of time. Indeed, despite being overwhelmed by emotions of anger and despair during the early sentence phase, many of our participants were surprised at their own resilience. Several recounted specifically that when on remand, they had told other prisoners or staff that they would take their own life, lose their minds and be generally unable to cope were they to be convicted and sentenced to life imprisonment. However, most had fared much better than they had predicted. In terms that were typical of such individuals, Kathryn, for example, recalled telling a staff member: 'If I get lifed off I'm going to kill myself because I can't cope - I can't go away for life', but went on to explain:

> Literally, as soon as I got convicted - it's like a very strange thing - like something switches in you where you like find this inner strength that you never ever knew you had. (Kathryn, 20s, early)

Eileen's reflections were similar:

> At the beginning you just think, 'oh my God, how on earth am I going to get through this? How am I going to do all these years? Why me? [...] I'm never going to cope?' But you kind of just find the will from somewhere. I can't explain how you actually cope with it, you just do, you've got no other choice. (Eileen, 30s, late)

As Eileen suggested, then, there was little option other than to cope. While adjusting to decades of confinement was a bleak and difficult task, it was preferable to psychological disintegration and was, in this respect, a *necessity*[13]:

> You don't really have much choice. You know, it's like saying 'd'you want to be shot in the head by a gun or d'you want to be stabbed in the heart by a knife?' (Bernard, 40s, post-tariff)

What follows in Chapter 5, then, is an attempt to convey how prisoners learned ways to move on from the period of emotional turmoil and reactive adaptation that we have described in this chapter—from survival to adaptation.

References

Adams, J. S. (1965). Inequity in social exchange. *Advances in Experimental Social Psychology, 2*, 267–299.

---

[13]As we noted in Chapter 2, however, 191 men and women who met the criteria for our study had been transferred to secure psychiatric hospitals during the course of their sentence.

Adshead, G. (2011). The life sentence: Using a narrative approach in group psychotherapy with offenders. *Group Analysis, 44*(2), 175–195.

Adshead, G., Ferrito, M., & Bose, S. (2015). Recovery after homicide: Narrative shifts in therapy with homicide perpetrators. *Criminal Justice and Behavior, 42*(1), 70–81.

Archer, M. S. (2003). *Structure, agency and the internal conversation.* Cambridge: Cambridge University Press.

Averill, J. R. (1983). Studies on anger and aggression: Implications for theories of emotion. *American Psychologist, 38*(11), 1145–1160.

Baumeister, R. F., Dale, K., & Sommer, K. L. (1998). Freudian defense mechanisms and empirical findings in modern social psychology: Reaction formation, projection, displacement, undoing, isolation, sublimation, and denial. *Journal of Personality, 66* (6), 1081–1124.

Beijersbergen, K. A., Dirkzwager, A. J., Eichelsheim, V. I., Van der Laan, P. H., & Nieuwbeerta, P. (2015). Procedural justice, anger, and prisoners' misconduct: A longitudinal study. *Criminal Justice and Behavior, 42*(2), 196–218.

Blagden, N., Winder, B., Gregson, M., & Thorne, K. (2014). Making sense of denial in sexual offenders: A qualitative phenomenological and repertory grid analysis. *Journal of Interpersonal Violence, 29*(9), 1698–1731.

Boninger, D. S., Gleicher, F., & Strathman, A. (1994). Counterfactual thinking: From what might have been to what may be. *Journal of Personality and Social Psychology, 67*(2), 297–307.

Bryant, R. A., Creamer, M., O'Donnell, M., Silove, D., McFarlane, A. C., & Forbes, D. (2015). A comparison of the capacity of DSM-IV and DSM-5 acute stress disorder definitions to predict posttraumatic stress disorder and related disorders. *The Journal of Clinical Psychiatry, 76* (4), 391–397.

Bury, M. (1982). Chronic illness as biographical disruption. *Sociology of Health & Illness, 4*(2), 167–182.

Camus, A. (1954). *The stranger.* New York: Vintage Books.

Clements, P. T., & Burgess, A. W. (2002). Children's responses to family member homicide. *Family & Community Health, 25*(1), 32–42.

Clore, G. L., & Centerbar, D. B. (2004). Analyzing anger: How to make people mad. *Emotion, 4*, 139–144.

Cohen, S. (2001/2013). *States of denial: Knowing about atrocities and suffering.* Hoboken: Wiley.

Condry, R. (2007). Families outside: The difficulties faced by relatives of serious offenders. *Prison Service Journal, 174*, 3.

Cramer, P. (2000). Defense mechanisms in psychology today: Further processes for adaptation. *American Psychologist, 55*(6), 637–646.

Crewe, B. (2009). *The prisoner society: Power, adaptation, and social life in an English prison.* Oxford: Oxford University Press.

Crewe, B., Hulley, S., & Wright, S. (2014). *Written evidence provided to the House of Commons Justice Committee on Joint Enterprise: Follow up.* Available online: http://data. parliament.uk/writtenevidence/committeeevidence.svc/evidencedocument/Justice/ Joint%20Enterprise%20followup/written/10886.html. Accessed 29 October 2018.

Diehl, M., Chui, H., Hay, E. L., Lumley, M. A., Grühn, D., & Labouvie-Vief, G. (2014). Change in coping and defense mechanisms across adulthood: Longitudinal findings in a European American sample. *Developmental Psychology, 50*(2), 634–648.

Douglas, J. D. (1984). The emergence, security, and growth of the sense of self. In J. A. Kotarba & A. Fontana (Eds.), *The existential self in society* (pp. 69–99). London: The University of Chicago Press.

Ferrito, M., Vetere, A., Adshead, G., & Moore, E. (2012). Life after homicide: Accounts of recovery and redemption of offender patients in a high security hospital–A qualitative study. *Journal of Forensic Psychiatry & Psychology, 23*(3), 327–344.

Fitchett, G. (1980). Wisdom and folly in death and dying. *Journal of Religion and Health, 19*(3), 203–214.

Flanagan, T. J. (1980). Time served and institutional misconduct: Patterns of involvement in disciplinary infractions among long-term and short-term inmates. *Journal of Criminal Justice, 8*(6), 357–367.

Freud, A. (1937/1993). *The ego and the mechanisms of defence.* International Psycho-Analytical Library, No. 30. London: Karnac Books.

Hackmann, A., Ehlers, A., Speckens, A., & Clark, D. M. (2004). Characteristics and content of intrusive memories in PTSD and their changes with treatment. *Journal of Traumatic Stress: Official Publication of the International Society for Traumatic Stress Studies, 17*(3), 231–240.

Haines, J., & Williams, C. L. (2003). Coping and problem solving of self-mutilators. *Journal of Clinical Psychology, 59*(10), 1097–1106.

Harvey, J. (2012). *Young men in prison.* Collumpton: Willan.

Hulley, S., Crewe, B., & Wright, S. (2016). Re-examining the problems of long-term imprisonment. *British Journal of Criminology, 56*(4), 769–792.

Hulley, S., Crewe, B., & Wright, S. (2019). Making sense of 'joint enterprise' for murder: Legal legitimacy or instrumental acquiescence? *British Journal of Criminology, 59*(6), 1328–1346.

Irwin, J. (1970). *The felon.* Englewood Cliffs, NJ: Prentice-Hall.

Irwin, J. (2009). *Lifers: Seeking redemption in prison.* New York: Routledge.

Jewkes, Y. (2005). Loss, liminality and the life sentence: Managing identity through a disrupted lifecourse. In A. Liebling & S. Maruna (Eds.), *The effects of imprisonment* (pp. 366–388). Cullompton, UK: Willan Publishing.

Johnson, R. (2019). *Condemned to die: Life under sentence of death* (2nd edn.). New York: Routledge.

Johnson, R., & McGunigall-Smith, S. (2008). Life without parole, America's other death penalty: Notes on life under sentence of death by incarceration. *The Prison Journal, 88*(2), 328–346.

Kashka, M. S., & Beard, M. T. (1999). The grief of parents of murdered children: A suggested model for intervention. *Holistic Nursing Practice, 14*(1), 22–36.

Kübler-Ross, E. (1969). *On death and dying.* New York: Scribner.

Kübler-Ross, E., & Kessler, D. (2005). *On grief and grieving: Finding the meaning of grief through the five stages of loss.* New York: Simon & Schuster.

Kübler-Ross, E., & Kessler, D. (2014). *On grief and grieving: Finding the meaning of grief through the five stages of loss.* New York: Simon & Schuster.

Leigey, M. E., & Ryder, M. A. (2015). The pains of permanent imprisonment: Examining perceptions of confinement among older life without parole inmates. *International Journal of Offender Therapy and Comparative Criminology, 59*(7), 726–742.

Liebling, A., Tait, S., Durie, L., Stiles, A., & Harvey, J. (2005). A summary of the main findings. In *An evaluation of the safer locals programme.* Cambridge: Cambridge Institute of Criminology Prisons Research Centre.

MacKenzie, D. L., & Goodstein, L. (1985). Long-term incarceration impacts and characteristics of long-term offenders: An empirical analysis. *Criminal Justice and Behavior, 12*, 395–414.

Maercker, A., Bonanno, G. A., Znoj, H., & Horowitz, M. J. (1998). Prediction of complicated grief by positive and negative themes in narratives. *Journal of Clinical Psychology, 54*(8), 1117–1136.

Mathiassen, C. (2016). Nothingness: Imprisoned in existence, excluded from society. In J. Bang & D. Winther-Lindqvist (Eds.), *Nothingness: Philosophical insights into psychology.* New Brunswick: Transaction.

Meichenbaum, D. (1996). *A clinical handbook for assessing and treating posttraumatic stress disorder.* Chichester: Wiley.

Modell, A. H. (1961). Denial and the sense of separateness. *Journal of the American Psychoanalytic Association, 9*(3), 533–547.

Moskowitz, A. (2004). Dissociation and violence: A review of the literature. *Trauma, Violence, & Abuse, 5*(1), 21–46.

O'Donnell, I. (2014). *Prisoners, solitude, and time.* Oxford: Oxford University Press.

Owen, B. A. (1998). *In the mix: Struggle and survival in a women's prison.* Albany: State of New York University Press.

Pai, A., Suris, A., & North, C. (2017). Posttraumatic stress disorder in the DSM-5: Controversy, change, and conceptual considerations. *Behavioral Sciences, 7*(1), 1–7.

Pollock, P. H. (2000). Eye movement desensitization and reprocessing (EMDR) for post-traumatic stress disorder (PTSD) following homicide. *The Journal of Forensic Psychiatry, 11*(1), 176–184.

Quigley, B. M., & Tedeschi, J. T. (1996). Mediating effects of blame attributions on feelings of anger. *Personality and Social Psychology Bulletin, 22*(12), 1280–1288.

Richards, B. (1978). The experience of long-term imprisonment. *British Journal of Criminology, 18*(2), 162–169.

Shear, K., & Shair, H. (2005). Attachment, loss, and complicated grief. *Developmental Psychobiology: The Journal of the International Society for Developmental Psychobiology, 47*(3), 253–267.

Sorensen, J. R., & Reidy, T. J. (2019). Nothing to Lose? An Examination of Prison Misconduct Among Life-Without-Parole Inmates. *The Prison Journal, 99*(1), 46–65.

Stroebe, M., Schut, H., & Boerner, K. (2017). Cautioning health-care professionals: Bereaved persons are misguided through the stages of grief. *OMEGA-Journal of Death and Dying, 74*(4), 455–473.

Suyemoto, K. L. (1998). The functions of self-mutilation. *Clinical Psychology Review, 18*(5), 531–554.

Sykes, G. (1958). *The society of captives: A study of a maximum security prison.* Princeton: Princeton University Press.

Toch, H., & Adams, K. (1989). *The disturbed violent offender.* New Haven: Yale University Press.

Toch, H., & Adams, K. (2002). *Acting out: Maladaptive behavior in confinement.* Washington: American Psychological Association.

Toch, H., Adams, K., & Grant, J. D. (1989). *Coping: Maladaptation in prisons.* Piscataway: Transaction Publishers.

Tyler, T. R. (1980). Impact of directly and indirectly experienced events: The origin of crime-related judgments and behaviors. *Journal of Personality and Social Psychology, 39*(1), 13–28.

Tyler, T. R. (2003). Procedural justice, legitimacy, and the effective rule of law. *Crime and Justice, 30,* 283–357.

Ugelvik, T. (2014). *Power and resistance in prison: Doing time, doing freedom.* Berlin: Springer.

Vaillant, G. E. (1971). Theoretical hierarchy of adaptive ego mechanisms: A 30-year follow-up of 30 men selected for psychological health. *Archives of General Psychiatry, 24*(2), 107–118.

Vaillant, G. E. (1994). Ego mechanisms of defense and personality psychopathology. *Journal of Abnormal Psychology, 103*(1), 44–50.

Wickie, S. K., & Marwit, S. J. (2001). Assumptive world views and the grief reactions of parents of murdered children. *Journal of Death and Dying, 42*(2), 101–113.

Williams, S. (2000). Chronic illness as biographical disruption or biographical disruption as chronic illness? Reflections on a core concept. *Sociology of Health & Illness, 22*(1), 40–67.

5

Coping and Adaptation

All you've got is hope. That's all I've got, is hope, and it's like no matter what plans you make, you're not in control of any of them. You're not in control of anything and anything can change it at any moment. So you can't build a life while you're in here, all you can do is prepare yourself for when you get out of here. [...] It's like an athlete, isn't it, training for their Olympics. [...] This is my home right now, this is my life right now. [...]

So you're kind of caught in two different worlds?

Yeah. [...] And how do you maintain a world out there when you're living in here? [...] I'm still trying to figure that out.

But at the start of the sentence, you said to me, you wanted to cut everything off?

Yeah, I did. [...] I wanted to protect myself from the pain and the hurt, and now I'm dealing with the pain and the hurt on a daily basis, do you know what I mean? I have to face that stuff, I have to deal with it. Whereas before at the start I could just smoke some drugs and numb my brain, and not care what's going on out there: not care if my girlfriend's sleeping with someone, and not care if my brother's been in a fight or my dad's close to death, or whatever, I don't have to focus on that. And that's painful stuff, that's hard stuff to go to your cell every night and be alone in your cell with that kind of stuff every night going through your head. Especially where there's nobody to share it with, and no one to talk to, no one who could understand where you're at. (Ashley, 30s, mid)

© The Author(s) 2020

B. Crewe et al., *Life Imprisonment from Young Adulthood*,
Palgrave Studies in Prisons and Penology,
https://doi.org/10.1057/978-1-137-56601-0_5

In the previous chapter, we argued that the initial period of the sentences was dominated by feelings of shock, anger and despair, as a result of the stark and sudden dislocation from the prisoner's sense of self, social networks and future aspirations. In this respect, the early sentence phase was characterised by prisoners' attempts to manage acute affective reactions to their new predicament. This chapter outlines the ways that prisoners coped with and adapted to their sentence in the years that followed the initial period after their conviction. Building on Chapter 4, it describes the first few years of the sentence as a period of 'coping-survival', in which prisoners continued to exist in a state of 'fractured reflexivity', with a limited, defensive and reactive form of agency. It goes on to outline the ways in which, over time, precipitated and sustained by a range of experiences and discourses, long-term prisoners began to find hope and meaning in their existence, establish some sense of control over their life, and come to terms with both their sentence and their offence. A significant part of this process involved finding ways of managing the emotional burden of their circumstances. In this respect, Ashley's comments are emblematic of the substance of the chapter: his transition from defending against to processing his feelings of loss and pain; his reflective contemplations; his cautious optimism; his agentic orientation to his time in prison; and his acknowledgement that the prison had become his home, and therefore the place where his life needed to be lived.

Stasis and Survival

In discussing their situation, early-stage prisoners drew on a set of connected metaphors that conveyed their feelings of stasis and stagnation. For example:

I'd say I'm at a place now where I'm neither at the start or the end [of my sentence]. I'm neither here nor there, neither coming nor going. [...] So it's just, like, I'm here, rotting, as such. [...] You just stagnate. That's what it is. Just existing for pretty much no purpose at all, really. (Billy, 20s, early)

[The early phase] was just dead time: you're not progressing, you're not going backwards, you're sort of stuck in limbo, you're treading water. (Gibson, 20s, mid)

Terms such as 'just existing' and 'dead time' indicated a state of extreme passivity and purposelessness (see also Johnson 2019: 98). Others, such as 'stuck in limbo' and 'treading water', implied a sense of contortion and effort: being between two states (see Jewkes 2005), or expending energy to counter the flow and direction of the current, in a manner that is ultimately unsustainable. Indeed, the experience of being sentenced to a very long period of imprisonment was often conveyed using the language of sinking and swimming:

> You've got two choices when you're faced with a sentence like this: sink or swim, really, and there's a multitude of ways to sink and only one way to swim. (Neil, 30s, mid)

> [When found guilty] It just felt like I was sinking with no way to stop it. [...] All of a sudden everything's taken away from you, and everything that you spent your whole life clinging to has been ripped away. And you can't remember how to swim, but the other half of it is you're not sure you want to. And it takes a long time to start figuring out how to swim again, and sometimes you can do it and you swim a little way, and then you start to sink all over again because it just consumes you. I have some days where I want to swim, and some days where I am swimming, and then I have lots of days where I can't and then I have days where I just don't want to. (Maria, 20s, early)

The tropes noted above were indicative of a particular mode of agency, one that was limited and reactive, in relation to a context that was stultifying and overwhelming ('it just consumes you'). Martin, for example, believed that he would never be able to come to terms with his situation and was engulfed by his own distress:

> I will never come to terms with it.
> *No. And how much time do you spend thinking about it?*
> The majority of the day. (Martin, 20s, early)

Here, Archer's (2003, 2012) notion of 'fractured reflexivity' and Bottoms's (2006: 265) elaboration of the idea of 'reactive emotionality' are highly pertinent. Both relate to forms of agency that are oriented to 'the demands of short-term living in a fairly unstructured environment' (Bottoms 2006: 268), and are associated with 'people lacking "rooted forms of life"' (p. 273), preoccupied with a form of day-to-day living and unable to escape from fixation on their own suffering. In such circumstances of disorientation, people are unable to engage in productive forms of emotional self-commentary or projective forms of reflection that might help them to 'move "beyond themselves"' towards a different trajectory or future (Bottoms 2006: 270–271). To borrow Vaughan's (2006: 397) summary:

> Rather than the internal conversation supplying a commentary on emotional reactions, it spins around these affects in 'inconclusive circles' (Archer 2003: 303) that intensifies a person's lack of control. […] People feel buffeted by the environment and rendered passive by circumstances.

Here, then, Maria's comments are striking:

> It's just so hard to see the positive in anything you do, and I suppose maybe that's just because it is so early on in my sentence for me, but I don't know. It's strange, because 'I don't know' seems to be my answer for most things just lately. (Maria, 20s, early)

At the early sentence stage, prisoners facing long sentences struggled to invest in constructive activity, plan ahead, or develop a set of concerns beyond the everyday present. As the comments above highlight, early-stage prisoners were engaged in an ongoing effort to survive and were paralysed both by their affective desolation and by being thrust into an unfamiliar environment in which their habitual modes of thinking and conduct could not provide a guide to action (Maruna et al. 2006).

The process of adapting to the prison environment has been discussed primarily in terms of physical threat and survival. For the short-term prisoners in Schmid and Jones's (1991) study, the construction of a 'false identity […] created for survival in an artificial world' (1991: 150) related primarily to the need for self-protection. Accounts of prison life have consistently reported that, to avoid exploitation and physical assault, male prisoners need to engage in forms of 'masking' and 'fronting' that reify a particular version of taut masculinity (e.g. Sykes 1958; Jewkes 2005; de Viggiani 2012). Among our participants, statements about the need to avoid exhibiting weakness, to 'be assertive' in response to tests of personal confidence (Antone, 20s, early), and to communicate aggressive potential were expressed by both female and male participants:

I got scared as anybody else, I just never showed it, you know. I had the same fears and that. But I masked that with a 'fuck you' attitude. You know, 'I'll attack you'. (Campbell, 30s, mid)

If [prisoners] do show a lot of weakness they will get targeted. Vulnerable people. And I suppose you have gotta make your stand, like you're not gonna take any shit. That can make you a bit guarded. (Jill, 40s, post-tariff)

You need to have a certain amount of… not power, but you need to be able to just show people that you're not a dickhead, basically. (James, 20s, early)

However, in comparison with other problems, concerns about physical safety were considered to be relatively unproblematic. 'Feeling worried about your personal safety' was rated as the 37th (out of 39) most severe problem overall by the male participants and as the 36th most severe by the female participants. Some interviewees reported that their index offence itself secured them from exploitation— 'everybody's killed someone, so you don't need to prove no more to no one else' (Leonard, 30s, late)—although this was not the case for those who had committed murders against women or children, particularly where such offences had a sexual component.

More significantly, as Dan clarified, early-stage prisoners emphasised the importance of psychological as well as physical survival:

Being in prison, your primary concern is survival, that's really it, you know, and making it through however long I have to be here. […]
And is the survival that you talk about…
… it's physical and psychological. (Dan, 20s, early)

For female prisoners in particular, performances of coping were also strategies of emotional self-fortitude: a way of getting through the day, despite acute emotional anguish. As Liz stated, 'I put on a front. I just tried to get through the day the best I could, and I struggled every day' (Liz, 20s, early).

Such comments highlighted the affective burdens experienced by almost all participants, as they sought to navigate the waters of their first few years in prison. As we noted in Chapter 4, early-stage prisoners were often overwhelmed by anger and distress, and engaged in a range of defensive actions in order to cope with their emotional states. The need to keep emotions 'up' or to hold them down was identified by participants at this sentence stage as being among the most challenging aspects of the sentence (see Laws 2018):

> *What have you found to be the three most difficult things about serving your sentence?*
> It's being away from family. Being able to cope with all the situations in jail, not just certain things, but everything.
> *What sort of things?*
> Emotionally being able to control yourself, like not being down all the time, that's about it. (Ignacio, 20s, early)

These affective struggles were highly characteristic of the early sentence stage. Overall, they represented a form of coping-survival, in which, to return to the metaphors above, prisoners were barely able to keep their heads above water as they tried to absorb the various shocks and dislocations of having been convicted of murder. As Arkaan's recollections illustrate, at this stage, they could focus on little more than surviving their emotional tumult (see O'Donnell 2014):

> You're just surviving. You're just, kind of, taking every day as it comes, and it's not a nice place to be cos you're just… you know, you survive. I remember writing to [other] people in prison and I always used to say to them 'yeah, I'm fine, just surviving', […] and I realized later that it was a theme. Why did I always used to write 'I'm surviving, I'm surviving'. Suddenly realized, 'bloody hell, that's what I'm doing'. (Arkaan, 20s, mid)

Many prisoners in the later stages of their sentence continued to engage in forms of suppressive thinking, fearing descent into despair: 'I try and pull myself away from thinking about things too much, because I don't want to get caught in that cycle' (Deena, 20s, mid). Some recognised that many of their activities were forms of displacement, or what O'Donnell (2014) labels 'removal': 'anything just to stop you from thinking. […] Anything to get you out of here' (Arkaan, 20s, mid); 'sometimes [being busy] is about avoiding, so that you don't have to think too much, because sometimes your own mind is your worst enemy' (Gail, 30s, late). For example, female prisoners who had become Listeners—peer support workers, trained by the Samaritans—acknowledged that doing so was, in part, a way of deflecting their own issues or placing their pain in comparative perspective (see Perrin and Blagden 2014):

I'm a Listener, [...] and it's weird because by thinking about somebody else is probably sort of distracting yourself from your own, so that's good for me as well. (Kathryn, 20s, early)

I suppose a Listener hearing other people's stories it's like, 'phew, mine isn't that bad'. A lot of people in a lot of situations have had a lot worse to deal with. So I've kind of thrown myself into things, because I felt, for me, that was the only way I could get through it. (Gail, 30s, late)

Here, Ashley (30s, mid) also provides an indicative example. At the start of this sentence, as well as using drugs to anaesthetise his anxieties, on feeling pain or hurt within the prison, his immediate response was to 'seek revenge. I'm going to hurt someone back'. Having spent time in HMP Grendon—the democratic-therapeutic prison community, which we discuss in more detail below—he had become aware of 'the real pain I felt, and the real hurt and the real damage it did to me', particularly in his family life, and the hurt he had caused to others, primarily through his offending. 'Now', he said, 'I'm dealing with the pain and the hurt on a daily basis [...] I have to face that stuff, I have to deal with it'.

Looking back on the early phase of their sentence, mid- and late-stage prisoners implicitly identified this distinction between coping-survival and a form of 'coping-adaptation', in which they had begun to actively confront and address their issues:

> *Did you feel like you were coping?*
> I was just ignoring it. Because it just made life easier, I think, to ignore it. I think it takes a while before you can say you're coping. Coping is later on when you've started doing your courses and you've started doing your therapies and everything like that. That's when you're coping because you're working with the tools you've been given. [...] And to, sort of, face it, to have it in your head, rather than keeping it out of your head, yeah. (Tori, 30s, late)

That is, as the 'fog' of fractured reflexivity lifted, prisoners were better able to engage in forms of reflexive emotional processing.

Emotional reflexivity, then—dealing with trauma, shame and the acute distress of long-term confinement—was key to the adaptive process. As Jill summarised:

> They say it normally takes a few years to actually get into your sentence. And it does, you know. You've got a load of feelings, grief or anger or frustration, whatever,

drug addiction, you've got all that when you first come in. [...] You know, you're in this horrible world, alien to you, so your emotions are gonna be all over the place, and I suppose it depends on the individual how long it takes them to get past that and think 'right, OK, it's time I got myself together now'. (Jill, 40s, post-tariff)

In the extracts that follow, Merle and Gail provide accounts of this arduous transition from emotional paralysis and passivity to existential deliberation and agency:

It's been a long journey and a hard journey. When I first got my sentence I was in a daze, and then I went to an angry individual, not angry towards people but angry of the situation I find myself in, and then I went from where I had to console myself, I had to reflect on my behaviour, and I had to get involved and participate in courses, and change the way I was thinking, change my attitude, and then I started to be a positive role [model]. (Merle, 30s, mid)

You've got to motivate yourself to get through the length of sentence, and in amongst that you've got to try and grow as a person, look at everything that was wrong pre-jail and [the reasons] you came to be in prison, and work on that and try and emotionally develop. Quite often we're emotionally kind of stunted, from whatever traumas have happened in our younger years, and when we've had the trauma of coming to prison and what we've experienced to get to prison, it's like being dropped into an alien world [...] and you're expected to grow up within jail, and within the environment and it's really difficult. It's really difficult to try and find who you are. (Gail, 30s, late)

As these quotations demonstrate, this transition had two main dimensions. One required prisoners to come to terms with their sentence, and with the burdens of serving many years in a world in which their previous guidelines for action were incongruous (Archer 2003, 2012). The other required them to find ways to process their emotions, resolve their feelings of shame, and reconstitute themselves as new kinds of people (see Vaughan 2006). This aspiration to change was therefore an outcome of the imperatives of the environment, a desire to disavow the past and the need to project themselves into the future. To quote Vaughan (2006), writing about desistance processes more broadly:

human agents constitute their identity by plotting their own lives within a narrative that exists between a past that is denounced and a future ideal towards which they strive. The experiences of a past life seem foreign yet are indispensable for providing an impulse to reach for a different kind of life. Attempts to change are based upon the shame involved in reviewing the past and deciding that a fundamental adjustment to criminal inclinations is required which can only be achieved by dedicating oneself to a new ideal. (2006: 396).

Doing so involved a profound and prolonged reflexive confrontation with the self—to use Archer's term, an 'internal conversation', or what John Irwin (2010: 67) refers to as 'critical introspection' (see also Aresti et al. 2010). Mid- and late-stage prisoners consistently described the importance of 'knowing' themselves as a way of moving on from what they had done, the person they had been, and their initial reaction to being convicted. Emotions were reconfigured as existential questions:

And how do you maintain [hope] over that length of time?
You've got to know yourself, you've got to look into yourself, reflect, think, challenge yourself, really looking hard. You've got to go into places where you may not want to go. [...] That's what it's all about - acceptance. If you can accept yourself, right? And you've come to know yourself during your sentence; it's an emotional and a spiritual journey, but if you do those then you really are doing well and it makes it easier. (Ray, 50s, post-tariff)

At first I was angry with the victim. [...] then I went through blaming myself, hating myself thinking: 'Why am I like this? [...] Why am I stuck here? What have I done to myself? What have I done to all these people?' And after time I started to say: 'Do you know what, I am the problem. Let's fix the problem'. [...] I wanted to fix myself, I was broken. This thing had tore me apart. I haven't got nothing now. And, you know, I'm thinking about loads of bad things that have happened to me in my life, and thinking 'why has this happened to me? Why did I do this?' (Stephen, 20s, mid)

The forms of emotional and existential reflection that are detailed here are neither automatic nor evenly available. As Margaret Archer's work emphasises, reflexivity takes different forms according to biographical experiences, and some individuals are 'so preoccupied by [...] traumatic events' that they are unable to reflect upon themselves in ways that enable 'purposeful action' (Archer 2012: 249). As we argue below, among our participants, alongside the basic distress caused by a life-changing sentence, factors such as mental health problems, childhood abuse and environmental stressors led to emotional blockages and obsessions that impeded productive internal conversations.

Here, it is worth noting that, in the extracts above, Gail declared that 'It's really difficult to try and find who you are', while Merle noted that change had been 'a long journey and a hard journey'. In this regard, while reflexivity and personal reconstitution were impelled by the breach in the taken for granted that long-term imprisonment engendered, and by the desire among prisoners to disown their previous selves, they were far from easy (Akram and Hogan 2015). Often, reflexive capacity had to be freed or fostered, through what Akram and Hogan (2015: 15) refer to as 'consciousness-raising', i.e. 'bringing into consciousness those issues which are usually taken for granted, exist as doxa or are in the pre-conscious' (p. 15). Archer (2012: 267) herself notes that 'self- knowledge and self-transformation [...] involve a great deal of learning'. As we describe below, then, to release themselves from cognitive flooding and reflexive immobility, prisoners needed deliberate resources that provided ways of making sense of complex emotions and offered an alternative perspective on the self. While some forms of suppression and denial continued to feature in the lives of mid- and late-stage prisoners, in general, they operated less defensively than in the early phase of imprisonment. In comparison with early-stage prisoners, those further into their sentence were more able to examine issues relating to their backgrounds and offences, to confront the pain of their situation, and to come to terms with long-term confinement.

'Coming to Terms'

I think it took five years before it hit me. [...] I was playing on the computer and I just started going weird, I couldn't breathe or nothing. [...] And the next morning I ran out my cell to one of my mates, and I said, [...] 'something's not right' and he said, 'What?'. I said, 'Everything...' and he said, 'Oh, you're just, your sentence, your tariff, it's just the length of time you're doing, it's just hit you'. [...] A lot of lifers probably won't admit it to you, but they do get it.
They get what, sorry?

That moment. [...] It's a feeling of being enclosed, of being unable to love, hug your loved ones, being able to do... your liberty has been taken, and you stop understanding what your liberty's about and things have been taken away from you. Nothing makes any sense, no reasoning makes sense, so it's a feeling of being alone. (Leonard, 30s, late)

As we documented in Chapter 4, early-stage prisoners engaged in various forms of psychological defence so as not to have to fully acknowledge the gravity and ineluctability of their situation. While in the initial period of their sentence, some had begun to accept that the prison was their long-term residence, and talked of making it 'home' (e.g. by customising their cells with posters and photographs), their comments were often made with considerable ambivalence. For example, rather than conveying a sense of having fully 'come to terms' with his sentence, Darrin exhibited a posture of resigned fatalism:

> *Do you think you have come to terms with your sentence?*
> Yes and no.
> *[...] You said when you first got it you thought it was a bit of a dream or something.*
> Because when you are in your cell you have got a lot of time to think. You just think 'wow this is a long time. It is mad. You have actually got a long time, this is your life now'. You have got to accept this is your life, this is your life now. (Darrin, late teens, early)

Carl's claim that his life had shifted from the community into the prison was also strained:

> It doesn't matter where you're living, you're still living a life. Life is just the environment you're in ... and if I was on the outside, I would probably, I'd still be doing the same things, I'd still try to be learning academically. I'd still try to be forming friendships. The only real thing about prison is that, one, there's no girls, and, two, you don't get to see your family whenever you want. And those are the only two things that really I miss. (Carl, 20s, early)

Re-framing prison as his primary life domain required Carl to downplay the deprivations inherent in his predicament ('those are the only two things that really I miss'); the declaration that, in essence, he was leading the same life that he would have led had he been free was unconvincing. Both represented a continuing form of denial—'Even if I'm treading water or treading mud, at least I'm fooling myself into thinking I'm doing something' (Samuel, 20s, early)—and a reluctance to fully acknowledge the reality that life had been derailed.

Among other prisoners, terms such as being 'accustomised' to prison (Samuel, 20s, early) or being 'so used to prison now [that] it just feels like home' (Jonathan, 20s, early) reflected a pragmatic orientation to the present. Such prisoners were no longer seeking to deny their new reality, but nor were they reconciled with it emotionally. Just as often, prisoners at this sentence stage rejected the idea that prison could ever be considered a permanent home: 'I hear people say "oh, you're coming up to my room". And I'm thinking "that's a cell not a room", and I can't convert to that style of thinking because prison's prison, and it would never be my home' (Clark, 20s, early).

Those further into their sentence were more often reconciled to the permanence of their circumstances. Leonard's recollection—above—of the point at which he was fully struck by his predicament was unusually intense (resonating with Russo's concept of a delayed, 'chronophobic' panic about what O'Donnell (2014: 189) calls 'the immensity of time ahead'). However, the main features of his experience—a clear-sighted recognition, a few years into the sentence, of the reality of his situation—were common (see Liem 2016). In this respect, 'coming to terms' with the sentence meant no longer being in denial about having to serve it in full, starting to process it emotionally, and developing a stronger and more proactive sense of agency. Looking back, mid- and late-stage prisoners consistently described this process as having taken between two and eight years, following a period in which it had been difficult to 'register' (Gail, 30s, late) or fully absorb. Almost all commented that, after a period of a few years, the stark reality set in that they were 'persons living in prison rather than offenders doing time' (Zamble 1992: 423–424).

Among prisoners who regarded themselves as guilty, there was virtual unanimity that coming to terms with the sentence preceded, and was easier than, coming to terms with having committed or been involved in a murder:

Coming to terms with your sentence, you do that pretty early. [...] The sentence, you know you can't change that, that's what the judge has given you. [...] But coming to terms with what you've done is a completely different ballgame. And I don't think it really happens in that first stage, not for me anyway. It took me a long time for me to even realise. (Asad, 30s, mid)

The hardest part for sure was the first five years of my sentence. It took me a long time to come to terms with it: I'd got this sentence. It took me even longer to come to terms with what I'd actually done, which I still do struggle with now. (Jenny, 20s, mid)

So how long did it take before you came to terms with the sentence?
The sentence, no problem. No problem at all.
And the crime, is that what you were going to say, it takes longer to come to terms with…?
I've never come to terms with it, and I don't think I'll ever come to terms with it. (Nathaniel, 30s, mid)

The strength and sentiment of Nathaniel's statement were widely shared. The great majority of mid- and late-stage prisoners who were not maintaining innocence felt deep and ongoing remorse about their crime, and talked emotively about the enormity of what they had done, the difficulty of reconciling themselves with their actions (see Chapter 7), and the profound impact on them and others of having committed murder (Zehr 1996; Irwin 2010). For example:

I killed someone. How could anyone ever come to terms with that type of offence? How could they? (Arkaan, 20s, mid)

Do you think there is a point at which you come to terms with the offence?
[Pause] Learn to live with it? I don't think coming to terms [with a situation where] somebody's lost their life is ever possible, because somebody died. And nothing you can do, no matter how hard you work, no matter what you do, it can never ever bring them back.
Do you still think about it now?
All the time, yeah. All the time. It's never something that goes away, ever. (Gail, 30s, late)

For many prisoners, the offence was unambiguously shameful—'the worst thing that I've ever done in my life' (Stephen, 20s, mid)—and dominated their experience of imprisonment. Early-stage prisoners who were not engaged in the defensive psychological manoeuvres that we outline in Chapter 4 existed in highly distressed emotion-states. Jamie (20s, early), for example, described questioning 'whether I was human or not', as a result of having taken someone's life. Explaining that, because of his offence, he put little value on his own life and never wanted to be released, he admonished himself for being alive while his victim was dead. 'I still think that now. [...] This is something that's with me all the time'. He had self-harmed, undergone what he called a 'psychological breakdown', experienced frequent nightmares and had rejected the option of suicide only because he considered it insufficient payback. No amount of punishment, he felt, was proportionate to his wrongdoing: 'People don't understand the seriousness, the effects I've caused on other people, and things like that'.

Some prisoners in later sentence stages continued to experience the kinds of reactions that we described in Chapter 4—including nightmares and intrusive recollections—or coped with unceasing feelings of guilt through acute forms of sublimation:

> *So how much time do you spend thinking about the offence?*
> Ha, well I suffer from obsessive compulsive disorder, [...] so mostly all the time. This is why I scrub my cell out five times a day. I go down the gym, throw the weights around as much as I can, you know, just try anything to take my mind off it.
> *So it plays on your mind a lot.*
> Yeah.
> *And you deal with that through…the cleaning is part of that process, is it?*
> Yeah.
> *And the weights as well?*
> Yeah, because I tire myself out then when I hit my pillow I'm not thinking about it, I'm out cold, I'm gone. (Nathaniel, 30s, mid)

Accounts of this kind illustrate the degree to which many prisoners were preoccupied with matters of guilt, conscience and existential anxiety. Kelvin (20s, mid), for example, described the hardest part of his sentence so far as 'Just trying to sort myself out and become a human being, a person, and come to terms with my offence even more, and a better understanding of it even more'. By illustration, among mid- and late-stage men who considered themselves guilty of the offence for which they had been convicted, 'Thinking about the crime you committed' was the 6th most severely felt problem (compared to 26th among those in the very early sentence stage).

For the majority of prisoners, then, dealing with the offence, and moving on from it, was a very significant component of the sentence and required a profound and sincere confrontation with the self. Early-stage prisoners who were not maintaining innocence often struggled to meet their emotions face-on:

> Yeah, of course I feel bad, do you know what I mean? I took someone's life, I killed the guy, you know what I mean? But it was an accident. And I'm trying to move on from it. It sounds kind of bad, but […] I don't let things like that get to me, because it'll fuck my head up. So I try not to dwell on it, really. (Oscar, 20s, early)

> *Do you spend a lot of time thinking about the victim and the victim's family and things like that?*
> At first you do. […] but I think they're the people that start having problems, you know what I mean. Start thinking about it all the time and that. I mean, don't get me wrong, you don't forget it. You, sort of, let it go, to try and sort your life out in here. You put it to one side and just leave it. […] cos you still have your life to get on with, get through. (Noel, 20s, early)

The acceptance of guilt, while a step on from seeking to 'blame silly little things' (Clark, 20s, early), was not the same as taking full, moral responsibility and working through complex feelings of shame. Representing a widely held view, Aaron argued that the latter required: 'being able to talk the truth about your crime, and not hide anything. […] And basically just be truthful with yourself'. At the same time, to move on from the offence meant learning to live with it: neither just reacting to its affective charge, through forms of anger and denial, nor being overwhelmed and hobbled by guilt. As Aakif suggested, dislodging oneself from the past in this way was far from straightforward:

> I struggled to let it out and even until now I struggle to let it out what I'm in for. You know, not just the murder word, but the rest of it. I think [I'm] embarrassed, [though] that's a bit of a weak word for it […]. The chaplaincy said 'you've got to leave the past where it is.' I said to the chaplaincy, 'well, I can't and that's the thing, I can't really move on, I can't really sit here and tell you why I did it or anything like that, because the thing is, I don't know why I did it'. There was so much going on I didn't know why I did it, but the main thing is I can't, I don't think I could live my life. There's only one basically thing in my head right now, and for the past couple

of days I just somehow want to go back in the past and change all that. (Aakif, 20s, early)

For prisoners who were maintaining their innocence, coming to terms with both the sentence and the offence was much more difficult[1]:

How long did it take before you came to terms with the sentence?
I can't come to terms with the sentence, never [...]. I'm just trying to live and trying to get acclimatised to the system, but...I can't get used to it. [...] If I [had done] it, I could get used to it, but... (Bentley, 30s, mid)

How long did it take you to come to terms with your sentence?
I don't think I'll ever come to terms with it, if I'm honest. Never, ever. I think now I've accepted I'm doing it. I've accepted that I'm doing this sentence and that's it, but I've never really come to terms with it. [Because] I don't think I should have been convicted of murder, and that's the truth. (Scott, 30s, mid)

Such reflections highlight important distinctions between accepting the reality of the sentence, regarding it as justified, and being at peace with it emotionally.

For prisoners who claimed innocence entirely, or who had been convicted as secondary parties under joint enterprise, coming to terms with the offence was particularly challenging: many had not committed the fatal act or were not present at the scene of the offence, and some denied any awareness at all of the offence. Such prisoners faced the double burden of not feeling themselves to be guilty and struggling to engage in the kinds of interventions that expedited progression through the system.

All these offending behaviour courses that you do are all based on the premise that you committed the crime, so it was kind of hard to do a victim awareness course when you're maintaining your innocence. (Linwood, 20s, mid)

---

[1] Fifteen of the 39 problems within the survey were reported as significantly more severe by participants who considered themselves to be not guilty of the offence for which they had been convicted, compared to those who considered themselves to be guilty. These included 'Feeling that your life has been wasted', 'Feeling angry with the world', 'Feeling that you are losing the best years of your life', 'Feeling that the system is ignoring your individual needs', 'Feeling frustrated that you are not progressing through the system', 'Thinking about the amount of time you might have to serve' and 'Feeling that the length of your sentence is unfair', which was the second most severe problem for prisoners who did not consider themselves guilty, compared to the 30th most severe among those who did.

Nonetheless, whether they considered themselves guilty or innocent, most prisoners found themselves able to move on from their initial period of turmoil. In the sections that follow, we document in more detail the specific factors that precipitated and sustained this transition—an acceptance or 'awakening' (Irwin 2010; Herbert 2018)—relating to both the sentence and the offence.

'Settling Down' and Moving On: Precipitating Factors

For many prisoners, acceptance of the sentence was deferred by the process of appeal. Engaging in legal action absorbed the mental space that might otherwise be filled by despair, while also offering a shard of hope that the conviction would be overturned. Both functions allowed prisoners to defer the point at which they had to accept that their long-term future was within the prison. When asked what he would do if his appeal failed, Siffre (20s, early), for example, stated that he was 'just going to keep going, I think I'll never stop until they let me out'. As a result, the time at which avenues for appeal had been exhausted was often the beginning of a new phase of adaptation. For some prisoners, the short-term impact of a failed appeal was crisis: 'I just broke down emotionally' (Paul, 20s, early); 'I just thought, you know, "what's the point of trying anymore?" [...] I didn't want to speak to my friends or anything' (Jeremiah, 20s, early); 'I started smoking weed, and after that I just couldn't be bothered. I just give up on everything' (Kendrick, 20s, early). However, once prisoners had overcome their initial distress, the longer-term consequence was to force them to 'move on':

> You have your first appeal and lose, yeah. [...] Well, up until that stage, in your head you're still saying you're going to win your appeal, until you lose it. Then you're thinking, 'well, this is a reality now and it sets in'. (Sim, mid, 30s)

> I've got an appeal in, but I'm not banking on it and I'm not even thinking I'm going to get it, because I don't think I will get it. But it's just hanging on to that little bit of hope, and if I didn't try then I'd always be living the sentence thinking, 'well, what would have, what would…'. It would always be if I did appeal would I have got it? So I'm doing it as the final straw, so that I can move on without…
> *Yeah, without always thinking 'what if?'*

Yeah, 'what if', yeah. (Liz, 20s, early)

Second, for a number of prisoners, 'settling down' and coming to terms with the sentence had not been possible until they had been transferred to prisons that were themselves relatively settled or held a high proportion of people serving similar kinds of sentences. Being among young offenders made future-thinking difficult, due to a culture of 'immaturity', 'bad influences' (Loren, 20s, early) and casual violence ('mental; fights every day' [Harris, 20s, early]). Likewise, many prisoners who had progressed out of the high-security estate (into Category B training prisoners) depicted it as a tense and volatile environment, in which everyday survival had required constant and considerable effort and energy:

> I've seen some horrible things going on [in high-security prisons]. I've seen guys getting hot oil thrown on them. I've seen guys get cut up, slashed. Just everything. […] I can't even put into words how hard it was, honestly. […] You had to watch your back all the time. […] I'd say I've been given a massive opportunity here [in a lower-security prison] to better myself, and better my sentence really. In [high-security prison], absolutely not. (Shaafi, 30s, mid)

In such contexts—'headaches, drama' (Asad, 30s, mid)—prisoners were preoccupied with daily survival and unable to find contemplative space; some emphasised the difficulties of planning ahead in circumstances where 'anything can happen at any time' (Kendrick, 20s, early), not only because of the intense politics of the prisoner world, but also the perpetual risk of being transferred to another establishment and the overbearing concern with security matters: 'everything's subject to security, security, so you could plan it and then it goes completely the opposite way' (Sim, 30s, mid). Although some prisoners reported that being transferred from a local prison to the high-security estate was when the sentence effectively started, their explanations pointed to the primacy of shared experience in easing the process of 'settling':

> I think that's when I settled into my jail properly. […] There were older people in there. That was a more settled jail. There was people in there who'd done years and years and years in jail. (Kenny, 20s, mid)

> A third stage started when I finally reached [a lifers' prison], when I was surrounded by people with a similar background and I know I'm gonna be here for a long term

so I can settle in. [...] You've taken someone's life and it's not something that you can easily talk with people [about]. It took me a long time to learn how to talk about it, plus it took me being surrounded by the people in the same situation; that makes it easier because they know what you went through, [they] know where you're coming from. (Antone, 20s, early)

As suggested here, what was shared among long-term prisoners was both the predicament of serving a particular kind of sentence and the experience of having been involved in a particular kind of offence.

A third factor that precipitated the ability to 'move on' was the passing of time and its impact on prisoners' social horizons. As we noted in Chapter 4, in the initial period of their confinement, some participants remained preoccupied with issues and relationships that were external to the prison. Yet, after a time, friends and memories from the outside world began to fade away and dwindle (see O'Donnell 2014, and Chapter 7). As they did so, prisoners came to realise that the world beyond the prison was moving on in their absence:

You start off your sentence and you think about the outside world, things you miss, your family, if you're in a relationship and stuff like that. You do miss that, but then as time goes by, because you have no real contact apart from visits with the outside world, this becomes your world. (Victor, 30s, late)

I think it hits you after about three or four years [...]. It's when you start losing things, when you start losing people, when you start realising life goes on, when people out there start getting married, [...] start progressing in life. (Cary, 20s, early)

In such circumstances, prisoners experienced a growing divergence between their everyday concerns within the prison and their engagement with the external community. Loren (20s, early), for example, explained that 'when you first come to jail, obviously everything's about staying in touch with the outside world', but that, soon, 'you forget about the outside world and it's all about the inside world'. Elaborating, he said that, having at first used the phone frequently to stay in touch with what was going on outside, he now only made calls that were 'relevant': when he needed 'to be sorting out something. [...] like my appeal, [or] money getting sent to me'. Here, then, he communicated the way in which, over time, prisoners became distanced from their previous life domains and drawn into the lifeworld of the prison.

A fourth kind of turning point related to matters of mental health, medication and drug use. In particular, for some prisoners, adaptive transformation resulted from or coincided with a recognition of problematic substance abuse, a rejection of heavy medication, the accurate diagnosis of an underlying mental health condition, or a shift in psychological well-being. Tori, for example, explained that 'When I got over my depression and I stopped letting it run my life, and the medication run my life, that was when I was able to take control of my life' (Tori, 30s, late). As suggested here, surmounting states of depression and anxiety was a key step for many prisoners in moving on from their initial phase of psychological stasis. Some did so organically: 'The third year, I've got over the depression and I'm getting myself back together' (Julius, 30s, mid); others required assistance and intervention. Jamie (20s, early) described himself as having 'acted up' until a psychological breakdown resulted in a diagnosis for post-traumatic stress disorder that was then appropriately medicated. Similarly, many prisoners identified the cessation of drug use—whether illegal drugs or prescribed medication—as a key point in their adaptive trajectory. Jill (40s, post-tariff) described herself as 'a bit of an arsehole … anti-authoritarian', until she came off Largactil and 'got into the gym'. Jenny (20s, mid) explained that her sentence had first felt survivable only after she 'finally got clean off all the drugs and everything'. Rafe (30s, mid) could recall the month, several years earlier, when he had undertaken 'detox' for a heroin habit, an act that led him to abandon his claims of innocence, begin to engage with the system and 'start reflecting': 'When I stopped taking heroin, that all come quite quickly; the thoughts of "oh my god what have I done?", came quite quickly to me'.

Some participants described undertaking courses relating to alcohol or drug misuse as key moments in their sentence:

> I think when I done [the] RAPT [course][2] it, kind of, opened up that emotional door.
> *[…] What inspired you to go on the course?*
> Eight-year heroin habit in prison. […] Knowing that the drugs were keeping me in longer. (Shane, 40s, post-tariff)

---

[2]RAPt: a drug treatment programme, delivered by the Rehabilitation for Addicted Prisoners Trust.

The termination of drug use was often accompanied by a social transition, away from other drug users and related activities, and towards a new peer group. On rejecting what she called 'the medication route', Jill (40s, post-tariff) had found 'a different circle of friends who were more pro-active and, you know, doing education and the courses and things like that'. Others described a narrowing of concerns, from the social to the individual: that is, from peer loyalties and prisoner politics to personal burdens and priorities. Meanwhile, in disavowing substances whose effects were absorptive and suppressive, prisoners found the energy and headspace to contemplate their actions ('start reflecting'), deal with submerged, disquieting feelings, and make more active decisions about their futures ('take control of my life'). Here, then, we find the themes of agency and emotional processing that feature throughout this chapter.

A fifth driver of adaptive transformation was participation in victim aware-ness courses, restorative justice programmes, and other kinds of interventions (see also Herbert 2018). Such activities enabled prisoners to think beyond their own interests, gain self-understanding, look at their offence from the viewpoint of its victims and consider the wider ramifications of their acts. Attention shifted from the suffering of self to the suffering of others. Jill (40s, post-tariff) attributed the offending behaviour courses she had undertaken with having made her 'look at [her]self ... and then accept what I'd done and my part in it'. Likewise, Asad explained that:

> ...the big turning point of my sentence was when I could put myself in the victim or the deceased's family, and put myself in their shoes. That's when I started to realise it's bigger than just me, and it's not just about me - the action that I took on that day has affected so many people's lives. [...] I've destroyed not just one life [...]. There's a mum out there, there's a dad out there, there's brothers, sisters grieving every single day for the action that I had taken. And from the time I started looking at things from their point of view, my whole outlook has changed on my sentence and how I feel about my sentence. [...] My thinking process has changed. [And] once my thinking process changed, then naturally everything else around me change[d] as well. (Asad, 30s, mid)

For Asad, transformation was essentially cognitive ('my thinking process'). A num-ber of other prisoners recalled their turning point—or what Lempert (2016) refers to as 'decision points'—as a singular moment of intense cognitive or emotional epiphany. Bernard (40s, post-tariff), for example, had a 'mystical experience'—'probably the pivotal moment in my life'—which 'just made me wonder what life was about and who I was. I had to question everything about myself and it was like I was seeing things for the very first time'. Stuart (40s, post-tariff) 'totally switched' one day, after his drug supply route had dried up: 'I went and seen the drug worker basically, and I said "look, I've had enough of this" [...] and I never really looked back'. For both Tommy and Stephen, being placed in a segregation unit precipitated a radical shift in orientation, the former coming to recognise that 'I had a problem, not everybody else', following an unprovoked assault on a prison officer, and the latter reflecting on his desolation and lack of self-efficacy:

> I think when it really hit me was when I was sitting in the segregation unit and I suddenly thought, 'what the hell have I done with my life? Why have I allowed all of that shit, and why couldn't have I just spoken to somebody, or had the balls to get up and say, "Look, I'm out of control".' [...] I couldn't blame it on [my] family because they hadn't been around for ages, I couldn't blame it on drink because I hadn't had a drink, and it kind of left [me to realise] 'ah, it's possibly me'. [...] And I was in the seg for about six months and I thought, 'no, I can't do this anymore'. (Tommy, 50s, post-tariff)

> I was in the block at one time, [...] and I was just thinking to myself: 'why do I do all this stuff? What am I doing with my life?' Then I started to think, 'I need to make my way out of prison', and things like that. [...] I just thought, 'look at me, I am in this little room within the world. [...] I am stuck in this little room, and I am just isolated from everyone and everything, and I can't actually make anything materialise'. So I started to think a bit about getting out: how do I get out? (Stephen, 20s, mid)

Lengthy periods of segregation were fateful because they represented a 'rock-bottom' moment, and because endless hours spent alone in a cell generated a great deal of time for existential reflection (Maruna et al. 2006; Comfort 2008; Appleton 2010; O'Donnell 2014; Schinkel 2014).

For other prisoners, the trigger for change was relational. Ashley described his meeting with his victim's mother as follows:

> She wanted to speak to me about why her son ended up getting killed on the night. [...] And I told her what had happened, [...] and we spoke about that. [...] She

spoke some more about how she copes on a day-to-day basis, and the loss. And then she asked me if she could give me a hug, and she got up and she came over and gave me a hug and I just burst into tears, man, I was like a mess in the place. And it was emotional and overwhelming, and it wasn't what I expected. [...] I was just expecting her to shout at me and scream at me, and that would have been easier for me to deal with that kind of thing; it's easier for me to deal with those kind of emotions and that kind of stuff. What she did, it was like... it was just too much for me to deal with on that day, man.

And how did that stay with you and affect you?

The last thing she said to me [was that] she did not want two lives to be wasted. [...] She said that she wanted me to make sure that my life turned out with something good, and not waste it, you know, partly in the memory of her son who died that night. And it was like taking a deep breath for a first time, you know, like when I breathed in, it was like I felt some new life in my lungs. (Ashley, 30s, mid)

The unexpected affective intensity of Ashley's experience ('it was emotional and overwhelming ... too much for me to deal with') was significant, opening up reflexive space, and making him confront his feelings of shame in relation to the vision of a different future.

A similar function was provided by establishments such as HMP Grendon, which featured very prominently in the change narratives of a large number of participants (for further details on Grendon's ethos and effects, see Genders and Player 1995; Stevens 2013).[3] Many male prisoners credited Grendon with fundamentally changing their orientation to their sentence. Phil (60s, post-tariff), for example, reported that being transferred to Grendon was the point at which he was first able to 'see a bit of light ahead', while Mahmood (30s, mid) noted that it was only on reaching Grendon that his 'journey started'. Sites such as Grendon offered a more humane environment than most other prisons, making prisoners more inclined to 'work with' rather than against the system. More importantly, they compelled prisoners to engage in forms of therapy that contributed significantly to key processes of emotion management and existential deliberation.

---

[3]The preponderance of such narratives was, in part, the outcome of our decision to identify a sample of participants within Grendon, although this decision reflected the fact that it is one of the seven Category B training prisons in the England & Wales prison system (another of which, HMP Dovegate, itself houses a 200-bed therapeutic community). That is, while prisoners in Grendon were over-represented in our sample relative to the population, many prisoners serving long sentences enter its community, or ones that are similar (such as the smaller therapeutic in HMP Gartree), at some point during their confinement.

Often, prisoners used metaphors of 'burial' to express the ways in which their emotions had been suppressed prior to being in therapy. Marcus (50s, post-tariff) explained that Grendon had helped him deal with 'issues that I've been carrying for years [...]. All the secrets that you've held onto and you bury'. Joseph (40s, post-tariff) recalled having been 'extremely bitter and angry' in the early years of his sentence, for reasons that he could not grasp until his engagement with psychologists and transferral to Grendon had induced a period of psychological introspection:

> It really opened up my mind to a lot of things, and I finally could put a lot of things together which I had no insight of for a long time, because I had buried a lot of stuff. [...] So that all started to make sense: why I had such issues with male authority, where all that really came from and why it is embedded in my thought patterns and how I deal with things. (Joseph, 40s, post-tariff)

For Joseph, and many others, Grendon helped unlock, explore and make sense of issues from childhood. Other prisoners, such as Mahmood, emphasised the impact of being able to talk frankly about their offence, in ways that had felt impossible elsewhere in the prison system:

> It helped me so much to talk about my crime, because I have held in a lot of guilt about what I've done. [...] I really wanted people to talk to. I really wanted people to understand what was going on inside of me because I kind of created my own world with myself, my own bubble, which I could escape in, that I could cry, I could be emotional and be down and depressed. [But as] soon as that [cell] door would unlock I would be smiling and hide behind my work and show no vulnerability. Coming here has helped me to actually show that side of myself. [In other prisons], I spoke to people on a superficial level, but never about my feelings and my thoughts, if there were problems at home or anything. [...] It's been a hell of a journey since then, to the person I am now. (Mahmood, 30s, mid)

As suggested here, Grendon's culture of trust and mutual support encouraged prisoners to show vulnerability, opening up space for them to identify and analyse emotional matters relating to their childhoods and offending. Of particular significance is that, in doing so—that is, in helping prisoners to liberate themselves from the grip of emotions such as shame and anger—it helped advance them from a state of reactive agency and fractured reflexivity.

Similar processes were described by prisoners who had not been through Grendon, but who had found other ways of confronting emotional trauma: for Justin (20s, early), a key step had been to 'forgive my dad and get over all of that'; Bryant (40s, post-tariff) described his driver of change as the point at which he decided to open up about and seek treatment for childhood abuse. These processes of emotional reflection involved and enabled an ongoing dialogue with the self:

> *Was there a particular turning point [...] where you thought 'this has got to change'?*
> I think for me it was during my time at Parkhurst and [...] I thought, 'why was I doing it? What is all this about?' Then the more it went on, the more I realised that I needed to understand for myself. There's so much stuff that I ain't talking about, that I've buried; Where is all this anger coming from? Where is all this hate coming from? Because I have buried a lot of the abuse, so I couldn't even see that myself. [...] I knew my behaviour was abnormal, but I couldn't work out why. So it started from there. (Joseph, 40s, post-tariff)

> Anger management's been the biggest one, it was where I realised why I was angry and what I was angry at and who I was angry at, [...] and I'm not that angry person any more, it's not my go-to response, because it used to be my go to response...shout, scream, and people would go away and leave me alone, whereas now if there's an issue I will deal with it and face it. (Jenny, 20s, mid)

Dialogue of this kind—the attempt to understand the self and work out patterns of emotional response—led prisoners to a fundamental reassessment of who they were and wanted to be.

In such respects, participants who were some years into their sentence resembled Archer's (2003, 2012) description of meta-reflexives. They were 'contextually unsettled' (2003: 257) and 'reflexively pre-occupied' (2003: 269), striving to transform themselves through knowing, monitoring and cultivating the self. Internal deliberation enabled them to construct themselves as particular kinds of people, propelled by idealistic objectives—wanting to 'make a difference' in the world, rather than merely satisfying immediate needs. We return to these issues in due course.

Discourses of Adaptation

The transitions described above were accompanied and sustained by a number of common discourses.[4] The first—'things could be worse'—was a form of comparative positivity, whereby prisoners asserted their good fortune relative to their victims, to prisoners in other jurisdictions, or to people whose circumstances were worse than their own. For example:

> In my country where I'm from, if I'd have taken a life my life would have been taken. An eye for an eye. So it's like I'm grateful that I get a second chance to do good with my life. (Asad, 30s, mid)

> In spite of everything, I do count my blessings because actually it could be a lot worse. My life could be worse, my health could be worse, my physical being could be worse, the conditions that I am in [...]. We all have our afflictions in life. [...]. Everyone suffers in some fashion. [...]. Things happen to people and if it hadn't been this maybe it would have been something else. (Dan, 20s, early)

> There's places a lot worse than mine, and that makes me feel a bit better inside. [...] It makes me feel my life wasn't that bad. People are out there suffering, people who can't even feed themselves. (Victor, 30s, post-tariff)

The second was a view that 'prison saved my life', by intervening in a lifestyle of addiction, violence or serious criminality that would otherwise have led to death:

> If I didn't come to jail, I would have carried on living life wrong anyway; I'd probably end up dead or [...] physically hurt, you know. (Luca, 30s, mid)

> This has been the best thing for me. I think I was a hazard to myself. I would have been dead now, I think. [...] Someone probably would have killed me or I would have killed myself with the drugs and drink. (Tori, 30s, late)

---

[4]We refer to these discourses as adaptive, rather than as forms of denial, partly because they did not involve dismissal of the reality of the situation, and partly because they helped prisoners to 'move on' rather than 'stand still'. It should be noted, however, that the causal and temporal pathway of these transitions and discourses varied or was unclear.

Such beliefs were asserted by some prisoners with considerable confidence. John (20s, mid) stated that 'there was only two ways I was living my life: jail or the graveyard'. Jenny (20s, mid) declared that she knew 'for a fact' that both she and her daughter, with whom she had been pregnant when arrested, would be dead had she not been imprisoned: 'so in a way prison's kind of saved my life and my daughter's really. [...] In one way I am grateful that I come in as young as I did, because if I'd stayed out I'd never have got to that age'. As suggested here, though ('In one way....'), not all prisoners expressed such beliefs in terms of unambiguous gratitude. Many recognised the tragedy of their circumstances, in which long-term confinement was both saviour and disaster:

> I never thought I'd end up in prison, but on the flipside of that prison saved my life, because of the road I was going down. If I didn't end up in prison, then I probably would have been dead in a gutter somewhere, because it was spiralling out of control quite a bit. [...] So it's weird where you could actually say a life sentence has ruined my life, [but] has also saved me. (Eileen, 30s, late)

A third trope was that 'I came to prison for a reason', and that, however unjust or bewildering, the predicament had some cosmic purpose. Some prisoners—particularly those who were maintaining innocence—reasoned that their sentence was, in effect, a reckoning for a range of offences for which they were guilty but had never been prosecuted (i.e. a form of accumulated guilt):

> You're just getting punished all at once. For every little thing that you might have done that was not only stupid little things like driving without a licence. (Julius, 30s, mid)

> I've broken lots of laws and done lots of bad things in my life, so I have this thing where I look at it and say, 'maybe it's just karma, for all the things I've done and got away with'. (Ashley, 30s, mid)

Others expressed a more spiritual logic that their conviction was fated, even if its grounds were not yet apparent to them:

> I've got more in touch with my religion while I've been here. So I started believing that - I don't know, like maybe God sent me here for a reason...
> *So has that helped?*

Yeah, it has helped. [...] Instead of being angry at the world or angry at everybody else, and feeling sorry for yourself and depressed [about] what's happened to me, the way I'm thinking of things now, like it's all happened for a reason and if God wants me to get out, then he'll help me with my appeal and I'm getting out. (Kendrick, 20s, early)

Everything happens for a reason, I come jail for a reason. I wish that someone didn't have to die, maybe something else I'd have come jail for, because we all need that wake-up call in life. (Cary, 20s, early)

As noted above, this perception—'everything has a reason'—was often linked to religious faith. For current purposes, our emphasis is on the fatalism that it shared with the other rationalisations elaborated above. Each offered a means by which prisoners could reconcile themselves to an unavoidable reality and persuade themselves that circumstances were less bad and more psychologically manageable than they ostensibly felt. Paradoxically too, although each offered a means by which prisoners could reassert some sense of agency over the future (by helping them to come to terms with their predicament), they did so by positioning prisoners as non-agents: their experiences defined or determined by external forces.

Prisoners convicted as secondary offenders under joint enterprise often resorted to such reasoning as a form of what Schinkel (2014: 72) calls 'coping acceptance', in which guilt is expressed more due to the need to cope than because of a sense that the sentence is 'normatively just' (p. 72). As well as expressing the modes of reasoning described above, some secondary offenders talked up their contribution to the murder for which they had been convicted as a way of justifying to themselves, and thereby coming to terms with, their ongoing detention. Having spent many years interrogating their recollections for traces of culpability, some emphasised their failure to prevent death ('because in the eyes of the law if you don't stop something then you are guilty'. [Carly, 30s, late]), while others redefined their actions as having contributed directly to the victim's death. Such rationalisations were often unconvincing, producing rather inconsistent accounts of moral and legal guilt, in which prisoners sought to persuade themselves of the legitimacy of their punishment at the same time as they disputed the fairness of their conviction. For example:

Do I think [the conviction is] fair? I mean [sighs] I don't know if 'fair' is the right word. I've accepted it. For the fact that somebody's lost their life. And I think I have done that for me to be able to get through my sentence. […] Yeah I was there, yeah, I […] met up with some people, but I didn't actually pull the trigger. I didn't shoot anybody. And I had no intention of doing that. So it's not fair in that type of way, you know? (Campbell, 30s, mid)

The point of such cognitive manoeuvres was to find a form of acceptance that enabled psychological survival by minimising the conflict between prisoners' sense of injustice and their unchangeable circumstances (see Park 2010). Persuading themselves of their guilt (even if it meant compartmentalising feelings of acute resentment) allowed them to accept their legal status, acquiesce to their confinement, and cope emotionally, rather than living with the corrosive effects of permanent embitterment (see Hulley et al. 2019).

This motivation was shared by prisoners who did not dispute their guilt. As suggested above, most prisoners recognised the need to evade or overcome emotions such as anger and resentment, and to avoid mind-states such as depression, for fear of where they could lead. Such concerns were sometimes instrumental, based on an understanding that those who could not contain their rage would languish in high-security prisons and delay their progression through the system. On the whole, however, the primary concern was the risk of psychological decomposition:

I'm here too long to be depressed and always like that. […] you can't let yourself get mired down in that kind of thinking, do you know what I mean? […] I can't really afford to be depressed. (Carl, 20s, early)

You can't be sitting there feeling sorry for yourself because that would just eat you away. You'll rot in your cell, innit? (Asad, 30s, mid)

Anger […] just drains you and makes it depressing. It's something that…you know if you got a rotten piece of fruit, it just keeps on deteriorating. (Bentley, 30s, mid)

In some respects, then, as phrases such as 'I'm at peace with it' or 'you just have to accept it' implied, 'coping' required a degree of resignation. With great consistency, prisoners explained that accepting the sentence was necessary to avoid what Scott (30s, mid) called the 'downhill slope' of depression. Paradoxically, however, they were in effect prohibiting themselves from sitting with the kinds of emotions that were a rational outcome of their situation. To have such emotions was hazardous, yet—as we discuss in Chapter 8—to suppress them brought risks of its own.

To summarise briefly at this point, in their early years of confinement, most prisoners could do little more than seek to survive the experience and remain psychologically intact. Most existed in a state of fractured or stunted reflexivity, in which they were unable to see beyond their day-to-day needs, reflect productively on their circumstances, or project themselves beyond the present. In time, they began to come to terms both with their sentence and with their offence. That is, they came to recognise that they needed to adapt to a new lifeworld, and to confront a range of emotions relating to their offence and their penal circumstances. In the next sections of this chapter, we continue to explain how prisoners moved on from their initial state of 'coping-survival' to what we call 'coping-adaptation', focusing specifically on the differences between how early- and later-stage prisoners discussed three key matters: control, hope and purpose.

Control

The first area in which early-stage prisoners expressed a stunted form of agency was in relation to control and autonomy. These matters were of huge significance (see also Johnson and McGunigall-Smith 2008). 'Having to follow other people's rules and orders' and 'Feeling that you have no control over your life' were reported by our female survey participants as the most severe and 12th most severe problems that they experienced, and by the male survey participants as the fourth and 20th most severe. With striking consistency, men and women in the initial period of imprisonment felt themselves to be almost completely lacking in power and control:

> *To what extent do you feel that you have control on your life in here?*
> None. (Antone, 20s, early)

> Got no power in here, ain't got no power. Got no power here. [...] The only power we've got in here is our rights, the things that prisoners are allowed to have, that's it, that's all we're allowed. That's the only power we've got. (Miguel, late teens, early)

> *Do you feel like you have got control of your life in here?*

No. [...]
Is there any areas that you take control of, that you feel like you can?
No. (Darrin, late teens, early)

In interviews, when asked specifically about the most difficult aspects of the sentence, responses from prisoners at all sentence stages very often focused on such matters, coalescing around two main areas. The first related to limitations on everyday control and autonomy—'not being able to do anything you want to do' (Toby, 20s, early)—and the fundamental trauma of being deprived of liberty. As Drake (2018) suggests, the apparently obvious painfulness of the loss of liberty and autonomy means that there is a tendency for it to be downplayed. Yet such pains are 'the foundation of all prison experiences' (Drake 2018: 5) and were often described as such by our interviewees, in terms that were extremely raw:

The three most difficult things? Well, two of them is obvious, really. Freedom, or lack of freedom and lack of liberty, basically. (Neil, 30s, mid)

There are lots of people that think prisons are easy and 'they've got a telly, and they've got this, and they've got that'. But do you know what? This is such a harsh, hard punishment and I'm not saying it shouldn't be, but I have got to spend every day for the rest of my life with what I did. [...] And wherever I go there is a great big fence and a great big wall that'll stop me going any further. [...] Your freedom and your liberty are something so precious, and my punishment is that I will miss so many firsts and so many lasts of everything my family will do. And I live with the realisation that members of my family may well die before I get to see them again, and that's hard. And, actually, having the TV and having it so easy as everybody seems to think it is, I would swap it in a heartbeat for five minutes at home. (Maria, 20s, early)

In such ways, prisoners highlighted both their spatial confinement and a basic loss of power to engage in daily practices that were normal in the free community. While male and female respondents described their lack of control in similar terms, female participants were more likely to dwell on the multitude of ways in which the prison exerted control over daily and intimate practices. For example:

To what extent do you feel that you've got control of your life in here?

Haven't really got much control at all …you can't even pick what food you want because they dictate to you what's on the canteen sheet, they dictate to you your menu. […] Your clothes are restricted because you're only allowed a certain amount. You're not allowed an electric toothbrush. […] Your meals are sent over when they send them over. If you're poorly you can't control what medication you take [and] I find that quite difficult, not being in control of my own life. (Kathryn, 20s, early)

You don't have control, you get told when to get up, you get told when to go to the dining room, you get told when to eat and when to go to work, when you can get your mail. You get told when you can get your medication. You get told when and where to do everything. (Eileen, 30s, late)

In this respect, it was telling that women reported 'Wishing you had more privacy' as the sixth most severe problem they faced, compared to 23rd among the men.[5] That is, loss of privacy related in part to the loss of control over practices that female prisoners considered to be highly personal.

Compared to male participants, our female participants more often discussed loss of control in relation to relationships with their children: not being able to phone them at preferred times, being unable to find out about their health and welfare ('I'm not allowed to know where he is, I'm not allowed a number, I'm not allowed nothing' [Fiona, 20s, early]), and feeling helpless and uninformed with regard to custody issues. A higher proportion of the female prisoners also made reference to the difficulty of adjusting to having so little control relative to their levels of autonomy and responsibility prior to confinement, either as parents (or surrogate-parents to younger siblings) or because they had been self-reliant from an early age. More often than the men, they objected to being 'suffocated' (Karen, 20s, mid) or infantilised by institutional power (see Genders and Player 1990; Carlen 1983, 1998). To quote Nadia (20s, early): 'They were asking me to do, like, "go to your room, go and get your food". […] I might be in prison and I might be getting punished, but I'm not a child, I'm a fully-grown woman'. The men in the sample had less often been living independently of parents or as primary carers for children, and expressed such feelings far less frequently.

The other factor of relevance here was the prevalence in female participants' lives of assaultive and abusive relationships. Such experiences made them particularly

---

[5] 'Having to follow other people's rules and orders' (women: 20.50; men 14.71); 'Feeling that you have no control over your life' (women 14.58; men 10.17).

sensitive to the way that power was exerted upon them.[6] As other scholars have noted, the prison environment itself reproduces a dynamic of abuse (e.g. Girshick 2003; Gartner and Kruttschnitt 2004), and in their testimonies of powerlessness, our female participants—more often than the men in our sample—made explicit connections between their family dynamics and experiences of abuse prior to imprisonment and their feelings about the use of authority in prison. Ostensibly, such sentiments did not seem to reflect a sense that prison staff wilfully overused their authority: the problem of 'prison officers making life harder' was ranked as the 30th most severe by the women and as the 22nd most severe problem by the men. Rather, it signalled an intense sensitivity to the erratic use of power and to issues of trust (see Chapter 6).

A second set of difficulties derived from dependence on or subordination to authority: 'not having control to do things when you want [to get] things done' (Bentley, 30s, mid). The emphasis here was on helplessness, and the frustration of the individual's everyday life and future being controlled or determined by other people. Billy (20s, early), for example, stated his hatred for prison, elaborating that 'I belong to the government, I belong to these lot'. In conceptualising 'control', early-stage prisoners often used binary terminology of this kind: whether they were free or un-free, and the power of prison officers both to exert authority over their everyday lives and, specifically, to lock them up.[7] In describing his lack of control, Blake (20s, early) stated that 'you've got minor control, but whatever they say goes'; Andre (late teens, early) referred to 'getting told what to do twenty-four hours a day'; Oscar (20s, early) likewise commented that, beyond some everyday choices he could make over his attitude and self-presentation, 'everything else is dictated by these'. Implied here was a rather passive discourse, in which the prisoner was, in Jeremiah's terms, 'programmed' by institutional authority and timetabling, i.e. more object than agent:

Do you feel that you're in control of your life in here?
No. I think the guards, they're controlling you. Sometimes it's like I'm programmed in here, and that's how it feels like I'm a robot. [...] Basically you're just programmed to do the daily...as soon as you get up in the morning you know this is going to

---

[6]The connection between such experiences and feelings of powerlessness is well established (see Campbell et al. 1995; Finkelhor et al. 2007).

[7]For prisoners at this sentence stage, the significance of legal appeal was that it was an outcome that, in a single step, would overturn current circumstances.

happen, you know that's going to happen [...]. You know exercise is at this time and you know that food is at this time. [...]

So are there any parts of your life where you do feel that you've got control?

I've got control over my freedom of speech and my education, but other than that, everything else, no. (Jeremiah, 20s, early)

Early-stage prisoners also noted with consistency the continuous and oppressive possibility of life being interrupted by being sent without warning or explanation to the prison's segregation unit or to another establishment:

I'm not in charge of my own liberty [...]. Anything can happen, one day the officers can come to me in gear and say to me 'you're going to the block'. That happened to me last time. I was in the block for about two months for no reason, they still haven't told me today. They just take you. (Cary, 20s, early)

I know right now they could come to me and say, 'Right, come on, you're moving'. [...] You've just always got that in the back of your head, that you could be moved at any time, or your cell could be searched. (Kenny, 20s, mid)

As Kenny's quote suggests, a further feature of early-stage prisoners' perceptions of control was their emphasis on the private sphere. Like Paul, most felt that their primary—or only—domain of autonomy was their cell, because this was the only space in which they could not be told what to do or how to conduct themselves. Often, they referred to the control they exerted over what they were able to read, study or watch on television once they were locked in:

To what extent do you feel that you have control of your life in here?

There are certain things which are permanent aspects which you can't control, but the things that you can control is, for example, like, what I can watch on TV, what I wanna study, what I wanna learn. [...] It's nice to... like, when I get locked up and that, I can... the time's mine. [...] The door's locked, it's just me. (Casper, 20s, early)

Again, then, power and control were understood in terms that were rather dualistic: inside the cell, they were in the hands of prisoners; beyond it, they belonged almost entirely to the authorities.

Similarly, subordination was often expressed with reference to the possession of cell keys: the essential reality that, to use Martin's (20s, early) terms, 'You ain't got no control, unless you have got a set of keys'. Paul offered a detailed explanation of why he considered himself to have so little control over his life, which centred on such matters:

> You have no control over anything.
> *No control over anything?*
> Not really. [...] You can think you have control but in the end the officers have control. [...] Everything you do in prison is down to whether the officers let you do it. So, in reality, you can think you're in control but you're not. At the end of the day, the officers are still locking the door, so they're in control. All it takes for the officer to kick the door open and close it theirself again, they're still in control [...] The only thing you're in control of is whether you choose to top yourself or not.[8] That's your decision. That's about the only thing you're in control of, [and] when you want to go to the toilet when you're in your cell. Cos when you're not in your cell, if you're in Education, you have to go at a certain time, so you're not in control of when you can go to the toilet any more. You're not in control of when you want to have a shower. You have a certain time period where you can have a shower. (Paul, 20s, early)

In discussing the forms of control that they had retained or appropriated, early-stage prisoners generally referred to mundane matters, or efforts to control their affective state. Many felt able to control only their anger, their emotional reactions, their everyday decisions—such as whether or not to attend gym sessions, or what clothes to wear—or aspects of their personality, such as their sense of humour. In doing so, they tended to qualify their statements by noting that these were their sole areas of control ('everything else is up to them' [Hugo, 20s, early]), were relatively trivial or—as matters of personality and selfhood—were the last territories that could be defended against the encroachment of institutional power:

> Joking or laughing is like the one thing that the system can't ever take away from you. Your sense of humour, who you are as a person, they can't change that unless you let them. [...] So I want to hold on to as much of my sense of self as a I can, because that's all I've got. (Carl, 20s, early)

---

[8] 'Top yourself': take your own life.

As a corollary, early-stage prisoners felt themselves to have relatively little control over aspects of life that were most significant, including their future prospects and the unfolding of their lives:

Do you feel that you're in control of your life here?
Not at all, no. [There] are superficial, minor things, you know, that you do on a day-to-day basis but ultimately you look at the bigger picture and you know you're not in control of life. [...] I'm not in control of my future. Ultimately, the decisions lie with people beyond these walls. [...] My future is not in my hands, and that's very demoralizing. (Dan, 20s, early)

The differences between what mid- and late-stage prisoners said about their feelings of control compared to those at earlier sentence stages were, to some extent, a matter of degree. In practice, prisoners operated within the same institutional structures regardless of their sentence stage, and those who had served many years in prison had no more control over the nature of the regime or the use of staff authority than those whose sentences had recently begun. However, their reflections revealed significant differences in perception (O'Donnell 2014) and feelings of self-efficacy, including greater confidence that there were elements of life over which control could be exerted, a revised definition of control, and an altogether stronger sense of agency (Appleton 2010).

One difference related to the perception of the fundamental extent to which they had control over their daily life. Many mid- and late-stage prisoners expressed a similar sense of powerlessness as their less experienced peers, and of having control mainly over minor, everyday matters.[9] However, they were less likely to present this powerlessness in terms that were absolute, rarely responding to questions about everyday control with answers of blunt negativity. More often, they stated themselves to have control 'to some extent', albeit within obvious limits. For example:

Do you feel like you've got control of your life in here?

---

[9] In discussing the activities that did produce a sense of control, being able to cook one's own food was cited most regularly as something that provided a degree of choice, and some sense of normalcy and commensality: 'it just makes a massive difference, you know, that being able to like socialise with someone at dinner time' (Linwood, 20s, mid).

To a certain point, you know. You can't control everything that happens, but with my things I've set out that I want to do and the way I go about things I think I've got a fairly good handle on it. (Curtis, 20s, mid)

Do you feel that you've got control of your life in here, or certain aspects of your life?
I've got control of certain aspects. I've got control in my reactions and how I react to people, and how I interact with people; my plans for the future and getting myself prepared and ready for that. I've got certain control over my education and I've got certain control over staying healthy, and staying fit, staying positive. (Ashley, 30s, mid)

Such prisoners understood control less in relation to external constraints or institutional demands than the internal freedoms that were possible within the parameters of incarceration. In this respect, as Johnson and Dobrzanska (2005) report, they recognised their powerlessness to control their general predicament and the futility of trying to do so:

You have said 'It is what it is' quite a few times, and it seems to be quite an important mantra for you [...].
Yes because I know how much time and energy I would waste, when I first come away, about things I couldn't change, and I would never be able to change. [...] You are wasting that time, when you could be using that time on something else that you could change [...]. And that's what I've tried to do ever since, is not go over old ground that you can't work out any different to what it is. Some things are what they are, and you ain't never going to change it ever, [so] you have got to be able to put it to bed and move on. (Joseph, 40s, post-tariff)

This attitude—what O'Donnell refers to as 'acceptance', or 'yielding to rather than opposing the flow of life' (Tolle 2005: 171, cited in O'Donnell 2014: 252)—was common. Prisoners who were some years into their sentence had learned to live with frustration and avoid dwelling on matters beyond their grasp: to 'swim with the tide', as such (Crewe et al. 2017). Compared to early-stage prisoners, they were much less preoccupied with basic matters of freedom and confinement. As Kenny (20s, mid) said, 'Anything that's out of my control, there's no point in stressing about it'. This process involved a broader shift, in which they relinquished the unalterable past, submitted to those aspects of the present that they could not alter, and sought instead to exercise control over personal conduct and selfhood:

Any other areas of your life where you try to retain control, or gain back some control?
Yeah, my behaviour. My behaviour: other people controlled my behaviour and my temperament before. I will blame you, it was your fault that I'm crazy - that's how I used to think. Whereas, now, no one can make me mad, only I can make myself mad. You can be a dickhead and do whatever you want to me, but it's up to me how I react to it. (Asad, 30s, mid)

Do you feel like you've got any control over your life in here?
Yes. […] Like, I have no liberty, but the person I am, the person I've grown to become is in spite of this place, these people.
So you feel like you've been in control over the person you've become?
Of course, well, I am in control over the person I've become. I made the person I am. (Neil, 30s, mid)

Compared to early-stage prisoners, this focus was less emotionally reactive, more oriented to the future and more agentic. As we discuss below and in Chapter 7, it was grounded in a sense of who participants wanted to be or become, their desire to reconstruct themselves as ethical beings, and their aspiration to build a life that was constructive. Like Archer's 'meta-reflexives', then, mid- and late-stage prisoners were 'fiercely individuated and insistent upon being the authors of their own values' (Archer 2012: 211).

Describing an epiphanal moment in his sentence, Bernard used this language of authorship to convey a key shift in his orientation to life:

I felt in control of my life. It was, like, I were writing in my own pages of my book, now. You know, it wasn't someone else writing them for me. I didn't feel like - fate didn't have this in store for me. From this point on, I was in control of where I went. (Bernard, 40s, post-tariff)

The sense of agency that Bernard expressed was typical of prisoners who were further into their sentences, who spoke a more coherent language of forging their selfhood and having some control over both their sentence and their future. Shaafi (30s, mid), for example, stated that he had 'a lot' of control over his life, noting that 'everything's down to you really. If you put work into it, and be open and honest, then you're going to get a massive amount from it'. Nathaniel (30s, mid) likewise proclaimed that 'You make your sentence how you want to make it; either you can have it hard or you can have it easy'. Asked to what extent he felt in control of his life in prison, Scott replied:

> I think I'm in charge of my own destiny in a way, because if I stick to what I'm doing, hopefully I shall get a positive move and I shall have progressed through the categories and go home. But in another sense, it's the screws [officers] and that, psychology, all them are in charge of whether you get your move, your categorization, things like that, so you're never totally in charge of your life. (Scott, 30s, mid)

Scott underscored the limits of control for prisoners who were confronting the prospect of release, with all of the uncertainties attached to a sentence that was indeterminate. Compared to early-stage prisoners, those later in their sentences were much less preoccupied with the control exerted by prison officers, and much more concerned by the arbiters of release, such as probation staff, prison psychologists and the Parole Board. With consistency, they contrasted the control they felt in determining their everyday existence with their relative powerlessness over decisions about progression and release:

> *To what extent do you feel in control of your life in here?*
> I'm really in control, as I've said before, that the only time I don't feel in control is the parole board, because that's out of my hands. (Haashim, 30s, post-tariff)

> There's obviously certain things that you've got restrictions on and that, and basically these [staff] are in control of your life ultimately, of decisions and your future, or whatever. [...]
> *So who is it that's got the main control over your future that you mention?*
> Well, the Parole Board, really. Psychology and parole, cos it's them that are gonna make the decisions about what happens, you know. Where you go, whether you get [recategorized] or whatever [...], what courses you have to do.
> *And what about control over your everyday life?*
> I've got a lot of control over that. (Curtis, 20s, mid)

Accordingly, one area where some mid- and late-stage prisoners felt relatively helpless was in relation to the reports that contributed to decisions about their progression and release. As Willis (30s, mid) commented, 'you don't know what's being written behind your back, and you don't know what the decision's going to be at the end'. Reflecting on the 'tightness' of institutional power, and, in particular, the influence of the bureaucratic file (Crewe 2011), some prisoners declared themselves indifferent to what was written about them, because this was beyond their control or because they regarded their behaviour as, in any case, pro-social. Often, however, they expressed anxiety and frustration about living 'in a goldfish bowl' in which 'everything you do, you say, you don't do, is documented' (Jenny, 20s, mid), and where the content of reports often felt unfair, arbitrary, difficult to challenge and highly consequential: 'a couple of sentences wrong on one report can lead to another two or three years in jail' (John, 20s, mid). We return to such matters in Chapter 7.

Hope, Meaning and Purpose

Hope has been defined as believing in one's own capacity to work towards goals and having the ability to 'produce plausible routes' to meet them (Snyder 2000: 9, cited in Martin and Stermac 2010: 694), and is known to be a 'coping mechanism in dire situations' (Martin and Stermac 2010: 694). For early-stage prisoners, however, the bleakness of their circumstances was reflected in expressions of deep hopelessness:

> *Can you tell me a little bit about how you felt when you found out about the length of the sentence you'd be serving?*
> I just thought 'that's it, innit?', I thought 'there's kind of no hope now. I'm never going to see outside again'. (Shaafi, 30s, mid)

> A life sentence kills your hope, man, it takes it, it takes it, it takes it easy, it swallows it. You've got no hope and no future, no life, no nothing. You're in your cell crying, 'Oh, my girl is going to leave me, my mum and my dad will probably be dead, my brothers will have all moved on with their wives and their kids. I'm going to get out of jail broke, homeless'. (Ashley, 30s, early)

One reason why levels of hope were so low (and levels of depression so high) was that so many prisoners had not expected to be found guilty. Having been convicted unexpectedly, and often feeling a deep sense of injustice, they were highly despondent about the future. Johnnie (late teens, early) had 'learned not to put hope in this justice system. Because I was hopeful I was going to go home, [and] it didn't happen'. Likewise, when asked how hopeful he was about this future, Martin (20s, early) replied: 'I have been let down already once so I couldn't tell you'.

As we discussed in Chapter 4, for some early-stage prisoners, hope lay in the possibility of short-term release, through the process of appeal. Even in this regard, however, expectations were subdued. While some prisoners expressed absolute—perhaps desperate—confidence that they would see success, most were cautious. James's comment that he did not 'want to get my hopes up' (20s, early) was representative of a common orientation towards appeal, in which the fear of disappointment was palpable. Hope was therefore counterbalanced by a form of protective pragmatism:

> The way I think about it is that I'm not going to get it, and if I do get it then it's a bonus, because if I put my mind in the state of 'yeah, I'm going to get it', and then I don't, it will be heart-breaking. [...] Just shatter your dreams. (Toby, 20s, early)

Not all early-stage prisoners were quite so despondent. Yet even those who expressed some degree of optimism communicated considerable ambivalence about their prospects. Terms such as 'you've got to [feel hope]' (Cary, 20s, early) and 'I have to be hopeful' (Bruce, 20s, early) were an acknowledgement of both the dangers of sinking into despair and the effort required not to do so.

Feelings of hopelessness and disorientation were compounded by a lack of institutional support. Several prisoners did not, for some time, understand the meaning of the 'minimum tariff' or the implications of serving a life sentence, such as being on permanent license after release. Many reported deficits in information and emotional support that left them feeling confused, alone and unsupported in dealing with their situation:

> The lifer governor come to see me when I was on the YOs before I moved up,[10] and tried to tell me about [lifer] stages and things like that. But I didn't really understand none of it, like what's stages...? (Deena, 20s, mid)

---

[10] 'YOs': young offenders [prison/unit].

Does it feel like they know how to cater for young guys who come in for these long sentences?
No, no. A lot of people like me, you feel like you are just left in a corner.
What could they do?
I don't know. (Damien, 20s, early)

With great consistency, when recalling the distress and bewilderment of their early months in custody, mid- and late-stage prisoners reflected that they would have benefited from having an opportunity to share their emotions—ideally, in person and in private. Asked what would have been of value, Erwin (40s, late) replied: 'Being able to talk to somebody who could help [me] understand some of the feelings that I was having'. As he went on to explain, however, there appeared to be neither appetite nor provision for such assistance:

Nobody was willing to sit down and have a one to one conversation with [me] – 'we haven't got time for it or we can't, no, we haven't got the facilities to do that'.
And what would you have liked to have talked about?
All sorts of things. My feeling guilty about my friend, what happened the night [my victim] was killed… the way I felt at the time, you know. […] All sorts of things that I hadn't been able to speak about. (Erwin, 40s, late)

Erwin's disappointment that support was indispensable but unavailable was widely shared. Merle (30s, mid) asserted that the 'biggest problem in prison today' was that 'there's no outlet, no one to speak to, no one to trust, no one to share their thoughts with'. Nadia (20s, early) attributed the disruptive behaviour of her early months in custody to the need 'to communicate: "Look, I'm hurt, I need help. […] I can't do it. Everyone around me is not listening"'.

However, at the same time that they criticised these deficits in care and information, mid- and late-stage prisoners conceded that, had it been on offer, they might not have accepted it, due to the profound state of shock in which they found themselves. In such circumstances, expressing emotions and taking on board advice and reassurance was difficult, as Bernard explained:

They describe it as like a grieving process. It's like saying to someone 'it'll be OK', you know, when a loved one just dies and stuff like that. They're not gonna listen to you. At that moment their world's just crumbled around them and they're gonna respond to it however they wanna respond to it, however they feel, whether it's isolating themselves, whether it's bawling their eyes out, whether it's acting out, you know, and I think that's the reality, particularly early in the sentence. (Bernard, 40s, post-tariff)

In the absence of institutional support, early-stage prisoners relied on alternative sources of hope and positivity. By far, the most important was family members (see Chapter 6). As the following quotations demonstrate, families provided a vital lifeline, through both direct contact and the ongoing sense of being loved:

What do you think matters to people when they start a sentence like this?
You know what, all that really matters is if your family have got you, if your friends have got you, and if you've got something to come out to at the end of it: is there a light at the end of the tunnel? (James, 20s, early)

So how did you manage to keep your hopes up at that point?
Family. Family. To me, that's what kept me going through my sentence, that's what kept me strong, that's what kept me not losing my damn mind. It's my family, it's the love of my family. (Asad, 30s, mid)

Another source of hope for early-stage prisoners derived from religion. In particular, faith made it possible to imagine a more positive future: a chance of release and an afterlife without pain. For Miguel (late teens, early), faith helped by giving him belief 'that down the line there's a light for me, yeah. Somehow I will get out of jail'. Damien stated that, without his belief in God, he would have taken his own life:

So it has been your faith that has got you through the hardest times, has it?
Yeah. I know that, obviously, there's a hereafter. This life, it is nothing really, that's the way I look at things. And if I am wrong, when I am dead I will be resting in peace. I won't be suffering like this, so that's what keeps me motivated. (Damien, 20s, early)

Such statements of hope gestured towards an underlying desperation: the need to look *beyond* the present. As we discuss in more detail in Chapter 8, early-stage prisoners were able to think about a future beyond the prison only by avoiding contemplation of the time in-between.

Most often, participants at this phase of their prison term described their faith as having fortified them, made them more emotionally resilient, and enhanced their ability to cope in the present:

> Obviously, I've been able to manage it a lot better in terms of how I feel, because I go to chapel every week and stuff like that. And a lot of the coping, a lot of how I've managed to cope with it has been spiritually. (Carl, 20s, early)

Other prisoners provided similar explanations, noting that their faith made them 'calmer, a lot, lot calmer' (Ignacio, 20s, early), by assisting them in making some sense of what they had done and the situation in which they now found themselves. A common discourse here was that their punishment was God's will (Clear et al. 2000; Maruna et al. 2006), and that God would not place them in a situation they would be unable to withstand:

> I don't even know if I've come to terms with it now, but the way I see it, I just say that God does everything for a reason […]. God plans out everything… if this is what he had planned for me then there's a reason for it. That's how I pick myself up. (Toby, 20s, early)

> I believe that God never gives us more than we can bear. So, me, within myself I know that I can… however long I have to do here. (Carl, 20s, early)

> I have faith in God. He ain't going to put me in a situation that I can't handle. […] I am a bit upset because I am getting punished, but I have faith in God. (Damien, 20s, early)

Fatalistic rationalisations of this kind enabled early-stage prisoners to confront the present with some degree of stoicism, to 'find meaning in a seemingly incomprehensible situation' (Maruna et al. 2006: 176). Faith in a higher purpose helped them to believe that there was some point to their suffering: '[Whereas] if there's nothing at the end, then it seems almost pointless' (Carl, 20s, early).

Within prison, hope and fortitude were also drawn from seeing people who had already served a number of years progress through the system or simply endure what was otherwise assumed to be un-endurable. Few prisoners described having mentors, as such, but many referred to reassuring conversations with more experienced peers, or uplifting encounters with 'survivors':

Occasionally I speak with the people that have done a long time and that puts your mind at a little bit of ease because you think 'well, he's done it, he's got through, so...' [...], and anyone that's done a long time says it goes quickly so...
[...] So it helps talking to others?
It helps talking to people that have done long sentences, yeah. (Dean, early)

We were doing a course [and] they brought this girl that had done a life sentence; she'd finished it. I swear, that was the best feeling I've probably ever had in jail. Because she showed me it could be done, and before then I don't think I believed it could actually be done. (Fernando, 20s, mid)

A further basis of hope lay in the belief that one of the only benefits of receiving a long sentence when young was that there would be 'plenty of life to lead' once released. For example:

Hope? I know I'm getting out, I've got some time, even if I went five years over my tariff, I'm still young. (Clint, 30s, late)

I think me age has helped, that I'm young... and I've still got a chance. I can rebuild, perhaps. (Sean, 20s, early)

Not all prisoners were able to project themselves forwards in this way, however, and some regarded middle-age as exceptionally aged: 'I'm not really going to have a life, to be honest, when you're 38 years old' (Eloise, 20s, early). Most felt that they were losing the key years of their life (see O'Donnell 2014; and Chapter 8) and would have to restart from a position of great disadvantage:

You're basically starting where you left off, kind of thing. [And] it's not like as if you're starting off again as fresh. [...] You're actually below that – no relationships as such, no actual material possessions or anything like that. (Billy, 20s, early)

Everyone's started their own families, they're paying their mortgages, they're paying money. And when I do get released, I'm going to be 20 years behind them. I'm going to be back where they were first, but without anything, without any funds for the foundation. (Willis, 30s, mid)

This attitude of despondency was also reflected in a widespread sentiment among early-stage prisoners that there was little they could do to make their sentence constructive. Often, participants who were in the initial years of their sentence expressed an attitude of ennui and apathy, declaring themselves uninterested in the activities on offer, or finding it impossible to imagine that anything in prison could be purposeful: 'it's just so hard to see the positive in anything you do' (Maria, 20s, early). Most stated with blank certainty that they had no goals at all while in prison, for example:

> *How do you build a life for yourself in here?*
> You can't really build a life in here, can you?
> *[…] What would make it feel like you were doing something meaningful or constructive?*
> I wouldn't want to be doing anything meaningful for this place. […] Nothing constructive will help me, I think, to be honest with you. Because I am still in the same place, I am still within these walls. I am not going anywhere. […]
> *Do you have any short- or medium-term goals in here?*
> I don't have nothing in here.
> *[…] What about jobs and stuff? Is there any job that you would like, or any of the vocational courses and stuff, can you do any of those?*
> Yeah. I can do the courses, but I don't want to do the courses, they are not going to benefit me. […] I might not get out so there is not much benefit is there. (Martin, 20s, early)

Martin's lack of motivation derived from his belief that there was little point committing to building a life while confined. This view, that the prison was a temporary life domain—'a breather in my life' (Thomas, 20s, early)—and was unworthy of personal investment, was widely shared. Noel provided a similar rationale: 'You can't really build a life in prison. You can get things to help you build a life when you get out. […] But while you're in jail you're on standby'. Likewise, Oscar (20s, early) described his work in the prison kitchens with enthusiasm, commenting that it was an effective way to 'pass the time' and a 'good crack … there's a few good boys down there'. Shifting register, however, he stated that 'I don't want nothing to do with the place, to be quite honest. I'm just here to do my time and go home'. His aim in the meantime was to 'just make myself as comfortable as I can in my cell', while life was essentially 'on hold'.

Prisoners whose thinking was suffused with sentiments of hopelessness and listlessness were highly sceptical about the value of investing time and effort in education and training. Martin (20s, early) described such activities as 'pointless', arguing that, since he would not want a 'normal job' on release, they had no benefit. Hugo (20s, early) had given up his studies in history because 'I know I'll never want a job in history anyway, but who cares if I've got a degree or not'. Jonathan (20s, early) had decided not to pursue his interest in psychology, because 'if I get out, when am I gonna use that?'. Several early-stage prisoners reasoned that they had so long left to serve that there was little need to engage in purposeful activity until further into the sentence: 'I know I've got a long time, so [...] I can just relax for a bit' (Rufus, late teens, early). Many other early-stage prisoners used terms such as 'chilled out' to describe a shift from a state of expressive anger to an orientation in which they sought, in Jonathan's (20s, early) words, to 'do my time as easy as possible as I can'. Phrases of this kind communicated a degree of withdrawal from involvement in the informal economy, and its associated stresses: 'I find time goes faster for me when I'm just chilling. Just have a chat with a few mates and chill, watch a bit of telly, have a smoke' (Noel, 20s, early). Nonetheless, the sense was of passing time in ways that were relatively aimless.

Responding to questions about what made their life constructive, most early-stage prisoners specified activities whose purpose was mainly to occupy them in the present: 'having a routine' (Cary, 20s, early); 'just getting on with things, doing courses, doing jobs and mixing with people' (Connie, 20s, early); 'just keeping busy, keeping my head down' (Ruby, 20s, early). Typically, in discussing their motivations, they made explicit reference to expending rather than using time: 'I just see it as passing time' (Connie, 20s, early); 'I'm not trying to build no houses. [...] I'm just doing [bricklaying] because they tell me I've gotta do bricks. [...] I'm just doing anything to kill the time, to be honest' (Andre, late teens, early). The benefits of filling time and occupying headspace were also relevant to the ritual dimensions of faith practices: prayer 'makes your time fly, because you've finished one pray [and] by the time you know it's time for your next one' (Zubair, 20s, early).

Such practices reduced the amount of time spent in contemplative solitude. Long periods of inactivity or time in cell generated distress in part because they left prisoners in a state of continuous rumination:

Have you ever tried to commit suicide while you've been in prison?
Yeah. [...] I was thinking too much at the time. I was just thinking and thinking and thinking, and thinking and thinking. [...] If I've got things to do, it kind of occupies me, so I'm not thinking about things. [...] When you've just been found guilty, you're in shock, and then you start thinking: 'I could have done this, but I could have done this, I wish I never was involved in this', do you know what I mean? (Eloise, 20s, early)

In particular, as Eloise indicates, early-stage prisoners were prone to 'brooding': backwards-looking counterfactual thinking in which they imagined alternative outcomes (Gilbar and Hevroni 2007) and berated themselves for the minor and cumulative decisions that had led to their offence. These forms of reflection—both about 'what could have been' and how things had turned out—only added to the raw and surreal nature of the experience.

Every night I think about it... fucking... 'why I didn't chuck the knife; why, you know, everything. Why - why did I go in the house in the first place? Why didn't I just drop the gear off? Where would I be in this if my son would have been born?' Yeah. Like, it just don't seem real. (Sean, 20s, early)

Reflections of this kind were primarily expressive. They betrayed a continuing preoccupation with the past, and ongoing feelings of helplessness and despair, and they did little to help prisoners move on psychologically. Keeping busy and consuming time were less emotionally reactive. Nonetheless, they were still relatively passive responses, oriented mainly to the present, and with a limited sense of purpose.

Some prisoners explained that their educational involvement was an attempt to imitate what they would have been doing had they not been sentenced, in a parallel version of their life. More typically, however, participants reported negative experiences of schooling ('obviously, I left school with no GCSEs' [Asad, 30s, mid]; 'I left school with fuck all' [Tori, 30s, late]) and talked of having 're-educated' themselves since being sentenced. Wearing their pride like a garland, they reeled off the courses they had attended and the qualifications they had obtained since coming into prison, accompanying such statements with testimonies of the benefits of training and education: improved self-confidence, a sense of achievement, and the acquisition of skills. In addition, they referred to the importance of gaining qualifications that would be of value either *for* or *on* their release, i.e. by enabling their progression out of prison and increasing their prospect of employment once in the community[11]:

> I want to get qualification in jail, stuff like that, when I get out hopefully one day and…
> *What kind of qualifications do you want to get?*
> All sorts, anything that's going to help me. […] Everything's worth doing, everything's going to help you, it's not going to go against you, it's going to go in your favour. (Ignacio, 20s, early)

> My plan is do as much education as humanly possible. […] I might as well use that time the best I can, so if I focus on education that's something that will stay with me when I finally get out and will benefit me. […] I want to get out as early as possible, and to do that, I need to have stuff in place for when I get out. (Antone, 20s, early)

In this respect, though, motivations were rather narrow and instrumental, based on the anticipation of a future that was vague and distant.

Hope, Meaning, Purpose and Coping: Faith and Education

Prisoners at all sentence stages identified music, exercise, cookery and education as things they could not manage without, particularly as a means of modifying their mood and freeing themselves from the grip of the institution. More significantly, in contrast to early-stage prisoners, mid- and late-stage participants referred with great consistency not just to 'keeping busy' but to being 'pro-active' in the development and pursuit of interests—or, following Archer (2003), what we might call 'projects'. Many asserted the importance of finding a hobby, usually in the form of physical

---

[11] With great consistency, prisoners of all sentence stages commented on the limited or 'very basic' (Clark, 20s, early) nature of educational provision. Many reported with great disappointment having 'exhausted' (Neil, 30s, mid) their educational opportunities, particularly when the alternatives to seeking to further educate themselves were mindless forms of labour in workshops:

> I've come to the point where there's nothing for me to do that's educational, so now they just want to put me in workshops where you're just sat there like a machine. […] I can't do it. It just draws all the energy out of me. (Siffre, 20s, early)

Prisoners who had served a number of years of their sentences often complained that they were being asked to repeat courses or qualifications that they had already completed. Those who were keen to engage in higher-level qualifications were highly despondent that funding for Open University degrees had been cut.

or creative activity: 'you need to find something you're good at, or you need to find something that you enjoy doing and stick with it' (Gibson, 20s, mid). In doing so, they deployed a future-facing language of 'goals' and 'targets', the substance of which provided hope, direction and a key source of coping:

> For me, coming into prison [taught] me that I need goals. I need something to aim for, I need something to hope for, I need something that pulls me forward and drives me along. [...] You've got to have a reason to drive you through that next year. So, for me, setting those targets has always been about getting through that next portion of time, and driving myself forward. (Gail, 30s, late)

> I have a target, I have an aim in my mind. I want to be able to memorise the Qur'an before I come out of jail. That's my goal. [...] Because 20 years of my life, that's a big chunk. And if I've come out and I've achieved nothing, then I'm a bum. (Mohammed, 20s, mid)

When mid- and late-stage prisoners discussed their most important coping mechanisms, and their main sources of hope, purpose and meaning, they referred to three matters in particular: family—which we discuss in Chapter 6—faith and (to a lesser degree) education. For example:

> If it wasn't for God and my family I wouldn't be here. (Shaafi, 30s, mid)

> *What [...] things could you not manage without in here?*
> My family, my faith (Mahmood, 30s, mid)

> Family support and my belief, I've got my faith and I think that's massive as well. I think without those two then it's not really a reason to aspire to anything beyond what I was, in a sense. (Alan, 30s, mid)

In discussing the role of religion—and sometimes non-religious spiritual practices, such as yoga and mindfulness—prisoners often made direct reference to sanity and survival. Neil (30s, mid) said that his faith had 'kept me alive, it's kept my buoyant'; Bentley (30s, mid) stated that 'If I didn't have religion or I didn't have any family out there to go to and I weren't thinking positive I would have maybe lost my whole mind'.

For mid- and late-stage prisoners, faith and education continued to provide many of the same functions as they did for those in the initial period of their sentence, including hope, perspective, mental distraction and the constructive use of time[12]:

> It gets you out of your cell, you have to go and work or education. And it keeps your mind occupied, and I'm a big believer of keeping your mind occupied, so it don't wander and fall in on itself. (Fernando, 20s, mid)

> I realised when I had my head in my books, I could shut out everything else and mentally tire out myself so come the night I could sleep.
> *So it's escapism?*
> Yeah, it was, it started out as that and then evolved into a lower learning, and obviously then I was lucky enough to find the area or the subject that I was meant for. (Neil, 30s, mid)

> It just puts life in perspective for me. I think about the hereafter as well, not just from jail to outside, I think about when I'm gone and then, do you get what I'm saying? Is there something more to this life, or is that it? (Asad, 30s, mid)

In these respects, educational, spiritual and religious activities supported forms of everyday coping (Liebling et al. 2011). Both practically and philosophically, through a variety of means, they helped prisoners to 'make the best out of [a] bad situation' (Jill, 40s, post-tariff) (see Clear et al. 2000), by increasing their resilience and helping them accept and alleviate the burdens of the present. Erwin, for example, explained his identification with Taoism:

> Taoism just sort of fits because it's like live and let live, don't get angry, try not to get angry, don't curse, don't swear, try not to influence people by the things you say or the actions that you do, just try and live life. (Erwin, 40s, late)

---

[12] Many prisoners described having converted to religion while in prison, discovered spiritual practices and philosophies, or found that their existing religious commitments had strengthened as a result of their sentence. As noted above, the same was true of education: typically, participants' experiences of schooling had not been positive, but, since re-discovering the benefits of learning, knowledge and self-knowledge, many had become passionate advocates for educational engagement.

Expressed more broadly, spiritual and religious practices—including yoga and meditation—helped prisoners to find 'peace and comfort' (Kelvin, 20s, mid), free themselves from excessive worry and minimise destructive forms of rumination (Clear et al. 2000):

> I will just shut my curtain, and I will just kneel, do my prayers, say my prayers, I will do a little bit of chanting sometimes. At other times I will just sit and just meditate and just go into my own zone. [...] Once I am in my own meditative state, then my body relaxes. (Joseph, 40s, post-tariff)

> I tell myself: 'don't dwell on it, you're here and now. Here and now. This is what you're dealing with now'. And that's it, that solves the problem. [...] And I meditate. [...] So that's how I cope with things. What goes in your mind is an illusion. (Walter, 60s, post-tariff)

> *What makes a slow day for you, or a bad day?*
> I don't really have like bad days you know, to tell you the truth. But I think that's down to my religion as well. [...] It's part of my religion to be content. That's why you see a lot of people getting long sentences becoming Muslim [...]
> *What else does it offer you?*
> Just peace of heart, just being peaceful. (Bruce, 20s, early)

Such statements signalled the role of faith, and other spiritual systems, not just in helping prisoners to survive the present, but in some ways to transcend it, through states of meditation, philosophies of acceptance, and the possibility of seeing goodness and godliness in the otherwise profane.

In this regard, one function of religious practice was 'removal' (O'Donnell 2014). Ritual practices such as prayer enabled prisoners to surmount the customary burdens of time: 'I reach that state where I'm content with everything. And at that time [clicks fingers], time's just kind of like that. [...] That's why I pray. That's why I might fast' (Mohammed, 20s, mid). Prayer also opened up reflective space that helped prisoners 'refresh' themselves (Stephen, 20s, mid) and offered mental sanctuary from the prison landings (Kerley and Copes 2009). Mahmood (30s, mid), for example, explained that, during his time in an establishment that was highly volatile, his prayer routine had helped him to 'keep my mental state sane'. Prisoners involved in educational activities often referred to the state of mental freedom that reading and thinking helped them to achieve.

Compared to their role in the lives of early-stage prisoners, then, faith and education were productive as well as reactive, for example: 'Instead of me serving time, I've let time serve me, by doing education, trying to put right what I've missed out on, getting my qualifications' (Eugene, 50s, post-tariff). Similarly, references among mid- and late-stage prisoners to faith and education more often made reference to personal drive—'it's kept me focused, motivated' (Neil, 30s, mid)—and the future:

> I put my time within religion and try to understand the Lord, so that helps to pass a bit of my time and a significant part of it is to make all this thinking about my family and I'm going to get out, I'm going to change my life around to try to make up for the time that I lost with my son and my family, and practise marriage and believe there is hope for a change. That makes me feel much better. (Bentley, 30s, mid)

Faith and educational practices also had a social and relational dimension, often linked to the nature of the spaces in which organised worship and educational activities occurred (see Clear et al. 2000; Kerley and Copes 2009; Liebling et al. 2011). Karen (20s, mid) described the appeal of going to the chapel in terms of meeting friends, 'and because they give us tea and coffee', while Victor (30s, post-tariff) explained that 'when I'm down there it's a bit time off the wing, it's a bit of relaxation, [...] it just takes the edge off it, really'.[13] Caspar (20s, early) described the chapel as the place where he could most easily be himself: 'It's just a different atmosphere. They're just people I trust, to be honest with you'. More specifically, as suggested here, places of worship were havens for forms of engagement and relational normalisation—'being treated like a human being' (Caspar, 20s, early)—that were rarely found elsewhere in the prison:

> It's like men and women and they're all walking over and giving you hugs. And every two minutes coming and [asking] 'do you want a cup of coffee? Do you want this? Do you want that?' Like that, helpful, and I ain't felt that in a long time since I've been in jail. (Kendrick, 20s, early)

---

[13] For some prisoners, however, the sociability of places of worship was off-putting. John (20s, mid), for example, had stopped going to religious services because others were 'going down not for the service, but for association, and they were laughing, taking the mick'; likewise, Jeremiah (20s, early) disapproved of some Muslim prisoners using services as a basis for social life rather than worship.

As in education departments, prisoners referred to the significance of the concern and mundane kindness that was shown to them by civilian staff and volunteers. Similarly, in recalling their turn towards Islam, several prisoners commented on the pull of relational warmth, community and mutual care (Kerley and Copes 2009; Liebling et al. 2011):

> Maybe it was their Muslim etiquette that I found that so warm. And that, kind of, warmed my heart towards the religion. I said, 'Yeah, these guys, they're really caring about each other,' you know what I mean? Like, prison can be a dog eat dog world. So, yeah, that's what attracted me to the religion. (Mohammed, 20s, mid)

> The appeal was being a part of something, you were a part of a group, you were part of something. [...] And everybody, they would always call you 'brother' - 'you're my brother' – they'd always ask how your family are. (Ashley, 30s, mid)

In this regard, both spatially and relationally, religious and educational practices enabled escape from the normal emotional terms of imprisonment (see Crewe et al. 2014).[14]

In discussing the benefits of both faith and education, mid- and late-stage prisoners, far more often than their early-stage peers, also talked a language of personal development and self-improvement. That is, rather than discussing educational attainment in terms of specific skills, they emphasised the broader set of intrinsic goods that learning delivered: 'I just want knowledge. [...] I don't really care about degrees, and things like that' (Stephen, 20s, mid); 'Anything to do with education, anything to better myself' (Asad, 30s, mid). Curtis (20s, mid), for example, reflected that some of the best experiences of his life had been gaining qualifications while in prison: 'all the educational stuff I've done since I've been in, you know, sense of achievement and all that'. Such comments were more about 'bettering myself' (Eloise, 20s, early) than simply 'bettering my skills' (Terrance, 20s, early). Learning was an end in itself. As Liebling et al. (2011: 39) noted, in their study

---

[14]At the same time, many prisoners were cynical about the true functions of religion, particularly Islam. Ashley (30s, mid), for example, went on to explain his disillusion with 'prison Islam': 'I realised that they're just a big gang [...] because it's safety in numbers and it's protection, and they're looked after'. Errol (20s, early), a committed Muslim, no longer attended Friday prayer, because of his antipathy towards some other worshippers: 'I don't go down there. These terrorists, I fucking hate them, man. I hate them'. The idea that Islam was a screen for drug dealing, violence and radicalisation was expressed very frequently, particularly by prisoners who were within, or had been transferred from, high-security establishments (see Liebling et al. 2011).

of a high-security prison in England & Wales, prison education 'was about much more than knowledge acquisition. It was about identity, cognitive transformation, and meaning'.

Self-improvement also had a moral component. For many mid- and late-stage prisoners, faith provided daily guidance for everyday personal conduct, in particular, resisting temptation (see Kerley and Copes 2009) and living life ethically (Liebling et al. 2011; Williams 2018). Neil (30s, mid) claimed that his faith had protected him from 'contamination'; others attributed to their faith their ability to 'stay away from drugs' (Mahmood, 30s, mid) and stay 'on the straight and narrow' (Arshad, 30s, late), either directly (through religious strictures) or through new peer groups (Kerley and Copes 2009). Religious teachings and philosophical traditions prescribed how to live virtuously, including how to be kind, sensitive, self-disciplined and other-oriented. Luca stated that his faith had 'shown me how to be a decent human being', elaborating that:

> I used to live in a lot of darkness. [...] But now I understand about God, I feel like there's more light in my life. And the other thing is, I used to do the things I'm not supposed to do, and that's why my life was so full of destruction and I've gotta work with that. And now I'm trying to do what I'm supposed to do, and that's what God says. And it's made a huge impact on my life. (Luca, 30s, mid)

As suggested in Luca's terminology, faith and education also helped prisoners cope with their offence, by offering channels for expiation, atonement and moral growth (see Clear et al. 2000; Maruna et al. 2006; Irwin 2010). That is, a key dimension of spirituality and religious practices related to helping prisoners 'find peace' not only with their state of long-term detention, but also with their offence and thereby with themselves. Several female prisoners—including some who had no religious belief, as such—specified the importance of ritually lighting candles in memory of their victim:

> Without fail every week I light a candle for [the victim], and so [the victim is] a really big part of my life and it's not something that's ever diminished over time. (Gail, 30s, late)

> I say, 'Peace be with you' and all this. [...] I do light candles a lot for [the victim], so she knows that I'm still caring for her. (Eloise, 20s, early)

Education, offending behaviour programmes and faith practices helped some prisoners to identify and process their moral emotions, via direct learning, analytic insight and religious teachings about matters such as vice, sin and virtue. For others, religion and spiritual philosophy offered a direct path to reparation and forgiveness (Clear et al. 2000). Haashim (30s, post-tariff) said that his admission of guilt was the result of his allegiance to a form of yoga that emphasised 'austerity, truthfulness, cleanliness of the mind'. Similarly, Mahmood linked his commitment to religious education with his acceptance of guilt and the subsequent 'turning around' of his life (Bottoms 2019):

> I made a vow to myself that, you know what, I'm gonna sort my life out, [and] I dedicated myself to [religious] learning and it's turned my life around. The way I do that is to look on my errors, mistakes and make amends. […] I think my spirituality, kind of, helped me to soften that blow. You know, to accept that what I'd done was wrong. (Mahmood, 30s, mid)

Ray's enthusiasm for education was based in a similar logic of restitution:

> I've done bad and I'm trying to do good, I'm trying to show that, really, I'm trying to do good out of this. […] There was more to it than just the wanting to take the opportunity for examinations. (Ray, 50s, post-tariff)

A further dimension of personal growth, then, was the discovery or development of a life philosophy, which could provide prisoners not only with a way to 'reinterpret their current living conditions' (Kerley and Copes 2009: 231), but their place in the world more broadly. As Maruna et al. assert (2006: 163), one reason why prisoners often 'find god behind bars' is that the prison is 'one of the social contexts in which self-identity is most likely to be questioned'. Processes of mortification, and the fact that imprisonment alters 'the basic parameters of everyday life' (p. 163), lead prisoners to reconsider their existing guidelines for action and reflect on previously unexamined 'issues of existence, life, and death, which are usually bracketed from everyday consideration' (p. 169).

For those facing the existential shock of committing a serious offence, and seeking to come to terms with its implications, this reinterpretation of self takes on particular significance. In the context of the enormity of both their offence and their predicament, then, another crucial function of faith and religion was to help prisoners in their quest for sense-making and understanding (Liebling et al. 2011). Faced with a range of questions about 'life, death, meaning and the individual's place in the world' (Maruna et al. 2006; Clear et al. 2000), many participants found answers in the teachings and philosophies of organised religion and other life-systems:

> I couldn't get the answers and it was leaving me frustrated, and then all of a sudden I came to Islam, I started reading it in depth, started asking questions, and I was getting the answers, and it's made me feel peace, and it's helping me be humble, you know, that sense of… completeness. (Arshad, 30s, late)

> [Christian belief has] helped me to question life and the value of life, the value of my life, love, relationships, my attitude towards people who in the past I've disliked or have even to some degree had hatred for. […] How to carry yourself, how to behave towards others. (Alan, 30s, mid)

As O'Donnell (2014) argues (and see Frankl 1959), coming to see oneself as part of 'something bigger' (p. 256) can make it easier to carry on.

The relative popularity of the philosophical systems attached to Taoism, Paganism and Buddhism spoke of the need among long-term prisoners to find a broad philosophy of life that could place in context their questions about who they were, what they had done, and the implications of taking a life. In their moral 'self-auditing' (see Irwin 2010) and their attempts to make sense of their long-term circumstances, prisoners were attracted to comprehensive systems of thought that helped them to weigh up and move on from their complex ethical and biographical histories, as Karen implied:

> I'm not actually a Pagan, just I find Paganism interesting because it covers such a broad spectrum of different beliefs, [and] it just seems so full and […] it balances the positive and the negative aspects of life. (Karen, 20s, mid)

Education—comprising reading, taught courses and the forms of knowledge gained through offending behaviour programmes—represented a secular version of these offerings. In particular, it gave prisoners both a better understanding of themselves and a sense of a world beyond their immediate circumstances. Mahmood (30s, mid) described his growing understanding of psychology as having 'opened my eyes to a whole different world out there'; Yvette (30s, mid) explained that courses had helped her 'see things very differently'; Jenny (20s, mid) credited an enhanced thinking skills course with having given her insight into 'where I was going wrong [and] the difference between the rights and wrongs of certain decisions and the possible consequences of my actions'.

Phrases of this kind were recurrent, and their optical terminology was indicative of the transformative potential of knowledge. It provided enlightenment, illumination and a lens for reinterpretation (O'Donnell 2014; or what Laws (2018) calls a form of 'alchemy'):

> In the end I just thought 'right, I'm gonna go to the library and I'm gonna start reading', and I started getting metaphysical books out, religious books out, psychology books, reading anything that I could get me hands on, history, sociology, everything and anything [...] and I just devoured books. [...] I was getting high from all this knowledge. It was like a new world had opened up to me. (Bernard, 40s, post-tariff)

> [Someone from the prison education department] started giving me [books] about politics, and current events, and stuff. I was happy with that, because that's what I was interested in: [...] I want to know about the world. I've never been anywhere. I need to be aware of who's who in the world, and who has power, and who's fighting for power [...].
> *And why was that important?*
> Because I didn't know my place in the world. [...] So now I'm starting to think more about current events, and society as a whole, and where do I fit within society. And this is like a driving force now to actually understand what am I, what am I here for? (Stephen, 20s, mid)

> Obviously through studying as well certain parts have been more, you know, it's helped open my eyes to a certain part of me and helped me to understand. (Neil, 30s, mid)

Again, in such statements, the offence provided a significant backdrop. Stephen went on to explain that, when first convicted, he had not regarded himself as 'part of the wider world. I didn't really actually care or have any feelings regarding anyone else really'. As he had learnt more about himself and the world beyond him, he had experienced 'an awakening. I was starting to wake up to who I was, and what was going on around me' (Stephen, 20s, mid). In similar terms, Mahmood

(30s, mid) reflected that 'knowledge was important, cos I guess my actions in the past have been down to lack of knowledge, lack of understanding, whether it be empathy or whether it be sympathy'. Here, then, the link between knowledge, empathy and the construction of humane selfhood was apparent. In the early sentence stage, then, faith and education served mainly to help prisoners suppress their affective distress. For prisoners who were several years into their sentences, their most significant function was to assist participants in situating themselves in the world, both morally and existentially.

Doing Time, Authority and Compliance

The early-stage orientation we have described above, of 'chilling', passing time and minimising stress, bears close resemblance to Irwin's (1970) concept of 'doing time': that is, avoiding trouble, securing minor luxuries, forming a small friendship clique, and 'doing what is necessary to get out asap'. Once prisoners had moved beyond their initial period of 'jailing', most of their non-compliant behaviour was directed at making the sentence more bearable. Some engaged in low-level trade to improve their living standards (e.g. to afford extra tobacco or food items). Ashley claimed that he had dealt drugs in order to 'survive' without having to request financial support from his family:

> I don't like asking them. It's a pride thing, I think. It's always part of me, always being used to looking after them. [...]
> *So the stuff that you were doing, it wasn't that you were trying to carry on the life that you had before?*
> No.
> *It was surviving?*
> Yeah, I was just surviving, it was just surviving. (Ashley, 30s, mid)

Prisoners who admitted to having owned mobile phones claimed that their main motivation was to maintain ties with loved ones. Zufar insisted that he was compliant in all regards, apart from this one:

> I comply with everything else, I don't hate prisoners, I don't hate officers, I don't swear at officers, or swear at anyone else, I don't use things where I shouldn't be using, don't take drugs, don't take alcohol, drink alcohol, I don't thieve other peoples'

prison stuff, which is not compliant with prison rules, I comply with everything apart from the mobile phone. (Zufar, 20s, early)

As he went on to explain, his fear that his family members might not be alive by the time of his release made this form of non-compliance a worthwhile risk:

Yes, you're taking a risk, and for me it's a risk well taken. [...] What is going to be more difficult for me say in 10 years' time, when my parents pass away? It would be more difficult to me that I couldn't speak to them every day [than] screw up my parole for another say three years, after 25 years. [...] I'd be thinking 'look, I spoke to my family every day, I had a connection with my mum before she passed away'. That's more important than anything else in this world.

A third form of non-compliance was oriented towards alleviating the tedium of prison living: 'Being bored' was the 14th most severe problem among early-stage prisoners and the 19th most severe overall. Many prisoners engaged in minor forms of gambling (on sports events, for example) to add some colour to long periods of inactivity: 'I'm not doing it because the jail says I can't; I'm doing it because it's something I enjoy doing, it gives us something to sit there and watch over the weekend' (Clark, 20s, early).

As suggested above, when probed about the nature of their non-compliance, very few participants expressed any intention to undermine the prison regime, as such. Further, in response to the statement 'I am completely compliant with the system', while 47% of survey participants either agreed or strongly agreed, only 15% disagreed or strongly disagreed. Often, compliance was instrumental, to make life easier. However, many participants described their behaviour in terms that were normative, based on personal values. This was particularly the case for those who were engaged in ethical self-projects, and who therefore regarded compliance as something consistent with their general orientation to life. Such prisoners frequently found themselves frustrated with bureaucratic inefficiencies and regulations, or with staff who they found lazy or indifferent. However, their primary concerns were personal, and they had no interest in tying themselves up in battles with the system.

Most often, participants reported that their compliance was based on attachment to significant others. Even when they felt themselves to be simply 'ticking boxes', they were often doing so in order to be reunited with people they loved:

So it sounds like you comply with the system.
Yeah. I jump through all the hoops.
Why do you do all the things that they want you to do?
Because I wanna get out for my children as early as I can.
So it's pretty simple in that sense?
Yeah. I've gotta get out for them. That's it. (Terrance, 20s, early)

The long-term goal of freedom—being released at the earliest possible opportunity—was a stronger motivator than everyday benefits and privileges. That is, conformity was oriented to the future more often than the present. Once they became aware of the power of the prison file, and its impact on decisions about progression and release, the great majority of prisoners were keen to limit conflict and suppress frustration:

So you've got to bite your tongue sometimes?
Yeah, a lot of the time I have to.
What are the things that you have to hold back?
A lot, like certain things that people do you don't agree with, you have to hold back, and certain things that people write that you don't agree with, you have to hold it back.
So you've got to be compliant?
You've got to be, you've got to be.
Because you want to get out?
Because you want to get out. (Cary, 20s, early)

In this respect, despite very long sentence lengths, prisoners were aware of the long-term risks of non-compliant behaviour:

People talk about life sentence prisoners as having nothing to lose…
Got more to lose. I suppose certain people might have nothing to lose, like, a lot of people here now, there's a lot of fifty year-olds getting life sentences and even if they do get out at sixty-five, seventy, you're life's finished, really. You've had another life, so they probably haven't got anything to lose. If I got a sentence at that age I'd probably still be in a high security jail cooking me food and just going on not giving a fuck or whatever. That's the truth. If I didn't have a life to get out to I'd be a lot worse than I am now, probably. (Scott, 30s, mid)

This attitude of pragmatism was consistent with our participants' attitudes towards authority in general, and prison officers specifically. Many had grown up with very cynical views about the police and other authority figures, due to feelings of having been repeatedly targeted by the former and 'let down' by the latter. As Victor (30s, post-tariff) summarised: 'All my life they've let me down. I felt my parents had let me down, I felt the police let me down, I felt loads of people let me down. So I've never really trusted society and authority figures'. These feelings were often compounded by prisoners' perceptions that their convictions were a result of having been 'set up' by the police. Zubair (20s, early) captured this sentiment as follows: 'I don't trust the coppers. […] Obviously, they gave me a thirty [year sentence] for something which I don't agree with'. Hostility towards the criminal justice system was exacerbated by joint enterprise sentencing, which fuelled a searing form of resentment about being found guilty or given a tariff that seemed grossly disproportionate.

During the early years of the sentence, these orientations often endured. Many prisoners acknowledged a resistance to being told what to do, in part because of adverse childhood experiences of parental and legal authority. Others maintained a view, during the early years of their sentence, that prison officers and the police were analogous.

Do you trust any members of staff?
No.
Would you ever?
Never.
Why would you not trust them?
No way, because they are prison officers. They are like police. […] That's how I think of it. They are police, innit. (Darrin, late teens, early)

Why did you hate officers?
I just saw them as the police. (Gibson, 20s, mid)

Over time, however, relationships with officers had generally improved and views of authority had softened, due to maturation, positive experiences, and shifts in self-identity (Sapsford 1978; Zamble 1992).[15] Mohammed (20s, mid) explained

---

[15]Relatively few participants expressed hostility towards uniformed staff, but some late-stage participants recalled incidents of brutality in the past, and minority-ethnic interviewees who had spent time in some

that he no longer felt 'hatred towards authority' because he no longer considered himself 'a criminal'. Phil (60s, post-tariff) had come to see prison officers as 'just blokes doing the job'; Kendrick (20s, early) had 'got to know one or two' and now talked 'to every single officer on the wing'. Accordingly, very few prisoners held officers responsible for the perceived injustices and degradations of the criminal justice system. Dan summarised this view as follows:

> I respect their role, because any misgivings about the validity or my conviction or anything like that, it's beyond the scope of the prison. It's not their responsibility. [...] So I respect the role that they play, which is [that] for as long as this conviction remains safe, they have to keep me in here. [...] It's not their fault. There's no point in rioting or protesting or taking it out upon them or the prison in any way because it has nothing to do with them. (Dan, 20s, early)

Relationships with officers tended to be detached but courteous. Many prisoners reflected that they 'didn't really have much to do with' officers (Jackie, 30s late), primarily because they became self-sufficient relatively quickly, and did not rely a great deal on officers for help. On the whole, they described their treatment as humane and respectful, and regarded officers as relatively fair and 'decent'. 'They've got a job to do', said Campbell (30s, mid), 'It's purely professional'; Terrance (20s, early) used a similar discourse: 'I don't hate them. They're just doing a job, at the end of the day'.

Yet with great consistency, when asked whether they felt that officers cared about them and their futures, they were highly sceptical, especially those in the early phase of their sentence:

> *Do you ever get the sense that the staff in here care about you and your future?*
> Ha ha... do I fuck! No, no they don't care about that, [...], they don't give a shit. (Toby, 20s, early)

---

high-security establishments reported experiences of racism, directed particularly against Muslims. While we did not identify any overall difference in the adaptive patterns of white and minority-ethnic participants, in the survey, 17 of the 39 problems were reported to be significantly more severe by black and minority-ethnic prisoners compared to white prisoners, while severity scores were significantly higher for Muslim prisoners compared to prisoners with either 'other' or no religious affiliations for the items: 'Feeling that the system is ignoring your individual needs', 'Prison officers making life harder', 'Prison psychologists making life harder', 'Feeling frustrated that you are not progressing through the system' and 'Thinking about the amount of time you have to serve'. Prisoners with no religion reported 'Losing your self-confidence' and 'Being worried about your mental health' as significantly more severe than Muslim prisoners and Christian prisoners, respectively.

Do they care about you and your future?
No. Course not, no. [...] No, they're just doing their job. (Cary, 20s, early)

Do you feel that the staff in this prison truly care about you and your future?
No. No. It's just a profession for them, innit, really? (Liz, 20s, early)

Here, then, the 'professional' disposition that life-sentenced prisoners associated with uniformed staff implied a limited commitment to care.

Prisoners who were further into their sentences were more likely to identify individual officers who had made a difference to them, by showing a personal interest in their life, encouraging them to 'better themselves', offering compassion during a time of crisis or demonstrating some form of humane concern. A number of participants recalled specialist 'lifer officers' who had comforted them simply by reassuring them that there was 'light at the end of the tunnel'. More often, the personnel whom prisoners attributed with having the most positive influence were civilian staff, working in prison education departments or chaplaincies, who had provided hope or inspiration. Prison psychologists were generally disparaged, but some participants identified transformative individuals among them who had helped them enormously in addressing their demons.

Yet, on the whole, staff featured very little in narratives of transformation. Typically, as the excerpts below illustrate, when asked whether any staff had been a positive influence on them, prisoners responded with straightforward negatively:

Do you think that - has there been any staff that's had a really positive influence on you, or a particular negative influence on you?
No, not really. (Connie, 20s, early)

Have you had any staff who've been a big influence on you over the years, good or bad?
No. (Sim, 30s, mid)

Are there any that have had a particular influence on you either positively or negatively over the years?
Not really. (Haashim, 30s, late)

Change derived less from staff relationships, and much more from the support and resources provided by faith and education, as we now move on to discuss.

Enduring and Emergent Problems

In Chapter 4, we noted a general pattern in which problem severity diminished according to sentence stage. Nonetheless, some problems endured, others emerged, and some—mainly those relating to progression and release—were felt more strongly by mid- and late-stage prisoners than by those who had been more recently imprisoned (see Chapter 8).

Both Arkaan (20s, mid) and Leonard (30s, post-tariff) had been diagnosed during their sentences with very serious health problems and described their illnesses as being the worst experiences of their lives, and the most difficult aspect of their time in prison. Leonard said that he had 'not had a good day for years', since the emergence of his health problem several years prior, and 'almost gave up' as a result of his daily health concerns. Few prisoners were in such an acute state of distress about their personal health, but complaints about the quality of prison health care were very frequent, and many prisoners communicated a preoccupation with matters of fitness and conditioning:

> I do the gym regularly […] to keep fit and to maintain my physical and mental wellbeing to get out, so that plays a part in my everyday life - my exercise is one of them crucial ones to my health. (Bentley, 30s, mid)

> As long as I keep myself fit and healthy, and I don't get in any more trouble, I'm going to come out of prison and I'm going to be in good health, I shouldn't have any health worries. (Gibson, 20s, mid)

Accordingly, reasons for using the prison gym were more often related to fitness than strength and muscularity ('It don't really matter how big you are. It's fitness. […] I don't wanna be using a walking stick, I just wanna be healthy when I'm walking out the gates' [Diego, 20s, early]).

Such comments indicated a wider anxiety about personal deterioration and decomposition (see O'Donnell 2014; Cohen and Taylor 1972). 'Being worried about your mental health' was rated the 37th most severe problem by the male prisoners and the 31st most severe by the female prisoners. Yet, as we detailed in Chapter 4, many prisoners had direct experience of depression and anxiety, or expressed fears about the deterioration of their mental health in the future. This was especially the case for those in the early period of the sentence:

What are the main things that you worry about?
Becoming crazy, I do worry about that. […] I see people go cuckoo, they go crazy, go mental, […] I'm scared that I might come out like one of them one day, walking around in stinking, dirty clothes, looking like a zombie. […] I do think a lot about my health: […] mental health, my physical health. (Zufar, 20s, early)

Is there anything else that you worry about?
Going mad. I'm worried about it, and if I think about it now I probably will.
In what way?
[…] They want you to spend more time in jail than you've been alive for something you ain't done. How long can you block it out for? How long can you cope with it for? What's going to happen when something serious happens to your family out there? (Kendrick, 20s, early)

Some observed that their cognitive functions had already deteriorated: 'In terms of mental capacity, I do feel like an idiot' (Rafe, 30s, mid); 'My memory's so bad since coming to prison [and] I struggle to concentrate sometimes' (Billy, 20s, early). Often, anxiety derived from witnessing lifers further into their sentences who were 'dead behind the eyes' (Jill, 40s, post-tariff), 'a bit brain dead' (Bruce, 20s, early), who had 'cracked up' (Campbell, 30s, mid), been 'destroyed' (Harold, 40s, post-tariff) or had rapidly aged or failed to mature: 'when you see 35 year-old men acting like little kids and that, it winds me up. […] Because I don't want to be like that' (Damien, 20s, early). Concerns about becoming 'docile' (O'Donnell 2014: 211) or institutionalised—'desensitised to the violence' (Dan, 20s, early) or unconcerned by the prospect of release—were also common. A minority of male prisoners expressed considerable fear about being seriously assaulted, especially after having witnessed incidents of extreme violence: 'I hope I get out in one piece physically. […] I've seen what's happened to people and it scares the shit out of me, really' (Dan, 20s, early); 'Sometimes I think I am going to be dead before I come out of jail. […] I could get into a fight and someone might hit me in the wrong place. […] Every day I think about that' (Damien, 20s, early).

Death by natural causes also featured prominently in prisoners' concerns. The possibility of dying within prison generated considerable dread (see Appleton 2010: 151–152) and was depicted in terms such as becoming 'another statistic' (Arshad, 30s, late), connoting a fear of non-existence, non-significance and non-achievement:

I just didn't wanna die in prison. [...] Cos you just think you're a nobody and that people have... many people have died over the years and they'll have somebody in their cell the next day, or two days after. Like they never existed. And I suppose the thought of that is, like, you know, you're nothing. You're just a number. (Jill, 40s, post-tariff)

You kick the bucket and who cares, it moves on.[16] By the time your body's cold on the slab there's someone else in your room, you know, that's it, it's over, and that was my biggest fear. (Arshad, 30s, late)

I would hate to die in here. It would be a disaster for me. Like I said earlier, my life has got to amount to more than this. (Stephen, 20s, mid)

Some events and experiences had a highly disruptive effect on lives that were otherwise relatively settled; each entailed a significant form of relational dislocation. One such experience was the termination of an intimate relationship some years into the sentence—that is, beyond the early phase, when many participants deliberately 'cauterized' their relational ties (Flanagan 1980: 155). Bernard, for example, recalled the deep dislocation and sense of hopelessness that was precipitated by being left by a girlfriend:

So what would you say has been the hardest part of the sentence?
I think one of the hardest parts was when me and Chantel broke up. I believed I would be unhappy for the rest of my life, so trying to find focus again at that point was really, really hard. (Bernard, 40s, post-tariff)

Similarly, a number of female prisoners had been propelled into states of extreme anguish as a result of losing custody of their children:

Earlier this year, when I essentially lost my baby, because she was what was keeping me going, I did get to a very dark place where I did lose the will to live, and I shut everybody out. I didn't speak to my mum, I didn't speak to my sister, and I took weeks off work, [...] and on a couple of occasions I have been sitting there with a razor and cutting myself thinking 'I've got nothing left to live for, [upset] what's

---

[16]To 'kick the bucket': to die.

the point in me even being here? I really don't care if this razor cuts so deep and I don't wake up'. (Kathryn, 20s, early)

Loss in the form of bereavement featured most regularly in prisoners' accounts of what they feared most, in terms of their ability to cope and the events that had already knocked them off course (see Herbert 2018). 'Being afraid that someone you love or care about will die before you are released' was ranked by male prisoners as the 10th most significant problem that they faced, and by female prisoners as the 13th most significant. Asked what he felt he would be missing out on, while serving his sentence, Blake (20s, early) noted: 'Well, my nan's seventy. My mum's fifty. I don't know if I'll be out there with them again, so…'. Bentley (30s, mid) expressed dread that he might 'get up one day and hear my son… that something dreadful's happened. That is my deepest-seated nightmare. […] That would hurt me in my brain'.

For others, the concern was that, should they lose a loved one while confined, they would struggle to cope with the sentence itself. Such fears were born out by those who had been bereaved at some point during their time in prison, many of whom identified family deaths as having been the hardest part of their prison term, for example:

You're helpless. […] When my mother died, fucking hell. Like, it was… [sighs] my world collapsed, you know? Like, there's nothing I could do. It's the hardest thing that's ever happened to me, man. […] Because she was everything to me. […] And to lose her, it was fucking… [exhales] it was hard. (Campbell, 30s, mid)

Managing grief within the context of the prison was exceptionally difficult, for a number of reasons. Prisoners were separated from fellow grievers, almost always denied permission to attend funerals, and unable to participate in the 'normal rituals' of death (Jill, 40s, post-tariff); several explained the feeling of alienation that resulted from being 'surrounded' by fellow prisoners, yet unable to express grief in front of them—what Doka (2002) calls 'disenfranchised grief': 'I really can't find the space to [grieve]. You've got everyone around you, so it's really hard' (Eloise, 20s, early). None felt that they had been given sufficient institutional support in dealing with their feelings, often describing being made to engage in normal prison activities, such as work, on the day when the funeral was held:

Was there space in the prison for you to openly express your grief, or talk to someone?
No one helped me, no, not at all. On his funeral day they made me go to work [...];
they chuck you in the deep end and let you get on with it. I should have been in
healthcare, really, like my head was proper twatted, really bad, and *nothing* - they
just chucked me on this wing, and just left me to get on with it. (Liz, 20s, early)

Being absent from the funeral contributed to the sense that the death was 'not
real' (Jill, 40s, post-tariff). At the same time, bereavement made the implications
of serving a very long sentence all the more apparent. For Carly (30s, late), it was
only when her uncle died that 'my sentence hit me. [...] It triggered something';
likewise, for Arshad (30s, late), the death of his father was the point when 'reality
sort of kicked in, you know, that my mum needs me, and I can't be there for her'.
This sentiment of powerlessness was echoed by Jill (40s, post-tariff): 'your world
caves in, because you can't do anything'. Meanwhile, Deena outlined the way that
death shattered the illusion that the world outside might be preserved until the
point of release:

When you come to prison you think that life stops. Because your life has stopped,
in a way, and you think that when you get out everything's going to be the same,
everything's going to be there. And it's not until something like that happens that
you realise, no, it's kind of changed. And it's not going to be the same anymore.
(Deena, 20s, mid)

Some prisoners reported that such experiences led to a re-evaluation of life (Herbert
2018). Campbell (30s, mid), for example, was so shocked by his brother's death,
and so devastated that he was unable to attend the funeral, that he reappraised his
priorities: 'I just thought "Fuck this. I need to get out of here"'.

More typically, bereavement plunged prisoners into crisis, as they struggled not
only to deal with their feelings of grief, but also to suppress emotions relating
to their sentence. Terms such as 'caving in' (Gail, 30s, late) and going 'off the
rails' (Deena, 20s, mid) signalled this sense of no longer being able to cope.[17] As
Ashley outlined, irrepressible feelings of anger, distress and helplessness often had

---

[17] For Rafe (30s, mid), the death of his father helped him achieve 'some victim empathy [...], to sort of think
to myself I have made other people feel like this, you know', but this was account of the positive impact of
bereavement was unusual.

regressive effects, driving prisoners to the kinds of coping mechanisms that were more typical of early-stage prisoners:

> You know the worse thing that's happened since I've been in jail? I'd say one thing was when my dad got a tumour. I wanted to just tear down the jail walls and I wanted to batter everybody in. I went back to smoking drugs just to calm me down, and I failed about three [urine] tests in that 12-month period. I was in such an angry place, and I was angry at myself for being in jail and not being there for him, because he supported me through this sentence. [...] I felt so guilty and so bad, and so I just started smoking drugs again just to calm me down, man, and just to keep me sane because I was losing it. I was just raging. I was just raging and raging and didn't know what to do. (Ashley, 30s, mid)

For female prisoners in particular, complex mental health needs and the impact of trauma often eclipsed the concerns with imprisonment itself that preoccupied other long-termers. Several female participants stated that their conviction was a less painful or momentous life event than experiences that had preceded it. One explained that she could never move on from the death of her son, stating she was unconcerned by her sentence because its significance was subordinate to the trauma of burying her child. Liz (20s, early) noted that 'my life had always been so tough, it was hard, but I'd been through tough things before, so I'd say the mental health was worse than being sent to prison for murder'.

Others described the struggles that they faced in working out who they were, or in feeling 'normal', due to personality and mental disorders or the psychological adjustments they had made in the community in response to acute distress: 'I learned to be somebody else [...] and over time I totally forgot who [I] used to be, and now I'm this other person' (Karen, 20s, mid). Certainly, more often than the men, the women used a language of 'losing' themselves, due to trauma, substance abuse and potent medication (see Chapter 7). Several claimed that it was only in prison that they had been able to find themselves and act as full agents in their own lives:

> [Prison] gives you the skills to actually make decisions about your life. Whereas outside, when you're younger, life just happens to you and you deal with it. Whereas, I suppose, now, you can actually make conscious choices about what you will allow to happen. [...] I don't think I ever made a conscious choice out there; I never made a choice to be with my babies' dad, it just happened and I just went along, because

I didn't have a choice. [...] When you've been in that background of violence, you daren't really get up and have a voice. When you do actually find your voice - prison's a funny place to find your voice in. (Gail, 30s, late)

As we now discuss, this process of self-discovery led to a reconsideration of life projects and priorities, and to a sense of a future.

Projects and Concerns

Describing their imprisonment as a kind of 'wake-up call', many early-stage prisoners reflected that their sentence had given them a greater appreciation of matters that they had previously taken for granted ('like freedom and people around you [who] you love' [Clifford, 20s, early]), or had helped put into clearer perspective what mattered in life: 'how valuable certain things are, how valuable your families are' (Zufar, 20s, early). As Neil summarised, 'you start to re-evaluate what's important to you, and what's really important to you' (Neil, 30s. mid).

Reflections of this kind were significant in echoing conventional narratives of the clarifying power of bereavement. Indeed, several prisoners referred to a form of grief that they felt for themselves—'the life that I could have had' (Carl, 20s, early)—as a result of their sentence, or drew directly on discourses of 'loss': 'It kicked me so hard up the arse, you know. What I'd lost. I'd lost everything' (Campbell, 30s, mid). As we discuss in the final sections of this chapter, this awakening—an outcome of the social and existential dislocations that we have highlighted (see Aresti et al. 2010)—prompted the radical reappraisal of prisoners' 'ultimate concerns' (Archer 2003, 2012) and the daily projects in which they invested to fulfil these priorities. In particular, projects and concerns were focused on matters of family relations and ethical selfhood: making amends, being good, and doing good.

Prisoners who were beyond the first few years of the sentence also talked consistently about wanting to 'give something back: what Erikson's (1982) calls 'generativity'. Generative concerns related to both life inside the prison and beyond it (see Appleton 2010; Liem 2016; Bullock et al. 2018; Kazemian 2019). With regard to the former, a very high number of participants had become Listeners, taken counselling courses, taken on roles as violence reduction or safer custody representatives, or involved themselves in schemes designed to impress upon schoolchildren the perils of crime (see also Irwin 2010; Herbert 2018). Others reported having assumed nurturing roles by 'talking therapeutically' (Arkaan, 20s, mid) to their peers or taking younger prisoners under their wing: 'Even in jail I try and help people, the little youngsters that's coming in jail getting long sentences' (Asad, 30s, mid).

Some prisoners were motivated by a desire to 'give back' the help they had received from others, or reflected that, had they received the forms of advice that they were now providing for others, they might have avoided their current circumstances. Most often, generative ambitions were expressed in a language of redemption (Irwin 2010). Using terms derived from offending behaviour courses, such as 'ripple effects' (Arkaan, 20s, mid), prisoners explained the importance of counterbalancing the negative things they had done in their lives by becoming 'a better person', providing inspiration, and preventing others from reproducing their own mistakes. Often, these sentiments were rooted in a sense that, in effect, two lives risked being 'lost' as a result of someone's death: those of both the victim and the perpetrator. For example:

> All I can do is I can take the positives from this situation. A person of 19 years old died, you know, and I can never ever take that back. [...] The only thing I can do is change, make myself a better person, and obviously try and affect people in beneficial ways. [...] I have to make something happen, you know, like a shining star come out of something bleak and black. (Stephen, 20s, mid)

As suggested here, many prisoners were haunted by the impossibility of being able to change the past and 'bring someone back' (Mahmood, 30s, mid), something often referred to directly and with sorrow. Instead, as a partial form of restitution, they felt that they might be able to prevent similar kinds of tragedies in the future, using a language of salvation to describe their hope of delivering others from their fate: 'guiding someone to Christ' (Luca, 30s, mid), or simply 'stop[ping] one youngster from going down the same path that I did' (Mahmood, 30s, mid). Many prisoners struggled with the awareness that these forms of reparation were inevitably partial:

> There's no other way for me to make amends of what I did. [...]. I can't bring him back ever. If I could I would, but I can't, so... I can do what I can do, man, and that's the only thing that I can do. (Luca, 30s, mid)

Other prisoners expressed their mission to do good in terms of leaving a positive legacy that might supersede the act of murder that otherwise defined them. Doing so would grant them an identity beyond being a murderer or simply being forgotten: 'a page in a book' (Frank, 40s, late).

Generative objectives—being 'an agent of positive change' (Herbert 2018; Maruna 2001)—were almost always related to feelings of profound remorse and self-loathing about the offence. Doing good for others was bound up with attempts to absolve feelings of shame and produce a more positive narrative of selfhood: to 'feel better about myself' (Mahmood, 30s, mid). As we describe in Chapter 7, some prisoners pursued these ends not through activities that were explicitly generative, but by cultivating themselves as ethical agents (Foucault 1986), expressed in a 'code' for living: being polite, respectful, stoic in the face of frustration and provocation, and able to 'have a decent conversation'. Such aims also reflected the highly constrained environment in which projects had to be formed. In their daily practices and projects, mid- and late-stage prisoners were highly purposeful and agentic but had limited resources with which to pursue their goals. In this context, personal conduct—interpersonal decency, conversational ability, affective discipline and so on—was among a very limited set of options through which to demonstrate ethical selfhood.

The desire to live a mundane ethical existence or 'give something back' was also relevant to post-prison aspirations. A large proportion of prisoners expressed a desire to work with 'delinquents and problem families, all this stuff' (Arkaan, 20s, mid). Jill (40s, post-tariff) described her 'dream' of 'working with young offenders … teaching them how to grow their own veg, be self-sufficient'; Andre (late teens, early) wanted to 'talk to young people, just coming in [to prison] - hold their hand and that'. Such goals shared the same features as those of generative ground projects: the hope of 'inspiring others' (Arkaan, 20s, mid), proving oneself 'a better person' (Yvette, 30s, mid), 'counterbalancing' previous misdeeds (Neil, 30s, mid), and ensuring that the index offence was not 'the definition of my life' (Karen, 20s, mid).

Although aspirational, such hopes were rarely grandiose. When asked about their goals on release—their ultimate concerns—prisoners generally listed ambitions that were modest and highly conventional. This finding is consistent with Appleton's (2010: 215) statement that, among her sample of life-sentenced prisoners, 'what stood out most was the aspiration for normality [and] their resilience and determination to achieve a life more ordinary'; likewise, in their research into the post-release lives of long-term prisoners in Canada, Munn and Bruckert (2013) report a common 'quest for normalcy' (p. 105): being 'an indistinguishable part of the social fabric – an average guy' (p. 168; see also Bullock et al. 2018). As in such studies, our participants typically spoke of wanting to lead lives that were 'settled', uneventful and relatively parochial: to reunite with loved ones, stay away from drugs and alcohol, get a place of their own, run their own businesses or get a 'decent' job ('I can do dustman and cleaning and that' [Arthur, 50s, post-tariff]), and lead a simple life with simple pleasures.[18]

Some explained these ambitions by reasoning that it was unrealistic to expect much more, in the sense that it would be 'too late' (Nathaniel, 30s, mid) or too difficult to achieve anything further: 'when a lifer leaves prison, how much of a successful life has anybody ever heard of?' (Julius, 30s, mid). More often, prisoners craved the forms of routine activity and fulfilment that the deprivation of liberty precluded:

And what do you hope life looks like for you?
Normal. Just normal, mundane, everyday, getting up, going to work, coming home, eating, sleeping, breathing…. just the normal stuff.
Yeah, and being able to do that when you want?
Yeah. Being able to lock my own door. (Jenny, 20s, mid)

Just a normal life I suppose, like […] you get up in the morning and go to a job and then after work go to the gym and have a dog and walk the dog, just normal things, and a relationship and cook food and sit and watch TV or go out, just normal things. (Jackie, 30s, late)

What do you most want to achieve from your life after this sentence?
[…] I would like to take my dog for a walk, that's one thing. That will just be the pinnacle for me, because it would mean […] that I would be living, at least, in a place of my own, where I would be capable of looking after a dog. The house […] would be of a certain standard, and I would have the freedom just to say: 'Come on mate, we will go out for a walk'. […] and maybe I will be able to have a relationship and a child… I don't know from then on, but I think you could sum it up by just saying that. Yeah. Take my dog for a walk. (Rafe, 30s, mid)

---

[18]The aspiration to be self-employed or run one's own business was partly explained by the desire to achieve 'something on your own' (Deena, 20s, mid), and partly by the knowledge that the stigma and disqualifications resulting from a life sentence would make it hard to find many other forms of paid work.

Rafe's hesitancy about having an intimate relationship was not unusual. Julius (30s, mid), for example, observed that 'Everyone that I know that leaves prison as a lifer just wants to be left alone'. Mid- and late-stage prisoners who were not already parents more often expressed the aspiration to have children, or 'get to know my family again' (Deena, 20s, mid), than to find romantic or sexual partners (though some female prisoners recognised that their sentence had deprived them of the possibility of carrying children [see Walker and Worrall 2000]). In doing so, they often stated their credentials to be good parents and their drive to teach their children not to replicate their own mistakes. For some, forging a family life was the paramount goal:

> I'm just looking forward to being out, and just starting again and just starting a family now. Because that's the only thing I'm going to do, I don't care about nothing else like, all I care about is just like getting me a wife, have some kids and just be like a proper good dad like what I couldn't be when I was in jail. [...] I'll just be like a proper good dad and best friends with my little boy or girl or whatever, just like... just have fun and enjoy life. (Olin, 20s, mid)

The ultimate concerns of those who already had children were to become reacquainted with them and re-occupy roles of nurture and love; to 'be a good mum' (Yvette, 30s, mid) or father:

> My long-term goal, my ultimate long-term goal is, you know, they're all interrelated, but generally at the forefront it's getting out and caring for my children. And obviously getting out relates to everything else. (Neil, 30s, mid)

Aspirations of this kind brought into relief the primacy of liberty as an ultimate concern. Nonetheless, among most mid- and late-stage prisoners, optimism about the future was cautious. Although more positive about their lives than they had been at earlier sentence stages, many did not trust the prison system and were all too aware of the unpredictable nature of prison life. They were reluctant, therefore, to invest too much hope in the prospect of their own liberty, for fear of disappointment (see Munn and Bruckert 2013). The result was a discourse that was fatalistic precisely because of the intense hope underlying it:

> If it happens it happens, if it doesn't it doesn't.
> *Is it that you don't want to get your hopes up in case you're then disappointed?*

Yeah. (Nathaniel, 30s, mid)

I wouldn't tuck all me eggs in a basket because you never know what's gonna happen. [...] Life is unpredictable. And human behaviour is the same, so you never know what tomorrow is gonna bring to your table. (Shane, 40s, post-tariff)

I do think about the future, but I don't think about it too much because I'm not there yet so I don't... I'm not optimistic enough.
Are you worried to get too excited about it?
Yeah, in case it like gets took away from me. (Jackie, 30s, late)

Often, it was only when they were in open conditions that prisoners allowed themselves to feel optimistic about being freed: 'you know you're on the home run there, you're on your way out' (Eileen, 30s, late). At this point, however, anxiety shifted to the realities of life post-release. For prisoners beyond their tariff point, for example, 'Worrying about how you will cope when you get out' was the 14th most severe problem, compared to 25th and 28th among very early-stage and mid-stage participants, respectively. Among such prisoners, trepidation about what Gail (30s, late) called 'all the unknown and starting from scratch' was pervasive. For example:

And how do you feel about your release itself?
Quite hopeful that everything will go well and that I will manage to stay out. But slightly scared, like I said earlier, because there's a lot of stuff that I've not done, I've not been an adult in the outside world, I've not been clean and sober outside for a long time, so it's going to be a big hurdle and it might well be a struggle, but hopefully I will manage it. (Jenny, 20s, mid)

Prisoners who were well beyond their tariff point (or who were nearing it, but without any imminent prospect of release) talked about hope in terms that echoed those of early-stage prisoners. Walter (60s, post-tariff) declared that he had 'no future. But I'm not bothered about it. [...] There's nothing outside for me. I don't feel sorry about this, or unhappy. I'm a realist, I face reality'. Stuart (40s, post-tariff) noted that almost all of the life-sentenced prisoners he knew were over their tariff point, and felt a sense of 'desperation' and 'hopelessness' about their powerlessness with regard to release: 'there's not even a tunnel, let alone a light there'. Marcus had given up pushing for release, explaining that:

There's a bit of, you know, I'm tired. Because there's always the desire to get out. I'd like to get out. I'd like to meet my friends at the… But I don't believe that I have motivation for it, that I'm motivated for it. I think something's died inside me. *[…] And the bit of you that you say has died inside, what is that bit? What is it that's died?*
Hope. (Marcus, 50s, post-tariff)

Even prisoners who were more sanguine recognised the difficulty of envisioning and enacting a set of ultimate concerns while sequestered from the world in which their goals could be realised. Aware that the world outside was not congruent with the world of the prison, and unable to try on different roles for size—what Bottoms (2006: 266) calls 'toe-dipping'—often, the most they felt they could do was 'prepare'. Kenny (20s, mid) stated that his life beyond the prison was 'on hold' and that he did not 'plan anything in jail. I just want to do as good as I can while I'm in jail, what will help me when I get out'. As stated in the quotation with which this chapter opened, Ashley's reasoning was similar: while it was possible to build a life in prison, the construction of a life beyond it was an altogether different matter. At most, one could 'prepare':

I educate myself, I'm trying to get a degree, I'm trying to get a diploma in counselling, because counselling is what I want to do. So I'm educating myself and getting what I need to give me an upper hand. And I know I've got a criminal record and all the rest of it, but if I can get to the level I need to be at I can possibly achieve something. (Ashley, 30s, mid)

For prisoners who had been removed from the community for very long periods, merely imagining the outside world was difficult. To quote Gail (30s, late), 'I haven't got the ability to imagine that world and me in that world, you know?' Memories had dulled, society had moved on, and it was hard for such participants to 'envision their lives beyond their immediate carceral environment' (Munn and Bruckert 2013: 62) or project themselves imaginatively into a future that was pixelated and unreal (c.f. Bottoms 2006). Some were optimistic about having a future beyond the prison, but were unable to picture it:

I wanna be, one day, just sitting somewhere which is not prison and feeling normal, you know, and I just long for that moment, that one day. I know it's gonna happen, but I just can't imagine it right now. (Mahmood, 30s, mid)

My life has got to amount to more than this, and I hope it does. Right now it's not possible for me to actually think beyond these walls, in the sense of making plans and that. But I know there is going to be a time when I will be out. (Stephen, 20s, mid)

Discussion

Much of what we have described in this chapter is broadly consistent both with previous scholarship and prisoner memoirs (e.g. Carceral 2006; Hassine 2011). In their article on 'mature coping', Johnson and Dobrzanska (2005: 8) argue that, following an initial period of 'unsettled adjustment', life-sentenced prisoners 'typically come to a realistic assessment of their grim situation'. Specifically, they 'come grudgingly to accept the prison as their involuntary home for life' (p. 8), 'consciously submit to the prison rather than fight battles they cannot win' (p. 8), and 'fashion a life at least partly on their own terms, giving them a sense of control and hence personal autonomy' (9). In addition, the authors argue, their interviewees managed to find some sense of meaning and purpose in their existence, often through mentoring activities or the development of deep religious faith (see also Johnson 2019). Liem's (2016) findings indicate a similar transition. Drawing on Irwin's (1970) typology, she characterises life-sentenced prisoners in the United States as initially 'doing time', but, after a period of several years, exhibiting an adaptive style more like Irwin's concept of 'gleaning', in which prisoners use the resources available to them within the prison to pursue a goal of personal change and self-improvement.

What is more distinctive is our emphasis on the particular forms of agency and reflexivity that characterised these phases. Prisoners in the early sentence stage conveyed a mode of agency that was stunted, defensive and reactive, as they engaged in a basic process of psychological survival and sought to deflect and deny the realities of their situation. Those who were further into their sentence were—like Archer's (2003, 2012) meta-reflexives—more actively attempting to overcome their difficulties through forms of reflexive contemplation and productive agency. This process of 'coping-adaption' involved coming to terms not only with the sentence itself, and with the long-term confiscation of their freedom, but also with the moral and existential implications associated with the offence. Rather than trying to suppress the resulting emotions of anger, distress and shame, or avoiding a frank confrontation with reality, they reflexively deliberated on their circumstances. This mode of deliberation—a kind of reckoning with the self—involved an increasing orientation to the future, in which prisoners sought to dedicate themselves to 'course[s] of action congruent with their [ultimate] concerns or commitments' (Vaughan 2006: 392). That is, they made decisions about their present actions that were oriented to a sense of who they wanted to be and how they wanted their lives to develop (Archer 2003). Doing so often required a midwife, and many years of nurture, provided by practices of faith, education and therapy, and supported by loved ones external to the prison. It is telling that these resources, and the forms of ethical self-reflection that they generated, were relatively unrestricted. As Archer notes, 'certain intentional human activities, like private prayer, can never be the objects of structural and cultural constraints' (2003: 8). Such processes allowed prisoners to find some degree of hope, despite their exceptionally grim circumstances, to feel some degree of control, despite the severe restrictions placed on them, and—as we discuss in subsequent chapters—to cope with the burdens of time, and 'construct a new, positive life and self-identity' (Maruna et al. 2006: 173). The need and drive to do so was produced by the radical dislocations we have identified throughout the book so far, and therefore by the desire and requirement to reconstruct a set of social relations, become a different kind of person, and imagine a different kind of future. We turn to these matters in the chapters that follow.

References

Akram, S., & Hogan, A. (2015). On reflexivity and the conduct of the self in everyday life: Reflections on Bourdieu and Archer. *British Journal of Sociology, 66*(4), 605–625.

Appleton, C. (2010). *Life after life imprisonment.* Oxford: Oxford University Press.

Archer, M. S. (2003). *Structure, agency and the internal conversation.* Cambridge: Cambridge University Press.

Archer, M. S. (2012). *The reflexive imperative in late modernity.* Cambridge: Cambridge University Press.

Aresti, A., Eatough, V., & Brooks-Gordon, B. (2010). Doing time after time: An interpretative phenomenological analysis of reformed ex-prisoners' experiences of self-change, identity and career opportunities. *Psychology, Crime & Law, 16*(3), 169–190.

Bottoms, A. (2006). Desistance, social bonds, and human agency: A theoretical exploration. In P.-O. Wikstrom & R. Sampson (Eds.), *The explanation of crime: Context, mechanisms and development* (pp. 243–290). Cambridge: Cambridge University Press.

Bottoms, A. (2019). Penal censure, repentance and desistance. In A. du Bois-Pedain & A. Bottoms (Eds.), *Penal censure: Engagements within and beyond desert theory*. London: Hart Publishing.

Bullock, K., Bunce, A., & McCarthy, D. (2018). Making good in unpromising places: The development and cultivation of redemption scripts among long-term prisoners. *International Journal of Offender Therapy and Comparative Criminology, 63*(3), 406–423.

Campbell, R., Sullivan, C. M., & Davidson, W. S. (1995). Women who use domestic violence shelters: Changes in depression over time. *Psychology of Women Quarterly, 19*(2), 237–255.

Carceral, K. C. (2006). *Prison, inc: A convict exposes life inside a private prison* (Vol. 14). NYU Press.

Carlen, P. (1983). *Women's imprisonment: A study in social control*. London: Routledge & Kegan Paul.

Carlen, P. (1998). *Sledgehammer: Women's imprisonment at the millennium*. Houndmills: Macmillan Press Ltd.

Clear, T. R., Hardyman, P. L., Stout, B., Lucken, K., & Dammer, H. R. (2000). The value of religion in prison: An inmate perspective. *Journal of Contemporary Criminal Justice, 16*(1), 53–74.

Cohen, S., & Taylor, L. (1972). *Psychological survival: The experience of long-term imprisonment*. Middlesex: Penguin.

Comfort, M. L. (2008). *Doing time together: Forging love and family in the shadow of the prison*. Chicago: Chicago University Press.

Crewe, B. (2011). Depth, weight, tightness: Revisiting the pains of imprisonment. *Punishment and Society, 13*(5), 509–529.

Crewe, B., Hulley, S., & Wright, S. (2017). Swimming with the tide: Adapting to long-term imprisonment. *Justice Quarterly, 34*(3), 517–541.

Crewe, B., Warr, J., Bennett, P., & Smith, A. (2014). The emotional geography of prison life. *Theoretical Criminology, 18*(1), 56–74.

Doka, K. J. (Ed.). (2002). *Disenfranchised grief: New directions, challenges, and strategies for practice*. Research Press Pub.

De Viggiani, N. (2012). Trying to be something you are not: Masculine performances within a prison setting. *Men and Masculinities, 15*(3), 271–291.

Drake, D. H. (2018). Prisons and state building: Promoting 'The fiasco of the prison' in a global context. *International Journal for Crime, Justice and Social Democracy, 7*(4), 1–15.

Erikson, E. H. (1982). *The life cycle completed.* New York, NY: W. W. Norton & Company, Inc.

Finkelhor, D., Ormrod, R. K., & Turner, H. A. (2007). Poly-victimization: A neglected component in child victimization. *Child Abuse & Neglect, 31*(1), 7–26.

Flanagan, T. J. (1980). The pains of long-term imprisonment: A comparison of British and American perspectives. *The British Journal of Criminology, 20*(2), 148–156.

Foucault, M. (1986). *The care of the self: The history of sexuality* (Vol. 3). New York: Pantheon.

Frankl, V. (1959). *Man's search for meaning.* NY: Simon & Schuster.

Gartner, R., & Kruttschnitt, C. (2004). A brief history of doing time: The California Institution for Women in the 1960s and the 1990s. *Law & Society Review, 38*(2), 267–304.

Genders, E., & Player, E. (1990). Women lifers: Assessing the experience. *The Prison Journal, 70*(1), 46–57.

Genders, E., & Player, E. (1995). *Grendon: A study of a therapeutic prison.* Oxford: Oxford University Press.

Gilbar, O., & Hevroni, A. (2007). Counterfactuals, coping strategies and psychological distress among breast cancer patients. *Anxiety, Stress, & Coping, 20*(4), 383–392.

Girshick, L. B. (2003). Abused women and incarceration. In B. H. Zaitzow & J. Thomas (Eds.), *Women in prison: Gender and social control* (pp. 95–118). Colorado: Lynne Rienner Publishers.

Hassine, V. (2011). *Life without parole: Living and dying in prison today.* New York, NY: Oxford University Press.

Herbert, S. (2018). Inside or outside? Expanding the narratives about life-sentenced prisoners. *Punishment & Society, 20*(5), 628–645.

Hulley, S., Crewe, B., & Wright, S. (2019). Making sense of 'joint enterprise' for murder: Legal legitimacy or instrumental acquiescence? *British Journal of Criminology, 59*(6), 1328–1346.

Irwin, J. (1970). *The felon.* Englewood Cliffs, NJ: Prentice-Hall.

Irwin, J. (2010). *Lifers: Seeking redemption in prison.* Abingdon: Routledge.

Jewkes, Y. (2005). Loss, liminality and the life sentence: Managing identity through a disrupted lifecourse. In A. Liebling & S. Maruna (Eds.), *The effects of imprisonment* (pp. 366–388). Cullompton: Willan.

Johnson, R. (2019). *Condemned to die: Life under sentence of death* (2nd ed.). New York: Routledge.

Johnson, R., & Dobrzanska, A. (2005). Mature coping among life-sentenced inmates: An exploratory study of adjustment dynamics. *Corrections Compendium, 30*(6), 8–9.

Johnson, R., & McGunigall-Smith, S. (2008). Life without parole, America's other death penalty: Notes on life under sentence of death by incarceration. *The Prison Journal, 88*(2), 328–346.

Kazemian, L. (2019). *Lotus in the mud: Positive growth within our prisons.* London and New York: Routledge.

Kerley, K. R., & Copes, H. (2009). "Keepin' my mind right" identity maintenance and religious social support in the prison context. *International Journal of Offender Therapy and Comparative Criminology, 53*(2), 228–244.

Laws, B. (2018). The return of the suppressed: Exploring how emotional suppression reappears as violence and pain among male and female prisoners. *Punishment & Society.* https://doi.org/10.1177/1462474518805071.

Lempert, L. B. (2016). *Women doing life: Gender, punishment and the struggle for identity.* New York: NYU Press.

Liebling, A., Arnold, H., & Straub, C. (2011). *An exploration of staff-prisoner relationships at HMP Whitemoor: 12 years on.* London: Ministry of Justice, National Offender Management Service.

Liem, M. (2016). *After life imprisonment: Reentry in the era of mass incarceration.* New York: NYU Press.

Martin, K., & Stermac, L. (2010). Measuring hope: Is hope related to criminal behaviour in offenders? *International Journal of Offender Therapy and Comparative Criminology, 54*(5), 693–705.

Maruna, S. (2001). *Making good.* Washington, DC: American Psychological Association.

Maruna, S., Wilson, L., & Curran, K. (2006). Why God is often found behind bars: Prison conversions and the crisis of self-narrative. *Research in Human Development, 3*(2–3), 161–184.

Munn, M., & Bruckert, C. (2013). On the outside: From lengthy imprisonment to lasting freedom. Vancouver: UBC Press.

O'Donnell, I. (2014). *Prisoners, solitude and time.* Oxford: Oxford University Press.

Park, C. L. (2010). Making sense of the meaning literature: An integrative review of meaning making and its effects on adjustment to stressful life events. *Psychological Bulletin, 136*(2), 257–301.

Perrin, C., & Blagden, N. (2014). Accumulating meaning, purpose and opportunities to change 'drip by drip': The impact of being a listener in prison. *Psychology, Crime & Law, 20*(9), 902–920.

Sapsford, R. J. (1978). Life-sentence prisoners: Psychological changes during sentence. *British Journal of Criminology, 18*(2), 128–145.

Schinkel, M. (2014). *Being imprisoned: Punishment, adaptation and desistance.* New York: Springer.

Schmid, T. J., & Jones, R. S. (1991). Suspended identity: Identity transformation in a maximum security prison. *Symbolic Interaction, 14*(4), 415–432.

Snyder, C. R. (2000). *Handbook of hope: Theory, measures, and applications.* London: Academic press.

Stevens, A. (2013). Prisoners' motivations for therapeutic community treatment: In search of a 'different' approach to offender rehabilitation. *Probation Journal, 60*(2), 152–167.

Sykes, G. (1958). *The society of captives: A study of a maximum security prison.* Princeton: Princeton University Press.

Vaughan, B. (2006). The internal narrative of desistance. *British Journal of Criminology, 47*(3), 390–404.

Walker, S., & Worrall, A. (2000). Life as a woman. *Prison Service Journal,* 27–36.

Williams, R. J. (2018). Finding freedom and rethinking power: Islamic piety in English high security prisons. *British Journal of Criminology, 58*(3), 730–748.

Zamble, E. (1992). Behavior and adaptation in long-term prison inmates: Descriptive longitudinal results. *Criminal Justice and Behavior, 19*(4), 409–425.

Zehr, H. (1996). *Doing life: Reflections of men and women serving life sentences.* New York: Simon & Schuster.

6

Social Relations

The social transition imposed on prisoners as they enter custody is one of the most significant dislocations that they encounter. All prisoners are required to adapt to enforced separation from family and friends, restricted communication with loved ones, and living within an alternative social community. For those serving long life sentences, this fracturing of social relations is particularly 'critical' (Flanagan 1981: 210), requiring both a reframing of existing relationships and the establishment of new social bonds and networks.

This chapter explores the changing nature of long-term prisoners' kinship relations and friendships, following the radical rupturing of their social existence caused by their conviction and sentence. For prisoners who had recently entered custody, adjusting to physical separation from loved ones, and the associated anxieties, felt acutely painful. As noted in Chapter 4, this was evidenced by 'worrying about people outside' and 'missing someone' being among the most severe problems reported by both male and female participants in the study. Most commonly, in the absence of long-term partners and dependent children, the men wrestled with concerns about how to be 'a good son' and reported improvements in their relationships with parents. Meanwhile, the women who had dependent children were tormented by the challenges of fulfilling maternal roles while in custody for a very long period.

© The Author(s) 2020
B. Crewe et al., *Life Imprisonment from Young Adulthood*,
Palgrave Studies in Prisons and Penology,
https://doi.org/10.1057/978-1-137-56601-0_6

While some family members remained present in most prisoners' lives, the majority of pre-prison friendships either dissipated or were jettisoned, demonstrating the 'distinctive obligations' of the kin network, particularly at times of crisis (Paylor and Smith 1994: 134). A few loyal friends remained in contact, sometimes unexpectedly, tethering prisoners to some aspects of their pre-prison social world. Meanwhile, in adapting to their new social domain, many prisoners developed a small number of 'meaningful' friendships with their peers in custody. This development took time, and for some it never occurred, but for most long-term prisoners it was important to foster some degree of social existence to satisfy the need for 'relational goods', such as companionship, trust, care and intimacy (Donati 2011). The following sections discuss these experiences in more detail.

Dislocation of Social World—Natal and Nuclear Family

Separation from loved ones and close friends was among the most painful aspects of long-term imprisonment for the men and women in our study, as in others (see Flanagan 1980; Richards 1978). As Table 6.1 shows the acuteness of this pain was

Table 6.1 Mean scores and ranks of problem statements related to social relations—female and male survey respondents

Problems	Mean score Female	Mean score Male	Rank (out of 39) Female	Rank (out of 39) Male
Missing somebody	18.63	17.17	2	1
Worrying about people outside	18.21	15.30	3	2
Feeling that you are losing contact with family and friends	15.39*[a]	10.46	7	17
Being afraid that someone you love or care about will die before you are released	14.58	12.43	13	10

[a]The mean severity score for female prisoners was significantly higher than the score for male prisoners (* $= p < 0.05$)

illustrated in the survey results: 'missing somebody' was reported to be the most severe problem for male prisoners at all sentence stages, except for those who were post-tariff. For female prisoners, 'missing someone' was the second most severe problem overall—with an absolute severity score that was higher than for male prisoners—and was among the eight most serious problems across all sentence stages. Similarly, 'worrying about people outside' and 'feeling that you are losing contact with family and friends' featured among the ten most severe problems for the female prisoners, while 'worrying about people outside' and 'being afraid that someone you love or care about will die before you are released' featured in the male prisoners' ten most severe problems.

For most prisoners, being forcibly separated from loved ones for many years was excruciating, and it was this severance that many struggled to cope with most of all:

> I just felt really shitty [a few years in] and I thought 'what the fuck am I going to do all these years in prison?', do you know what I mean? Away from my kids, away from my family. And I've got to stay in this fucking prison for fucking how many years, and, do you know what, I just thought 'I'll just end it' [i.e. take my own life]. (Eloise, 20s, early)

> When I get stressed out, I get really stressed out, just, kind of, find it hard to cope, and you just need someone to talk to, but not just anyone, someone who genuinely cares and loves you. [...] You know, when you're feeling that raw, I just wanted to be with my family. That's all I wanted. (Mahmood, 30s, mid)

The pain associated with the dislocation from loved ones had a number of implications for prisoners, including daily suffering, emotional conflict, and ultimately the loss of some relationships, particularly those that had been intimate prior to their imprisonment.

The Rupturing of Intimate Relationships

Schinkel (2014: 75) argues that, for men, ceasing contact with loved ones during a long prison sentence 'solves several problems: it reduces thoughts of those outside, thereby minimising the pain of missing them, it helps to maintain control over relationships and means that they are not diminished through superficial interactions' (see also Toch 1992). This was certainly the case for many of the men in our study were in intimate relationships when sentenced, most of whom terminated their commitments relatively quickly: during the trial, when sentenced, or following a failed appeal.

As noted in Chapter 4, such decisions were often presented as altruistic, to protect partners from putting their lives 'on hold' for many years. However, most prisoners also disclosed motives of psychological self-protection:

> So when I was sentenced, I went 'it's over'. [...] cause obviously, it ain't fair on her, is it?
> *So [...] you wanted to end it [...] so she could move on?*
> Yeah, really. Cos it takes a bit of stress off you, doesn't it? Being in prison when you've got someone on the outside and you start [thinking] 'what's my baby [girlfriend] doing outside?'
> *[You] worry that they might cheat on [you] or...?*
> Exactly. You don't want none of that while you're in prison. (Zubair, 20s, early)

The reciprocal bond of pre-prison relationships was rarely strong enough to survive the prospect of long-term separation. Since these relationships tended to be fairly casual and non-committed, the initial force of imprisonment was often decisive. Most prisoners reported that intimate partners could not cope with the stress of their being in prison or that they themselves could see little point in trying to maintain the relationship under the circumstances:

> *A week after [being sentenced], what was going through your head in those days?*
> I was distressed. I had a girlfriend, [and] when I got 18 years she broke down, she started crying on the phone, and I was, like, 'you're not doing 18 years with me, are you?' and obviously she said 'I am, I am'. I said 'you're not, I'm going to let you go'. So that's what I've done. (Miguel, late teens, early)

> I was, like, 'I can't cope with you out there and me in here, and this don't make no...'. To me, it just didn't make any sense staying together, what are we staying together for? (Fernando, 20s, mid)

As Fernando's comments suggest, many prisoners were in a state of psychological turmoil that precluded the kind of mutuality needed to maintain relational goods (Donati 2011).

Female prisoners' relationships with partners outside prison were also brittle, but broke for different reasons. Compared to the male prisoners, many women reported being in more serious intimate relationships prior to imprisonment, but— reflecting the experiences of women in prison more generally (Corston 2007)— these relationships were very often highly abusive. For example:

> A massive, serious incident with [my partner] was he tried slashing my throat. […] He'd smashed the window and tried to drag my throat across it, but I kicked back. And my house was like - the windows were huge, and he'd wrote all over the walls in blood, 'I'm going to kill you. I'll be back', and all this. At this point, he's threatening to kill me and my children, […] he just went mental, and he pulled out this commando knife and things and it was like, 'oh my God, this time I'm dead. This time I'm not getting out'. (Gail, 30s, late)

Almost all female interviewees reported experiencing domestic violence, including at the hands of men who were their co-defendants:

> I was with [my ex-boyfriend (and co-defendant)] for eight years and he beat me every day. (Tamara, 20s, early)

> I met my co-defendants, and then I got [together] with one of my co-defendants, and I couldn't even stand him; I hated him to be honest. He was violent, and I was scared of him. (Carly, 30s, late)

Typically, these relationships were dissolved during the early stage of custody, due to extreme resentment at being implicated in an offence committed by the partner, recognition that the relationship was dysfunctional and unhealthy, or because contact was difficult to maintain when both partners were in prison.

For both male and female participants, the fracturing of intimate relationships felt acutely painful, but often this pain was relatively short-lived, not least because prisoners were still reeling from their conviction and trying to cope with the initial shock of the sentence:

What have you found to be the three most difficult things about serving your sentence?
Splitting up with my girlfriend was the worst.
So how do you deal with that in this environment?
You just get over it, yeah, just have to get over it.
Did it take a long time?
I can't really remember. I remember I spoke to her…it took about a week, that to be fair was long enough! (Craig, 20s, early)

I split up with him [a week before being sentenced]. I turned around and said to him, 'I can't do this no more', and I was like, 'And I'm getting guilty. I can't be with you if I get guilty'.
And was that hard?
It was really hard, because I'd been with him such a long time and I really did love him. […] I was crying my eyes out and I was like, 'I'm so sorry' […]
And what happened then with you here and how were you coping then?
I don't really remember, I think I just chucked myself into doing stuff, like I just didn't want to think about [the conviction]. (Tamara, 20s, early)

For most prisoners, then, cutting intimate ties was necessary either for psychological survival or because the paralytic state produced by the shock of the sentence made it impossible to maintain a relationship of co-produced intimacy.

Estrangement from Family

Compared to the sharp but relatively brief distress caused by detachment from intimate partners, the impact of separation from deeply embedded familial relations was, for the majority of prisoners, both agonising and enduring:

On remand, there's always hope; there's always that chance you'll go home. But once you're convicted, your home seems further away from you than it's ever been in your life. And you're suddenly not the only one that's being punished, because your whole family is then being punished. And it doesn't matter what anybody says or does to try and help you, it was like being sucked into a black hole and you think the pain's never going to end, and it doesn't. (Maria, 20s, early)

You said you were devastated when you got the sentence - can you describe to me what it's like?
I was devastated, well, not for myself, I was just devastated that my nan [primary carer], you know, I was devastated for her. I was devastated, yeah, I was devastated. [...] Knowing that I won't be there in her later life, and she dedicated her life to bringing me up. (Asad, 30s, mid)

Male prisoners' ruminations about such matters focused principally on their natal families—the families they were born into—primarily their parents, but also siblings and extended family members (such as grandparents), some of whom were, as for Asad, their primary carers. Here, our findings depart somewhat from the existing research literature, in which 'The psychological bias is to think of males as sons when they are little and as husbands and fathers when they grow up' (Barnett et al. 1992: 508). Since many of our male participants were barely adults when they were sentenced, few were married or in long-term relationships; those who were fathers were rarely primary carers (see Richards et al. 1994) and often lived apart from the 'baby-mother'.

Nonetheless, for these men, being away from their children was devastating:

And not seeing my daughter grow up, that kills me that does. She's 10 this year, bless her. [She was] six weeks old she was when I got arrested. Yeah, it kills me, that does. (Robert, 30s, mid)
How does it feel for that role [as a father] to be the way it is?
Well, it's devastating, you know. I'd love to, you know, be out there and... I, kind of, feel like I'm missing on a lot of things, missing out. Every time I get a picture, he gets bigger, you know, my son. That hurts. (Terrance, 20s, early)

Some men managed to maintain contact with their children, through the efforts made by former partners to bring them to visits. However, communication was difficult, particularly for those who had not featured consistently in their children's lives. Merle (30s, mid), for example, explained ruefully that he 'tr[ied] to do what I can as a father', through phone calls and visits, but 'it's difficult because I haven't been there in their life, throughout their life I haven't been there'.

During their sentences, many men limited visits with children or withdrew contact altogether, to avoid exposing them to the process and emotionally austere environment of prison visits; to maintain a pretence that they were 'at work' or 'on holiday', rather than in prison (see Richards et al. 1994)[1]; or because of the emotional pain of failing to fulfil a paternal role:

> *Are there any particular challenges about being in this kind of environment?*
> Not seeing my son as much as I can.
> *Is it difficult to remain a father in…?*
> Of course it is. You don't feel like a father, you just feel like an idiot. (Martin, 20s, early)

> I don't really want to see them. […] It's very, very hard, but it's for the best I think, […] because I can't be a father to them. […] I can't really call myself a father, can I really? (Merle, 30s, mid)

Faced with this issue of a highly compromised role identity, then, most men chose to withdraw altogether (cf. Schinkel 2014). As we discuss below, this was in contrast to the response of female participants to similar concerns.

Female prisoners were less likely than male prisoners to describe missing their natal family members. Previous research shows that they tend to have poorer relationships with their mothers than male prisoners and are more likely to be estranged from their parents, often having experienced local authority care (Richards et al. 1994) after having suffered abuse or neglect (Prison Reform Trust 2015a, b). However, some women did report their natal relationships in positive terms, including parents who fought legal battles for them and campaigned on their behalf, for example, against joint enterprise convictions:

> My mum and dad - I speak to them on the phone every day. […] They're like my support. If I've got any problems, I'll just get on the phone to them and just let it all out to them. […] My mum, we're all very close and so I just tell her everything. (Connie, 20s, early)

Mothers were the primary sources of support, and a small number of our female participants described their relationships with their mothers as having improved, often as a result of the transfer of caring responsibilities for their own children:

---

[1] The length of the sentences that the prisoners in our study were serving made maintaining such a pretence extremely difficult. Doing so was only possible among those who retained some hope that they would be released on appeal, prior to their children becoming aware of the shattering reality.

My mum has kept me alive, you know, by talking about me all the time [to my son] and [sending] pictures and photos [of my son] and things like that [...] so she's kept me alive. (Jill, 40s, post-tariff)

More typically, however, women's relationships with their parents were highly strained or already estranged. In relation to the male parent or parental figure (e.g. step-father or mother's boyfriend), this was often due to the perpetration of sexual and physical abuse. Carly (30s, late), for example, 'cut [her] family off' at the start of her sentence because of her growing sense of anger at the way her father had regularly beaten her and her sister during their childhoods. Tori described similar experiences:

My dad was always... he was...
Violent to you?
Yeah. [...] He was always ... [...]. He saw it as he was the punisher.
The disciplinarian?
But there's a difference between discipline and physical abuse. [...] I don't talk to him anymore. Haven't spoken to him in years. (Tori, 30s, late)

Female prisoners' relationships with their mothers were often frayed too, due to mental health and addiction problems, direct physical abuse, or because of feelings of resentment that their mothers had ignored or disbelieved the abuse to which others had subjected them. Such feelings of maternal neglect and abandonment had often been submerged or suppressed prior to the sentence, when most female participants' lives had been highly chaotic, and had emerged during extended periods of contemplation in prison:

[My mum's] an alcoholic. She chose her drink over me a lot of the time. She used to beat me with a rod on the bottom. [...] She used to get violent when she drank vodka, so she hit me over the head once. [...] It's hard, because when we're locked behind our door, we've got so much time to sit and think, and sitting there thinking about it and it just breaks me. It just makes me boil and then I start self-harming. *And who are you angry with about that stuff?*
Everyone: my mum, dad, social services, just the foster people that [sexually abused] me; him, my baby-father, everyone. (Tamara, 20s, early)

For the women in our sample, as we discuss in greater depth below, it was estrangement from children that caused the most pain:

> Well obviously my best [experience in life] was having my kids, that's standard. And then obviously my worst was leaving them. (Fiona, 20s, early)

> *You said that it was hard to stop being a mum. How does that happen, and do you have to completely stop that?*
> I don't think you completely stop, I don't think you can ever completely stop. [...] I think you kind of almost lock that part of your heart away, and lock that hurt away. [...] It never goes away that missing them, and that kind of ache'. (Gail, 30s, late)

The searing pain of being dislocated from children was associated with missing key life experiences, the loss of physical intimacy, and feelings of guilt about being absent from children's lives. Kathryn (20s, early), for example, whose daughter was only a few months old when she was imprisoned, had missed 'her first steps, her first words, all her firsts, and that's quite difficult'. Others expressed sorrow that their children were, in Eloise's (20s, early) terms, 'missing out on their mum', or were concerned that their children's well-being was compromised by their custody arrangements. For example:

> I've got to come to terms with my mum was looking after my son, and at the time she was suffering from depression badly. [...] And she's looking after my child. She's tried to kill herself numerous times and there was one point where she was going to kill herself and kill my son at the same time, and it was all, like, heavy, heavy. (Jill, 40s, post-tariff)

For both male and female long-termers, as we now move on to discuss, many of the difficulties associated with being separated from loved ones focused on worries about their family members and changes in their own role identities.

Worries About Family

'Worrying about people outside' was the second and third most severe problem for male and female survey respondents, respectively. While such matters felt painful for prisoners at all phases of the sentence, for the men, it was particularly severe at the earliest stages. Concerns related to three main issues: the impact of their imprisonment on family members' psychological and physical well-being; its consequences for family life; and its wider social repercussions, including shame and social judgement. We discuss these issues in brief below.

Impact on Family Members' Psychological and Physical Well-Being

Both male and female participants were cognisant of the significant distress experienced by their family members (Murray 2005). Carrying the knowledge of how much hurt they had caused was a very significant burden, as Ray testified:

> Last year, my mother died and [my sister] said to me, she said, 'Mum said something strange', and I said, 'What's that?' She said, 'You broke her heart'. Well, that was very, very heavy and so I put the phone down, went upstairs, shut my door and I sobbed my heart out. [...] And I thought, 'my God, 37 years down the line and it's still causing pain'. (Ray, 50s, post-tariff)

In many cases, prisoners believed that their long-term imprisonment had exacerbated the existing vulnerabilities or mental health issues of family members, including depression and acute anxiety, especially for mothers. Many expressed considerable guilt, and a sense of powerlessness, about the impact on others of prolonged separation (see Murray 2005):

> ...my dad died about five years ago or something. So my mum got left on her own and, like, it's hard. I don't like ringing home now. Just for the fact that my mum's in the house. She's still upset by it cos they were together so long. [...]
> *But why is it that you don't like phoning?*
> It's just the fact of I'm sitting here in jail, she's at home depressed and crying and upset, and I can't help her, do you know what I mean? (Kenny, 20s, mid)

> *Has it had an impact on your life [beyond the prison]?*
> Yeah. Massively, to be honest with you. My family have had to deal with everything, all the like shame and stuff, it's kind of landed on my family, really. So what I've put

my family through is kind of... it's going to hurt me for the rest of my life. (Shaafi, 30s, mid)

Opportunities to mitigate these problems—through prison visits, for example— did not offer a straightforward solution, particularly in relation to family members at either end of the lifecourse. As indicated above, having to expose children to intrusive searches, to the strict (and often confusing) regulation of movement and contact,[2] and to the distress caused by abrupt and unwanted goodbyes caused prisoners to question, limit and, in some cases, altogether forego prison visits:

...when [my girlfriend and my son] come up on a visit here, you can't take [my son] to the toilet. So when he asked 'Take me to the toilet', [...] I just have to tell him that I can't go through there. I have to make something up. [...] I find it hard. That's why lately I haven't really been making her come up, because every time they go to leave it is stressful. (Martin, 20s, early)

I really want to see [my son], because I haven't seen him for ten months. But, no, it's awful, but then I think, 'oh my God, like coming in here', and I just think of him like getting searched, but I really want to see him. (Ruby, 20s, early)

Prisoners also worried that the lengthy period of custody would have a deleterious effect on family members' physical well-being. Those with elderly relatives, as well as young children, were reluctant to put them through the strain of long journeys and extended periods of waiting. Many were concerned that longer-term psychological stress would have physical consequences. Most often, however, as suggested in Chapter 5, the overarching anxiety was that family members would deteriorate or pass away over the course of a long sentence. Seeing decline in others—with regard to both health and personality—was highly burdensome, as Shane detailed:

---

[2]During standard visits, prisoners cannot leave their seat and are usually allowed only 'minimal physical contact'—a hug and (non-passionate) kiss with their loved one once on arrival and once on departure (Offenders Families Helpline 2015). These are very different experiences to 'family visits', which are less regular and more limited, but allow longer visiting periods (sometimes a whole day), in a more relaxed environment, during which prisoners have greater freedom of movement and can engage in more physical contact.

[Mum] contracted multiple sclerosis in the last five years so [she's] not how I remember her when I came away, you know, the able-bodied woman standing up for herself, doing what she's doing and not caring who had something to say about what she was up to. But now, everything's 75 per cent slower. Her movements, cos she's got crutches now and…
Yeah, that must be difficult.
Mm. (Shane, 40s, post-tariff)

Impact on Family Life

A second set of worries related to the impact of indefinite absence on family life. Scott (30s, mid), for example, reported that, since he had been sentenced, his family had 'never celebrated Christmas'. A further concern was the financial burden that imprisonment imposed on parents or grandparents, and the feeling of psychological debt and dependence that this produced. For example:

I used to have money sent into prison to me all the time and I used to rely on that all the time. And I said to myself, [my parents are] getting old now, I've just got to start saving like a few pound here. […] My dad can't afford to send it in no more. […] It kind of hits you after a while, and you think, you can't keep relying on people outside, because they've got it hard, to send you in money. (Aaron, 40s, late)

For prisoners with children, a significant source of stress was their exposure to people of whom they disapproved. Clint, for example, was upset at hearing that his son did not like his ex-partner's new boyfriend: 'I got angry [with my ex-partner] because my son came to visit me and says, "Dad, mum goes out with blah, blah, blah and I don't like him, and he stays at the house"' (Clint, 30s, late).

Repercussions for Family

Prisoners also worried about the repercussions for their family members, in terms of stigma and direct harm, of having a loved one in prison for murder (see Johnson 2019). Such anxieties were exacerbated in situations where their cases had generated media interest. Kathryn (20s, early), for example, expressed concern about 'the backlash for my mum' that might result from her victim's family discussing their feelings in a newspaper. Being 'guilty by association' placed some family members at risk of considerable harm, particularly during court cases or in the period following conviction:

> I had to tell a few of the lads to 'make sure you're in court every day', you know. [In the end] Nothing happened to my dad, [because] no one turned up on the other side, the victim's side.
> *Is that something you were a little concerned about then?*
> Yeah, cos [the victim] was a gang member. (Zubair, 20s, early)

> The first few weeks were hard after I got sentenced, because I felt bad for my dad and he's coming up here, he's trying to calm me down, and then he's going through a lot out there. A lot of people egged my dad's house, smashed his car windows.
> *Because of your conviction?*
> Because of my crime. Saying to them that I was a murderer, and my brother's got into so many fights because he's trying to say to them, 'No [Tamara's] actually done nothing wrong, and we've all proved our innocence'. My sister […] got stabbed in the arm because of it. (Tamara, 20s, early)

While rumination about such problems and possibilities played on prisoners' minds, greater anguish was caused by compromises to their role identities. As we now discuss, for male prisoners, this tended to relate to the difficulty of remaining a 'good son' over many years of imprisonment, while for female prisoners who had children, it was the effort to remain a mother that felt particularly harrowing and challenging.

Compromised Role Identities

'Role identities are important for self-conception. They are conceptions of oneself in terms of where one fits in the social structure' (Simon 1992: 26). When people are highly committed to a particular role, they experience more distress if ongoing problems threaten their sense of self in that role (Simon 1992). In contrast, '[s]atisfactory enactment of roles not only confirms and validates a person's status as a role member (Callero 1985) but also reflects positively on self-evaluation' (Hogg et al. 1995: 257). As the role of intimate partner waned, the men and women in our study most often invested social and emotional energy in the roles of son and mother, respectively. As such, it was these roles that had the greatest potential to either cause distress or enhance self-esteem (Hogg et al. 1995).

Male Prisoners as Sons

Criminological research has foregrounded the weakening of relations between prisoners and their families during incarceration (Murray 2005; Hairston 1991), although recent research has acknowledged the potential for the imprisonment of sons to help '*rebuild* or stabilise family-prisoner relationships' (McCarthy and Adams 2019a: 378). Prior to their imprisonment, relationships between male participants and their immediate families had typically been fraught or distant, aggravated by their offending behaviour, addiction issues and lifestyle choices (such as being out until late), or because of mental health issues among parents. A significant number of our male participants therefore reported that relationships with their parents had *improved* during their sentence, albeit from a low baseline (see McCarthy and Adams 2019a):

> If anything, [the relationship with my dad and step-mother] grew stronger, because when I was out, yeah, I couldn't sit in my house and have a conversation with them cos I was either high or [...] coming down [from drugs] or too busy trying to earn money or trying to steal from them to even chat. (Jonathan, 20s, early)

> I was hardly at home, if I'm honest. I went to my room and from my room I'd just come down the stairs and just walk out. (Aakif, 20s, early)

While friends fell away (see below) and partners were discarded during imprisonment, parents (and mothers in particular) offered unconditional love and support—unbounded relational goods. Despite the fact that their sons had often generated significant problems prior to their incarceration, and some had admitted to committing murder, most parents afforded their children special status: to quote Paylor and Smith (1994: 135) 'he's still my son, whatever he's done' (cf. McCarthy and Adams 2019b). Mothers, in particular, remained loyal:

My mum, my family, regardless of where I've been they've always just supported me and said that they loved me, and they're here for me. Obviously, [my mum's] not happy with what's happened to me, but she said she'll always be there and stuff like that. (Carl, 20s, early)

At the same time, incarceration provided the time and opportunity for prisoners to redefine their role as sons, reassess their priorities, and change their orientation towards the family. Errol explained that he had 'matured a lot', become less selfish and come to recognise 'what I put [my mum] through, [and] now I care enough to change' (Errol, 20s, early). Casper reported that his relationship with his parents had strengthened both because he saw them more frequently and had more time for the kind of reflexive contemplation discussed in Chapter 5:

When you're outside, life is so busy that you don't really get a chance to sit back and look at your relationship with that person and how you can improve it. In here you've got a lot more time to think about them sort of things: 'how can I be a better son?' (Casper, 20s, early)

Thomas likewise described the impact of receiving a life-changing sentence on his sense of his ultimate concerns:

It's allowed me to recognise what's really important in my life, what I'm grateful for. When you're a life sentenced prisoner your whole world comes crashing down, you realise just how important family is, and you learn to appreciate them, and you just feel so lucky to have a mum and dad who [...] love you the same, and that feels amazing, absolutely amazing. (Thomas, 20s, early)

Thus, although imprisonment represented a 'crisis' (Morris 1965: 22), it also enabled and encouraged prisoners to take stock of their lives and reformulate their ultimate concerns:

[A] crisis can be a wake-up call, heightening attention to what matters. It can become an opportunity for reappraisal of priorities, stimulating greater investment in meaningful relationships and life pursuits. [...] Many families report that through weathering a crisis together their relationships were enriched and more loving than they might otherwise have been. (Walsh 2003: 3)

The greater salience of, and commitment to, family relationships led to many male prisoners becoming more emotionally 'present' and expressive with their parents, willing to demonstrate and vocalise their feelings for them. Noel explained that he had previously taken his parents for granted—'cos you know they're always there'—but was now much more inclined to express his appreciation for them: 'I never used to really tell my mum that I loved her that much, when I was on road, but now obviously every time I see her I always tell her I love her' (Noel, 22, early). Some prisoners extolled 'the power of the letter' as a means of expressing emotions in permanent form (Christopher, 20s, mid). Most maintained their relationships through regular phone calls and visits and considered themselves to have become 'better sons' as a result—more communicative, emotional and attentive than they had been in the community.

However, a number of challenges placed limits on this heightened emotional investment. First, being physically absent from the family made it difficult to perform the filial role:

> I'm the oldest male in my household, and, in a way, me coming to prison I've lost that title, I've kind of forfeited that title. Because now I'll always be the older male in the *family*, but I'm no longer the oldest male in the *house* because I am not there right now. So in that sense, I've had to give that up because my mum got married last July and my brother had to give her away. (Carl, 20s, early)

Physical presence is not required to perform the role of a son, and most families 'reorient' themselves once children leave the family home (Turner 1969). Some male prisoners reported having found ways of maintaining established roles, in particular, by using phone calls and letters to provide guidance to younger siblings or members of their extended families—often using their imprisonment as the basis for dispensing advice on how *not* to live life. Through such means, they were able to remain at the centre of family life, participate in collective decision-making, and continue to act as 'fathers of the household'.

However, forced and total physical absence from their parents' daily lives and restrictions on contact were difficult to endure. Many men described a kind of protective impotence: a feeling of powerlessness that resulted from being unable to protect their parents and siblings from physical and emotional harm:

In terms of losing that role that you had as the man of the family, is that something that bothers you?
I mean obviously it does bother me, because now, for example, God forbid, if anything ever happened to my brother, or if anything happened to my mum I wouldn't be able to do shit about it. [...] So in that sense I feel helpless, I feel helpless. (Carl, 20s, early)

Worries relating to the impact of the conviction on loved ones led to complicated and guarded flows of communication. Paradoxically, while prisoners reported being more emotionally explicit with their parents, very often they also described withholding information to protect them from anxiety: 'I tell them "everything's rosy and calm"' (Arshad, 30s, late). Pretence of this kind was reciprocal. Prisoners understood that their families refrained from disclosing information that might upset them:

> I've talked to me family about a lot more things. I open up with them about a lot but on the other hand, I keep a lot of things from them, what I think will get them upset or worried as well. [...] I know they try and put on a brave face for me as well, but I know behind the scenes that they're upset, so I just try and look brave for them and they're trying to look brave for me, I think, both with the same aim. (Scott, 30s, mid)

Non-disclosure also reflected the fear of being judged or letting family members down. As we discuss in Chapter 7, this often meant fudging or distorting the truth about the index offence:

> I couldn't tell my mum, because, I mean, how do you start that conversation? You know: 'hi mum, what's for breakfast today? I might have killed someone', do you know what I mean? [...] That's why I think some things are easier to tell the people in here than your mum. Because, for example, you can tell someone something and you'll probably never see them again, or you probably won't build that bond with them. So any judgments they may or may not make, it doesn't really affect you. Whereas your mum... I mean there's things I've said to my mum as a little kid in anger that she said she still remembers now. And I don't want to be in that position where I end up upsetting her. (Carl, 20s, early)

While these forms of emotional masking were undertaken as a means of maintaining family ties, they also placed considerable strain on some relationships. A number of prisoners described awkward interactions and difficulties in 'relating', as a result of the disconnection between the worlds that they and their family members inhabited. Billy (20s, early) noted that his mother's visits were, if anything, too frequent, because while she had 'all the world to talk about', his everyday reference points were much more limited: "'been to the gym today… I mopped the floor today, again", for the X amount of times. So there's not much to talk about in that respect'. Mohammed (30s, mid) expressed ambivalence about his visits, for very similar reasons: 'How much can you tell them? […] "Oh, yeah, I got searched today"'. Here, the complexities that resulted from the disjuncture between the domains of the prison and the community—and the difficulty of trying to exist in both worlds simultaneously—were particularly apparent.

Male prisoners' attempts to be 'good sons' were also affected by feelings of guilt. Hugo, for example, had ceased visits with his mother, to defend himself against his feelings of failure:

> I never acted like a son. […] I love her to bits, and I'm always going to have that guilt for what I did. I fucking destroyed her whole life. […] It sort of sets me back to stage one every time she comes up to visit. She's become the symbol of my fuck-up and it destroys me completely. (Hugo, 20s, early)

However, this example was atypical. Unlike the men in Schinkel's (2014) study of long-term prisoners, few of the male participants adopted a strategy of cutting off contact with their parents to 'maintain circumscribed horizons' by 'living their life as if there were no outside to miss' (p. 75). As we note below, this kind of relational dissolution more closely reflected the experience of friendships. Overall, male prisoners' relationships with their parents tended to be well-maintained and were often reconfigured in ways that continued to provide them with a sense of filial fulfilment.

Women as Mothers

> I think the hardest thing for me when I came into jail was nobody told me how to not be a mum - I had spent so many years being a mum, I didn't know how to switch that off. (Gail, 30s, late)

For many female participants, as Hairston (1991: 95) summarises, 'being stripped of the mother role was one of the most traumatic factors in women's adjustment to institutionalization'. Women's sense of self is more closely tied to parenthood and more emotionally invested in the parental role than men (Simon 1992). For women in prison, being physically and emotionally estranged from children is particularly painful, because 'awareness of the life that goes on without them makes their prison time doubly difficult' (Owen 1998: 129). In our study, many of the resulting difficulties were exacerbated by the nature of our participants' offences and their very long tariffs.

For female prisoners generally, 'family ties' and contact are frustrated by practical problems including: distance from home (exacerbated by the small number of women's prisons in England and Wales); complicated relationships with a 'heterogeneous group' of carers acting as gatekeepers to their children (Richards et al. 1994)[3]; and a lack of control over the separation from their children (Hairston 1991; Murray 2005). Fiona, for example, conveyed her feelings of powerlessness in relation to one of her children failing to attend a visit:

> I see my eldest [son], [and] I was meant to see him Saturday but he never turned up, and I don't know why. [...] I'm not allowed to know where he is, I'm not allowed a [phone] number, I'm not allowed nothing. (Fiona, 20s, early)

These difficulties were particularly hard to manage because they contrasted with women's experiences of being primary carers prior to incarceration—'when I was with them all the time' (Fiona, 20s, early)—and were felt most acutely when children were young or were subject to custody disputes. Absence from their children's lives was in sharp tension with women's desire to protect and care for their children on a daily basis. The pain caused by being unable to do so, and by

---

[3]The children of male prisoners are most often cared for by partners or ex-partners (Richards et al. 1994).

problems maintaining contact, generated very high levels of distress, and had a significant impact on well-being and mental health:

> I only get to see [my daughter] three times a year, so in a sense I've lost the main part of her, but she's still alive, and then that makes it really difficult because every time I see her it brings up all my feelings for her again, and then I spend the next four months grieving, and that's really difficult because you're constantly going through it, so you're breaking your heart a little bit more every time. (Kathryn, 20s, early)

> I was a bit suicidal because my daughter had decided not to talk to me as well, so everything kind of culminated at one point and I just went downhill. [...] My daughter...the one thing that holds me to this earth, had decided she disliked me. (Jenny, 20s, mid)

Children were a significant source of both strength and pain. For some women, their children were a key protective factor—the only thing that made life worth living and restrained them from trying to take their own life. Yet many of the primary pains of imprisonment related to the very long-term separation from these children and sometimes total loss of contact. As Gail (30s, late) said, 'I haven't spoken to [my children] for a couple of years. [...] It kills me a little bit more each day'.

'In the prison context, active, close parenting is extremely difficult to achieve' (Murray 2005: 455), and a key challenge for the women who had children was to redefine their maternal role and remain present and involved in their children's lives. Visits, letters and phone calls all had limitations. Small children could not write letters and those who were older were uninterested in this 'old-fashioned' form of communication: 'I've only had, like, four letters off my son in 20 years' (Jill, 40s, post-tariff). Initiatives such as 'Storybook Mums' (and Dads) offered parents the chance to fulfil parental duties, by recording bedtime stories for their children, but were mainly suited to children who were young. Family visits provided enhanced opportunities for women to actively inhabit maternal roles—'it's nice because you're a mum and daughter, and you're together' (Yvette, 30s, mid)—but the potential presence within visits halls of people convicted for offences against children made some parents wary about such opportunities.

For a number of women, contact was also limited by court orders or obstructive primary carers. Kathryn (20s, early) said that she was prohibited from phoning her daughter, was allowed only three visits per year, and was only able to write every two-months, plus cards for birthdays, Christmas and Easter. Jenny (20s, mid) had been involved in a custody battle for her daughter with her own parents and had not seen her for several years: 'I don't know what she looks like now. I wouldn't know her if she walked into a room'. Most women in such situations continued to fight through the courts or made plans for a time in future when greater contact might be possible, for example:

> I am allowed to contact my daughter, but my ex-partner is just being an idiot who won't answer the phone, [...] and every time if I would write a letter he'd just rip it and put it in the bin. [...] I didn't bother sending her a [birthday] card, but I've been keeping them so…when she's going to come and see me all her birthday cards are there for her. (Laura, 20s, early)

For many of the female participants, maintaining positive relationships with children was made more difficult because of the nature of their offence and any associated publicity. Some women explained that newspaper reports, 'real-crime' books and other publications had demonised them and exaggerated or misrepresented their culpability. At least two women's children had severed contact as a result of such depictions:

> I know my parents kept all the newspaper clippings and everything because they give it to my daughter who read it when she was nine, which caused a whole lot of drama. [...] I've only read bits, and it would traumatise anyone that reads stuff like that, and she was nine. [...] The first thing I knew that she'd read anything was [being told that] I was dead to her and I'm not her mum any more, and then I decided that I was going to try and kill myself after, and everything went to pot again. (Jenny, 20s, mid)

Jenny's reference to her decision to try to take her own life was indicative, highlighting the burning pain of separation that many other women reported.

Dislocation from Social World—Peers

During the early period of custody—in the initial months and years—most participants found that the majority of their pre-prison friendships began to dissipate and fade. In some cases, prisoners actively chose to sever contact (see below). For the most part, however, the disintegration of social networks was initiated by others. A small number of prisoners believed that they had been cast aside due to the anger, disappointment and deferred shame that their conviction had generated. Tamara (20s, early), for example, described a best friend who had broken off contact at the point of her conviction, 'because he feels that I've lied to him […], that I've took more part in [the offence] than I said'. More often, prisoners believed that friends found it too arduous to maintain a relationship under the circumstances of distance and long-term separation: visiting prisons located many hours from home communities required a significant financial and time commitment. As a result, most friendships simply 'dropped off' (Eugene, 50s, post-tariff), 'faded away' (Carl, 20s, early), 'moved on' (Joseph, post-tariff) or 'stepped back' (Dan, 20s, early).

For male prisoners, such experiences were both painful and surprising. Many of the men described friendships that they believed had been strong and solid with a tragic sense of nostalgia. Relationships had often been forged in early childhood or developed during teenage years with individuals who lived nearby, attended the same school, or were part of a wider family circle (often cousins or close family friends). Some described these bonds as being extraordinarily tight, involving an intense sense of loyalty—'I was willing to die for them' (Ashley, 20s, mid)—unwavering trust, deep affection and intimacy. Indeed, some—in particular, those who were younger, and involved in collective criminal activity—suggested that they were serving their sentence because their unbreakable sense of loyalty meant that they had not informed on the actual perpetrator:

I didn't actually do [the murder]. […] People know what happened, they know I didn't do it but I get more respect for not saying nothing. […]
You know who did it but you wouldn't say anything? I mean, it's a massive deal, saying you'll do eighteen years for someone. […] Would it be dangerous for you to say something?
[…] I could say 'I don't care [about being seen as an informer]. I'm not riding a life sentence for you'. […] I could do that [but] they wouldn't do that to me, so I'm not going to do it. (Andre, late teens, early)

Relationships of this kind were often represented in familial language. That is, friends outside were variously described as 'brothers' and 'like family'. For many prisoners, peer groups had functioned as surrogate families, providing deep and enduring emotional goods such as empathy and support to a degree that surpassed biological parents.

In this context, when relationships collapsed, prisoners were crestfallen by the realisation that they were, in fact, fragile, transient or conditional. Such sentiments were often expressed in terms that were strikingly intimate—'The love we had is gone' (Earl, 20s, early)—and the sense of abandonment produced considerable anger and resentment, particularly in the immediate aftermath of the conviction, as prisoners reflected on their unrequited loyalties:

> There's people that I used to roll with every day, I've grown up with them.[4] We've lived on the same estate, we've gone through the same shit. We've gone through the same struggle. I've been to their mum's house, they've been to my mum's house, they've been to my dad's house, I've been to their dad's house - we were raised together, from the roads. Every single day you'll see us together. And now I'm in jail, I ain't spoken to them since I've been in jail. They don't write to me. They don't send me money. [...] And it's like if we're going to go through all of this, and you're not even going to help me when I'm in jail, you might as well have just told me that from the beginning. I would have not been fucking … I would have not been here. I would have not rolled with you lot. (James, 20s, early)

For James, loyalty was an inviolable, masculine pledge. The withdrawal of contact and failure to offer financial support represented an affront to this sense of allegiance, demonstrating a lack of commitment and care that was painful and bewildering:

> It felt like the hardest time in my life. [...] People were just turning their back on me. The times I needed them and they're not there, and yet if the shoe was on the other foot I've always been there. (Willis, 30s, mid)

> Because I'm in here for such a long time, it hurts a lot more really, in terms of the fact that the people that I thought were always going to be there are not. (Carl, 20s, early)

---

[4] 'Roll with': spend time or hang around with.

Both men and women described being deserted by people they had considered to be friends as a brutal revelation, and stated dolefully that, in Connie's words, 'you realise when you've come to prison who really is your friends and who isn't. [...] You realise a lot when you come to prison' (Connie, 20s, early).

Accordingly, then, many participants described discovering which of their pre-prison friends were 'real': a minority of individuals who stuck around, remained loyal, and showed they 'really got love for you' (James, 20s, early), including some who had 'stepped up' unexpectedly (Carl, 20s, early):

> Certain girls, yeah, that when I was on road I used to think, 'you're just a girl' [...], I never used to appreciate them. Now I'm in jail, they're the ones sending me money, sending me brand new clothes, coming to visit me all the time. Telling my friends: 'You lot are dickheads, why don't you write to him?'. And it's like [...] now I'm in jail I'm seeing who ... I can't believe that girls are writing to me and contacting me more than my so-called friends who I thought I would have chosen over any girl in the world. (James, 20s, early)

As a result of enduring contact, some friendships strengthened, particularly when individuals went 'above and beyond' normal expectations, by travelling for many hours in order to visit, offering mutual candour and support, or maintaining contact over many years through letters, birthday cards and Christmas messages—gestures that were at least as meaningful as the provision of material support, precisely because they demonstrated emotional concern.

Female prisoners generally described their friendships outside as intense, but rather transitory and instrumental, entangled with long-standing patterns of drug and alcohol use. Such friendships—'drinking partners' (Connie, 20s, early)—were shaped by, and often exacerbated, the women's vulnerabilities, and perpetuated coping mechanisms that were highly destructive. As a result, when female participants 'got clean' during their sentence, they 'knifed off' these relationships fairly swiftly. In retrospect, such relationships were regarded as inauthentic, or as liabilities, and were terminated without compunction or sentimentality:

> Some of my friends from outside, they all came up [to visit at the prison] about four or five years ago, and I hadn't seen them for a while. And I looked at them and I just thought 'you've never changed, you've never moved on and I'm not part of that world anymore'.

So what does their world look like?
Still all doing the things they did when we were young.
Drugs and stuff?
Yes. And it was just like, 'no, I don't like, no'. (Gail, 30s, late)

Some men reported breaking off friendships when they found it too difficult to cope with being a spectator in the lives of friends who were at liberty. Observing from distance the ways in which friends were progressing with their lives—for example, by giving up crime and reaching conventional milestones like buying houses and starting families—was too painful a reminder of 'what might have been', the parallel existence that was evidently out of reach. The forward trajectory of friends, advancing along the traditional path of young adulthood, contrasted sharply with the sense of stagnation prisoners felt, particularly in the early phase of the sentence (see Chapter 8). Retreating from this world and limiting their 'temporal horizon' (Schinkel 2014) were means of psychological self-protection:

> Most of my friends on the outside, I've cut off, and I don't want to speak to them, […] because that could have been me, you know what I mean? […] Like a lot of my friends have kids, they're all settled down, they're buying their own houses. Really, I don't want to be knowing about them, because I've got a long time to go before I can start planning my stuff. […] I don't want to hear what they're doing. (Oscar, 20s, early)

For prisoners like Oscar, then, it was less painful to cease contact with friends, limit reminders of their progress and focus on their trajectory within the prison.

The disparity between prisoners' everyday experiences and concerns, and those of their friends outside, could also render them almost strangers to one another and unable to relate (see Grounds 2005). Kenny (20s, mid), for example, noted that 'My mates say they know me. I'm like "you don't know me, I grew up in jail"'. Jared highlighted the difficulty of maintaining interest in external dramas whose significance felt somewhat trivial in comparison with his own burdens:

> It can get distressing sometimes. A lot of people like talking about their problems outside, or whatever. […] It's a bit of a wind-up sometimes. If I'm in a bad mood one day and my mate, she goes on about how bad she's got it with all her boyfriends she's had. Since I've been in jail she's had a countless amount of boyfriends, and one day I just kicked off and went, 'I don't care. Stop writing to me about all your

fucking problems. Well, you should appreciate life and what you've got right now. I mean, do you want to spend your life in here, and do you want to take over my time in here and do a swap and see how you like it?' (Jared, 20s, early)

Most participants commented mournfully that, as time passed, relationships became not 'as close' (Darrin, late teens, early) or more 'distant' (Willis, 30s, mid). As prisoners experienced a gradual but significant drifting from their social moorings, friendships became increasingly difficult to preserve or simply dwindled.

Changes in prisoners' sense of self also affected the extent to which they attempted to maintain friendships with those who remained in the community. Participants who were some time into their sentence felt that they had grown up and matured during their incarceration (see Chapter 7) and were judgemental of friends who they felt had stagnated, as evidenced by continuing engagement in activities that they now considered to be destructive, such as crime and drug use. This made continuing with some friendships risky or unappealing:

Most of the friends that I did have on the outside, they were criminals. Like they were all criminals. [...] So any person that's still trying to do crime or anything like that, I just cut people off [from] my life, because I don't need that in my life and I'm not part of all that anymore. (Asad, 30s, mid)

I put my life on the line for [my friends] and the gang was like my family. That was like my family.
So you did have strong feelings for those people?
Yeah I wouldn't be in a gang unless I cared about them; I was willing to die for them [...]. But when you are out of it you can look at it for what it really is, and see I was brainwashed by these people to a certain degree. They were controlling me to a certain degree. If a man can put a gun in my hand and say, 'Yo shoot' or 'Yo! Come down here I've got some trouble', and I'm not asking any questions [...] they must have some kind of control over me. [...] There was some controlling nature within that relationship, and it was unhealthy and it was wrong. (Ashley, 30s, mid)

Here, the contrast was not just about divergent social worlds, but also divergence in identity and moral character: that is, while long-term prisoners tended to feel that their *social lives* were stunted and inert, conversely, over time, they generally felt *themselves* to have changed considerably in terms of personal values and orientations (see Chapter 8). They were not just living in a different domain, with different preoccupations, but were different people, with a new set of ultimate concerns. The dislocation of long-term imprisonment thereby produced two quite different dynamics: one resulting from social stasis and the other from personal change. Both pushed prisoners towards a reconsideration of the purpose and basis of their friendships.

While many prisoners did not make sense of these shifts until many years into their sentence, some had a sense from a relatively early point that their social commitments needed to change. For these prisoners, decisions about which friendships to continue to invest in were based on who offered a positive outlook or was living a law-abiding life. Jeremiah, for example, saw no point in phoning friends from outside because 'they've got nothing positive to say to me. So I'd rather distance myself and then speak to the people that's just moved on, getting on with their lives and going to college and whatnot' (Jeremiah, 20s, early). Olin (20s, mid) kept in contact only 'with people that's on the straight', because of his aspiration on release to avoid returning to crime. As suggested in Chapter 5, this objective—like Gail's earlier—was significant in that it indicated a shift in perspective, from the past to the future, and from a form of agency that was reactive to one that was productive.

For both male and female participants, the emotional and psychological repercussions of the fracturing of pre-prison friendships continued to reverberate for many years. Some found it extremely difficult to trust others or invest in friendships in prison, particularly those who felt they had been betrayed by friends (often co-defendants) during their trial (see below). In this sense, the termination of long-standing friendships contributed to the affective turbulence, bewilderment and fractured reflexivity that many early-stage prisoners expressed and exhibited. Yet most prisoners needed to satisfy an innate need for relational goods, such as care, kindness and companionship, as Carl outlined: 'You're always going to need that sort of human quality; you're always going to need people to talk to, you're always going to need people you can glean advice from' (Carl, 20s, early). As a result, most were motivated to develop a new set of relationships, within the social world of the prison.

Reforming a Social World in Prison

During the very early period of the sentence, male prisoners tended to form relationships based on existing networks (i.e. people already known to them from the community or sometimes from prior prison sentences) or commonalities such as shared hometowns. These initial peer relationships were somewhat instrumental, based on the need to pass time, find a form of loose companionship and ensure personal safety. Although emotional trust and intimacy were lacking in such relationships, the assurance of mutual protection meant that prisoners felt that these companions were more than just associates[5]:

> *The guy that you know [in prison], do you trust him?*
> Yeah, but not to a full extent, because I don't know him from outside. [...] In jail I trust him, because I know him, I feel comfortable around him. [...] I know I can go anywhere with him and I know he's going to get involved in my fights. (Johnnie, late teens, early)

Nonetheless, men in the early years of their sentence repeatedly stated that people they had befriended within prison could be 'good friends, but not road friends' (Blake, 20s, early). As Paul (20s, early) summarised, 'You can never be friends with people in here. Friends are people you've known for years'.

Distinct from these were the 'real friendships' described by men who were further into their sentences, which entailed more complex emotional interactions, involving mutual disclosure and trust. For these men, friendships were often based on ultimate concerns that were oriented to the future—'going home' (Olin, 20s, mid) or 'sorting [one's] life out' (Phil, 60s, post-tariff)—rather than cemented by the past or based on the need to navigate the prisoner society. Accordingly, it was also important to ensure that friends were not a risk to progression or eventual release. Significantly, then, the establishment of such friendships coincided with what Zamble (1992: 414) describes as a 'conscious and deliberate policy [among long-term prisoners] of withdrawing from the flow of institutional social activity', particularly 'the mix' of the drugs economy and prison 'politics' (Owen 1998), in order to sidestep the possibility of 'trouble':

---

[5]Prisoners descriptions of 'friends' and 'associates' inside prison reflected the distinction identified elsewhere in the prison literature between 'friends' and 'acquaintances' (Hartup and Stevens 1997: 358; Crewe 2009).

I surround myself with books. And that's what I do. I stay away from badness. Like, from the drug scene or whatever. And all these kind of things. And I'm just, I'm very religious, I suppose, in that context. (Mohammed, 30s, mid)

How do you, in general, build a life for yourself in here?
I keep myself to myself; I don't get involved in anything that I don't need to get…
I don't get involved in things that I used to get in before. (Leonard, 30s, late)

As suggested in the quotations below, prisoners were often upfront with their friends about the limits of their loyalties, which were circumscribed by the overwhelming desire to progress through the prison system towards release:

You've gotta pick your friends well, I think, because […] I had a good mate in Frankland [prison] and he was always in trouble. I'm kind of a mate so you feel like you've gotta back [him] up, but then he's getting you in trouble for your sentence so you've gotta try and think of yourself first. […] I just said to him, 'listen, I'm not being funny. I can't have a hand in this'. […] He understood. (Scott, 30s, mid)

No-one can ever get me involved in anything. […] As I said, all my friends now, we've all done near enough the same time in jail. So we're all at the same time, we're all at the same stage, we all know what we want. (Kenny, 20s, mid)

Such sentiments were demonstrated in the survey: 30% of male prisoners in the very early stage of their sentences agreed that they would be willing to 'get involved' on behalf of a friend, whatever the consequences, compared to nine per cent of those at the mid-stage. Similarly, while 50% of prisoners at the very early stage agreed that a prisoner should 'always be loyal to another prisoner rather than staff', among mid-stage prisoners, this figure was considerably lower, at 26%.

These findings were indicative of the extent to which prisoners who were some years into their sentence were more concerned with personal goals and existential concerns than with prison dynamics and social relations. Compared to prisoners serving shorter sentences (see Crewe 2009), most participants who were beyond the early sentence stage were indifferent to prisoner politics. As Zamble (1992: 421) commented in his study of long-term prisoners, 'In effect, they sometimes seemed to be living within a world of their own, inside the prison but separate and apart from its ordinary discourse'. The importance of social interactions and external reputation was eclipsed by preoccupations with internal conversations, personal projects and existential contemplation. Forced to think through the implications of being involved in someone else's death, and faced with the burdens of the sentence, their primary concerns were 'interior'. In this regard, long-term imprisonment for murder relegated most social matters within the prison—the lifeblood of most prison sociology—to a secondary consideration, behind personal projects and concerns relating to the self. To refer back to Archer's (2003, 2012) work, like meta-reflexives, mid- and late stage participants were very much *individuals*, almost immune to normative group pressures.

This is not to say that friendship and intimacy were superficial or unimportant. While almost all participants repeated a mantra that no one in prison could be trusted (Crewe 2009), most reported a small number of valued and intimate friendships, characterised by trust, care, emotional warmth, generosity, and a bounded form of loyalty:

[I] walk around the yard with a few mates. You feel part of something, I suppose. And I think that's what a lot of people crave in prison, you know. Because it can be a lonely place, man, if you ain't got nobody, or no support or anything like that. It can be real lonely. (Campbell, 30s, mid)

We've got the same tariff, come in at the same time, and he's one person I can honestly say that 100% I'm going to stay in contact with all day long, and if he didn't get his parole and I did and I got out before him, he wouldn't need nothing, I would do everything for him, as he would do for me. (Olin, 20s, mid)

Reciprocity was central to these 'bilateral friendships' (Crewe 2009: 349). While often expressed in practical terms, such as the lending of goods or the joint preparation of meals, it also had important emotional dimensions, linked to coping with the demands of the sentence:

I'm so glad I've met people on this wing, and people in the system, and I think, 'wow, man! If I had a million pounds, I'd give it to you'.
And how important is it when you're going through your sentence to have those people around you?

Massive [...]. They support you or listen and talk, and just be with you every step of the way. It's to ensure that you keep above water, you don't drown and you're floating. (Arkaan, 20s, mid)

Over time, then, relationships between male prisoners developed that—at their best—allowed for deep disclosure. These friendships were crucial, particularly at difficult periods in individuals' lives, such as times of bereavement or when reminded of someone from home who was intensely missed. 'Bonded' by the mutual 'life experience' of long-term imprisonment (Asad, 30s, mid), friendships provided much-needed support, care and love, often expressed through veiled forms of intimacy:

Sometimes my friends do iron my things for me [like] my shirt. I'm not gonna lie. Like I had a visit on Saturday. My friend had to iron my shirt for me. (Christopher, 20s, mid)

Something got said, [...] and it made me think about my son and that, and I says, 'Yo, I'll shout you in a minute' and he's like, 'Yeah, yeah, yeah'. We had a laugh about it afterwards, but I put my music on loud and I had a cry. And then I shouted him up about 20 minutes later, and he was like 'What's going on?' [...]. And then the next day he was like, 'Yo, you had a cry last night, innit?' And I was like, 'yeah, yeah'. Like, 'Fucking pussy!' and I was like 'Yeah, right mate!'. We just had a laugh about it afterwards, but obviously I think he sort of knows how I feel, do you know what I mean? Because he's from up north, and he hasn't seen any of his family for four years being in here. And his little sister has had two kids and he hasn't ever seen them. So I think he sort of knew how I felt about my kid. (Harris, 20s, early)

Here, the use of humour offsets the potential for social embarrassment, while enabling mutual acknowledgement of a shared and profound emotional predicament. Similarly, Joseph explained that affection and support were often communicated indirectly (see Hartup and Stevens 1997; Crewe 2014):

You just want each other to know that someone is there for you. It is a nice thing, I suppose. It is not something that we say to each other, but I think it is unsaid. They know that you have got each other's back and if you need support then it is there. It is unsaid, but said, so a strange way of doing it but.... (Joseph, 40s, post-tariff)

Such forms of mutual care—shaped by physical proximity and mutually recognised pains and aspirations—meant that some prisoners described their prison friendships as being richer and more valuable than those they had experienced prior to their imprisonment. Willis, for example, was adamant that a close friendship in prison was 'even better than a friendship outside', because of the context of what Goffman (1961) called 'mortification':

> You haven't got all the luxuries you do outside to… you know, some people you're friends [with outside] because you're going out and you're a good laugh, and you've got money and you look after people. In prison, without that, then you're stripped down to your bare essentials, really, and if people can be good friends with you through that, through the tough times, then… (Willis, 30s, mid)

In this respect, prisoners in the mid- and late-sentence stages considered their friends in prison—forged through time, and the experience of long-term imprisonment itself—to be *real friends* or even 'like family': in one prisoner's terms, like an 'older brother' (Alan, 30s, mid). Such references to kinship, although less common than among the female participants (see below), reflected feelings of care, intimacy and acceptance, particularly in relation to the personal shadow of the index offence. For example:

> A couple of lads that I started to hang around with, […] they didn't judge me or anything like that […]. I felt a really good kinship with them. […] I felt really close to them and a proper friendship. I'd never experienced true friendship before. Even outside, yeah. And I saw these lads as my brothers. I felt closer to them than any of my own family. […] We all understand the situations that we're all in. We're all tired of talking about the same things, and I would like to maintain that friendship throughout my life. We've kept each other out of trouble and I think I started to trust myself a lot more and open up more and talk to people [about my offence], even when they didn't ask, you know. And they said 'we don't need to know. We accept you for who you are', sort of thing. (Bernard, 40s, post-tariff)

> It is a form of support, because you can speak to them on certain issues and it's like family, they become like family. (Bentley, 30s, mid)

The durability of such friendships varied. Some prisoners aspired to maintain them after release or were still in touch with men they had met in prison who were now in the community. More typically, though, participants were sceptical that relationships would endure, based on personal experience of being let down: 'they never write, they've promised to write back but they never do, you know, keep in contact, visit, and they never do' (Phil, 60s, post-tariff). Post-tariff prisoners, in particular, considered prison friendships to be insubstantial and unreliable, echoing the terms used by their early-stage peers:

> *So do you have people in here who you would count as friends?*
> That I like. I don't call them 'friends'. [But] They're more than associates. They're people that I like and that I deal with them every day.
> *And do you trust them at all?*
> No. (Marcus, 50's, post-tariff)

> *How far can you go in a relationship with someone in prison?*
> Well, very limited and distant, because you don't really trust people. [...] I've had people I'd hang around with, and they've got my back for certain reasons, I've got their back for certain reasons. But it's trusting them with personal life, how you're feelings and you can't do it. (Victor, 30s, post-tariff)

In reminiscing about the 30 years he had spent in prison, Arthur summed up the pragmatic view of many very long-serving prisoners with regard to social relationships: that, on the whole, they oiled the experience of coping with particular prisons during particular sentence phases:

> I've made good friends and I've got memories. [...] I've met good people inside, good and bad, but the majority of people are good people I've hanged around with and some nice people, genuine people. [...] I could be there four years in the prison with a few good lads, and we really get on staunch, and [then] I might not see them, I probably might see them 12 years later at the end of it, or never again. We might write, [but] it fades off, because it's just passing through, really, and surviving in them stages, do anything to survive each prison. And I think everyone's got that, a sort of strategy, surviving and making it as best as they can in them years they're there. You get the right people around and have a laugh, a joke, have your drink, your drugs and pretending you're partying and you're outside and forgetting, escape from this, that and the other. And that's how you do it [...]. And then it's the next chapter, that's how it works. (Arthur, 50s, post-tariff)

For the women in the study, in-prison relationships were generally considered to be stronger and more meaningful than those formed in the community. Connie (20s, early) stated that 'you find more decent people in here than you will out there', while Eileen (30s, late) said that she had 'met more people in prison that I know I will keep in contact with, and had more help and support from girls in prison than I ever did outside'.

The baseline for such comparisons was rather low: as noted above, for most of the women in our sample, pre-prison friendships had generally been based on shared destructive lifestyles, typically involving substance misuse, and were regarded in hindsight as having been superficial and highly damaging:

> I've got decent friends now, where before it was just junkie friends, you know, and it was all about drugs, whereas this time it's like decent conversations and we'll play scrabble or we'll give each other massages or we'll do each other's nails or pedicure or stuff, have a dance around, have a sing. I think I'm a happier person now I don't take drugs any more. [...] I'm not as moody and miserable. (Jackie, 30s, late)

In contrast with such accounts, previous research suggests a 'deep' and 'present' distrust in women's prisons (Girshick and Sharp 1999; Greer 2000), and 'not feeling able to completely trust anyone in prison' was ranked by our female participants as the fourth most severe problem that they experienced (compared to 16th, by the men). Such results were indicative of a *generalised* mistrust, the roots of which lay in women's pre-prison experiences of trust having been cumulatively eroded or multiply abused. As indicated above, with bleak consistency the female prisoners reported being let down or exploited by parental figures, intimate partners and representatives of the state—including those explicitly tasked with forms of welfare and protection, such as social services—in ways that produced what was described repeatedly and uniformly as 'trust issues'.

For female prisoners, then, there was a paradox of trust—a tension between embedded anxieties about extending trust to others alongside a deep yearning for intimacy. In the early phase of their sentences, far more often than the male prisoners and with much greater intensity, female participants explained their desire to establish intimate bonds and the centrality of trust to their interpersonal ties. Asked about the most important thing she derived from her friends in prison, Laura replied: 'The trust, the trust of somebody... That's the most important thing for me in here' (Laura, 20s, early). Describing a friend in prison, Liz likewise explained that she could open up to her emotionally, without risk: 'I can trust her without thinking that she's manipulating me, and sucking the life out of me at the same time' (Liz, 20s, early).

Some women reported prison friendships that were damaging or destructive. However, more often, prison friendships provided the first trusting relationships that participants had experienced in their lifetimes.[6] The strength of such relationships, and the degree to which they involved forms of care and emotional support, was reflected in 'kinship terminology' (Propper 1982: 127). While, as described above, a discourse of kinship was present in male prisoners' accounts of friendship, among the men there was no equivalent of the mother–daughter tropes that were commonly used by female participants. This language was not universal and did not reflect the kinds of stable 'pseudo-familial' structures reported in early sociological work on women's prisons (Giallombardo, 1966; Ward and Kassebaum 1965; Larsen and Nelson 1984). Rather, as Greer (2000: 461) observes, these were 'terms of endearment', used to designate relationships with particular individuals who offered almost unconditional love and commitment. For example:

> Sarah is like a mum to me; she's done so much for me. [...] As a mum I'd do anything for her. As a child, as a daughter to her, I'd do anything for her.
> *And you feel like it's a mother/daughter relationship?*
> Yeah. She even feels the same, she tells me, 'You're my little princess, you're my daughter'. (Tamara, 20s, early)

> My friend who was here with me, [...] she did behave towards me the way any mum would behave to their, towards their child. And I needed that, and at the time I needed somebody to look after me, because I couldn't do it myself. (Maria, 20s, early)

The prevalence of 'mother-daughter' terminology seemed to reflect the relative absence of 'real' mothers in many of these women's lives, at the time when they entered prison (Koscheski and Hensley 2001). One female participant described

---

[6]Friendships were often enabled by the relatively small female lifer population and the small number of women's prisons within the system, which meant that women often spent many years in each other's company in a particular prison, or re-encountered each other over the course of their sentences: 'I would describe [her] as a proper friend because I've known her since I was 21 when I first went to [prison X], and she's like... like a mother to me' (Jackie, 30s, late).

being 'mothered' by peers who had taught her how to read; another used terms that were explicitly infantile in depicting her relationship with her prison 'mother figure':

> We chat, listen to music, sometimes we watch films, like we have a film day. Like she'll sit on my bed and I'll get under my quilt all snuggly with my teddy bear. (Tamara, 20s, early)

Relationships of this kind were distinct from the intimate sexual partnerships that were also described by some women, which offered them alternative sources of relational goods (and contrasted with their intimate relationships in the community with men):

> [Having a girlfriend] it's just like having somebody to chat to and [...] I suffer really bad with night terrors and stuff, so [...] when I do have a nightmare it's one of them comfort things of knowing that you've got somebody to cling on next to or you can go and wake them up and say 'please will you come and sit with me till I get back to sleep?', and the nice things like having someone to stroke your hair while you fall asleep and just knowing that you've got somebody there who you can go to. (Kathryn, 20s, early)

> *So the relationships that you've had in prison, what's the most important thing that they've given you?*
> Attachments. Because I don't really have a family, do I? And I've sometimes felt quite detached from the world, from most things, and I need attachments in my life. It's good to feel loved and to be able to express my love to other people, and it's nice to feel intimate and close to someone and to feel connection. [...] I think that's one of those basic human needs. (Karen, 20s, mid)

In this sense, these relationships, and the mundane forms of company and care that they provided, made everyday life feel 'a bit more normal' (Jenny, 20s, mid).[7] Many had lasted for several years; some continued after partners had been released; and at least two women were now female parents to children to whom their female

---

[7] For the very small number of men in the study who reported engaging in sexual and intimate relationships with other prisoners, the benefits were similar: 'that sort of comfort and caring; [...] you've got respect, and it's just part of life' (Arthur, 50s, post-tariff).

partners had given birth since their release and were planning their futures within these nuclear units.

Similarly, there was a great deal of optimism among female participants that friendships would endure beyond the prison gates. This was despite the emotional intensity of the relational environment (see also Genders and Player 1990), which put considerable strain on close friendships and sexual intimacy:

> *What's it like to spend time in like an almost all female environment?*
> It's horrendous. It's horrendous. When you get in relationships and the girls find out, [or] even if you're friends with somebody who somebody else doesn't want you to be friends with, they come out with saying, 'Well she said this behind your back, she said this behind your back' or 'She said you're fat'. (Kathryn, 20s, early)

> I don't think you can have a healthy relationship in prison, because you don't have a relationship just with the person; you have a relationship with the person and the rest of the wing, because they've all got opinions. […] It's been a conscious choice not to anymore because they're too intense. It's too intense to be with someone all the time. And everybody else in the jail had an opinion on it, and I don't like my business public. You can't do anything in private in here. […] In prison you become such public property. (Gail, 30s, late)

As suggested in these quotations, this culture afforded little emotional privacy. That women ranked 'wishing you had more privacy' as the sixth most severe problem that they experienced (compared to 23rd among the men) was partly related to literal intrusions—in particular, being visible to male prison staff when using the toilet or getting dressed, for example (see Carlen 1983; Moran et al. 2009). But it also reflected a form of emotional claustrophobia (Genders and Player 1990), produced by the sheer amount of relational talk.

For some women, this culture of what Gail called 'constant bombardment' produced a preference for self-isolation:

> I don't mind lock-in and things like that… especially the weekend, I like it when that door is shut, that's you and that's your time. No one coming to your door; no one ain't going to come to your door and bother you and things like that. […] I do miss that, having that privacy and just sometimes when you just want to be by yourself, and you just don't want anyone around you. (Deena, 20s, mid)

I don't like it when it's free-flow and you've got so many bitchy, conniving, back-stabbing people in here. (Tamara, 20s, early)

While male lifers therefore provided accounts of prison life as emotionally repressive, female lifers inhabited an environment in which the ubiquity of emotional discourse could be overwhelming (see Greer 2002).

Conclusion

The social dislocation that prisoners experienced when sentenced to long terms of life imprisonment was crushing and sometimes catastrophic. Separation from loved ones, anxieties about how the sentence would affect them over such a long period, and highly compromised role identities meant that many of the most painful and devastating aspects of enduring confinement related to family members, particularly parents and children. At the same time, for a range of reasons—life divergence, identity change, moral judgement, the pain of 'missing out', and the sheer difficulty of staying in touch over long periods and substantial distances—most friendships were terminated or simply faded away. As prisoners became increasingly disconnected from their pre-prison social worlds, they were forced to turn to the inner world of the prison in order to satisfy their need for relational goods. Despite statements of mistrust, most were able, over time, to develop some relationships of intimacy, shaped by the demands of the environment and bounded by the shared understanding that the ultimate concern of release trumped other obligations and priorities. In this respect, these friendships were similar to those outside prison, in being based to a large degree on 'shared histories, accumulated experiences, and simultaneously moving through major developmental transitions' (Hartup and Stevens 1997: 358). Meanwhile, the development of friendships was consistent with three broader dynamics: first, a change in focus from the outside community to the domain of the prison; second, a shift in orientation from the past to the future; and, third, a reconfiguration of priorities, from the social to the individual, as prisoners distanced themselves from everyday prisoner dynamics and focused increasingly on internal matters of who they were and the kind of person they wanted to become.

References

Archer, M. S. (2003). *Structure, agency and the internal conversation*. Cambridge: Cambridge University Press.

Archer, M. S. (2012). *The reflexive imperative in late modernity*. Cambridge: Cambridge University Press.

Barnett, R. C., Marshall, N. L., & Pleck, J. H. (1992). Men's multiple roles and their relationship to men's psychological distress. *Journal of Marriage and the Family, 54,* 358–367.

Callero, P. L. (1985). Role-identity salience. *Social Psychology Quarterly, 48,* 203–215.

Carlen, P. (1983). *Women's imprisonment: A study in social control*. London: Routledge & Kegan Paul.

Corston, J. (2007). *The corston report*. London: Home Office.

Crewe, B. (2009). *The prisoner society: Power, adaptation, and social life in an english prison*. Oxford: Oxford University Press.

Crewe, B. (2014). Not looking hard enough: Masculinity, emotion, and prison research. *Qualitative Inquiry, 20*(4), 392–403.

Donati, P. (2011). Modernization and relational reflexivity. *International Review of Sociology, 21*(1), 21–39.

Flanagan, T. J. (1980). Time served and institutional misconduct: Patterns of involvement in disciplinary infractions among long-term and short-term inmates. *Journal of Criminal Justice, 8*(6), 357–367.

Flanagan, T. J. (1981). Dealing with long-term confinement: Adaptive strategies and perspectives among long-term prisoners. *Criminal Justice and Behavior, 8*(2), 201–222.

Genders, E., & Player, E. (1990). Women lifers: Assessing the experience. *The Prison Journal, 70*(1), 46–57.

Giallombardo, R. (1966). *Society of women: A study of a women's prison*. New York: Wiley.

Girshick, L. B., & Sharp, S. (1999). *No safe haven: Stories of women in prison*. Boston, MA: Northeastern University Press.

Goffman, E. (1961). *Asylums: Essays on the condition of the social situation of mental patients and other inmates*. London: Penguin.

Greer, K. R. (2000). The changing nature of interpersonal relationships in a women's prison. *The Prison Journal, 80*(4), 442–468.

Greer, Kimberly. (2002). Walking an emotional tightrope: Managing emotions in a women's prison. *Symbolic Interaction, 25*(1), 117–139.

Grounds, A. T. (2005). Understanding the effects of wrongful imprisonment. *Crime and Justice, 32,* 1–58.

Hairston, C. F. (1991). Family ties during imprisonment: Important to whom and for what. *Journal of Sociology and Social Welfare, 18,* 87.

Hartup, W. W., & Stevens, N. (1997). Friendships and adaptation in the life course. *Psychological Bulletin, 121*(3), 355.

Helpline, O. F. (2015). *Visiting a prison.* http://www.offendersfamilieshelpline.org/index.php/visits/. Accessed 30 September 2015.

Hogg, M. A., Terry, D. J., & White, K. M. (1995). A tale of two theories: A critical comparison of identity theory with social identity theory. *Social Psychology Quarterly, 58,* 255–269.

Johnson, R. (2019). *Condemned to die: Life under sentence of death* (2nd edn). New York: Routledge.

Koscheski, M., & Hensley, C. (2001). Inmate homosexual behavior in a southern female correctional facility. *American Journal of Criminal Justice, 25*(2), 269.

Larson, J. H., & Nelson, J. (1984). Women, friendship, and adaptation to prison. *Journal of Criminal Justice, 12*(6), 601–615.

McCarthy, D., & Adams, M. (2019a). Can family–Prisoner relationships ever improve during incarceration? Examining the primary caregivers of incarcerated young men. *British Journal of Criminology, 59,* 378–395.

McCarthy, D., & Adams, M. (2019b). "Yes, I can still parent. Until I die, he will always be my son": Parental responsibility in the wake of child incarceration. *Punishment & Society, 21*(1), 89–106.

Moran, D., Pallot, J., & Piacentini, L. (2009). Lipstick, lace, and longing: Constructions of femininity inside a Russian prison. *Environment and Planning D: Society and Space, 27*(4), 700–720.

Morris, P. (1965). *Prisoners and their families.* Woking: George Allen & Unwin.

Murray, J. (2005). The effects of imprisonment on families and children of prisoners. In A. Liebling & S. Maruna (Eds.), *The effects of imprisonment* (pp. 442–492). Cullompton: Willan Publishing.

Owen, B. A. (1998). *In the mix: Struggle and survival in a women's prison.* Albany: State of New York University Press.

Paylor, I., & Smith, D. (1994). Who are prisoners' families? *The Journal of Social Welfare & Family Law, 16*(2), 131–144.

Prison Reform Trust. (2015a). *Prison: The facts* (Bromley Briefings Summer 2015). London: Prison Reform Trust.

Prison Reform Trust. (2015b). *Keeping children in care out of trouble: An independent review.* http://www.prisonreformtrust.org.uk/ProjectsResearch/CareReview. Accessed 21 September 2015.

Propper, A. M. (1982). Make-believe families and homosexuality among imprisoned girls. *Criminology, 20*(1), 127–138.

Richards, B. (1978). The experience of long-term imprisonment: An exploratory investigation. *British Journal of Criminology, 18,* 162–169.

Richards, M., McWilliams, B., Allcock, L., Enterkin, J., Owens, P., & Woodrow, J. (1994). *The family ties of English prisoners: The results of the Cambridge project on imprisonment and family ties.* Cambridge: Centre for Family Research.

Schinkel, M. (2014). *Being imprisoned: Punishment, adaptation and desistance.* Basingstoke: Palgrave Macmillan.

Simon, R. W. (1992). Parental role strains, salience of parental identity and gender differences in psychological distress. *Journal of Health and Social Behavior, 33*(1), 25–35.

Toch, H. (1992). Violent men: An inquiry into the psychology of violence (Rev. edn). Washington: American Psychological Association.

Turner, C. (1969). *Family and kinship in modern Britain: An introduction.* London: Routledge & Kegan Paul.

Walsh, F. (2003). Family resilience: A framework for clinical practice. *Family Process, 42*(1), 1–18.

Ward, D. A., & Kassebaum, G. G. (1965). *Women's prison: Sex and social structure.* Chicago: Aldine.

Zamble, E. (1992). Behavior and adaptation in long-term prison inmates: Descriptive longitudinal results. *Criminal Justice and Behavior, 19*(4), 409–425.

7

Identity and Selfhood

[In] my [first] prison I was very introvert. I think I was still recovering. You know, character wise, I'd been completely demolished, in every sense, by what had happened, and I had to rebuild myself emotionally in terms of my principles and beliefs, considering that everything that I'd held dear in my life, everything I held to be true, had been challenged by the events that took place. [...] So I had to reformulate that life. (Dan, 20s, early)

Erikson (1959) argues that individuals begin to shape their identities during adolescence. Teenagers pass through a 'psychosocial moratorium', during which they 'try on' various possible selves 'for size'. At this time, young people are 'developing their own view of themselves and the paths down which they would like to go in the years ahead' (Shapland and Bottoms 2011: 271). For around a fifth of both the men and women in our study, being sentenced to life imprisonment when they were adolescents (i.e. 18 years old or younger) meant that this crucial phase of psychosocial development occurred within the constraints of the prison environment. Even the majority of prisoners, sentenced in their post-adolescent years, were still 'struggling towards' their 'sense of life' or *modus vivendi* (Archer 2012: 113) at the point when they were convicted.

© The Author(s) 2020
B. Crewe et al., *Life Imprisonment from Young Adulthood*,
Palgrave Studies in Prisons and Penology,
https://doi.org/10.1057/978-1-137-56601-0_7

As outlined in Chapter 4, not only did individuals suffer the well documented 'assaults upon the self' (Goffman 1961: 40) experienced by all prisoners on entry into custody, but their relative immaturity and the gravity of their situation posed additional threats to the development of their sense of self. Specifically, they were forced to confront understandings of what it meant to be—or be seen as—a murderer and work out how they could move beyond the symbolic and existential implications of this designation. In this sense, what we have called the 'offence-time nexus' was highly pertinent to ongoing matters of identity and selfhood: perpetrating an act of murder, and/or witnessing distressing scenes of violence *as well as* the cataclysmic outcome of being condemned to prison for many years, had a particular and profound impact on prisoners' identities and sense of self:[1] on their sense of who they were prior to their sentence, who they were now and who they would be in the future, after release.

The structure of this chapter broadly follows the shifts in selfhood, and personal and social identity, described by our participants at different stages of long-term life imprisonment. It reflects on the ways in which prisoners at the start of their sentence consistently described a sense of 'losing themselves'. Conceptualised in terms of the 'dislocation of self', the focus is on the various displacements and implications that resulted from being party to a homicide, defined as a 'murderer', and confined to prison for many years. The chapter then moves on to describe the forms of existential reflection reported by prisoners who were further into their sentence, and the process of re-narration by which they made sense of their experiences and who they were. The final section of the chapter considers the ways in which those participants towards the end of their sentence reflected on the development of their sense of self over time, towards becoming—in their own terms—a better and more 'authentic' person: 'the real me'.

---

[1] For clarity, while the terms 'identity' and 'self' are often used interchangeably, here we apply them with a subtle distinction. 'Identity' is understood as 'the traits and characteristics, social relations, roles, and social group memberships that define who one is' (Osyerman et al. 2012: 69), while the 'self' is considered to be the individual's view of the composition of those identities within themselves, so that 'identities make up one's self-concept variously described as what comes to mind when one thinks of oneself' (Osyerman et al. 2012: 69).

Dislocation of the Self

Being convicted of murder is a 'disorientating episode' (Lofland 1969: 290), and prisoners' descriptions of 'losing' themselves, feeling 'broken' (Karen, 20s, mid), or being 'demolished' (Dan, 20s, early) by their conviction denoted a loss of existential confidence in who they were and a feeling of a sudden loss in life purpose and meaning: 'I just lost myself completely' (Liz, 20s, early); 'that guilty [verdict], like, shattered me' (Christopher, 20s, mid). In Archer's (2003) terms, and as described in earlier chapters, being convicted of murder, with all its implications, fractured the ability of most interviewees in the initial sentence phase to hold an effective internal conversation about who they were and what mattered to them (see also Mathiassen 2016).[2]

For a number of prisoners, even before their current predicament, selfhood was incoherent or in turmoil: '[prior to prison] I wasn't anybody [...] I didn't know who I was anymore' (Liz, 20s, early). Overwhelmingly, this was due to traumatic life experiences and mental health and substance abuse issues (with drugs and alcohol used to self-medicate psychological distress). Prior to their sentence, 67% of women and 15% of men who completed surveys had self-harmed or attempted to take their own life, and 68% of the women and 43% of men had experienced a problem with drugs, alcohol or both. For the prisoners who were already affectively fractured prior to imprisonment, the multiple shocks and dislocations generated by the offence, conviction and sentence deepened an already existing existential crisis. For those whose sense of self was clearer, these shocks—primarily, the offence itself and the realisation of how many years they would have to spend away from the loved ones to whom selfhood was tethered—triggered a profound crisis.

This initial crisis was rooted in a number of cognitive and emotional struggles associated with 'guilt', anger and shame. In interviews, prisoners who did not consider themselves guilty of the offence for which they had been convicted expressed a range of affective responses to their predicament: anger, due to feelings that their convictions and sentences were illegitimate; shame, associated with being labelled a 'murderer'; and, for some, guilt, relating to the social and emotional impact of their situation on their families. For prisoners who were not disputing their guilt,

---

[2]This inability was no doubt compounded by their youth and relative immaturity (Criminal Justice Alliance 2011).

the self was fissured by the existential crisis and shame associated with coming to terms with *being a murderer* and their implications for family members.

The majority of male prisoners who disputed their guilt were in the early period of their sentence and/or were convicted using the principles of joint enterprise (see Hulley et al. 2019 for further details). 77% of survey respondents in the 'very early' sentence stage stated that they did not consider themselves to be guilty of the offence for which they had been convicted, including *all* those at this stage who had been convicted under the principles of joint enterprise. In interviews, such individuals expressed overwhelming feelings of anger and bitterness, directed primarily at the criminal justice system, and at other people whom they felt had betrayed them, such as parents, social workers and co-defendants. These feelings had changed who they were in important ways:

> I was expecting 'not guilty', so when they said 'guilty', I just went mad. I just went mad. [...] I started attacking my Co-D [co-defendant] every time I saw him. [...] When they found me guilty, I just went into panic and I started punching the jailors and that. I am not that violent – I'm more naughty than violent. It just- I don't know [pause]. I felt like a monster for that whole year. (Damien, 20s, early)

> I think I could cope with losing my child, [my] abuse and everything else, but prison has turned me into someone I don't know. I'm not the person that I used to be outside; like I'm a very angry, horrible person to be around. (Tamara, 20s, early)

Intense anger, rooted in feelings of injustice, was supplemented with sentiments of guilt, even among prisoners who considered their involvement in the index offence to be indirect. Such participants often felt a deep sense of responsibility for the impact of their conviction not just on their own family members but also on the families of the murder victim. These feelings weighed heavily and impacted significantly on their self-concept. Tamara, for example, grappled daily with the implications of having been involved in a murder, despite her belief that she was neither legally nor morally culpable of the offence:

> *You said a couple of times to me that you are a 'horrible person'. Did you feel like that before this, or has this incident made you feel [like that] in some ways?*
> I think it's affected me, yeah. [...] It's affected me in a way that it shouldn't have affected me, because I didn't know the [victim]. I understand someone's life's been

taken and I'm remorseful, like I feel guilty for his family, whatever, but I didn't *know* him. And to live with that on my mind every day, all day, all night, is bad for me, because I actually didn't do anything to him and I had no contact with him - I didn't even know who he was. And I'm sat here feeling guilty for something that [my co-defendants] did, because they thought it would be funny. (Tamara, 20s, early)

The public shaming that resulted from being branded a murderer was also difficult to reconcile with the prevailing sense of self. In particular, the 'social ramifications [and] stigma' (Dan, 20s, early) of the conviction, alongside representations in the media, often felt fundamentally at odds with the perceived self: 'The things that are written about you, in this kind of detached sense, doesn't seem to really relate to who I am' (Dan, 20s, early).

The disjuncture between the prisoner's sense of self and his or her ascribed identity as a murderer was highly disorientating and was resisted by many prisoners through recourse to legal appeal (see Chapter 4). As well as presenting a potential escape route from the prospect of years of imprisonment, appeal performed some important *identity* functions. First, it publicly communicated the prisoner's contestation of the identity of being a murderer. Second, as explained by participants who, sometime into their sentence had retracted initial claims of innocence, it reflected a sense of profound disbelief that one could be the kind of person who was capable of murder:

I used to deny my offence as well, maintain my innocence out of shame and embarrassment, because what I did was really serious. [...] My younger sister believed for the longest time that I was innocent, because it was so out of character, she couldn't see it, I couldn't see it. (Karen, 20s, mid)

[For two years] I didn't wanna admit it. I didn't wanna have to accept that I took a human life. [...] I couldn't believe I could be that person. (John, 20s, mid)

Ironically, then, the disjuncture between prisoners' self-identities as moral agents and the subjective implications of being regarded as a murderer was a significant obstacle to the acceptance of responsibility for the offence.

Those who did not contest their guilt also frequently grappled with the belief that their offence was fundamentally inconsistent with who they were.[3] For these participants, the sense of moral responsibility for the death of the victim felt overwhelming. This situation became more complicated and painful when the victim was known to, or in an intimate relationship with, the individual:

> I just completely lost myself again [after being sentenced], and I was just like really in on myself. I was just grieving for my boyfriend. I was missing him and it was horrible. [...] My head was properly twatted. (Liz, 20s, early)

Violating normative expectations of behaviour through involvement in a murder shattered most prisoners' sense of 'ontological security' (Laing 1965): their sense of having a continuous and reliable selfhood. That is, from an early point in their sentence, many found themselves facing an existential void and a 'flooding of anxiety' (Giddens 1991: 37), as they asked themselves 'who am I, if I am capable of *this?*':

> Once you're convicted, there's - I don't know what it is, but, there's something inside of you that changes. [...] I'm not the same person I was. Because you *can't be* [...]. I don't know who the real me is. I don't know what sort of person I am. Because everything I thought I knew about me *can't be true* for me to be here for what I'm here for. (Maria, 20s, early)

> Somebody's dead because of me, and because of this group that I was with. So now I'm evaluating how I react to situations, [...] and things like that.
> *Are you re-evaluating yourself? Your whole identity?*
> Yeah. I'm thinking, 'Why the hell am I in this situation. [...] Am I capable of something?' [...] I couldn't walk up to somebody and just kill them, like; that's not me. That's not what I've been about all my whole life. (Stephen, 20s, mid)

---

[3] Only 13% of male prisoners in the very early stage of their sentence reported that they considered themselves to be guilty of murder, compared to 32% in the early stage, around half in the mid- or late stages of their sentence and 70% of those who were beyond their tariff point. The discrepancy between these figures was due to a number of factors, including the high proportion of joint enterprise prisoners in the very early and early stages (who were significantly more likely to dispute the charge of murder) and the tendency for some prisoners to maintain innocence in the early years of their imprisonment before conceding guilt at a later point.

It took me about five years to come to terms with the enormity of what I had done. It really, really affected me deeply. [...] The taking of somebody's life was just so beyond my comprehension that I had done something like this, taking another human being's life. (Ray, 50s, post-tariff)

This feeling of ontological insecurity among long-term prisoners has been reported in other studies. Cohen and Taylor (1972: 109), for example, reported their participants coming to doubt 'the integrity of the self, the reliability of natural processes and the substantiality of others', due to fears about personal deterioration in the future. By contrast, our participants—during the first few years of the sentence, at least—expressed feelings of 'cognitive and emotional disorientation' (Giddens 1991: 37) as an outcome of acts they had already committed and a resulting distrust in their moral boundaries and self-definitions. Individuals who accepted responsibility for the victim's death commonly reflected that they had lost something of themselves when they took another person's life: a sense of innocence, their 'soul', self-esteem, or a connection to particular emotions. These sentiments— what Mathiassen (2016) refers to as a sense of 'existential nothingness'—were bound up with feelings of shame:

A big part of me died that day when my victim died. My whole confidence in myself disappeared, I just... I couldn't believe that I'd allowed myself to get into that situation and done what I'd done. (Jenny, 20s, mid)
It's like the shame inside of me. I feel weak. Even today it's part of my personality I have and, I mean, it's something I'll never get back again.
Can you explain what that means, like what part of your personality?
I used to be bubbly and have a good laugh when I was out there, and all that. But murdering [the victim], it's like part of me has gone, part of my feelings, like the soul – it's gone. (Victor, 30s, post-tariff)

With murder, you'll never come to terms with it, because it's an inhuman act, just like rape is an inhuman act. But murder is something else, it's completely different. [...] I don't really know how to explain it.
Does it change your identity?
It changes who you are. Definitely. [...] You lose something human inside of you once you commit a murder. You [...] lose a bit of yourself. (Leonard, 30s, late)

Forms of shame associated with the offence were expressed most strongly by certain subgroups: female prisoners (often described as especially 'shame prone' [Ferguson, Eyre and Ashbaker 2000: 134]); prisoners in the later phases of their sentence, who had been forced to confront the worst of themselves repeatedly through offending behaviour programmes and in preparation for parole; and prisoners—like Shaafi, below—who had spent time in therapeutic communities, where such feelings had been repeatedly scrutinised:

> [The offence is] the biggest thing in my life I feel ashamed of, and it's like taking your deepest, darkest secret and just putting it out there for everybody to have a look at. The one thing that you feel horrendously ashamed of, and have everybody look at it and pick it apart and go, 'ooh'. And it's like you just, you die a little bit and each time it's like a bit of you dies. And when they do the sentence plan boards it's like having a wound that you let scab over and every time they go back they pull the scab off. (Gail, 30s, late)

> I just wanted to hide away [during the trial]. I didn't want people knowing about me, or what I've done, obviously, you know, I just felt ashamed. [...] It's kind of a horrible thing to see your name in the paper as a convicted murderer. It's kind of... it's not something that you can kind of brush aside. It's really kind of... it has a massive impact on you. (Shaafi, 30s, mid)

In rare cases, participants wholeheartedly assimilated the offence into their personal identity, to such an extent that being 'a murderer' superseded all other defining characteristics. Tori, for example, explained that 'I never define myself as anything other than I'm a murderer. My crime defined me as a person' (Tori, 30s, late) (although as we discuss below, there were indications that self-identifications of this kind could change over time). More commonly, as the sentence progressed, individuals made it clear that being a 'murderer' was not all that defined them. This was particularly important in the quest to rebuild a more positive sense of self.

Yet the impact of being *labelled* a murderer—and knowing what the term communicated to others—persisted. The stigmatic connotations of this label were 'very difficult to integrate into [the] prisoner's self-concept' (Sapsford and Sapsford

1983: 83). Indeed, attempts to come to terms with the offence early in the sentence generated anger and distress more than they served to resolve them. During this sentence stage, at a time when most were still very young—and therefore less able to 'turn experience into narrative' (Singer 2004: 443)—participants consistently conveyed a form of self-reflection that was frantic, emotive and somewhat incoherent. Stephen recalled this period of his sentence as follows:

> *[Were] you re-evaluating yourself? Your whole identity?*
> Yeah, yeah, that's what happened. I'm thinking, 'why the hell am I in this situation. [...] Why did I allow this to happen? And what did I allow myself to do this? Why can't I read, why can't I do this, why can't I do that? Why am I in prison? Why is it always me?' you know?
> *Feeling sorry for yourself as well?*
> Not even, I'm getting angry with myself at that time. I'm thinking to myself, 'what the hell have I done man? I'm an idiot, I'm a fool'. (Stephen, 20s, mid)

While murder might be a 'high status' offence in the prisoner hierarchy (see Vaughn and Sapp 1989), among our participants, expressions of pride in having a murder conviction were virtually non-existent. Instead, most struggled with the awareness that they would be permanently regarded as someone 'evil', 'monstrous' or 'psychotic':

> I'm in for murder, aren't I? [...] Being labelled a murderer, [...] it's really difficult to deal with. You know? I took somebody's life, so [...] you can't really be proud of yourself. Do you know what I mean? If I got out tomorrow, above me, there's always going to be that label, isn't there? So it's something that has kind of hurt all my family. (Shaafi, 30s, mid)

These difficulties were compounded by wider social and penal processes: public stigmatisation, through media publicity; offending behaviour programmes, which required prisoners to repeatedly interrogate their offence; and the culture of therapeutic communities, which asked prisoners to introduce themselves in relation to the worst thing they had ever done:

> I feel like a killer and I feel like I'm one of those people that you see on TV - deranged! [...] If someone new comes on the wing we have to introduce ourselves, so I say: 'Hi, I'm Arkaan and I'm serving life for murder'. And you say that over and

over again, and it's almost as if you're reinforcing that act and that act reinforces and defines the person. (Arkaan, 20s, mid)

Such processes contributed to a crippling sense of self-stigma, as prisoners internalised the judgements of others (Corrigan and Watson 2002), and to acute psychological distress, including suicidal ideation:

[On conviction] suddenly everything is ripped away from you, and feels like it's been taken to a different planet. And I felt so alone and isolated and, actually, I felt like I deserved it and there wasn't a day - and there still isn't - that I don't think about my victim and his family, and my family. And the mental torture that I put myself through got worse; it didn't get better, every day got worse. And every day I spent planning to take my life, because I didn't know how to cope; I couldn't cope. (Maria, 20s, early)

In general, then, the feelings generated by the conviction threatened or annihilated the sense of self, both for those who disputed their guilt and those who did not. For while the latter were especially animated by feelings of anger about the illegitimacy of their conviction and the former by a profound sense of guilt, both groups had to confront being publicly identified as a murderer, process feelings of empathy for the family of their victim, and manage concerns about the impact of their conviction on their family members (see Chapter 6). Being untethered from these social relations and confined for such a long period to the social world of the prison produced a further dislocation, to which we now turn.

Social Dislocation and Self-Identity

Douglas (1984: 82) explains the role of 'looking homeward' when experiencing an identity crisis:

Home-grounding is often of intense emotional importance to individuals precisely when they feel most insecure ontologically. [...] Insecurity resulting from identity crises, such as those resulting from soul-wrenching divorces or from other failures and losses, often lead individuals to reground themselves by looking homeward and returning home. The feeling of homelessness and the conviction that 'you can't go home again' […] involves a feeling of being lost (uncentred) and, indeed, of losing a vital part of the self.

At precisely the time when secure connections were needed, long-term removal from family, friends and other loved ones left long-term prisoners feeling lost, existentially stateless (Mathiassen 2016), and unable to anchor their sense of self.[4] For some prisoners, during the early stage of their imprisonment in particular, this separation rendered it impossible for them to 'be themselves':

You just can't be yourself [in prison]. There's no possible way of being yourself […]
What stops you from being yourself then?
You need to have family around you. You need to have people that know you; you can't just be with some random people, who [you] have never met in your life, and be yourself. It is impossible. (Martin, 20s, early)

You're not the same person [inside prison and outside prison], are you? You're not functioning, you're not around your friends and family and… you're just not the same, are you? Because there's only part of me here. Like, the other part of that is, like, with my family and my son.
Do you feel that there's a sense that you left that part of you outside and hope you can pick it up again, when you get back out?
Yeah, that's what I mean - cos you're not really whole in here, are you? (Sean, 20s, early)

Sean described suspending his 'true', pre-prison self during his sentence and antic-ipated reviving it once released, when back among the people who made him 'whole'. Only 18 months into a 19-year sentence, his comments resonated with those often made by prisoners serving shorter sentences, who tend to describe selfhood within prison as temporary and inauthentic (see Schmid and Jones 1991; Crewe 2009; see Chapter 8). Again, both time and the offence itself were highly germane here. For prisoners whose pre-prison selves had been shattered by their

---

[4]On being convicted, prisoners lost sources of social identity besides established social and familial networks, including employment, the ability to demonstrate individuality through social artefacts such as clothing and shared cultural meanings. John (20s, mid), for example, described struggling to 'learn to stop who I am' within an environment in which his normal response to threat, in the form of violence, was institutionally unacceptable.

index offence or conviction, the very idea of a true self to which they could return was unsustainable (see below). For those who had been confined for some time and who recognised that release was still many years away, it began to feel inconceivable to suspend identity in perpetuity. As we have detailed in previous chapters, friendships wilted, priorities shifted, and the world of the prison progressively shaded out memories of, and references to, prior social domains. Gradually, prisoners' sense of who they *had been* began to fade, while the demands of the environment exacerbated the difficulty of connecting to the person they 'really were' prior to their imprisonment.

Environmental Demands

Prisoners did not passively experience the dislocation from their previous personal and social selfhood. Indeed, in many cases, institutional demands required them to actively reconstitute themselves as particular kinds of beings, in ways that were not necessarily aligned with their pre-prison sense of self. First, in order to advance through the prison system, they were expected to demonstrate changes in values, attitudes and behaviours (Robinson 2008). Risk reduction—a prerequisite for progression and release—meant actively engaging with cognitive behavioural programmes, in pursuit of a future self that was institutionally and socially acceptable (Crewe 2011):

> They want me to do the CALM [anger management] course. I don't feel like I really need to do it myself, but I'm gonna do it. I know that I've been assessed for it and they felt it suitable, so there must be a reason why they find it suitable to do so.
> *Does it force you to be different from the kind of person that you are?*
> Yes, because that's what they're trying to do. They're trying to change you from what you was. They try and change your thoughts, and the way you behave, so that if you're ever in the same situation, you don't do the same things again, you know? (Curtis, 20s, mid)

Some prisoners talked about offending behaviour courses and prison psychologists with contempt, particularly those in later sentence stages, whose progression to open conditions or release depended on positive reports. For example, 'prison psychologists making life harder' was the fifth most severe problem for male prisoners who were post-tariff (with a severity score of 11.44), compared to 27th among those in the early stage (severity score: 7.69) and 22nd among those in the late stage (severity score: 9.46). Similarly, women in the late stage rated this issue as the 12th most severe problem that they experienced (severity score: 10.00), compared to 33rd and 38th for mid-stage (severity score 6.50) and early-stage (severity score: 6.00) women, respectively.

Notably though, 'Feeling that you need to be careful about everything you say and do' was rated as a more severe problem by very early and early-stage male prisoners—15th and 24th most severe, respectively—than by mid- and late-stage prisoners and those who were post-tariff—31st, 25th and 27th most severe, respectively (severity scores: 11.66, 9.71, 7.50, 5.71 and 6.79, from very early to post-tariff). Among female participants, those at the mid-stage rated this problem as most severe (22nd most severe, compared to 29th and 28th among early- and late-stage prisoners, respectively). As suggested in Curtis's attitude of stoic acceptance, above, most prisoners did not regard institutional attempts to 'change' them as oppressive or entirely unwanted (cf. Warr 2019). Likewise, Nadia's comments suggested a sincere commitment to official programmes and interventions:

[The first five years was about] doing some programmes to sort myself out mentally and physically. [...] They haven't said to me 'you've got to do this, you've got to do that'. I'm the one sitting there saying [...] 'No, I'm doing it, I want to do it'. [...] Because some of them were drug-related, and I knew I had a drug issue and I needed to sort it. (Nadia, 20s, late)

Often, as suggested here—and in Chapter 5—the nature of their offence or pre-prison lifestyle meant that prisoners had a strong and intrinsic desire to change and were willing to use the resources offered by the prison in order to do so. While some used institutional language to describe changes in self-identity, few appeared to exhibit a form of 'audit selfhood' that was entirely imposed or internalised (Fleetwood 2015; Warr 2019). More often, in making sense of who they were, those who had served a number of years in prison used discursive resources deriving from educational and religious activities, which were provided by the institution but offered broad scope for interpretation and personal customisation.

Second, and relatedly, prisoners were expected to demonstrate an alternative, 'pro-social' self in their daily interactions. Again, many mid- and late-stage prisoners accepted this imperative, since it was consistent with their desire to demonstrate ethical selfhood (see below). For others, however, particularly early-stage prisoners who were struggling to contain themselves affectively, it was regarded as 'unrealistic' and emotionally oppressive:

> I think [the prison] expect[s] you to be a person that nobody ever can be.
> *And what's that?*
> Don't get angry, like, day-to-day things that can happen to anybody… it's a mood, innit?
> *So you think it's unrealistic, the kind of person you're expected to be?*
> Yeah, it's like they're trying to create a machine. (Jamaal, 20s, early)

In a similar vein, female prisoners, in particular, conveyed anxiety that to be entirely open in expressing their emotions was hazardous, because it might be pathologised, interpreted as 'not coping', or treated as an indicator of risk (see Laws 2018), as Jill explained:

> Sometimes we feel that you can't really show your true emotions because it would be twisted. 'Oh, they're not handling their sentence. Oh, they're still aggressive. Oh, they're crying their eyes out all the time. That's it, it's not coping'. (Jill, 40s, post-tariff)

Often, female prisoners' concerns about being candid related to mental health issues, and the risk of being labelled by the authorities as 'mad', and being indefinitely medicated as a result (see also Laws 2018). Such anxieties led some women to mask their psychological struggles:

> I've got this problem at the minute and I've had it on the out, and I don't know what it is and I'm scared to tell the doctor about it. I've had it a couple of times. […] I'm sat there and [I can see] these black balls going down the stairs, and I've had that since I was little […]. They're banging and banging and banging and it really scares me.
> *And why are you scared to tell the doctor?*

I don't know, because I don't want them thinking I'm mad. [...] They might put me on more medication and that's what I'm worried about. [...] Because I don't want to be a pill-head; I want to be off all that. (Eloise, 20s, early)

In a number of ways, then, institutional expectations produced a need to repress true selfhood, at least to some degree.

The demands of prisoner culture also required some degree of self-modification. For a minority, this involved 'dumbing down' (Tom, 20s, early) or not being 'as posh' (Paul, 20s, early). Overwhelmingly, however—and as widely reported in studies of prisoner culture (e.g. Jewkes 2005; De Viggiani 2012)—prisoners described a need to demonstrate emotional and physical fortitude and suppress signs of weakness, in order to avoid exploitation. These practices of emotional self-policing meant that it was not always possible for prisoners to be entirely 'themselves', although most—especially those further into their sentence—did not find these demands all-encompassing:

Are there particular places in the prison where you can be yourself?
Your own cell after lock up.
Right. Is that the only place?
That's the only place you can truly be yourself.
So that's where you're on your own.
Yeah.
So with the people that you're around, is there anyone that you can be yourself with?
Not hundred per cent. (Antone, 20s, early)
You can't show any weakness, cos then otherwise you become a target. So [...] in certain situations you've got to act a certain way, but most of the time you can just be yourself, you know. (Curtis, 20s, mid)

Often too, forms of emotional suppression were consistent with pre-prison behaviour, due to childhood socialisation or conditioned responses to early trauma. Kathryn (20s, early), for example, explained a long-standing practice of 'shutting everybody out', developed in her youth to ensure that no one could see when she was hurt by insults. Joseph (40s, post-tariff) attributed his ability to 'put up the shields' to his childhood experience of abuse.

Over time, though, faced with a dislocation of self, the severing of ties to the pre-prison social world, and the demands of the prison environment, long-term prisoners were impelled to find a way of making sense of who they were now.

As we suggested in Chapter 5, and will now explain in more detail, most found this possible by engaging in forms of intensive existential reflection about what they had done, who they were and who they wanted to be. To put this in Archer's (2012) terms, they began to reflexively reconfigure their ultimate concerns.

Self-Reconstruction (I): Implications of the Offence for Identity

> The challenge [of surviving extreme experiences] is to assemble a new – and stable – self that incorporates the additional fragments; a mosaic that brings [the] life story up to date. (O'Donnell 2014: 275)

As we argued in Chapter 5, the combination of the length of time spent in custodial conditions and the moral-existential implications of being convicted for murder often led to deep reflection on matters of identity and selfhood:

> If prison makes you do nothing else, it makes you look at yourself, and it makes you look at who you are. I think out there [in the community] you're bombarded with that much. [...] You don't stop and take a look at yourself and try and find out who you are, because you're still developing and you wouldn't know. [...] In here, the lock-in gives you space, it gives you time to think about who you are, about what you want, and what you want to do and things like that. And you're not bombarded with being other things to other people, because you're just you. And it's like you're stripped bare, it's like you are just you and you have to find who you are and you have to get comfortable in your own skin. And you have to learn to be able to live with you, and to be able to kind of come to terms with why you're in and be able to live with that, no matter how difficult it is. [...] You do become quite reflective, and [think] 'How the hell did this ever happen?' You really confront yourself and you can't get away from you. You're locked in a tiny room, I mean, you're locked in a little cell and it's just you. (Gail, 30s, late)

Gail's statement was telling both for her comment about being 'stripped bare' and for her initial reference to her prison cell as a 'room'. While the former indicated a common sentiment of being dispossessed and dislocated by the conviction and sentence length, the latter gestured towards the kind of adaptation that most interviewees were able to make, after the early period of confinement, as they began to reflect on themselves in increasingly lucid ways. That is—to revisit our central thesis—as the emotional fog of the early years lifted, prisoners found that they had the psychological strength and space to consider the existential questions that in the past they had been unable to contemplate or had judiciously ignored (see also O'Donnell 2014). Indeed, our interviews with prisoners who were beyond the early sentence stage were saturated with contemplation about the meaning of life and death, and soul-searching about their implications for selfhood. As Douglas (1984: 76–77) notes, self-crisis 'can produce the greatest possible self-awareness and self-searching (soul searching)' because it is experienced as 'a threat to the inner sense of self'.

For most prisoners, much of the challenge of 'coming to terms' with the offence was finding a way to situate it within a coherent biography: to integrate their past behaviour with their current sense of self (Giddens 1991). Aakif, still relatively early on in his sentence, conveyed the difficulty of this endeavour:

> I've sometimes asked myself 'could that be me? *Was* it me?' Because the situation I'm in now - clearheaded, no drugs, no alcohol, nothing - [...] there's no way I would do, or get to that stage. But that's the past, that's one of the good things I think people taught me - that you leave the past where it is and you don't have to forget, you can remember it. But there's times you've just got to move on, so I'm just - you learn from the past, that's all I could do, and then you could turn a negative into a positive and use them in the future, and that way, one day, you might forget your past completely. (Aakif, 20s, early)

Comparatively, prisoners further into their sentences acknowledged the pain of thinking about their offence, but described having reconciled it within their life narrative and redefined themselves as people who were in some way responsible for a particular act, without being defined by it entirely:

> So when people say 'I'm a criminal' or 'I'm a murderer', I don't actually like to say that because I have done that act and I was that person, but now I'm not. I'm not a robber now, I'm not a drug-dealer now and I'm not a killer now. [...] It's a part of what's contributed to me developing into this person, but it's not who I am now. (Arkaan, 20s, mid)

Significantly, then, coming to terms with the offence required a complex form of psychological adjustment: a distinction between actions and selfhood, and a need to honour the past without being swamped by a single episode and its moral implications, whatever their immensity. Being a murderer became *part* of the life story, but—crucially—not its sole or central narrative. As suggested above, many prisoners were frustrated by a backwards-facing institutional gaze, which focused on who they used to be and a particular act they had committed, rather than who they were now and what they might become. For example:

> All I want to do now is just focus on my future. I'm sick of people asking me about my past, and I just want them to realise it's not about that no more, it's about my future and that's all that should matter now, but, obviously, it doesn't. (Eileen, 30s, late)

Alternatively, the offence was reframed almost as a *necessary* event in the individual's life trajectory:

> And this is what happened, this is what got me here: spur of the moment, going for a stupid game, what cost someone's life. And [...] it does hurt. It does hurt, it really, really does hurt, you know, there's no getting away from it. But I have to live with that. And it's a good thing really to have that, because it's like a kick up the arse. It's a...[reminder]: you drink, [this is] where are you going to end up. (Eugene, 50s, post-tariff)

The way in which Eugene re-narrated his experience as 'a good thing really'—part of a 'redemption sequence' (McAdams and Bowman 2001: 471)—was common among prisoners who were some way into their sentence. In this regard, most prisoners did not place complete narrative and cognitive distance between their index offence and their current self-concept, as a way of managing shame (c.f. Maruna 2004). Rather, they sought to integrate their offence into their narrative of self and use this to help 'shape and guide' their future (Maruna 1997).

Nonetheless, engaging in existential soul-searching was often painful. As we noted in Chapter 4, 'thinking about the crime you committed' was a more severe problem for those later in their sentence, than those in the early stages. Living with the offence was an ongoing struggle:

When I talk about certain things, I can get a bit emotional, you know. I know some things and certain subjects are still a bit raw for me. Every day is a process for me, every single day is a process, every day is a road to bettering myself. So I try sometimes, yeah, sometimes I take five steps forward and take a step back, but I try every day. (Asad, 30s, mid)

As Asad's terms suggest ('I try every day'), despite the difficulties of doing so, most mid- and late-stage prisoners felt morally obligated to work through, and remain conscious of, what they had done.

Self-Reconstruction (II): Making Sense of the Changing Self

Some prisoners who had engaged in extended existential reflection described undergoing wholesale personal change—becoming a 'whole new me'—in part because of their reflections on the offence itself and a lifestyle associated with it.[5]

Do you think being a long-term prisoner has changed you as a person?
A million percent. [...] Prison's worked for me, basically, it's worked for me in the fact that I don't want to live that kind of life anymore, at all. Though not only does it not appeal to me, it kind of disgusts me now, and sometimes I have to remind myself that I used to live that kind of a life. Because I feel so separate from it now. [...] [This sentence has] changed my whole way of thinking. I've had to re-evaluate my whole life, really, pretty much, everything about my life. From the kind of things I used to do, my outlook on what I found acceptable ways of making money. [...] I never want to live like that again, I never wanted my kids to live like that. (Neil, 30s, mid)

The sense of agency implied here was in contrast to how such prisoners recalled life in the community, where—with hindsight—they believed their choices to have

---

[5] In surveys, of the fifty male prisoners who were late stage or post-tariff, only three 'strongly disagreed' with the statement 'I have become/am becoming a better person' and only five 'disagreed' with this statement. In interviews, this subgroup of prisoners suggested that they did not feel they needed to change and were maintaining their innocence or remained 'deep' in the system, as Category A prisoners. Of the six female survey participants who were at the latter stages of their sentences, only one strongly disagreed or disagreed with this statement. For this woman, any changes felt a natural part of growing up.

been highly restricted. Likewise, as suggested in Chapter 4, prisoners who were in the mid- and late stage of their sentence felt considerably more in control of who they wanted to be than they had done during the early years of their sentence. Neil (30s, mid), for example, stated: 'I am in control over the person I've become. I made the person I am'; similarly, Aakif, four years into his tariff, proclaimed that 'Prison hasn't changed me, I've changed myself' (20s, early).

Others described more modest developments, with subtle changes to their pre-prison characters or new attributes that had been combined with the durable aspects of their 'core' personality (Maruna 1997). These characteristics included such matters as 'moral code', sense of humour, or intelligence:

> *Are there things about you that you think have stayed the same since you've been in [prison]?*
> I'm still a proud person. I've still got morals and that as well [...] I'll always help a mate out of stuff. Mostly, I've just stayed the same really apart from I've gotta be careful about what I'm doing. I'm less impulsive than I was. (Scott, 30s, mid)

In line with narrative theory (McAdams 1993), prisoners' change narratives were often imbued with a sense of meaning and value. Most were able to 'rewrite a shameful past into a necessary prelude to a productive and worthwhile life' (Maruna 2001: 87). They did so through three distinct scripts, each enabling a form of positive self-regard, which provided 'shape and coherence' to who they were, what they had experienced, and how they had changed (Maruna 1997). The first was a script of 'ethical selfhood', in which prisoners recounted that they were 'a good person' who had made a mistake. The second was consistent with the concept of 'post-traumatic growth', characterised by a claim that the experience of imprisonment had made them a 'better person', with a greater appreciation for life. The third narrative was more passive, describing changes to the self as a process of maturation. These scripts were not mutually exclusive, but, for the sake of clarity, will be discussed in turn below.

The Ethical Self

The narrative of the inherently good person who had 'made one mistake' (what Presser [2010] refers to as a 'stability narrative') was most common among mid- and late-stage prisoners:

Reflecting back, would you say that you've discovered new things about yourself, or new sides?
I'm a good person. I did a bad thing, but I am a good person.
And is that something new for you?
It's something I've learnt over the last few years, that I am a good person. Although I've always known I am a good person. (Tori, 30s, late)

I wasn't a bad person, and I say, to this day, I wasn't a bad person. I didn't do nothing that bad out there that I was going around hurting people or causing some concern; it was just one night, one bad move, changed everything. (Arshad, 30s, late)

Some depicted the act of taking another life as an existential anomaly: an incident which was entirely inconsistent with who they were and how others perceived them, prior to the offence. As Arshad went on to explain:

If you ask anybody in my family, my friends and relatives, anyone who knows me, I'm one of them who's very [em]pathetic, you know. If I see something on TV, 'oh look, look what's happening to them', you know. I've always given money to charity, always go out of my way to help my neighbours and stuff, that's why all my family, relatives, friends and neighbours, they all love me, and that's why they were shocked as well, you know, they were going 'he wouldn't do that!' And that's what gets under my skin, you know, I'd never do that; to be honest, I could have made a different decision on the day, could have been right out of that situation, but you know, it's all ifs and buts again. (Arshad, 30s, late)

This self-narrative of essential and underlying goodness was relevant to ongoing conduct within the prison. Many prisoners sought to emphasise the routine ways in which being convicted of murder did not make them fundamentally immoral or unethical, emphasising in particular such matters as being courteous, generous, and able to conduct a 'civilised' conversation:

I'm not a bad person, not a bad person. I made a mistake - a *big* mistake - but a mistake. I had no intention of hurting anyone that night. I'm not a bad person. I've got quite a big heart, quite generous.
How do you show that in here?
I just be polite. I think manners is a big part, I was always brought up with manners, it don't cost nothing. I'm just a normal lad that just made a mistake, that's all, people

make mistakes; it's how you learn from them isn't it … but, yeah, I learnt I'm not a bad person and I'm not useless. (Gibson, 20s, mid)

Small acts of decency subverted the identity imposed on the individual by their conviction. Through mundane ethical practices, then, prisoners attempted to resist the essentialised version of who they were in the eyes of others. This struggle to resist being reduced to a label, and to publicly display ethicality, was, for some participants, completely critical. As Infinito (2003: 158) notes, '[h]aving one's identity defined for one is as restrictive to individual freedom as bars and chains'. In this regard, everyday courtesies were not only 'an accomplishment in the moment', but also represented a commitment to being an ethical subject, in the present and in the future (Williams 2018: 733; see Foucault 1997). For many prisoners, then, a commitment to generative pursuits on release—the aim of saving 'even just one' individual from a similar fate (Maruna 2001: 104; and see Kazemian 2019)—was deeply connected to the desire to re-write public identity through the demonstration of personal decency:

[I want to] make a difference in this world and at least when I die I wanna leave something behind, you know, a legacy. [So] That my legacy isn't that 'he took someone's life'. I wanna leave behind that: 'you know what, yeah, he done wrong in his life but he also did some good'. And I wanna [pause] I guess I wanna leave that on this world. (Mahmood, 30s, mid)

As suggested by the emphasis on 'legacy', public reputation and generative practices, bringing this moral self into being was a relational and dialogic practice. That is, it was made real and reinforced through interactions and feedback from others, including family and friends outside prison, peers within prison, and daily exchanges with prison staff. Aaron, for example, took pride in wing reports that provided approbation and supported his self-image:

Officers on the wing, I've never had - from day one, I've never had a bad report. It's always the same thing: 'model prisoner, good with staff, good with inmates, causes no problems, very polite person'. (Aaron, 40s, late)

Likewise, as discussed in Chapter 5, the discourse of personal virtue was reinforced by religious beliefs, which not only provided a set of 'prescriptions and guidelines' for living a righteous existence (Park 2005: 711), but also rituals and social communities through which ethicality could be enacted and mutually reinforced (see Williams 2018). In such ways, demonstrating their 'ethical self' allowed prisoners to assimilate who they were 'then' (when they were involved in an act of murder) with who they were 'now' and would be in the future—a good person who had learnt from an anomalous mistake.

Post-Traumatic Growth and the 'Stronger, Better Self'

Whereas prisoners who presented a script of ethical selfhood believed themselves to have 'made a mistake' in the context of having been always and essentially good, a second discourse presented the individual as having advanced from a state of moral or psychological deficiency (see Liem 2016). Within this 'reform narrative' (Presser 2010), the trauma of having been involved in a murder and/or endured a long prison sentence had given rise to something psychologically beneficial:

> I've got a better understanding of myself, of what I'd done in the past, what I'm doing now, and an understanding of why I did it. Do you know, this place [a therapeutic prison] has just been absolutely amazing for me. It's developed me as a human being and a person, and an individual and a man and that. (Kelvin, 20s, mid)[6]

Prisoners who described this sense of post-traumatic growth believed that their adverse experience was 'meant to be' (Maruna 2001: 97; and see, e.g., van Ginneken 2016), and that going through and learning from it had improved them:

> [This experience has] kind of made me stronger, and more like [pause] a better person, because I don't want to do anything remotely close to that. And I kind of want to learn from my mistakes, I want to lead a different life, I want to go down a different path. [...] So I think because of what I've done, and because twelve years I've had to think about it, it's kind of made me realise the person that I was, and the life that I was leading, and the changes that I need to make, needed to make. So in that way it's kind of made me a lot more [of] a better person. (Shaafi, 30s, mid)

---

[6] Joseph (2011) proposes that post-traumatic growth is more likely to occur when basic psychological needs are met, and it is telling that claims of 'improvement' were associated with more morally decent prison environments (and see Auty and Liebling 2019), such as prison-based therapeutic communities.

This sentence will make me stronger and when I come out I will learn from this and obviously I will follow the right path. [...] This so far has made me think more positive [pause] It's made me grow up. [...] I want to get out and show that I've changed and do something positive with my life and show them obviously that I've been in a bad situation and I've made something out of it, and I've turned a negative into a positive. (Dean, late teens, early)

This narrative corresponded with two of Janoff-Bulman's (2004: 30) three 'models of posttraumatic growth': 'strength through suffering' and 'existential reevaluation'. 'Strength through suffering' entails gaining from underlying distress, that is discovering new strengths, coping skills or resources that provided 'new possibilities in life' (Janoff-Bulman 2004: 31). Zufar (20s, early), for example, felt that his sentence had already made him 'tougher, mentally and physically, [...] to know I can cope with different things where I wasn't able to cope with when I was outside'. For other participants, personal progress was primarily intellectual, rather than emotional or psychological. This too generated new possibilities, with new skills and abilities projected into generative ambitions for the future:

Even though this is bad, what I'm going through now, I just believe that I'm a lot more intelligent than who I was. And at the end of the day, it's not all about me now, it's about the younger generation. I wanna try and do my best for them when I get out if I can. (Luca, 30s, mid)

Maruna (2001: 98) likens this perspective to Frankl's (1984) concept of 'tragic optimism'—'the belief that suffering can be redemptive'—or, as for our participants, the idea that actions for which one is personally responsible can, in due course, lead to greater strength and wisdom.

'Existential re-evaluation' involves a 'greater appreciation for life' (Janoff-Bulman 2004: 32) developing out of adversity. In research on meaning-making, this response has been associated with events and experiences such as rape, cancer, natural disasters and serious accidents (cf. Park 2010). While prisoners might not be conventionally regarded as 'survivors' of trauma, the processes that they described were analogous with the broad literature in this area. In particular, they involved grappling with 'questions of comprehensibility' in the 'immediate aftermath' of both a murder and a life-changing sentence, before turning to 'questions of significance' (Janoff-Bulman 2004: 33). For our participants, such matters included a new 'appreciation' for family, friends, faith, freedom and for life itself—the ultimate concerns that we described in Chapter 5 (and see Liebling, in press). This narrative of appreciation tended to be reported by prisoners earlier in the sentence than the other redemptive scripts:

> Your perspective on what really are the priorities in life completely changes in this scenario, and you cannot fully appreciate freedom until you've had it taken away from you. There's no way that you can simulate this kind of environment or these kind of conditions, and it is an eye-opener, and I think, looking back, I did take a lot for granted and, you know, I have regrets about that, and I know that moving forward I'm excited about the future because I know that my appreciation for life, for my friends, for the things that we do take for granted, even the smallest thing... something as simple as walking through a park, you know, or looking in the supermarket and having such a diverse range of foodstuffs, whatever, silly little things, are actually incredibly precious. (Dan, 20s, early)

> Has [being a long-term prisoner] changed me? [Pause] It makes you think more about the bigger picture. And it makes you appreciate life, freedom and other things. (Sean, 20s, early)

Trauma produced an inadvertent opportunity to reassess life. In this context, faith again provided a 'core schema', which informed the individual about their 'self, the world, and their interaction' (Park 2005: 711). Arkaan (20s, mid), for example, explained that his Islamic faith had 'helped me kind of look at my connection with the world, and my understanding of life'. As we detailed in Chapter 5, religious belief and reflection facilitated the development of new life concerns, helped show the path to their realisation, and gave prisoners the strength to pursue them. In doing so, they provided what Snyder et al. (1991, cited in Martin and Stermac 2010: 694) identify as a model of dispositional hope: belief in the ability to achieve personal goals (i.e. a sense of agency) and a sense of the pathways for doing so. Progressing towards these goals was part of the process of personal and ethical reconstruction:

> I have targets. [...] I have an aim in my mind. I want to be able to memorise the Qur'an before I come out of jail.
> *So the achievement for you is learning the Qur'an?*

Yeah. Cos I know having five GCSEs are not gonna help me when I get outside. Because who's gonna wanna hire someone that's been in jail for twenty years? But […] you know, if I wanna help other people, I know that's the angle that I want to come from.

So learning the Qur'an is what helps you to then…

From a religious perspective, yeah. Because that's my community now. The Muslim community. (Mohammed, 30s, mid)

Like the discourse of the 'ethical self', the narrative of 'becoming a better person'— wiser, stronger, more skilled, and with a greater appreciation of life—enabled prisoners to distance themselves from the person they *had* been, integrate their offence into a coherent self-narrative, and forge a new sense of self oriented to the future.

The More Mature Self

A third narrative, expressed in particular by prisoners late in their sentence, emphasised the role of maturity in changes to personality and self-identity. Here, feelings of greater wisdom were attributed not to the need to cope with adverse experiences, but to the natural process of 'growing up'. Indeed, prisoners who expressed such views tended to reject the idea that they had been changed by imprisonment itself, instead regarding themselves as facsimiles of who they would have been had they not received a long sentence:

How would you say that being a long-term prisoner has changed you as a person?
I don't know, because I don't think it's prison what's changed me, I just think I've grown up. […] I just finally grew up I suppose. (Jackie, 30s, late)

How would you say that being a long-term prisoner has changed you as a person?
I don't think it's just being a long-term prisoner that's changed me, I think I've just grown up myself. I think that's all it is, I don't think it's about prison changing you, I think it's about you're just growing up and becoming the person you were always meant to be anyway. […] Even if I'd never had this long sentence I would have still become the person I am today. […] I'd still be the person I am today, but probably with a different future, that's all. (Eileen, 30s, late)

These interpretations of change were more passive than those presented in the other narratives, described above. Prisoners like Eileen and Jackie did not feel that they had changed *themselves,* so much as been altered by the developmental effects of ageing. Other participants credited some aspects of their custodial experiences for aiding their maturation, in particular, for making them less reactive and impulsive:

> *So how would you say that being a long-term prisoner has changed you as a person?*
> Just the age. I think I've just got older. [...] Just got older and a little bit more wiser. [...] Just doing these courses. [...] It's helped me. I don't act irrationally now. I don't, 'I want to do this, I want to do that, I want to buy this…'. I stop to think now, I think 'oh, calm down. Take a deep breath, and just work things out', where I am, and where I want to be. [...] If I had this knowledge in my head years ago, I'd have been alright. (Eugene, 50s, post-tariff)

As suggested here, this discourse of maturation explained the index offence as a reflection of a less mature and rational self, rather than an aberration. The current self was both changed from and consistent with the past self, rather than being either entirely new (as in the case of the 'better self') or entirely continuous (as in the case of the 'ethical self'). What all three narratives offered—the ethical self, the better self, and the more mature self—was a coherent life story, a biographic analysis that was considerably more intelligible than the attempts at sense-making made by early-stage prisoners. They also provided a means of distancing the current self from the person or incident that had led to the life sentence, in a way that allowed the prisoner to look to the future. Almost exclusively, this self was presented as better and more authentic than versions that had preceded it.

Finding the 'Real Me': The Developed Authentic Self

Prisoners who had reflected on, and found meaning in, their experiences—and it is important to clarify that this was not universal—almost always described their current self as the 'real me'. Thus, while prisoners who were at earlier points in their sentence often emphasised that their true, pre-prison self had been obliterated, eclipsed or suppressed, those who had served more time no longer regarded the person who had entered prison as their authentic being:

Do you feel like the person you are in here is the real you?

I'd say the real person will be going out, the real person did not come in. […] I come in as what I'm not, and I'm going out as who I am in my opinion.

So what's happened to make that not the real you and this the real you?

Because it's self discovery isn't it? Because now I understand what my interests are, why I have kind of behaved the way I did. I was more concerned probably about what others were thinking and stuff like that, and you start understanding how shallow those things are, so really the other one, you had like a veneer, which is not real. (Haashim, 30s, late)

How does the person you are now compare to the person you were outside?

Well I'm a man now, and back then I was a boy. That's the truth. […] I think I've learnt a lot, I've grown a lot. And I've become who I am over these years.

So which one's the real you?

I think now. I think this is me, this is the me. […] And it's just like I think through experience, and through learning more about myself as well, […] I sort of like found that out about myself.

Do you think it's easier now you can articulate yourself better?

Yeah definitely. I can put my points across. I can put names to emotions, and things like that, in different situation. (Stephen, 20s, mid)

Notably, then, most mid- and late-stage prisoners had come to see their pre-prison persona as false and their prison identity as true—an inversion of what is said by most prisoners serving short sentences (see Crewe 2009). This 'real me' was regarded as a better and more positive self than the person who had entered prison: more tolerant, respectful and polite, better skilled, with fewer mental health problems, and greater optimism about the future (see Heather 1977; Zamble 1992).

These sentiments were reflected in the survey data. Tables 7.1 and 7.2 show a range of items relating to social maturity, personal maturity, well-being and skills that prisoners were asked to rate on a five-point Likert scale, ranging from 'strongly agree' to 'strongly disagree', with a higher score always indicating a more

Table 7.1 Mean scores showing perceptions of change among male survey respondents by sentence stage[a]

Question	Very Early (51–57)[b]	Early (83–98)	Mid (81–85)	Late (25–28)	Post-tariff (19–20)
I am becoming/have become less tolerant of other people	3.02	3.17	3.48	3.46	3.80
I am becoming/have become less respectful of other people	3.65	3.81	4.19*VE	4.11	4.35*VE
I am becoming/have become more polite and considerate towards other people	3.14	3.53	3.92***VE	3.82*VE	4.00*VE
I am becoming/have become a less mature person	3.80	3.83	3.91	4.32	3.90
I am learning/have learnt to deal with my emotions	3.43	3.87	4.11**VE	4.11*VE	4.10*VE
My mental health is better than before I came to prison on this sentence	2.22	2.63	2.96***VE	2.74	3.80***VE, E, *M, L
My life feels more stable now than before I came to prison	1.69	2.35***VE	2.99***VE,*E	3.18***VE,*E	3.90***VE, E, *M
I feel happier than before I came to prison	1.25	1.73***VE	2.07***VE	2.57***VE,*E	3.37***VE, E,**M
I am learning/have learnt how to avoid the things that get me into trouble	3.60	3.82	4.14*VE	4.25*VE	4.40*VE
I am learning / have learnt useful skills	3.54	3.88	4.29***VE,*E	4.36**VE	4.25*VE

(continued)

Table 7.1 (continued)

Question	Very Early (51–57)[b]	Early (83–98)	Mid (81–85)	Late (25–28)	Post-tariff (19–20)
I am gaining/have gained a good education	3.04	3.41	3.71***VE	4.04*VE	3.80
I am becoming/have become less positive about my future	2.87	2.88	3.42*E	3.57	3.45
I am becoming/have become a better person overall	2.83	3.44*VE	3.86***VE	3.64*VE	4.15***VE

[a]Significance is reported at the following levels: *$p < 0.05$, ** $p < 0.01$, *** $p < 0.001$. Initials indicate the group that the score is *significantly higher* than: VE—very early, E—early, M—mid, L—late, PT—post-tariff. For women, early is first third of their sentence, mid is the second third of their sentence and late is the final third of their sentence or over tariff

[b]The number in brackets depicts the number of prisoners in each group. This is expressed as a range because more prisoners responded to some questions than others

Table 7.2 Mean scores showing perceptions of change among female survey respondents by sentence stage

Question	Early (10)	Mid (3)	Late/post-tariff (6)
I am becoming/have become less tolerant of other people	2.50	3.33	4.17[*E]
I am becoming/have become less respectful of other people	3.30	4.67	4.17
I am becoming/have become more polite and considerate towards other people	3.50	3.33	4.00
I am becoming/have become a less mature person	4.11	3.67	4.33
I am learning/have learnt to deal with my emotions	3.00	4.33	3.83
My mental health is better than before I came to prison on this sentence	2.50	3.33	3.50
My life feels more stable now than before I came to prison	2.10	4.33	4.17[**E]
I feel happier than before I came to prison	1.50	2.00	3.17[**E]
I am learning/have learnt how to avoid the things that get me into trouble	3.90	4.33	4.33
I am learning/have learnt useful skills	3.56	4.33	4.50
I am gaining/have gained a good education	3.00	4.33	4.17
I am becoming/have become less positive about my future	2.33	4.00	3.67
I am becoming/have become a better person overall	3.00	4.00	3.67

positive response.[7] Prisoners who were at the mid- and late sentence stages reported scores that were generally higher than those of earlier phase prisoners (often to a statistically significant degree). For statements such as 'My mental health is better than before I came to prison on this sentence' and 'My life feels more stable now than before I came to prison', these differences were considerable. Most strikingly—though, for reasons we set out in subsequent chapters, we would warn against taking these data at face value, or reading them in bad faith—male and female participants who were further into their sentence were significantly more likely than those at the earliest stages to agree with the statements 'I feel happier

---

[7]To minimise response bias, some statements were worded positively and some negatively. Items worded negatively were recoded during analysis so that a higher score on an item represents a more positive response, regardless of how each item is worded, with a score of 3.0 interpreted as neutral (i.e. on average respondents neither agree nor disagree).

than before I came to prison' and 'I am becoming / have become a better person overall'.

In interviews, authenticity was defined primarily in terms of personal confidence, the ability to be honest with oneself, and having the strength to resist social pressure. For example:

> The 'me' that is close to the real me. I mean I've found what I like, what I don't like, who I am, I've found my voice, and I kind of like the sound of my own voice sometimes, it's quite nice. Ha ha. But yeah, I can stick up for myself, whereas before I was [pauses] I just moulded into whoever and whatever people around me wanted. (Jenny, 20s, mid)

This reflects the broader literature, which links authenticity to positive 'adaptive psychological functioning'. The benefits of feeling able to behave authentically are rooted in the individual feeling 'adequate acceptance [...] simply by being oneself' (Leary 2003: 53). Participants who had spent some time in prison described this ability to simply 'be themselves' and being accepted as such by others:

> Because I've been here so long, I'm just left alone to do my own thing, and people are pretty decent with me. And because [the people] I hang around with, they're not bad apples, they're the best of the bad apples I suppose, the ones that are respected more, so that I can just be myself and do my own thing, people won't bother me anymore about what I did. I've been here a long while, people are just used to me now. (Karen, 20s, mid)

In contrast with early-stage prisoners, those further into their sentences tended to claim that their pre-prison social ties had limited their self-expression, rather than allowed them to be themselves. This was particularly so for those who had spent time, or were currently located, in therapeutic communities, where space was provided for prisoners to engage in the 'ongoing production of themselves' (Infinito 2003: 168). In such contexts, where trust and emotional candour were encouraged and expected, expressing vulnerability felt possible in ways that it had not in the community:

> *So it sounds like you're saying you can be genuine, and you can be the person that you are...?*

Yes, that's the thing here […] that is totally different from other places. I've never spoken about [childhood sexual abuse] to any of my family, but it's something that was always burning deep inside of me throughout my whole life. Where I wasn't really sure about myself, and I'd been questioning myself a lot at the time. […] And there's people here who I was in [another prison] with and they're [now] doing the same things as me: they're open and talking about things and listening and hearing. And I've cried with them, I've cried in here and I heard my friend in there just last week speaking about himself being abused as a child. And I walked out of the room in tears because it just brought so much emotion for me, but I'm comfortable to do that. (Ashley, 30s, mid)

As Ashley suggested, for some prisoners, discovering the 'real me' meant accepting fateful life experiences that they had concealed for a long time. For others, it was about accepting aspects of themselves—such as their sexuality—that they had felt forced to suppress prior to their imprisonment. Such discoveries and reconcilements often brought considerable satisfaction (Douglas 1984) and were expressed with pride:

If I saw myself outside [as the person I used to be] I would have grabbed him by his scruff of his neck. I just want to give him a good shaking: 'Where the hell is your head at? Put your head up, you've got a head'. But his brain was dormant. You hear the saying, 'Lights on, but nobody's in': that was me years ago. But now lights are on, somebody's in, […] and I like myself right now. I like the new me now. I'm more confident. […] I am cheeky, but in a nice way. And when I do get something on my mind, […] I don't hold it back. I let it all out. And I talk. And I say, 'you know, I'm here now. You're going to listen now and listen good. This is me. You never listened to me before, never give me a chance, now here I am'. Do you know what I mean? This is me. […] He's not the same person as what he was [in the 1980s]. He's changed. (Eugene, 50s, post-tariff)

Conclusion

Eugene 'hated prison', reminding us not to conflate the time and space needed to engage in the internal conversations, re-narration processes and personal changes described above with the state of incarceration. The need to survive the experience, and construct a coherent life story, meant that, even in the most extreme penal circumstances, prisoners were able to find meaning and 'come to new understandings and accommodations' about their circumstances (O'Donnell 2014: 274). Much of this happened in spite of the carceral environment rather than because of it. For almost all prisoners, the experience of being convicted of murder when still relatively young had a shattering effect on their sense of self. Feelings of shame and stigma, the stripping back of life to some bare truths and features, and the de-coupling of selfhood from existing social and relational moorings combined to produce a deep existential rupture. A key challenge of the sentence involved reflecting on questions about selfhood, life and death—'who am I, if I was capable of killing someone? What is all of this about?' (see Mathiassen 2016)—and assimilating the offence into a coherent life story. The resulting narratives of ethical selfhood, post-traumatic growth and maturation were striking in presenting a positive version of self and in producing an almost universal belief that—despite years spent in a state of coercive confinement—compared to the pre-prison self, the present self was more authentic: the 'real me'. Indeed, rather than reporting deterioration, prisoners indicated what Kernis (2003: 1) calls 'optimal self-esteem', in part because they had survived such an extreme experience. As Arshad (30s, late) stated, 'I think I've done pretty well coming out at the other end with my head still screwed on and not turning out to be some sort of nutcase'. As we describe in the chapter that follows, however, regarding the prison self as 'the real me' was complex, representing a shift in the perception of the prison from being a non-place to a real place, and reflecting a highly contorted notion of selfhood, forged within the specific environment of the prison.

References

Archer, M. S. (2003). *Structure, agency and the internal conversation*. Cambridge: Cambridge University Press.

Archer, M. S. (2012). *The reflexive imperative in late modernity*. Cambridge: Cambridge University Press.

Auty, K. M., & Liebling, A. (2019). Exploring the relationship between prison social climate and reoffending. *Justice Quarterly*.

Cohen, S., & Taylor, L. (1972). *Psychological survival: The experience of long-term imprisonment*. Harmondsworth: Penguin Books.

Corrigan, P. W., & Watson, A. C. (2002). The paradox of self-stigma and mental illness. *Clinical Psychology: Science and Practice, 9*(1), 35–53. https://onlinelibrary.wiley.com/doi/pdf/10.1093/clipsy.9.1.35.

Crewe, B. (2009). *The prisoner society: Power, adaptation and social life in an English prison.* Oxford: Oxford University Press.

Crewe, B. (2011). Depth, weight, tightness: Revisiting the pains of imprisonment. *Punishment & Society, 13*(5), 509–529.

De Viggiani, N. (2012). Trying to be something you are not: Masculine performances within a prison setting. *Men and Masculinities, 15*(3), 271–291.

Douglas, J. D. (1984). The emergence, security, and growth of the sense of self. In J. A. Kotarba & A. Fontana (Eds.), *The existential self in society* (pp. 69–99). London: The University of Chicago Press.

Erikson, E. H. (1959). Identity and the life cycle: Selected papers. *Psychological Issues, 1,* 1–171.

Ferguson, T. J., Eyre, H. L., & Ashbaker, M. (2000). Unwanted identities: A key variable in shame—Anger links and gender differences in shame. *Sex Roles, 42*(3–4), 133–157.

Fleetwood, J. (2015). In search of respectability: Narrative practice in a women's prison in Quito, Ecuador. In L. Presser & S. Sandberg (Eds.), *Narrative criminology: Understanding stories of crime* (pp. 42–68). London: New York University Press.

Foucault, M. (1997). Technologies of the self. In P. Rabinow (Ed.), *Ethics: subjectivity and truth* (pp. 223–252). New York: New Press.

Frankl, V. (1984). *Man's search for meaning.* New York: Washington Square Press.

Giddens, A. (1991). *Modernity and self-identity: Self and society in the late modern age.* Stanford: Stanford university press.

Goffman, E. (1961). *Asylums: Essays on the social situation of mental patients and other inmates.* New York: Anchor Books.

Heather, N. (1977). Personal illness in lifers and the effects of long-term indeterminate sentences. *British Journal of Criminology, 17,* 378.

Hulley, S., Crewe, B., & Wright, S. (2019). Making sense of 'joint enterprise' for murder: Legal legitimacy or instrumental acquiescence? *British Journal of Criminology, 59*(6), 1328–1346.

Ievins, A. M. A. N., & Crewe, B. (forthcoming). *Lateral tightness and 'sex offenders'.*

Infinito, J. (2003). Ethical Self-formation: A look at the later Foucault. *Educational Theory, 53*(2), 155–171. https://onlinelibrary.wiley.com/doi/pdf/10.1111/j.1741-5446.2003.00155.x.

Janoff-Bulman, R. (2004). Post-traumatic growth: Three explanatory models. *Psychological Inquiry, 15*(1), 30–34.

Jewkes, Y. (2005). Men behind bars: "Doing" masculinity as an adaptation to imprisonment. *Men and Masculinities, 8*(1), 44–63.

Joseph, S. (2011). *What doesn't kill us: The new psychology of post-traumatic growth*. Philadelphia: Basic Books.

Kernis, M. H. (2003). Towards a conceptualization of optimal self-esteem. *Psychological Inquiry, 14*(1), 1–26.

Laws, B. (2018). The return of the suppressed: Exploring how emotional suppression reappears as violence and pain among male and female prisoners. *Punishment & Society*. 146247451880507.

Leary, M. R. (2003). Interpersonal aspects of optimal self-esteem and the authentic self. *Psychological Inquiry, 14*(1), 52–54.

Liebling, A. (in press). The moral grammar of prison life and questions of politics: An inquiry. In A. E. Bottoms & J. Jacobs (Eds.), *Morality, crime and criminal justice*. Oxford: Hart Publishing.

Martin, K., & Stermac, L. (2010). Measuring hope: Is hope related to criminal behaviour in offenders? *International Journal of Offender Therapy and Comparative Criminology, 54*(5), 693–705.

Maruna, S. (1997). Desistance and development: The psychosocial process of going straight. *British Society of Criminology conferences: Selected proceedings*. Available at http://britsoccrim.org/volume2/003.pdf.

Maruna, S. (2001). *Making good: How ex-convicts reform and rebuild their lives*. Washington: American Psychological Association.

Maruna, S. (2004). Desistance from crime and explanatory style: A new direction in the psychology of reform. *Journal of Contemporary Criminal Justice, 20*(2), 184–200.

Mathiassen, C. (2016). Nothingness: Imprisoned in existence, excluded from society. In J. Bang & D. Winther-Lindqvist (Eds.), *Nothingness*. New Brunswick, NJ and London, UK: Transaction Publishers.

McAdams, D. P. (1993). *The stories we live by: Personal myths and the making of the self*. New York: Guilford Press.

McAdams, D. P. & Bowman, P. J. (2001). Narrating life's turning points: Redemption and contamination. In D. P. McAdams, R. Josselson, & A. Lieblich (Eds.), *Turns in the road: Narrative studies of lives in transition* (pp. 3–34). Washington: American Psychological Association. https://doi.org/10.1037/10410-001.

O'Donnell, I. (2014). *Prisoners, solitude and time*. Oxford: Oxford University Press.

Osyerman, D., Elmore, K., & Smith, G. (2012). Self, self-concept, and identity. In M. R. Leary & J. P. Tangney (Eds.), *Handbook of self and identity*. New York: Guildford Press.

Park, C. L. (2005). Religion as a meaning-making framework in coping with life stress. *Journal of Social Issues, 61*(4), 707–729.

Park, C. L. (2010). Making sense of the meaning literature: An integrative review of meaning making and its effects on adjustment to stressful life events. *Psychological Bulletin, 136*(2), 257–301.

Presser, L. (2010). *Been a heavy life: Stories of violent men*. Urbana: University of Illinois Press.

Robinson, G. (2008). Late-modern rehabilitation: The evolution of a penal strategy. *Punishment & Society, 10*(4), 429–445.

Sapsford, R. J., & Sapsford, R. (1983). *Life sentence prisoners: Reaction, response and change*. Milton Keynes: Open University Press.

Schmid, T. J., & Jones, R. S. (1991). Suspended identity: Identity transformation in a maximum security prison. *Symbolic Interaction*, 14(4), 415–432. https://onlinelibrary.wiley.com/doi/abs/10.1525/si.1991.14.4.415.

Shapland, J., & Bottoms, A. (2011). Reflections on social values, offending and desistance among young adult recidivists. *Punishment & Society, 13*(3), 256–282.

Singer, J. A. (2004). Narrative identity and meaning making across the adult lifespan: An introduction. *Journal of personality*, 72(3), 437–460. https://onlinelibrary.wiley.com/doi/pdf/10.1111/j.0022-3506.2004.00268.x.

van Ginneken, E. F. (2016). Making sense of imprisonment: Narratives of posttraumatic growth among female prisoners. *International Journal of Offender Therapy and Comparative Criminology, 60*(2), 208–227.

Vaughn, M. S., & Sapp, A. D. (1989). Less than utopian: Sex offender treatment in a milieu of power struggles, status positioning, and inmate manipulation in state correctional institutions. *The Prison Journal, 69*(2), 73–89.

Warr, J. (2019). 'Always gotta be two mans': Lifers, risk, rehabilitation, and narrative labour. *Punishment & Society*. https://doi.org/10.1177/1462474518822487.

Williams, R. J. (2018). Finding freedom and rethinking power: Islamic piety in English high security prisons. *British Journal of Criminology, 58*(3), 730–748.

Zamble, E. (1992). Behavior and adaptation in long-term prison inmates: Descriptive longitudinal results. *Criminal Justice and Behavior, 19*(4), 409–425.

8

Time and Place

Prison's like a stand-still in your life, isn't it? I'm being taken out of the world, yeah, and put in here, and this is its own little world. [...] It's like you've been stuck in time, but everyone else is still moving. (Justin, 20s, early)

The hopes of a prisoner deprived of freedom are utterly different from those of a man living a natural life. A free man hopes, of course (for a change in luck, for instance, or the success of an undertaking), but he lives, he acts, he is caught up in the world of life. It is very different with the prisoner. There is life for him too, granted – prison life – but whatever the convict may be and whatever may be in terms of his sentence, he is instinctively unable to accept his lot as something positive, final, as part of real life. Every convict feels that he is, so to speak, *not at home*, but on a visit. (Dostoyevsky, *The House of the Dead*, 1915, 2004: 79)

As Moran (2012) has argued, geographers have tended to conceptualise incarceration primarily in terms of space, including the concentration of people and prisons in particular locations (Philo 2001; Che 2005; Engel 2007), the denial of movement from and within that location, and prisoners' use of space (Dirsuweit 1999; Baer 2005; Sibley and Van Hoven 2009). Prison sociologists have more often focused on the temporal dimensions of imprisonment, arguing that time is

© The Author(s) 2020
B. Crewe et al., *Life Imprisonment from Young Adulthood*,
Palgrave Studies in Prisons and Penology,
https://doi.org/10.1057/978-1-137-56601-0_8

the essence of imprisonment (Cohen and Taylor 1972; Flanagan 1981; Sapsford 1983; O'Donnell 2014), including the unit by which the period of confinement is measured; the centrality of timetabling and routine to prison regimes (Foucault 1979; Sparks et al. 1996); and prisoners' subjective experience of time (Cohen and Taylor 1972; Brown 1998; Wahidin 2002; Cope 2003; O'Donnell 2014; Middlemass and Smiley 2016). Justin's comments (above) alert us to the ways that time and space are, as Moran observes, mutually constituted (and described in each other's terms). To quote Parkes and Thrift (1980: 12), 'space is in its very nature temporal and time spatial'.

Time and space are relevant to two of the three dislocations that are central to our analytic framework. First, our participants were dislocated socio-spatially, from the lifeworlds that they inhabited prior to their sentence. Second, they were dislocated from the lives that they had imagined for themselves, that is from the futures that they had anticipated. Meanwhile, the issue of time was central to the experience of the sentence in the present. Prisoners serving long sentences are particularly burdened by the sense of having a surfeit of time to bear while incarcerated at the same time as 'losing time' in their lives beyond it (Jamieson and Grounds 2005; Jewkes 2005). As Flanagan (1981: 212) notes:

> the element of time exacerbates all of the deprivations in the case of long-term prisoners and transforms them from noxious characteristics of imprisonment that can be accepted over the short-term into major problems of survival over the duration of a long prison sentence.

In the chapter that follows, we describe the ways that our participants managed and conceptualised time and place. In some respects, our findings resonate with the ways that other scholars have portrayed prisoners' subjective experiences of time as endless and meaningless in the present (see Cohen and Taylor 1972; Jewkes 2005; O'Donnell 2014), and as overwhelming and incomprehensible when viewed prospectively (Flanagan 1981; Liebling et al. 2012). To cope with these burdens, prisoners in the early sentence stage engaged in a range of defensive strategies—similar to those that we detailed in Chapter 4—in which they sought to deny, compress or suppress time, in various ways. However, we argue that prisoners in the later stages of long sentences found ways of taming and transcending time, while no longer regarding the prison merely as a 'non-place' (Augé 1995) and increasingly coming to reorient themselves to the world inside rather than beyond it. We conclude the chapter by reflecting on the nature of the maturation that most prisoners described, arguing that this entailed an adaptive form of emotional suppression, whose features were highly contextual.

Temporal Vertigo

As noted in Chapter 4, in describing what it felt to be given such a long prison term at an early age, participants who were in the initial phase of their sentence conveyed a sense of *temporal vertigo*. One prisoner explained that, when the judge passed his sentence, his 'future flashed before his eyes' (Terrance, 20s, early). Others conveyed a feeling of dizziness and disorientation about the time that lay ahead of them:

> I was nineteen when I got sentenced. Basically, all them years I've just done, growing up, I've got to do them again in prison, and it's, like, *whoa.*
> *Could you get your head around it at all?*
> No, not at all, no. I just didn't want to think about it, cause I knew if I thought about it a lot then it would just mess up my head. (Curtis, late teens, early)

> My little girl's going to be, like, 30 by the time I even get out, and I'm thinking 'hang on a minute, I was 19 when I got my tariff, you have given me a tariff that was longer than I'd been alive'. And it's, like, *whoa.* (Yvette, 30s, mid)

Comments of this kind illustrated two main issues. The first was the sheer difficulty of conceptualising the amount of time due to be served. Samuel (20s, early)—one year into a 25-year prison term that he had received when aged nineteen—explained that 'it's a bit un- comprehensible, really, your sentence, kind of imagining that amount of time'. Similarly, Martin (20s, early) reported that he 'had no concept of eighteen years of life' when he was sentenced, and that it took him years to be able to 'imagine that amount of time. Before, it was fucking overwhelming'. Being given prison terms that were often longer the number of years they had been alive meant that many prisoners had no reference point for what they now faced. As Karen (20s, mid) summarised, 'I didn't know what it felt like to *live* 20 years'.[1]

Many participants could only make the length of their sentence meaningful with reference to the years of their own consciousness, or using children as a temporal yardstick. For example:

> It's a bit daunting at times. Because when I first went to jail, my friend just had a kid, and I'm thinking his kid is going to be my age, what I am now, when I get out. So it's mad, really, but you try not to think about it, you just try to take it day-by-day and crack on, really. (Oscar, 20s, early)

> The main thing I think about is my daughter. By the time I'm eligible for parole, my daughter'll be my age now. (Blake, 20s, early)

References to the growth of others, in terms of age or size, were common, as if participants were rooting an otherwise intangible sense of time in some kind of physical reality. Del (20s, early), for example, noted that: 'when I came [into prison], my nephew was a little short, fat thing, but now he's six foot, he's got a moustache, things like that'. As we discuss below, it was significant that the sentence was best gauged not through the development of self, but others.

The second issue was expressed in Curtis's final comment, above, that thinking about his sentence length 'would just mess up my head'. Some interviewees were relatively sanguine about life after release, commenting that re-entering the free community in their late thirties or early forties meant that they would still have 'plenty of life to live'. That is, one of the few advantages of being imprisoned at an early age was the possibility that there would still be time left to build a meaningful existence (see Chapter 5). However, for prisoners who were in the early phase of their sentence, to think about the intervening years—those that would be spent within prison—felt impossible or psychologically hazardous:

---

[1] Nineteen of the 39 problems included in the survey were reported to be significantly more severe by respondents with tariffs of 20 years or more, compared to those with tariffs of under 20 years. Prisoners with tariffs of over 25 years found a number of problems to be significantly more severe than prisoners with shorter tariffs, including: 'Feeling that your life has been wasted', 'Missing social life', 'Feeling that you are losing the best years of your life', 'Feeling that you have no control over your life', 'Not feeling able to completely trust anyone', 'Feeling that the length of your sentence is unfair', 'Feeling worried about your personal safety', 'Feeling that you have no purpose or meaning in your life', and 'Having to follow other people's rules and orders'.

> I try not to think about the length [22 years]; I don't wanna think about that. [I]
> just take it day-by-day. Cause I can't change anything, so the more I stew on it …
> it's just gonna mess my head up, innit? (Alfie, 20s, early)

> I just take each day as it comes and I think that's the easiest way, because if you start
> thinking too far ahead, then it's a lot harder. […] It's a lot harder if you take it in
> too big a chunk. (Carl, 20s, early)

Prisoners at this sentence stage were unable to consider the sentence in its temporal
entirety, either because it was beyond them to grasp or conceptualise it, or because
they feared that doing so would be damaging to their mental health. To quote a
female participant:

> I don't ever, ever, ever think about it as a whole because, as soon as I [do], I feel
> my head going west and I'm, like, 'oh no, I can't do that amount of time', and then
> that's when like the suicidal thoughts start coming into my mind. (Jackie, 30s, late)

Living 'Day-By-Day'

Flanagan (1981: 210) states that 'the most effective method to reduce the uncertainty and ambiguity of the future is to concentrate on the present'. With almost
total consistency, early-stage prisoners explained that they survived their sentence
by focusing only on the immediate here-and-now:

> I just go through. I'm here, and that's it. I don't look at it like I've got 25 years. I'm
> just living, yeah, at the moment. Cause it would play on my mind. (Jamaal, 20s,
> early)

> I take it day-by-day, take each day as it comes, and just try not to think about the
> outside world. (Liz, 20s, early)

> I get by day-by-day. I don't think in weeks. […] I count how many days to go
> [because] it is one day closer to freedom, that is how I feel. (Darrin, late teens, early)

Phrases such as 'I just take it as it comes' (Martin, 20s, early), 'one day at a time' (Fiona, 20s, early) and 'you just try to take it day-by-day' (Oscar, 20s, early) were recurrent among early-stage prisoners (see Zamble 1992). Often, they spoke of thinking of each completed day as representing 'another day closer to freedom' (Carl, 20s, early) or as 'a day less' (Kathryn, 20s, early). Such phrases indicated highly circumscribed time horizons. When describing how they managed their time, prisoners in this sentence phase generally referred only to a daily timetable, or short-term milestones, such as canteen day or the daily programming of television shows, such as soap operas. Rather than planning ahead, they lived a myopic existence, in an endless and repetitive present (Brown 1998; Cope 2003; Jewkes 2005; Marti 2017), perceiving even the short-term future to be irrelevant to their existence. For example:

> Today, innit. Today. Tomorrow is irrelevant. Tomorrow's gonna be similar to today, so there's no point thinking about tomorrow. (Andre, late teens, early)

> [The future is] just not something you think about. Today's the day. If you survive it, that's another day tomorrow. (Zubair, 20s, early)

> I don't think about I've gotta do twenty years
> *Do you ever think about that?*
> No, there's no reason to.
> *Because?*
> I just don't think about it.
> *Do you think if you did it would bother you or is it just…*
> No.
> *There's no point to it?*
> Yeah, there's no point to it. (Rufus, late teens, early)

Statements of this kind, and the affective flatness with which they were delivered, pointed to emotional desolation and a form of subsistence living: a bleak and immediate existence ('survival'), with little sense of purpose. In a state of overwhelming distress, seeing beyond the day felt virtually impossible, as Maria conveyed:

> When you're sat here like this and you've lost your whole world, what else have you got you can take away from me? […] I won't watch my brothers get married. I won't

have children of my own. I won't watch my brothers have children. I won't watch my mum get old and I may not see them before it's too late. So there are days when it consumes you, and there is no way that I could take it more than one day at a time. Because, at the moment, I don't see a future and I don't see a life. (Maria, 20s, early)

The orientation of early-stage prisoners towards the future was also shaped by the shock of an unexpected conviction. Having lost faith in the predictability of life, when asked where they saw themselves in five years from the present, many were unable or reluctant to project themselves ahead:

Looking forward four or five years from now, where do you see yourself?
I don't know, I couldn't tell you [...].
Is it too much, to ask what you hope life will look like in four or five years?
I don't know because if you would have said this to me four or five years ago when I wasn't in prison, I wouldn't have expected that I would be like this, so I can't say. You can never say. (Dean, late teens, early)

Can you imagine your life five years from now? Where will you be?
Probably be in jail sitting down man. I don't know. In five years from now anything can happen, innit. (James, 20s, early)

Here, the language is telling. Phrases such as 'you can never say' and 'anything can happen' reflected a discourse that was highly non-agentic, in which life was fated, and there was little that could be done to determine one's own destiny. In this regard, as in others, these prisoners resembled Margaret Archer's (2012: 249) description of the state of fractured reflexivity, in which individuals are 'so preoccupied by the traumatic events in question that they focus on the immediate needs of survival' and are incapable of planning their lives through reflexive engagement. It is particularly striking that Archer uses a terminology of time and place that is so redolent of the language found in the accounts of our participants: being 'adrift' (2003: 312), 'passively going with the tide' (2003: 312) and 'taking each day as it comes' (2003: 314). In the 2012 elaboration of her argument, she describes the 'expressive reflexive' (a sub-type of the fractured reflexive) as living by 'presentism', making decisions based on instincts and 'gut feelings' (p. 281), rather than through an interior dialogue directed to the future: 'to them there is no "big picture" but simply a succession of events that command their attention from day to day' (Archer 2012: 279; see also Shirani and Henwood 2011). In such circumstances, to cope with the burdens of time, prisoners expressed and exhibited a number of reactive strategies, particularly, although not exclusively, in the early phase of the sentence.

Time Strategies

As is consistent with the framework that we outlined in Chapter 4, the first of these strategies involved forms of *denial*. One way of denying time was to forego ways of knowing or measuring it. While some prisoners reported having started their sentence by marking off days on a calendar, most found that this merely made the sentence feel longer: 'I did a calendar and I crossed a day off. Then it just seemed to drag so I started flipping over the calendar every month or whatever' (Merle, 30s, mid; and see Middlemass and Smiley 2016). Although the organisation of calendars into daily units might seem consistent with a 'day-by-day' orientation, by representing the wider span of time, they illustrated to prisoners how little the passing of each 24 hours dented the overall mass of the sentence.

More often, prisoners described ways of deliberately avoiding time—their location within it, and the broader temporal domain—in order to accelerate it subjectively:

> You try and really not look at the calendars. [...] I'm covering the days with a post-it note, to be honest. [...] The more you focus on time, the more it drags. So if you lose track of time you get a perception that it goes much faster. (Antone, 20s, early)

> I used to have [a watch], but I don't have one, just don't keep track of time; it makes it go faster. Otherwise you're clock watching. (Thomas, 20s, early)

This strategy was made possible in part because of the repetitive, eventless and timetabled nature of the prison regime, in which there was little need to know the specific date or the difference between one day and the next. In such circumstances, losing track of time seemed neither difficult nor disadvantageous.

An alternative form of denial involved legal appeal. Processes of appeal consumed time, by providing focus and activity: 'when you're appealing, you're spending so much time and energy on it, that time does kind of go quick' (Sim, 30s, mid).

They also enabled prisoners to maintain some hope that they would not, in the end, serve the amount of time to which they had been sentenced (see Chapter 5). Alan (30s, mid) recalled that one reason why he had denied his offence at the beginning of his sentence was that he 'couldn't see that far into the future. I couldn't picture myself doing 18 years [...], couldn't accept that I would be in prison for that length of time'. Tom, a current appellant, explained that:

> I don't think about the future [in prison], because I have no intention of spending that long in jail. My focus isn't prison. It's the world beyond prison. And mentally I make an effort to transcend my existence here. (Tom, 20s, early)

Appealing helped prisoners to negate their fear of the future and remove themselves psychologically from the perpetual present. As suggested in the quote above, it also enabled them to relocate themselves in space, giving them a sense of existence outside the institution.

A second strategy entailed temporal *compression*: finding ways of rationalising time, in order to shrink the number of years to which the sentence amounted. Haashim, for example, argued that his sentence in effect reduced to just two years, once he factored out the amount of time he would spend sleeping, eating and engaging in activities that he enjoyed:

> Half of my day is basically gone, isn't it, through sleep, eating. I don't count that as my sentence. Therefore my sentence has gone to nine years. And when I'm talking to my friends or watching videos or reading my books, I don't count that because my mind is engaged, so when you start really breaking it down, your sentence is only like two years or whatever. (Haashim, 30s, late)

Liz explained that the only way to survive the early years, and the pain of being separated from her son for so long, was to knowingly shrink her period of absence:

> *You said [your son] is eight now?*
> Yeah, he is [pauses] He'll be 23 when I get out. I know.
> *That must... has that been hard thinking about the time you've got to serve in those terms, thinking about it in terms of his...*
> ...when I look at it like that, yeah. But I *don't* look at it like that [...] I'm looking at it like I've got eleven [years] to do and then I'll be in an open [prison], and I can get a job and that. It's not that long. [...] I think you've just got to kid yourself and

be in denial about things, because if you're not it'd kill you. You've just got to sort of see things in a different way than you would normally see it, do you know what I mean?

You've got to create a story for yourself that's acceptable?

[…] I think you've just got to live in a fucking fairy tale world and just pretend it's all right when it's not.[…] I mean, what else can you do? (Liz, 20s, early)

Liz's reference to needing to 'live in a fucking fairy tale world' was telling, both in implying that coping required a commitment to an unreal world (to which we return below) and in indicating her awareness of her own technique for coping. Other participants claimed to feel undaunted by long periods of custody. Terrance (20s, early), for example, breezily discounted the vast period of time that he would have to serve before reaching an open prison: 'I'll have another 3 or 4 years here. Then there will be close to 20 left. Then I'll be Cat B, and before you know it, you're in D Cat'.

Like Terrance, many early-stage prisoners truncated their sentence length by considering the endpoint to be transferral to open conditions, rather than release itself. Harris (20s, early), for example, declared that 'when I go to cat D, I class that as being at home', while Scott (30s, mid) claimed that, at the point of reaching open conditions, 'even though I've got another three or four years to spend in jail, that wouldn't bother me - I know the end's near'. Typically, prisoners further into their sentence recalled feeling 'ecstatic' (Tori, 30s, late) when they reached the halfway point, and considered the last decade of their sentence as 'the home straight' (Curtis, 20s, mid). Alternatively, Mohammed downplayed the remaining years of his sentence with reference to his learned ability to cope with sustained confinement:

It [feels] really easy. I've got about ten or eleven years left in jail. To anyone else it's a long time, but for me, I haven't got [sighs] it's not difficult, do you know what I mean? (Mohammed, 20s, mid)

Time, then, took on a relative dimension.

A third strategy—often described in retrospect—was characterised by *suppression*, or what O'Donnell (2014) calls 'reduction': principally, making use of drink, drugs or sleep to accelerate the passage of time (see Cope 2003; Crewe 2005) or inhibit awareness of place:

The whole point of taking heroin became that I didn't [have to] think about a minute [of the sentence], really. (Phillip, 30s, mid)

What can you do to make time pass more quickly?
Sleep. Constant sleep. (Earl, 20s, early)

In a similar vein, many early-stage prisoners highlighted practices of 'removal' (O'Donnell 2014), in which commitment to particular activities—most often, exercise—alleviated sources of stress and anxiety that might otherwise prolong the passing of time. Jamaal, for example, stated: 'When I'm in the gym I forget about everything. Time goes, like ten minutes and an hour's gone. I don't think about nothing' (Jamaal, 20s, early).

While suppressive practices produced blankness, other pursuits actively stimulated alternative experiences of time and place. That is, activities such as reading or playing video games served not just to block out reality, but, through immersive *escapism*, sped up the passing of time and removed prisoners psychically from the environment:

You can get lost in a good book. [...] I can just lose myself for an hour, or two hours or however long you want; a day, even. [...] It's amazing because you can take yourself off and you don't have to be constantly in jail. And that's a big thing for me; I don't think my head's ever been inside the gate properly and people say, 'Oh no, that'll really hit you hard when your head comes inside this gate'. I've been here for years and my head hasn't come inside the gate once, and I'm not planning on bringing it inside the gate because it's not where I'm meant to be, so I'm keeping my head out the gate. (Kathryn, 20s, early)

For those two hours or three hours that you choose to read, you're somewhere else, you're not in prison, you're in the story, and you're somewhere else. It helps a lot in terms of not only expanding your imagination and vocabulary. It just helps in terms of the time. (Carl, 20s, early)

With a video game or a book, you go into a sort of universe. [...] You're part of the story, so it gets you involved, it's sort of escapism. (Antone, 20s, early)

Activities of this kind helped prisoners avoid being overwhelmed by negative thoughts. As discussed in Chapter 5, one of the most difficult aspects of the sentence for many early-stage prisoners was that the abundance of time and solitude provided too much opportunity for thinking, for example about lost opportunities and the time that lay ahead. Long periods spent alone in cells required some degree of mastery, purpose or escape. Again, then, the terminology used in Kathryn's statement ('inside the gate' and 'out the gate') is significant, in suggesting that, to deal with time, prisoners also had to (re)locate themselves psychologically in place.

The Experience of Time

Common to all of the strategies described above was the limited sense of control that they conveyed. Accordingly, several prisoners who described themselves as doing their sentence 'day-by-day' justified their time horizon with reference to a sense of unpredictability and powerlessness. Cary (20s, early), for example, explained that he 'live[d] each day as if it's the last' because 'you don't know when you're going to die', while Bruce attributed the same orientation to the perpetual possibility of coercive re-location (see Chapter 5):

> I deal with things day-by-day in here, so it's not like I plan for the … anything in prison, you just deal with day-by-day. […] It's an environment where anything can happen. It's an unpredictable environment. One minute you could be here, the next minute you're in the block for nothing or something. (Bruce, 20s, early)

In their descriptions of how time *felt*, the over-riding themes—among prisoners across sentence phases, but particularly those in the initial stage—were repetition, monotony, and the merging of days into an eventless whole:

> It's the same shit every day, man. Like the same routine, so you know what to expect every day.
> *And does time go quickly or slowly?*
> Time? To be honest, time flies, man. (Zaid, 20s, early)

> It seems like it drags, but then when you look back it's flew because it's repetitive, it's the same, so there's nothing major that stands out. […] It's gone so fast, because nothing's happened. (Scott, 30s, mid)

In prison, your day-to-day is so similar. It's monotonous. The same old routine, different day. And you know, it just blends into one [but] it's frighteningly quick, how fast time goes. When you're in a routine and you're doing something. See, time in prison seems to fly as well, once you get into a routine. [...] The days become the weeks, come into the months, and before you know it, it's gone. (Campbell, 30s, mid)

Time in the present was painfully slow: 'endless, endless, barbaric' (Horace, 50s, post-tariff). Prisoners spoke very consistently about the days 'dragging': 'sometimes on a day-to-day basis it can seem, like, "shit, this day is lasting forever, man, why won't it hurry up and go"' (Ashley, 30s, mid). And yet, as also suggested in the quotations above, when they looked back at the passage of time, it appeared to have passed quickly: 'Time does fly. At the time you're doing it, it drags as hell, but when you look back....' (Asad, 30s, mid).

In *Prisoners, Solitude and Time*, O'Donnell (2014) explains this paradox as resulting from unchanging routine and habitual activity. In such circumstances, because life is devoid of significant events (i.e. is flat and untextured), when viewed retrospectively, time collapses into a homogenous unit, in a way that gives the impression of speed. As prisoners themselves identified, in the absence of episodic memory, time 'blends into one':

Because of the monotony, similarity, of every day, it's very hard to sort of pinpoint a particular date. (Bernard, 40s, post-tariff)

When you're outside, every day is different, but in prison every day is the same. You wake up at the same time. You go to bed at the same time. You have your dinner or your tea at the same time. Everything's the same. So when I look back on it you can't really differentiate the days. [...] It goes quick because [it's] like one long day. [...] Every day [in prison X] dragged out, and it was long. So in terms of the days, they were long, but when you look back at it through a long period, it's gone quick. (Shaafi, 30s, mid)

Some participants described becoming unaware of specific times and dates, knowing only their place in the prison's weekly timetable. Others described developing a 'completely different timescale' in prison (Dan, 20s, early), or time distorting and losing ontological meaning:

It feels like it doesn't exist. It feels like there is no time. (Stephen, 20s, mid);

It's like I have no perception of time and I just have no recollection [of events and when they occurred]. I think time gets distorted in jail, it gets kind of warped. (Nadia, 20s, early)

I think of time as being made up. I don't think there's such a thing as time, cause there's not. Time is just for appointments. Time is just for things, isn't it? Time's nothing to me. (Sean, 20s, early)

I look at the time, but time means nothing to me. It's twenty to three now, but it doesn't mean nothing. [...] You forget about time, otherwise you go mad. [...] I know I'm not going anywhere, so why should I worry about it? (Walter, 60s, post-tariff)

Such comments hinted at a profound sense of existential alienation. Indeed, in their descriptions of time, early-stage prisoners frequently drew on metaphors of death and decay, implying that long-term imprisonment was akin to being—like a zombie—both alive and dead at the same time (see Johnson 2019). Imprisonment was described as 'dead time' (Jared, 20s, early), 'a waste of life' (Aaron, 40s, late), 'like you're wasting away … you're not living, really. [...] You're just existing' (Sean, 20s, early). Descriptions of sleep as the best way to 'hurry up time' (Thomas, 20s, early; and see Cope 2003; O'Donnell 2014) emphasised the feeling that time was something to be expended, and that this was best achieved through a state of self-suspension. Jared (20's, early) explained that he would welcome 'being in a coma for the next 20 years', so as to 'wake up to my release date'. Recurring tropes of the need to 'kill time', as well as to time being something that 'just kills you' (Christopher, 20s, mid), reinforced the sense that time was an adversary—an agentic entity—something to be combatted through strategies of defence and aggression.

As we outlined in Chapter 5, the other dominant discourse in accounts of the experience of time was of 'treading water':

You know when you're treading water in a swimming pool and you're not going forwards, you're kind of not going backwards; it's like walking on fucking quicksand, like you have to speed up a little bit otherwise you'll sink, you know what I'm saying? It's just a lot of wasted years. (Gibson, 20s, mid)

You've gotta get hobbies or go to the gym or whatever. Find something constructive to do with your time. [Otherwise] you're left treading water. (Jill, 40s, post-tariff)

Here, then, space and time were entwined particularly closely. Such metaphors for time had a spatial dimension, implying a form of transit, in the sense of being 'swept along', as well as the constant risk and sensation of 'going under'. They also suggested a particular mode of agency, which required the prisoner to work hard simply to remain in the same place. What was absent was any sense of the possibility or desirability of remaining comfortably still or finding contentment in the present.

The Prison as a Non-place

For prisoners in the early years of their sentence, the prison represented a 'non-place' (Augé 1995). Augé characterises non-places as locations such as supermarkets, airports, motorways and hotel rooms: places of transience, entered *en route* to more significant locations. Because presence within them is fleeting, non-places cultivate no sense of belonging. People within them are simply passengers, customers or guests, and do not seek to develop meaningful relationships. In this respect, non-places are sterile, devoid of social significance, and are experienced as locations where real existence is suspended and people wait for time to pass, rather than as 'real places' where time has independent purpose.

Early-stage prisoners used terminology that was very suggestive of such ideas, and of the deadening and anaesthetising qualities of the environment (see Jewkes et al. 2017). As the following quotations demonstrate, 'real life' remained beyond the walls of the prison:

Life just stops when you are behind these doors, like. Like it's frozen the time. (Johnnie, late teens, early)

The life that I was living, or the life that I wanted to live on the outside, is on pause. [...] Because I'm in prison all I can ever affect right now is my inside [life], my prison life. So in that sense my life on the outside is on hold; I can't do anything to influence my life on the outside right now. (Carl, 20s, early)

> You are in a constant hiatus. Your life is on hold in that period. [...] I felt like time stopped the day I was put in prison. [It's] like I'm on pause at the moment. (Dan, 20s, early)

> It's just so slow; it feels like my life's been put on hold, like I've just pushed this button and my life's [on hold until] I go home. (Tamara, 20s, early)

Such metaphors are redolent of the ideas of 'deep freeze' (Zamble and Porporino 1988) and 'suspension' (Cope 2003) found elsewhere in the literature on time and imprisonment. Sapsford (1983: 76), for example, notes that 'prison time is an interruption of life, not a part of it, like a form of cryogenic suspension through which the patient remains fully conscious'. In this context, the idea that imprisonment entails a kind of intermission, in which the prisoner is 'frozen developmentally' (Zamble and Porporino 1988) and his or her life paused, is striking: while most non-places are occupied briefly, as staging posts or sites of transit, long-term prisoners faced decades in an environment that they regarded, at least initially, as static and un-real.

In contrast, prisoners recalled that, in the community, time moved quickly, in part because life was full, textured and developmental:

> Out there, you go to a party, you do this and you do that, and there's so many things out there that make you old, quick. [Here] it's like you're in hibernation, until you come out. (Cary, 20s, early)

> [My friend outside is] buying his own house. [...] He's high up in his job, he's got a kid now. So it just shows you how quick time moves outside. (Bruce, 20s, early)

> Life is fast, and then when you come into jail it just comes to a stop. (Mohammed, 20s, mid)

Jewkes (2005: 371) has argued that the feeling 'of being in stasis while the world moves on around you only serves to intensify the experience of ageing', and we will return to these issues—of maturation and development, and of existing in two parallel domains—below. However, very few prisoners could, over a long period, sustain this idea, that 'real life' lay elsewhere, or that they themselves were what Jewkes et al. (2017) call 'non-people'. As we argued in Chapter 5, coming to terms with the sentence meant acknowledging that the prison was now 'home', and the only place where life could meaningfully be lived.

Time Strategies II

Coming to see the prison as 'home' determined the ways in which prisoners who were some years into their sentence used and conceptualised time. While early-stage prisoners denied, compressed and suppressed it, those further into their sentence engaged with time more consciously and agentically, so as to 'own', control and transcend it. First, they found ways of taming their anxieties about the weight of time, through strategies of 'rescheduling' (O'Donnell 2014), in which they split the period ahead of them into manageable segments (typically, four- or five-year chunks). Often, this was done with reference to regular sporting events such as World Cups or Olympic Games. For example:

> They say every little bit [of your sentence] is like the World Cup comes on and the European Championship, then the Olympics. It's, like, certain things like [that make time pass].
> *Big sporting events, they make time go quicker, do they?*
> Yeah, yeah. (Scott, 30s, mid)

Even when their time horizons remained limited, mid- and late-stage prisoners were more capable than their early-stage counterparts of imposing a temporal rhythm onto each year, often in step with sports seasons (e.g. motor racing, football), or through seasonal patterns that they imposed themselves:

> Gymnasium has been the most constructive thing for me, because I started to train seasonally, so, like, in winter I would bulk up, in summer I would cut up.[2] And I started to think in seasons and just throw everything into my gym. [...] So you become focused, very focused on a period of time, and everything around your prison sentence is all shaped around that [...] and it's surprising just how one day merges into the next. (Bernard, 40s, post-tariff)

---

[2] 'Cut up': in this context, to exercise in a way that removes fat so as to reveal muscle definition.

Second, mid- and late-stage prisoners tended to have 'time anchors' (O'Donnell 2014), which enabled them to plan for specific target points in the future. Often, these were formed around predictions or aspirations about when they might progress to lower-security prisons. Typically, these prisoners carried precise temporal maps, in which they plotted the year when they would reach the halfway point of their sentence ('the home stretch') or 'single figures' (i.e. under ten years remaining before their tariff point), or would be in the more natural environment of an open establishment: '[you] can get outside, you can have normal things, you can start being a bit normal' (Fernando, 20s, mid). Such points, projected into the future, were significant psychological milestones. They gave texture to an otherwise distant and featureless future, and helped prisoners orient themselves to present action without minimising or discounting the years that lay ahead.

Third, prisoners who were further into their sentence had generally found active ways of managing, manipulating or making use of time: putting 'their own stamp on their temporal lives' (O'Donnell 2014: 195). Rather than experiencing the prison routine as unbearably repetitive, more often they described patterns of behaviour whose predictability made prison life tolerable and served as a 'counterbalance to the oppressive environment of prison' (Middlemass and Smiley 2016: 801). Their accounts were not marked by the despondency of early-stage prisoners, who felt marooned in the present and incapable of productive activity. Instead, activities such as reading, art, study, prayer, playing computer games and exercise were undertaken with a sense of purpose.

Some such activities, including spiritual rituals, forms of mindfulness and reading, lifted prisoners out of both time and place, transcending and taming the present (what O'Donnell [2014] calls 'raptness'). As suggested above, prisoners at all sentence stages referred to activities such as using weights or doing yoga as practices that enabled some 'escape' from time and rumination. However, those who were beyond the initial few years of their sentence were much more likely than those in the early stage to describe time as something that was to be *used* rather than simply filled, killed or expended (Flanagan 1981). For example:

> One of our [religious] scholars said, yeah, that, "Time's like a sword. If you don't grab hold of it, it'll split you in two." And that's exactly what happens in prison. [...] We've been given time. Prison is about time. [...] It's very important to use time well. (Mohammed, 20s, mid)

Contextual Maturity

While—as noted above—early-stage prisoners regarded themselves as developmentally static, mid- and late-stage prisoners consistently described themselves as having 'matured' within the prison. Both in interviews and through their survey data (as reported in the previous chapter), they reported having become more emotionally controlled, more respectful of others and more psychologically stable:

> I've become more educated. I've gained certificates, […] I've got older, I've got wiser, […] I've got a healthy head on me. I respect people, respect rules, regulations, I see the meaning of what things are about now, whereas I didn't really have that insight before. […] I understand the implications and consequence of my actions, deeds. I've definitely become a better person. (Stuart, 40s, post-tariff)

> Maturity-wise, yeah, I have grown up. I'm more rational now, I'm more aware of the consequences of my actions now. I feel more stable. [But] You've got one part of me that feels like I'm still 17 because that's the age of coming in, and I had no life experiences or expectations in life. (Victor, 30s, post-tariff)

Such statements were consistent with the narratives of personal improvement, post-traumatic growth and maturity that we described in Chapter 7. For current purposes, our aim is to stress the distinction they help draw between the dominant feeling among early-stage prisoners of being a developmentally inert 'non-person' to having grown into the 'real-me'.

However, the narratives of maturation that we have detailed so far merit further analysis. First, prisoners often framed maturity in terms of adaptive *survival*. Clark (20s, early), for example, explained that he 'had to mature quickly to keep myself sane and safe', while Yvette (30s, mid) employed a similar language of enforced maturation: 'I had to grow up quick'. In such regards, maturation was in many ways defensive: a reaction to the demands of the environment[3]:

---

[3] As we noted in Chapter 5, male prisoners who had served years in high-security establishments were clear that their experiences in such prisons were largely *non*-developmental, because of the levels of fear that they experienced. Time in these establishments was enervating and exhausting. It did not so much mature prisoners as age and exhaust them:

> When I was in the little wars I was in [in high-security], the time would go slow. I'd be thinking 'fucking hell, man, I can't get through tomorrow'. And that's hard, and I used to be anxious all day, adrenalin all day, all day long. (Arkaan, 20s, mid)

I've grown up, yeah, but I'm grown up prison way, like, if I got out now, I'd still be eighteen. The mentality I've got, I'm still gonna be feeling like I was eighteen because all that time I spent in jail, I've only grown up knowing jail things. I'm wise as in *jail* wise but I ain't *adult* wise now. (Jonathan, 20s, early)

I have had to mature intellectually and psychologically because I've had to learn how to cope with imprisonment. [...] And I think it's a remarkable example of what the human psyche's capable of withstanding. (Dan, 20s, early)

Second, as Victor implied in the quotation above, prisoners were all too aware that their maturation was limited and contextual. Typically, they reflected on having missed out on normal social experiences: these included rites of passage, such as learning to drive; periods of hedonism ('people say it's supposed to be the best time in your life' [John, 20s, mid]); life-moments that symbolised social and economic success, such as getting a mortgage; and the formative aspects of adulthood. For example:

I've missed out on the best part of my life. I've missed out on everything, going on holidays with your friends – you see it on TV all the time, a bunch of young guys heading off to some Spanish island to go and have fun. I've missed out on all of that. Getting married – I think I would have been married by now if I never came to jail, so I missed out on that kind of stuff. Having kids. [...] So that's a pretty painful thing to deal with. (Ashley, 30s, mid)

I am still 23 in here. [...] Because I have not had those experiences in the world that mature us. I have never been married, I have got no children. I've not had a significant or an intimate relationship. I've not had a mortgage, a Volvo or 2.4 kids, I've not held down a proper job. (Harold, 40s, post-tariff)

Third, as suggested in these quotations, prisoners recognised that they had been deprived of opportunities to construct a life, during the life-phase when most people set down roots, established stability, and laid the foundations for their future. Many expressed acute sensitivity about the importance of the decades during which they were (or would be) confined: 'it's when you set your life, isn't it?' (Scott, 30s, mid); 'the time when you're trying to make the foundations for the rest of your life' (Billy, 20s, early).

Of these deprivations, the most painful and debilitating related to relational and family life. Brodie (30s, mid), for example, reflected that 'I could have been married, got kids, and settled down by now – had a good life, really'; Jackie (30s, late) commented that: 'Obviously I wanted kids and I think like I'm getting on a bit now, so it could be too late'. Statements of this were recurrent. Our participants had entered prison when young, with relatively few life experiences or stable social ties. Most felt that their lives outside had barely begun. Rather than mourning the loss of relationships, accomplishments and forms of status that had already been established, as reported in studies of older prisoners (e.g., see Crawley and Sparks 2005; Jewkes 2005), instead these prisoners grieved for the loss of their potential, for events and experiences they had already or were bound to miss out on, and for the lives they believed they would have led had it not been for their imprisonment.

Moreover, the absence of intimate relationships was in itself an impediment to maturity:

> Prison holds you back. I'm immature in certain areas. And I'll always be immature in prison. Because it's the outside world that would help me mature.
> *So what are the areas where you feel that you're immature?*
> Intimate relationships. Friendships. Stuff like that. (Marcus, 30s, late)

Prison was a non-normal environment—'not the right environment to be growing up in, I suppose' (Jackie, 30s, late)—which placed remarkable limits on emotional and experiential possibilities. Hugo (20s, early), who had been in custody since the age of fifteen, expressed concern that he was 'going to be an emotional retard when I get out', because 'the life experience isn't the same as people on the out. You don't have your first car, or your first flat, all that sort of stuff'. Casper (20s, early) stated that he could not 'fully mature' and was 'stuck in time', because, within prison, there were 'no real new experiences to sculpt you into a more mature person'. Fernando (mid, 30s) felt as though he was 'stuck in a void [...] just stood still', because 'you don't get to see and live'. As he went on to explain, this sense of social stasis, during a key period of life (O'Donnell 2014), was exacerbated by the awareness that contemporaries outside prison were moving on in their lives:

> You hear of things outside: this person's had their trial, or this person's bought a house or got a promotion at work, and you can see people moving, progressing in their life. (Fernando, 20s, mid)

When you look in the mirror, you still think you're eighteen. [But] You haven't been in that society, where your friends have grew up with their families and things and have had children, and got married, you've stayed in this little capsule for years, so you're just locked in them thoughts. (Bryant, 40s, post-tariff)

Through statements of this kind, prisoners recognised not just that their maturity was contextual, but that maturity and development meant different things in prison and in the community:

[Some people say] you never grow up when you're in a prison. You do. You do, you just don't have the experience of being responsible, having to pay a mortgage and take your kids to school.
So you grow up in very different ways?
Yeah, you just grow up, you still mature. [...] How do you define maturity? It's just a different experience. (Kelvin, 20s, mid)

Often, participants reflected on the curious experience of 'growing up' in some respects, and yet at the same time still feeling the same age they had been on entering prison[4]:

In one way I've grown up massively, and I feel thirty-two, but in another way I still feel twenty years old. You see a programme, 20-year-olds on holiday, stuff like that, and think 'I should be doing that'. But then I think 'hold on, I'm 32 years old'. (Shaafi, 30s, mid)

I think the time change stops in here. [...] You sort of stop at the time you came into jail. [...] It conserves - your last experiences sort of get imprinted and whatever happens in jail goes in, like, a separate track. You're developing in a different direction, separate from what you have been on the outside. (Antone, 20s, early)

Here, metaphors of time and space were intertwined in complex ways, so that it was possible to 'mature' and 'stand still' at the same time. Shaafi (30s, mid),

---

[4]The view that, on entry into custody, prisoners were simply 'preserved' in their current state of maturity was expressed by a number of participants. Stuart (40s, post-tariff), for example, described himself as still having a 'young attitude' and feeling 'like I'm a young raver inside', conjecturing that this might be 'because I haven't experienced maturing in the community'. On the whole, however, when prisoners made such claims, they contradicted them elsewhere in their interviews, or made them with reference to other prisoners' immaturity: 'people over forty, and they act like twenty year-olds' (Antone 20s, early).

for example, observed that 'It feels like you're drifting away, because everybody's moving forward and you're kind of not there really'. Antone's terminology of life in prison and the community representing 'separate tracks' was also telling. For long-term prisoners, the nature of being was somewhat bifurcated, as they sought to exist in two domains—within and beyond the prison—whose temporal qualities did not feel in parallel.

Jamieson and Grounds (2005) suggest that this experience of existing in two different life-worlds or 'along two very different trajectories' (Jewkes 2005: 372) is one of the main burdens of long-term confinement. As Jewkes (2005: 372) highlights, one of the painful ironies of a life sentence is the simultaneous sense of time within prison feeling over-abundant or meaningless, while time outside being 'depleted, irrevocably lost' (see also Wahidin 2017; Armstrong 2016). For our participants, while the past faded and receded, the future too became increasingly intangible.[5] The loss was twofold: time that prisoners could not regain ('it's just slipping away, and you're never gonna get that time back' [Casper, 20s, early]), and an imagined future that felt increasingly tenuous (see Jamieson and Grounds 2005). As Ashley described:

Time is bad, because in one sense it's the most precious thing, more than any … you know, when I was out there robbing and selling drugs, you think money means everything. [Now you think] it's just being able to spend that time with the people who I love and I care about. And I think about, I hope my mum's still alive when I get out, I hope my dad is still alive when I get out, and will I be able to spend time with them? I see my brothers having kids and my nephews and nieces growing up and I hardly know them and they hardly know me. So that time there is so precious, but on the other hand somebody's took my time and just gone like *that*, and so easily. [So] on the one hand, [time is] just rubbish and on the other hand it's the most precious thing. It's like I'm in jail wishing my life away so I can get out to be with my family. (Ashley, 30s, mid)

---

[5]Prisoners often commented on the changes in technology that would render them of another time when released. Several talked about the possibility of 'flying cars', by the time they were freed. Others commented on the glimpses of change that they had seen when being transported between prisons or to external hospitals, for example:

… this fucking [advertising board], it moved. It had three pictures on it. And not only that, it had the time, and it had the temperature on it, and I was like, 'are you fucking for real?!' (Tori, 30s, late)

In noting the movement of time outside, developments in the lives of friends and relatives, and their own increasing separation from the external community, prisoners were in effect describing themselves not as non-persons *within* the prison but *outside* it. The battle for all participants to find the right balance between living in these two domains was palpable. Early-stage prisoners, in particular, described strategies for trying to 'keep their mind' outside prison, to some degree, to resist becoming too detached from the free community. Carl (20s, early) and Olin (20s, early) both described keeping up with the news, in order to ensure that, on release, they were able to 'function properly' and avoid being 'shocked'. Neil (30s, mid) declared that he had 'always lived outside' and was trying to 'life his life' within prison by engaging in the kinds of activities that he would have undertaken had he been free.

Yet many prisoners recognised that, from very early in the sentence, some degree of acculturation was hard to avoid. Loren (20s, early)—three years into a 20-year minimum sentence—reported feeling that, having 'got used' to prison and lost track of what was going on beyond it, he was already somewhat institutionalised, i.e. excessively accustomed to life in prison. Leonard argued that the process of coming to terms with the sentence was in itself a form of institutionalisation:

> We're all institutionalised. [...]
> *When do you think you became institutionalised?*
> As soon as you become comfortable with prison, as soon as you realise, 'yeah, I've got to do 15 years something'. As soon as you get your mind okay with prison, you become institutionalised. (Leonard, 30s, late)

As we discussed in Chapter 5, however, coming to terms with the sentence involved coming to see the prison as a place rather than a non-place. In essence, this required prisoners to make real an environment that they knew was unreal or distorted. As Deena (20s, mid) observed, 'a lot of my growing up I've had to do it in a false environment'.[6] Accordingly, as prisoners moved on in their sentence, their sense

---

[6]A small number of participants—mainly female prisoners—welcomed the unnatural nature of the prison environment, because it offered them forms of safety and structure that had been missing earlier in their lives:

> Prison, even though it's a surreal, it's not a real environment, you have that safety to grow in a healthy way without fear of attack or reprisal, or whatever. [...] I came in [young] and I was a mum [in my teens], and I didn't have any life experience. You know, those teenage years where you're out partying and being daft with your mates were gone - they were gone.
> *Do you feel like now you have life experience?*
> Yeah, I'm not sure it'd do me any good in real life. [But] I've got plenty of prison life experience. (Gail, 30s, late)

of the prison and the community was that *both* were real and unreal at the same time.

Schinkel (2014) suggests that institutionalisation might not be as apparent to people while they are serving their sentence as it is once they are released. Indeed, some prisoners expressed considerable uncertainty about whether they had become over-accustomed to their environment: 'I don't think I am, but I probably am, I'm probably institutionalised' (Merle, 30s, mid). Prisoners in the later stages of their sentence had far fewer doubts, and used the term or concept of 'institutionalisation' with anxiety or resignation. Frank (40s, late) described being 'frightened' of his own 'institutional traits'; Stuart (40s, post-tariff) called himself a 'jailhead' and considered himself to be 'fucked' by his alienation from the outside world (what Stearns et al. [2019] refer to as 'social death': 'the termination of a person's social existence in the dominant culture'). At this sentence stage, it was more common for prisoners to recommend 'keeping their head' inside prison rather than outside it, to minimise stress: 'if you put your head out there you mess your head up and you mess yourself up' (Gail, 30s, late). In its most extreme form, this could mean losing any sense of or interest in the external environment:

A lot of the time you forget why you're in jail. [...] Like, now, I very seldom look out my window, you know, I don't even notice the bars, you've been in jail that long, [...] you're just looking through the bars, and I'm always shocked when someone says... 'have you seen the snow outside?' I've said 'is it snowing?' And you don't know, because you're not remotely interested. (Haashim, 30s, post-tariff)

For prisoners like Haashim, as the outside world became irrelevant, it was only the prison that was real. Indeed, as he went on to describe, he had become so accustomed to his circumstances that the terms of the prison had infiltrated his selfhood:

We're instilled to having an emotional wall. [...] It's because subconsciously we are having to walk around the prison not showing any weaknesses. [...] You've actually conditioned yourself, it's probably become a part of your nature, your personality. (Haashim, 30s, post-tariff)

This observation is key to our thesis. In Chapter 5, we argued that coping involved finding ways of managing the affective impact of both the offence and the sentence. Here, though, we want to emphasise the way in which, over a long period of time, adaptation and emotion management entailed a form of emotional *suppression* whose impact was profound. That is, to avoid being overwhelmed with distress, and to deal with the enduring demands of the environment, prisoners learnt to 'shut down' and 'detach their feelings' (Deena, 20s, mid) in ways that reshaped them significantly. Almost uniformly, participants—across all sentence stages—talked of having become 'numb' (Alvin, 20s, early), 'hardened' (Aaron, 40s, late), 'desensitised' (Horace, 50s, post-tariff) and distanced from their own emotions:

> I think you become... not dead inside but you become immune to things. You're just, like, emotionally, physically, just because you're in that box for so long and you're so secluded you just switch everything off. The only way you can survive is to switch off. If you don't switch off then you struggle. [...] You don't survive and get stressed. (Bryant, 40s, post-tariff)

> *So you have to switch off certain emotions just to cope.*
> And because they're going to be switched off so long it's like something you stick in a cabinet, after a while it's going to be dusty, and it ain't going to work.
> *Yeah. And it's, like, can you feel that again?*
> Yeah. Can you turn it back on? (Jamie, 20s, early)

Some interviewees reported that emotional suppression was never entirely successful—'Sometimes I'll hit a wall [...] and I need to let it go: the hurt and the guilt' (Gail, 30s, late). Others were resigned to losing a part of themselves and their humanity. Luca, for example, explained that, having 'blocked' off his feelings, he no longer felt like 'a human being'. 'I lock myself up and I kind of block myself out from a lot of things. [...] I've been blocking a lot of things out that I shouldn't really block out' (Luca, 30s, mid). The key point here—as we discuss further in Chapter 9—is that the forms of emotional suppression that were 'adaptive', in terms of coping with a long sentence, had consequences that were not altogether positive.

Luca was referring primarily to the suppression of his sexual desires and frustrations. Male survey participants reported 'feeling sexually frustrated' as the 13th most severe problem that they encountered, while female prisoners reported it as the 33rd most severe. The difference between these ratings might well reflect the greater propensity for female prisoners to engage in sexual relationships while serving their sentences. Although our female participants generally explained the significance of such relationships in terms of intimacy rather than sexual relations, motivations ranged from 'casual fun' and 'needing to forget on the day of my trial' (Tamara, 20s, early) to 'falling in love' (Tori, 30s, late). A second explanation relates to the histories of sexual and physical abuse that most female participants had suffered at the hands of male partners.

When male prisoners were asked about how they dealt with sexual desire and frustration, some made reference to the circulation of pornography and the compensatory satisfactions of masturbation; only a very small minority reported having been involved in consensual sexual relationships while serving their sentence, either with other prisoners or with female prison staff. On the whole, sexual desire was simply suppressed:

How do you deal with sexual frustration?
You just put it to the back of your head. I don't really think about it to be honest.
(Gibson, 20s, mid)

You've got to choose not to feel certain things. You see a woman and think, 'oh she's pretty', but you've got to choose not to see that, because that will drive you mental.
(Jamie, 20s, early)

As Julius (30s, mid) also made clear, it was not so much that this frustration became less painful over time, but that it was possible to adapt to an environment lacking familiar forms of intimacy: 'I think men in here think about women continuously the first three or four years. [But after that], you don't tend to think about women, women, women - you just get on with your day'. The severity score for 'feeling sexually frustrated' diminished significantly in line with sentence stage, from 12.71 among very early-stage prisoners to 6.05 among those who were beyond their tariff point.

Time and Release

For prisoners who were close to release, the subjective quality of time changed again. As several participants explained, far from feeling that time was oppressively excessive, faced with the possibility of release, it began to feel more urgent and produced a set of new anxieties (see O'Donnell 2014: 208).

> [At the start of the sentence], trying to stay alive was an issue, so tomorrow wasn't going to come, as far as I was concerned. But once I'd got myself stable and able to deal with life in here and every day, it was kind of like… my parole has crept up on me and I'm shitting bricks because it's so soon, whereas in the past it was so far away. […] At the start, you take it, it just seems like there's too much time at the beginning. (Jenny, 20s, mid)

> At the start, [you think] 'I've got all this time'. And then eight years in, I have anxiety attacks that I'm not gonna be able to reach my goals before I come out of jail. (Mohammed, 20s, mid)

Among late and post-tariff prisoners, 'Feeling anxious about the uncertainty of your release date' was the 9th most severe problem, compared to 16th among prisoners at the very early and early sentence stages. For those who were many years beyond their tariff point, or who were very unclear about their release date, uncertainty and pessimism meant that time reverted to a more overbearing form, while the world outside became increasingly alien:

> What I do this day, you know, I do this day. I can't think of yesterday because it's gone. I can't think of tomorrow because it's not here. (Marcus, 30s, mid)

> It's like taking a monkey out of the jungle, and putting him in a big city. You've got to relearn to live outside. How can you do that after forty-two years in prison? (Walter, 60s, post-tariff)

Conclusion

Imprisonment tends to be regarded as a period of time that is discrete from the primary location of the individual's life (Pettit and Western 2004), while the prison environment is generally characterised as a highly distorted social domain (Crewe 2009). For our participants, much of the challenge of serving the sentence was about coming to terms with spending such a significant phase of life in a place that was therefore 'unreal'. In this regard, as Jewkes (2005: 367) argues, they existed in a state of 'permanent or near-permanent' liminality. That is, they were not moving from one clear life-stage or identity state to another, so much as reconciling themselves to a state of enduring limbo. Certainly, long-term prisoners were waiting to enter a new phase of life, on release, but initially this phase felt unreachable or unimaginable, and as it drew nearer its terms were increasingly fuzzy and unclear. In the meantime, the waiting period was so long that it impelled them to occupy a space of ambiguity and in-betweenness with growing commitment. Survival required that they make a false place 'real'.

To put this in alternative terms, their transition was from a state of transitional liminality, in which they were '*not-X-anymore-and-not-Y-yet*' to one of permanent liminality, which 'creates an enduring sense of being *neither-X-nor-Y* or indeed of being *both-X-and-Y*' (Bamber et al. 2017: 1516, italics in original): for current purposes, a person who was neither entirely inside nor outwith the prison, and in some ways was both.[7] For our participants, the balance between existence and non-existence in these domains shifted significantly over time, leaving them more certain of who they were, but more deeply embedded in the environment of the prison.

Our findings are consistent with Jewkes's (2005) assertion that, for life-sentenced prisoners, following a 'temporary suspension' of selfhood, reconstructing a narrative of self is still possible. Again, though, these narratives were ambiguous. While our participants considered themselves to have matured in many important respects, we have highlighted a critical distinction between personal-behavioural change and social-relational development—between *self* and *life*. Prisoners' narratives of change were often about interior development and behavioural change, of a kind determined by the need to adapt to imprisonment, rather than about social development, life progression or the kind of emotional growth that occurs through relational intimacy. As we discuss in the concluding chapter of this book, there are good grounds for believing that the nature of this maturation might be maladaptive for life after release.

---

[7]Moran and Disney (2017) suggest that, for all prisoners, the world from which they have been removed continues to exist for them as a kind of 'absent-presence', while their existence in the world outside likewise endures.

References

Archer, M. S. (2003). *Structure, agency and the internal conversation.* Cambridge: Cambridge University Press.

Archer, M. S. (2012). *The reflexive imperative in late modernity.* Cambridge: Cambridge University Press.

Armstrong, S. (2016). The cell and the corridor: Imprisonment as waiting, and waiting as mobile. *Time & Society, 27*(2), 133–154.

Augé, M. (1995). *Non-places: Introduction to an anthropology of supermodernity* (John Howe, Trans.). London: Verso.

Baer, L. D. (2005). Visual imprints on the prison landscape: A study on the decorations in prison cells. *Tijdschrift Voor Economische En Sociale Geografie, 96*(2), 209–217.

Bamber, M., Allen-Collinson, J., & McCormack, J. (2017). Occupational limbo, transitional liminality and permanent liminality: New conceptual distinctions. *Human Relations, 70*(12), 1514–1537.

Brown, A. (1998). Doing time: The extended present of the long-term prisoner. *Time & Society, 7*(1), 93–103.

Che, D. (2005). Constructing a prison in the forest: Conflicts over nature, paradise, and identity. *Annals of the Association of American Geographers, 95*(4), 809–831.

Cohen, S., & Taylor, L. (1972). *Psychological survival: The experience of long-term imprisonment.* Harmondsworth: Penguin Books Ltd.

Cope, N. (2003). 'It's no time or high time': Young offenders' experiences of time and drug use in prison. *The Howard Journal of Criminal Justice, 42*(2), 158–175.

Crawley, E., & Sparks, R. (2005). Hidden injuries? Researching the experiences of older men in English prisons. *The Howard Journal of Criminal Justice, 44*(4), 345–356.

Crewe, B. (2005). The prisoner society in the era of hard drugs. *Punishment & Society, 7*(4), 457–481.

Crewe, B. (2009). *The prisoner society: Power, adaptation and social life in an English prison.* Oxford: Oxford University Press.

Dirsuweit, T. (1999). Carceral spaces in South Africa: A case study of institutional power, sexuality and transgression in a women's prison. *Geoforum, 30*(1), 71–83.

Dostoevsky, F. (1915). *The house of the dead.* New York: The Macmillan Company.

Dostoevsky, F. (2004). *The house of the dead.* New York: The Macmillan Company.

Engel, M. R. (2007). *When a prison comes to town: Siting, location, and perceived impacts of correctional facilities in the Midwest.* Lincoln: The University of Nebraska.

Flanagan, T. J. (1981). Dealing with long-term confinement: Adaptive strategies and perspectives among long-term prisoners. *Criminal Justice and Behavior, 8*(2), 201–222.

Foucault, M. (1979). Authorship: What is an author? *Screen, 20*(1), 13–34.

Jamieson, R., & Grounds, A. (2005). Release and adjustment: Perspectives from studies of wrongly convicted and politically motivated prisoners. In A. Liebling & S. Maruna (Eds.), *The effects of imprisonment* (pp. 33–65). Cullompton: Willan Publishing.

Jewkes, Y. (2005). Men behind bars: "Doing" masculinity as an adaptation to imprisonment. *Men and Masculinities, 8*(1), 44–63.

Jewkes, Y., Slee, E., & Moran, D. (2017). The visual retreat of the prison. In M. Brown & E. Carrabine (Eds.), *Routledge international handbook of visual criminology* (p. 293). Abingdon: Routledge.

Johnson, R. (2019). *Condemned to die: Life under sentence of death* (2nd ed.). New York: Routledge.

Liebling, A., Arnold, H., & Straub, C. (2012). *An exploration of staff-prisoner relationships at HMP Whitemoor: Twelve years on.* London: Ministry of Justice.

Marti, I. (2017). Doing (with) time: Dealing with indefinite incarceration in Switzerland. *Tsantsa, 22*, 68–77.

Middlemass, K. M., & Smiley, C. (2016). Doing a bid: The construction of time as punishment. *The Prison Journal, 96*(6), 793–813.

Moran, D. (2012). "Doing time" in carceral space: Timespace and carceral geography. *Geografiska Annaler: Series B, Human Geography, 94*(4), 305–316.

Moran, D., & Disney, T. (2017). 'It's a horrible, horrible feeling': Ghosting and the layered geographies of absent–presence in the prison visiting room. *Social & Cultural Geography*, 1–18. https://doi.org/10.1080/14649365.2017.1373303.

O'Donnell, I. (2014). *Prisoners, solitude and time.* Oxford: Oxford University Press.

Parkes, D., & Thrift, N. J. (1980). *Times, spaces, and places: A chronogeographic perspective.* New York: Wiley.

Pettit, B., & Western, B. (2004). Mass imprisonment and the life course: Race and class inequality in US incarceration. *American Sociological Review, 69*(2), 151–169.

Philo, C. (2001). Accumulating populations: Bodies, institutions and space. *International Journal of Population Geography, 7*(6), 473–490.

Sapsford, R. J., & Sapsford, R. (1983). *Life sentence prisoners: Reaction, response and change.* Milton Keynes: Open University Press.

Schinkel, M. (2014). *Being imprisoned: Punishment, adaptation and desistance.* Basingstoke: Palgrave Macmillan.

Shirani, F., & Henwood, K. (2011). Taking one day at a time: Temporal experiences in the context of unexpected life course transitions. *Time & Society, 20*(1), 49–68.

Sibley, D., & Van Hoven, B. (2009). The contamination of personal space: Boundary construction in a prison environment. *Area, 41*(2), 198–206.

Sparks, R., Bottoms, A. E., & Hay, W. (1996). *Prisons and the problem of order.* Oxford: Clarendon Press.

Stearns, A. E., Swanson, R., & Etie, S. (2019). The walking dead? Assessing social death among long-term prisoners. *Corrections, 4*(3), 153–168.

Wahidin, A. (2002). Reconfiguring older bodies in the prison time machine. *Journal of Aging and Identity, 7*(3), 177–193.

Wahidin, A. (2017). Time and the prison experience. *Sociological Research Online, 11*(1), 1–10.

Zamble, E. (1992). Behavior and adaptation in long-term prison inmates: Descriptive longitudinal results. *Criminal Justice and Behavior, 19*(4), 409–425.

Zamble, E., & Porporino, F. J. (1988). *Coping, behaviour and adaptation in prison inmates.* New York: Springer-Verlag.

9

Conclusion

At the end of an interview conducted early in our fieldwork period with Phil Wheatley, former Director-General of the National Offender Management Service (NOMS), we asked him about the ways in which, were he still running the Prison Service, he would be interested in our study. Part of his reply was as follows:

> I think [politicians] have engaged in a [sentencing] experiment with prisoners, and lots of that's been about keeping the public happy, and I think people don't want to know what the reality has been for those that have been through it. [...] What's it like to be doing a very long sentence? What does it feel like? How are people reacting to it? How do they survive it? How do they feel about it? What does it look as though we're doing to them?

Any policy regime organised around a reductive reading of public sentiment is distasteful, particularly when the experimental objects are human beings, and the consequences for them are so extreme. There are good grounds for believing that public opinion in relation to sentencing is considerably more nuanced than politicians appear to believe (see e.g. Fitz-Gibbon 2013; Mitchell and Roberts 2011; Black et al. 2019; Marsh et al. 2019). In any case, if the aim of punitive sentencing is to satisfy a retributive urge or sate the legitimate anger of the bereaved, it seems liable to fail precisely because these feelings cannot be assuaged through

© The Author(s) 2020
B. Crewe et al., *Life Imprisonment from Young Adulthood*,
Palgrave Studies in Prisons and Penology,
https://doi.org/10.1057/978-1-137-56601-0_9

simple policy responses (see Victim Support 2010). We are doubtful that any sentence length can heal the trauma or cure the pain of victimhood; to suggest otherwise seems, if anything, to underestimate the depth of trauma that murders produce.

Our aim in this book is not to advocate for forgiveness, as such. As Cantacuzino (2015) suggests, the idea of forgiveness is too demanding of those who have undergone such profound trauma—too prescriptive about how they should react, too wrapped up in sentimentality and ideas of self-abnegation. Yet seeking to humanise our participants, by detailing their pain and remorse, and their ability to engage as moral agents, might go some way towards creating the space in which forgiveness might be possible. It certainly seems important to note that most of our participants recognised the moral enormity of their actions and wished sincerely to make amends. Accordingly, of those who considered themselves guilty, most did not dispute that they deserved significant punishment, even if they felt that its degree was excessive.

Meanwhile, descriptions of the conviction as a valuable 'lesson' or 'wake-up call' testified to the belief among many participants that some form of incapacitation or lifestyle dislocation might be beneficial. But these were very long lessons, and very harsh calls, and it is tragic that this reassessment of life occurred only at the point at which what lay ahead was many years of custody. As Billy (20s, early) reflected: 'I'm a lot better person now. [...] I'm in a lot better place. It's just a shame, really, that I'm here for the next thirteen years'. With striking consistency, when asked specifically what period of imprisonment would achieve and sustain change, prisoners believed that a sentence of more than a decade was counterproductive:

I did what I did, so I deserve to be punished for it, basically, so I deserve to be here, [but] I don't feel I deserve nineteen years. I don't think that amount of time is good for anybody, really. If you can't rehabilitate someone after ten years, then there's no hope for them, really. (Curtis, 20s, mid)

I think jail has done good for me. But, like, it gets to the point where you think, 'This is too long, this.' Now [having served 10 years], I'm at a good stage where I could get out and I know I could do well, and I could stay out. But in seven years' time, I don't know. (Kenny, 20s, mid)

Instead, sentence lengths for murder in England and Wales are, in the true sense of the term, wasteful, in that they expend something that is of value carelessly, extravagantly, or to no purpose. At the very least, their impact is to confuse the purpose of the sanction and undermine its rehabilitative objectives[1]:

> Don't say 'we're putting you in jail to rehabilitate you'. Because 30-years-to-life don't go with the word 'rehabilitation'. Because that's no hope. Do you understand?
> *Is that what it felt like: no hope?*
> Of course! [...] Because everything that you know, you're taken away from anyway. [...] And you just [sighs]... it just felt harsh. Cos at the end of the day I was a kid. Do you know what I mean? I was a kid. (Mohammed, 20s, mid)

Mohammed's reflections begin to answer the question of what it feels like, in essence, to serve a very long life sentence for murder. Most prisoners eventually find hope, but go through considerable despair en route to doing so. Some get 'lost' in the process. Matters of time, identity and personhood are brought into particularly sharp relief. Throughout the book, we have drawn on prisoners' own descriptive metaphors—of sinking and swimming, and of loss and stagnation, for example—to try to convey these experiences phenomenologically. The framework through which we have organised and interpreted these first-hand accounts has emphasised the triple dislocation or rupture that results from being incarcerated when young for at least fifteen years: from the prisoner's existing social relations, his or her sense of the self, and the future that he or she had anticipated. Within this framework, we have emphasised the existential, affective and moral dimensions of long-term imprisonment. That is, prisoners faced an existential threat whose magnitude extended well beyond the normal 'biographical disruption' (cf. Bury 1982) caused by a prison sentence. In the traumatic aftermath of having been involved in a murder (or feeling unfairly convicted of such an offence), and facing the realisation that life was changed forever, they were flooded by emotions of anger, confusion and shame, in ways that the established literature on the pains of imprisonment does not always capture or theorise.

---

[1] Considerable evidence now suggests that longer sentences produce little 'marginal benefit', in terms of future offending, and, if anything, might lead to increased recidivism (e.g. Loughran et al. 2009; Gendreau et al. 1999, 2000; Baay et al. 2012).

An adequate analysis requires recognition of the significance of the offence itself, with all of its moral implications, as well as the resulting sentence length (and, for female prisoners, the added factor of histories of abuse). This calls into question the tendency within prison sociology to disregard offence-type, or consider it of little relevance to prisoner adaptation (a matter for the legal system and the court, or a point of concern more suited to psychological approaches to criminology). Some offences are no doubt of greater significance than others: Shapland and Bottoms (2011: 270), for example, found that the short-term offenders they studied did not feel that their offence 'shaped and determined their whole persona and future'. In contrast, our findings are consistent with those of Munn and Bruckert (2013: 99), who note that 'for many of the men'—released after at least a decade of custody—'the crime they committed had a profound impact on their sense of self'. Acknowledging the relevance of such feelings is not meant to calcify prisoners as particular kinds of criminal offenders, defined by a single, unrepresentative act, but to acknowledge them as moral agents, capable of both normative breaches and normative reflection.

The nature of the offence contributed to our participants' adaptive orientations, as well as their sense of self. Along with the bewilderment of being in an unexpected context, and the traumatic prospect of a life-warping prison sentence, the psychic burden of having been involved in a murder was highly significant. In the early sentence phase, it produced a range of defensive reactions that protected prisoners from the implications of their offence and kept at bay the reality of their situation. Energy was expended in psychological survival—managing immediate and otherwise overwhelming forms of emotion—but at the expense of productive forms of agency and internal deliberation. As Casper (20s, early) summarised: 'The first two years … I just didn't know whether I was coming or going, you know. It was just letting my circumstances lead me, rather than taking control of what I'm doing'.

During this early phase of confinement, feelings of distress and unresolved shame (see Butler 2008) meant that prisoners were at their most unstable. It is not difficult to see the potential appeal of simplistic ideologies that offer to explain prisoners' circumstances, justify their resentment, and fulfil many of their human needs, for love and meaning, for example (see Liebling et al. 2011). In this respect, for all of the reasons that faith and self-education provide narrative lifeboats for those who are drowning, they also have the potential to drag prisoners towards adaptive orientations that are extreme and destructive. This risk will be heightened when the moral quality of imprisonment is highly compromised: when prisoners feel disrespected and misrecognised (see Liebling 2015). We encountered few prisoners whose anger and alienation had been yoked to toxic forms of ideology or transformed into outright violence, in part because such men and women are concentrated in particular corners of the system (and, no doubt, because radical views will have been concealed from us). Most participants portrayed themselves as highly compliant, breaching rules principally to ease the burdens and frictions of prison life (Rubin 2015), rather than to subvert institutional power. Although many were embittered by their convictions, and continued to feel a searing sense of injustice, most were eventually able to separate their feelings of illegitimacy about their conviction and sentence from their orientation towards the prison authorities. Nonetheless, we do not doubt that one outcome of growing sentence lengths is the exacerbation of 'political charge' (Liebling 2015), and a group of prisoners for whom the fracturing of existence and selfhood produces significant risk and vulnerability.

While this form of fractured reflexivity was characteristic of our early-stage interviewees, remaining in a state of affective stasis and denial was unsustainable and unproductive. The multiple ruptures produced by the sentence—their puncturing of the taken-for-granted (Akram and Hogan 2015), and the social and emotional space burst open as a result—produced a reflexive imperative, of the kind that Margaret Archer (2003, 2012) identifies with broader forms of contextual incongruity. In a state of anomie, and without guidelines for future action, prisoners were pushed into an extended reflexive conversation about who they were and the revised parameters of their existence. Like meta-reflexives—in circumstances of much greater extremity and intensity—their main preoccupations were personal and interior (see also O'Donnell 2014), bound up with efforts at self-transformation. As Victor (30s, post-tariff) commented:

> How much time have you got to actually stop and reflect on things? I've had that time and I've looked into myself. [...] I've had the chances to be able to sit or reflect, and analyse and look inward to myself and everything else. [...] I've had that opportunity, and I am a better person.

Cohen and Taylor (1972: 137–138) suggest that self-consciousness—'the need to make sense of one's experience' and 'understand what is happening to you'—is essential for surviving extreme circumstances. Certainly, for our participants, reflexive deliberation was a key part of the adaptive process.

This process involved a number of elements[2]: coming to terms with both the sentence and the offence, in part by finding ways of controlling, channelling and processing a set of otherwise inchoate emotions; finding sources of hope, meaning and purpose and some sense of control, often through forms of faith and education; the construction of a self-narrative that could integrate the past, provide some direction in the present, and work towards a different future; and a reframing and rebalancing of social existence inside and beyond the prison. To use a metaphor that has seasoned our analysis, while prisoners in the early sentence stage were, in effect, treading water, being passively carried by the tide, or trying to swim against its flow, those who were further into their sentences accepted that they would not escape the water. Instead, they submitted to the current, while at the same time seeking to use its energy to their advantage—making the most of a situation that was not of their choosing, but from which they believed they could derive some personal value (see Johnson and Dobrzanska [2005] on 'mature coping', and O'Donnell [2014] on 'acceptance'). Their use of time was constructive rather than merely depletive; their agency was future-oriented and productive, rather than backwards-looking, defensive or reactive. They swam with the tide, rather than against it.

These adaptations involved the acknowledgement and taming of some emotions and the suppression of others. To advance from a state of fractured reflexivity, prisoners had to identify and manage feelings of shame, control feelings of anger and handle feelings of loss. Adjusting to an unchangeable long-term reality required a kind of psychic splitting, in which emotions of bitterness, resentment and desperation had to be subdued or set aside. Yet this process of adjustment involved

---

[2]To repeat a point made in Chapter 3, our analysis is organised around a set of common, but not universal, adaptive patterns. While this results in some shearing away of variance, it is worth noting the similarities in findings between studies of long-term imprisonment conducted in different countries, over a very long time period (Richards 1978; Flanagan 1980; Leigey and Ryder 2015; and see Hulley et al. 2016). The implication is that, almost regardless of time, place and policy context, the deprivation of liberty over a sustained period of time creates a consistent set of pains and adaptive responses. As we have stated elsewhere (Hulley et al. 2016), we do not believe that the nature and intensity of these problems would be invariant regardless of context. Nor, therefore, do we think that these problems are entirely intractable, even if the implication is that they are almost inherent to extreme confinement.

its own forms of suppression, and the nature of imprisonment itself inhibited the development of certain kinds of emotional and relational competences. In this respect, we should be cautious in interpreting prisoners' accounts of their own development at face value. Like many previous studies (e.g. Zamble 1992; and see Kazemian and Travis 2015; van Zyl Smith and Appleton 2019 for comprehensive overviews), our findings appear to suggest that long-term imprisonment might not have deleterious effects, and, in fact, might produce improvements in mental health and emotional well-being. With regard to our survey results, 'problem severity' was generally highest among early-stage prisoners and lower for those who were further into their sentences, while prisoners who were further into their sentences reported higher levels of emotional and psychological well-being compared to those in earlier phases. Furthermore, in interviews, many prisoners presented themselves as having become 'better', stronger, more mature, and a more faithful reflection of their true self.

The typical interpretation of such findings is that, following an initial period of 'considerable psychological discomfort' (Zamble 1992: 42), long-term prisoners become accustomed to the pains of imprisonment and find ways of adapting to the environment that prevent the problems of long-term confinement from escalating over time (e.g. Flanagan 1981; Leigey and Ryder 2015: 736). To quote Sapsford (1983: 63):

> Prisoners did not deteriorate, because they found ways of coming to terms with the prison environment and using it for their own purposes. [Most men] managed to reassert some measure of control over their prison experience and a few managed effectively to 'negate' or 'escape from' it by forcing a redefinition of circumstance such that prison was an inconvenience rather than an environment exerting total control, or even became a facilitating environment.

As implied in this quotation, some studies conclude that, far from becoming 'institutionalised', life-sentence prisoners might develop skills that are of value on release. Indeed, a shallow reading of such studies is that long-term confinement might not cause enduring harm. This is not our interpretation. First, in light of the complexity of human existence, measures of change such as cognitive functioning or intellectual capacity (e.g. Rasch 1981) are limited and superficial. The human weight of imprisonment impacts people profoundly, in ways that are moral, existential and relational as much as they are cognitive and psychological. Second, as suggested in the very notion of post-traumatic growth, personal development may be the direct outcome of experiences that are acutely harmful and undesirable. In such a context, to regard growth is an unambiguous good is to trivialise the acute and manifold pains that this book has tried to convey. Relatedly, our analysis suggests a vital distinction between the forms of personal growth or psychological 'improvement' that prisoners report, and the forms of social and relational maturation that long-term imprisonment denies them. In this respect, it is perfectly possible for people to feel 'improved' in certain respects but damaged in others. As O'Donnell (2014: 276) emphasises, drawing on Breytenbach's (1984: 130) account of his experience of solitary confinement, alongside a range of positive effects and personal discoveries, 'parts of you are destroyed and these parts will never again be revived ... And this damage is permanent, even though you learn to live with it, however well camouflaged'.

Third, then, it is analytically deficient to suggest that long-term prisoners simply adjust to their situation, and alleviate the problems that they encounter, through a 'redefinition of circumstance'. Both assumptions—that these problems truly diminish, and that prisoners remain untouched by the process—seem questionable. Generally, our participants suggested that the pains of imprisonment did not, in any simple sense, ease. Rather, they became a taken-for-granted aspect of daily life, in the same way that any chronic form of pain—backache or bereavement—can become absorbed into daily life.[3] To use their own words:

> Those demons just become part of you. They become part of your everyday world and living with them becomes part of every day, and it doesn't get easier, but you get used to it. (Gail, 30s, late)

> I think what jail does do, especially when you are doing a long time, it does harden you. It does make you a bit more distant, because that's the life you are in. [...] People keep [emotions] to themselves. And so I think that's just sadly a part of prison. It is who you become, and if you are hardened in the beginning then you become even harder, you become even colder, you become more detached. (Joseph, 40, post-tariff)

Over many years, imprisonment alters prisoners in ways that are profound and enduring. The burdens of imprisonment might be felt less sharply over time,

---

[3] With thanks to Anna Kotova for this analogy.

but this is because, in some respects, they become internalised into the prisoner's being—part of his or her overall transformation into a different kind of person. Matters that are initially encountered as problems become less apparent, because, like the person who adjusts their daily movements and routines to deal with long-term back pain, the requirements of survival and adaptation have already reshaped the prisoner's being. To try to distinguish between the person and the problem becomes impossible: the former is deeply imprinted by the constant presence of the latter.

To make this case is not to suggest that prisoners become 'institutionalized', in the way that the term has been conventionally defined: that is, psychological dependent upon institutional structures and contingencies (Haney 2003; Sapsford 1978). Far from becoming more listless, passive and unable to take initiative, if anything, most participants felt themselves to be increasingly agentic: in control of their lives, and able to forge their futures. Instead, the principle feature of long-term institutional exposure was a particular kind of suppressive emotional configuration—what Joseph describes above in terms of 'hardening' and 'detachment', and others as 'numbing' or 'withdrawal'—resulting from the over-regulation of discomfiting emotions, the demands of the environment and the poverty of relational goods.

All of this suggests that the adaptive mechanisms that alleviate some of the pains and problems of imprisonment can themselves be debilitating. These secondary handicaps are not always visible to prisoners while they remain in the environment to which they have had to adjust. While our study can make no claims about post-release outcomes, it is instructive that our findings are consistent with the literature that does. Liem and Kunst (2013), for example, identify in prisoners who had experienced prolonged incarceration, a specific cluster of symptoms similar to post-traumatic stress disorder, supplemented with 'institutionalised personality traits', including hypervigilance, difficulties with intimacy and social interaction, feelings of 'not belonging' (p. 336), the suppression of emotion, self-isolation and a general distrust of the world (see also Haney 2003; Munn and Bruckert 2013). The 'emotional numbing' (Liem and Kunst 2013: 335) that composes one part of this disorder corresponds with the intimate distancing that Jamieson and Grounds (2005) describe among a sample of wrongly convicted former prisoners, who struggled to relate to their families. Likewise, Munn and Bruckert (2013) detail the ways in which, once released, prisoners who had served more than a decade in prison found themselves 'unprepared' for the world that they re-entered. Confused by social and technological change, and lacking in relationship skills, there was a significant disconnect between 'the lives they envisioned establishing while in prison' (p. 84) and the realities and constraints of life in the community and on parole.

Archer's (2003: 353) comments on the restless disappointment of meta-reflexives are also apposite. Since they 'can rarely be eremitic'—that is, entirely secluded in their social existence—'though the most important part of themselves may be vested in activities such as lone writing or solitary prayer, their ideal of a holistically integrated life [...] condemns them to life-long frustration as social utopians' (2003: 353). For our purposes, the point is that long-term prisoners may be able to pursue or imagine a life of relative idealism, devotion or purity within the prison—often organised around faith, education or personal ethics—but, on release, might well find that their aspirations and orientations are incompatible with the world as it is. Two key themes in our analysis are of relevance here: one is the difficulty of preparing for life in the community having been removed from it for so long. The other is the possibility that adaptations that are functional within prison are deeply dysfunctional on release, particularly in the realms of social and family life (Grounds 2005). One of the many tragic aspects of imprisonment is that, while it often produces a desire among prisoners to lead a different kind of life, it so often disables the possibility of doing so through the ties that it breaks and the traits that it generates.

Here, then, we return to the quotation with which the book started, and to Dan's metaphor of the chrysalis:

> We are trapped in a chrysalis while the outside world rushes on without us, yet within the chrysalis a metamorphosis is taking place. We change as people, we achieve certain things, removed from the real world. And so what emerges is a transformed individual, for better or worse. [...] One can never truly be the same or simply take off from where we left off. (Dan, 20s, early)

The butterfly emerges perfectly adapted to the environment. We are much less optimistic that long-term prisoners, despite their positive outlook, emerge back into society well-adjusted to its demands and requirements. More importantly, when men and women are spending decades of their lives in prison, we should be interested in the chrysalis itself: what it means to undergo the most extreme form of state punishment.

References

Akram, S., & Hogan, A. (2015). On reflexivity and the conduct of the self in everyday life: Reflections on Bourdieu and Archer. *British Journal of Sociology, 66*(4), 605–625.

Archer, M. S. (2003). *Structure, agency and the internal conversation.* Cambridge: Cambridge University Press.

Archer, M. S. (2012). *The reflexive imperative in late modernity.* Cambridge: Cambridge University Press.

Baay, P., Liem, M., & Nieuwbeerta, P. (2012). "Ex-imprisoned homicide offenders: Once Bitten, twice shy?" The effect of the length of imprisonment on recidivism for homicide offenders. *Homicide Studies, 16*(3), 259–279.

Black, C., Warren, R., Ormston, R., & Tata, C. (2019). *Public perceptions of sentencing: National survey report.* Edinburgh: Scottish Sentencing Council.

Breytenbach, B. (1984). *True confessions of an albino terrorist.* Faber and Faber.

Bury, M. (1982). Chronic illness as biographical disruption. *Sociology of Health and Illness, 4*(2), 167–182.

Butler, M. (2008). What are you looking at? Prisoner confrontations and the search for respect. *British Journal of Criminology, 48*(6), 856–873.

Cantacuzino, M. (2015). *The forgiveness project: Stories for a vengeful age.* London: Jessica Kingsley Publishers.

Cohen, S., & Taylor, L. (1972). *Psychological survival: The experience of long-term imprisonment.* Middlesex: Penguin.

Fitz-Gibbon, K. (2013). The mandatory life sentence for murder: An argument for judicial discretion in England. *Criminology & Criminal Justice, 13*(5), 506–525.

Flanagan, T. J. (1980). The pains of long-term imprisonment: A comparison of British and American perspectives. *The British Journal of Criminology, 20*(2), 148–156.

Flanagan, T. J. (1981). Dealing with long-term confinement: Adaptive strategies and perspectives among long-term prisoners. *Criminal Justice and Behavior, 8*(2), 201–222.

Gendreau, P., Cullen, F. T., & Goggin, C. (1999). *The effects of prison sentences on recidivism* (pp. 4–5). Ottawa, ON: Solicitor General Canada.

Gendreau, P., Goggin, C., Cullen, F. T., & Andrews, D. A. (2000, May). The effects of community sanctions and incarceration on recidivism. *Forum on corrections research, 12*(2), 10–13). Correctional Service of Canada.

Grounds, A. T. (2005). Understanding the effects of wrongful imprisonment. *Crime and Justice, 32,* 1–58.

Haney, C. (2003). The psychological impact of incarceration: Implications for post-prison adjustment. *Prisoners Once Removed: The Impact of Incarceration and Reentry on Children, Families, and Communities, 33,* 66.

Hulley, S., Crewe, B., & Wright, S. (2016). Re-examining the problems of long-term imprisonment. *British Journal of Criminology, 56*(4), 769–792.

Jamieson, R., & Grounds, A. (2005). Release and adjustment: Perspectives from studies of wrongly convicted and politically motivated prisoners. *The effects of imprisonment,* 33–65.

Johnson, R., & Dobrzanska, A. (2005). Mature coping among life-sentenced inmates: An exploratory study of adjustment dynamics. *Corrections Compendium, 30*(6), 8–9.

Kazemian, L., & Travis, J. (2015). Imperative for inclusion of long termers and lifers in research and policy. *Criminology & Public Policy, 14*(2), 355–395.

Leigey, M. E., & Ryder, M. A. (2015). The pains of permanent imprisonment: Examining perceptions of confinement among older life without parole inmates. *International Journal of Offender Therapy and Comparative Criminology, 59*(7), 726–742.

Liebling, A. (2015). Appreciative inquiry, generative theory, and the 'failed state' prison. In J. Miller & W. Palacios (Eds.), *Advances in criminological theory* (pp. 251–270). New Brunswick, NJ: Transaction Publishers.

Liebling, A., Arnold, H., & Straub, C. (2011). *An exploration of staff-prisoner relationships at HMP Whitemoor: Twelve years on.* London: National Offender Management Service.

Liem, M., & Kunst, M. (2013). Is there a recognizable post-incarceration syndrome among released "lifers"? *International Journal of Law and Psychiatry, 36*(3–4), 333–337.

Loughran, T. A., Mulvey, E. P., Schubert, C. A., Fagan, J., Piquero, A. R., & Losoya, S. H. (2009). Estimating a dose-response relationship between length of stay and future recidivism in serious juvenile offenders. *Criminology, 47*(3), 699–740.

Marsh, N., McKay, E., Pelly, C., & Cereda, S. (2019). *Public knowledge of and confidence in the criminal justice system and sentencing: A report for the Sentencing Council.* London: Sentencing Council.

Mitchell, B., & Roberts, J. V. (2011). Sentencing for murder: Exploring public knowledge and public opinion in England and Wales. *British Journal of Criminology, 52*(1), 141–158.

Munn, M., & Bruckert, C. (2013). *On the outside: From lengthy imprisonment to lasting freedom.* Vancouver: University of British Columbia Press.

O'Donnell, I. (2014). *Prisoners, solitude, and time.* Oxford: Oxford University Press.

Rasch, W. (1981). The effects of indeterminate detention. *International Journal of Law and Psychiatry, 4*(3–4), 417–431.

Richards, B. (1978). The experience of long-term imprisonment: An exploratory investigation. *British Journal of Criminology, 18,* 162.

Rubin, A. T. (2015). Resistance or friction: Understanding the significance of prisoners' secondary adjustments. *Theoretical Criminology, 19*(1), 23–42.

Sapsford, R. J. (1978). Life-sentence prisoners: Psychological changes during sentence. *British Journal of Criminology, 18,* 128.

Sapsford, R. (1983). *Life sentence prisoners: Reaction, response and change.* London: Open University Press.

Shapland, J., & Bottoms, A. (2011). Reflections on social values, offending and desistance among young adult recidivists. *Punishment & Society, 13*(3), 256–282.

Victim Support. (2010). *Victim's justice: What do victims and witnesses really want from sentencing?.* London: Victim Support.

van Zyl Smit, D., & Appleton, C. (2019). *Life imprisonment: A global human rights analysis.* Cambridge: Harvard University Press.

Zamble, E. (1992). Behavior and adaptation in long-term prison inmates: Descriptive longitudinal results. *Criminal Justice and Behavior, 19*(4), 409–425.

Index

Printed in Great Britain
by Amazon

68529339R00208